Stormy Years

SUN LI

FOREIGN LANGUAGES PRESS
BEIJING

First Edition   1982

Translated by
GLADYS YANG

ISBN   0-8351-0996-8

Published by the Foreign Languages Press
24 Baiwanzhuang Road, Beijing, China

Printed by the Foreign Languages Printing House
19 West Chegongzhuang Road, Beijing, China

Distributed by China Publications Centre (Guoji Shudian)
P.O. Box 399, Beijing, China

Printed in the People's Republic of China

Author's Preface

In the autumn of 1937 the Japanese imperialists invaded North China. My home was in the Central Hebei plain and I saw for myself how the people there, led by the Chinese Communist Party, rose up in their fury to launch the great resistance movement.

The people everywhere gave an immediate, selfless, stupendous response to the call for resistance.

The autumn and winter of 1937 were a period of mobilization and organization. The initial panic in the villages was overcome by systematic work of this kind. Then the people, all of one mind, pulled together and brought their strength into full play to inflict heavy blows on the invaders.

From its birth in 1921 the Chinese Communist Party exercised a powerful political influence in North China, and from this time on it had firm bases in the villagers. Before the outbreak of the War of Resistance Against Japan the Party had the foresight to strengthen the work in this region.

When my home town was invaded by the Japanese, the fine qualities of my people were clearly brought home to me. The eight years of the War of Resistance deepened my understanding of the Chinese peasantry's fortitude and capacity for hard work. With infinite courage, resourcefulness and optimism they threw themselves into the sacred War of Resistance. They had complete faith in their ultimate victory. Their confidence grew from day to day during the war.

i

The great War of Resistance Against Japan not only aroused our people and made them rise up, but also spread new ideas far and wide and brought forth a new culture.

This period deepened my love for my country and my people, their new moral standards and customs, each blade of grass of my home. All these had passed the cruel test of the war and triumphantly proved that they could not be overcome.

The profound impression all this made upon me pervaded and shaped my feelings.

So in 1950, when I was working for a Tianjin newspaper and had relatively quiet conditions in which to write, I knew more or less what I wanted to describe in my novel. Without any definite plan or carefully worked out plot, I set about writing, and the newspaper published each chapter as it was finished. The wartime happenings simply flowed from my pen.

Readers can see that the events of the first two dozen chapters seem to shape themselves. They are absolutely true to life, a faithful record of the life and feelings of people at that time.

Nothing has been exaggerated. Impressions from life combined and merged to make up the incidents of *Stormy Years*.

Let me repeat: The period of the War of Resistance deepened my love for my country and my people, for the work they did and the fine qualities they displayed.

Most of all I loved the splendid optimism they showed at all times. This deserves the name revolutionary optimism.

My story naturally reflects this spirit. For this was what made the deepest impression on me, what encouraged me most forcefully to write.

Owing to my limited experience of life and of writing and the lack of an overall plan, the construction of my novel is weak in many places, its range is too narrow and it has many other faults.

I hope generous readers will help me with their criticism.

September 1963, Tianjin

Principal Characters

Mangzhong, hired hand, who later joined the People's Defence Corps

Chun'er, Mangzhong's sweetheart and chairman of Ziwuzhen's Women's National Salvation Association

Old Chang, hired hand, chairman of Ziwuzhen's Workers' Union and later village head

Old Wen, hired hand, who later joined the People's Defence Corps

Gao Qingshan, commander of the Seventh Detachment of the People's Defence Corps

Gao Xiang, political commissar of the Seventh Detachment of the People's Defence Corps

Qiufen, Gao Qingshan's wife

Gao Sihai, Gao Qingshan's father

Li Peizhong, head of Gaoyang County

Bian Ji, propaganda chief of Five-dragon Temple's Peasants' Resistance Association, who later joined the People's Defence Corps

Wu Dayin, Qiufen and Chun'er's father

One-eyed Tian, landlord in Ziwuzhen

Old Jiang, One-eyed Tian's underling

Gao Ba, brigand regiment commander

Su'er, Gao Ba's wife

Tian Yaowu, One-eyed Tian's son and bogus district head

A great drought gripped the central Hebei plain all the spring and summer of 1937. That May the River Hutuo dried up and hot winds, laden with swirling sand, blasted the russet knot-grass and foxtails along its banks. Wild flowers opened at night to wither away the next day. Dry as it was, however, the peasants foresaw a bad flood later on in the year. But the rain held off right up to early July, when merchants from Beijing and Baoding coming home to spend the summer brought the villagers news of the Japanese invasion of northern China.

The peasants of Ziwuzhen used to rest at noon in the shade of trees on the big dike north of the village. Under a great elm at a curve in the dike two girls, sitting face to face, were spinning yarn. Judging by their clothes and appearance they were sisters, one in her mid-teens, the other in her late twenties. The elder was rather pale, her face somewhat care-worn. The younger, on the other hand, seemed bubbling over with optimism and enthusiasm.

The leaves above their heads were utterly still. Cicadas were shrilling. From time to time caterpillar droppings fell to the ground. Far off a covered cart came into sight and the girls caught glimpses of its red mudguards and wheels behind crops golden and green, some high, some low. Two large mules were pulling the cart at a spanking pace, swishing their tails in the broiling noonday sun.

The sisters turned to look.

"Someone's coming home," said the elder.

"Let's see if it's my brother-in-law." The younger sprang to her feet.

"Don't you miss our dad?"

"I miss them all, but missing them won't bring them back." She stood on tiptoe, straining her eyes, then sat down abruptly and picked up her spindle again.

"What a let-down!" she grumbled. "It's One-eyed Tian's carriage bringing that son of his back from Baoding. None of *our* men ever come back. I wonder if one of them will come this year?"

The cart bowled past them to the village gate and Old Chang, the carter, jumped down from one shaft to flourish his long, red-tasselled whip and called out a cheerful greeting. His young master, of whom nothing but one ankle in black silk hose could be seen, peered out to look at the girls, who bent their heads.

The sisters' name was Wu. The elder was called Qiufen, the younger Chun'er. The elder had married into a family at Five-dragon Temple.

Five-dragon Temple was a small village on the south bank of the Hutuo, where the river raging down from the southwest made a sharp, precipitate turn. The villagers had built a high dike reinforced with wooden piles at this bend, for it was a notoriously dangerous stretch.

Many a time flood waters had swamped the village. Sometimes they swept everything away, leaving only a gaping pit. Sometimes they silted the whole place up with sand as high as the roof tops. But the little village never gave in to the flood. As soon as gongs sounded the warning, all the men and women, old and young, rushed out to the dike. They battled to stop the breach with anything that came to hand, taking doors and window-frames, rafters and tiles from their

2

houses. Women lugged over cases, chests, tables and chairs, or even brought along their bedding and mats. One year, it was said, they did all they could, used everything there was, but still failed to stop the breach. Then five young fellows jumped into the angry waters and threw themselves into the gap, yelling to the others to shovel earth over them — and so the dike was saved!

The villagers built a large temple to these men who had saved their lives and property. It was called Five-dragon Temple. As the years went by, that became the name of the village.

This small village, seemingly so snug in the plain, was exposed to the fury of the elements. And life was so hard that for years there had been very little increase in the population or the number of households.

Each time their houses were washed away by the flood, without waiting for the waters to subside completely the villagers helped each other to bake bricks and tiles, fell timber and saw wood to start rebuilding. Foundations were laid more firmly, walls piled thicker, the new homes made higher than the ones swept away. They built no courtyard walls or outhouses, just single rooms facing south. From a distance the place seemed a cluster of little towers, for high steps led up to each door and entering a house from the yard was like going upstairs.

Qiufen's father-in-law, Gao Sihai, was a man of sixty. People in these parts were music-lovers, and while still in split-bottomed pants he had learned to play the flute, soon becoming an adept. The sound of his flute carried ten li* or more, and the boatmen who heard it at night as they plied up or down the Hutuo forgot the hardships and fatigues of their

---

* One *li* is equal to half a kilometre or roughly one-third of a mile.

journey. His flute could draw the audience away from an opera. Buddhists or Taoists, who were chanting masses, were reduced by it to abject, crest-fallen silence.

Old Gao was not merely a fine flutist but an enterprising, cheerful character, the organizer of most village activities.

Ten years earlier there had been a peasants' uprising here. It spread from Gaoyang and Lixian until all the villagers brought out red flags and held meetings in the fields. That was the first appearance, stirring and splendid, of the red flag on this plain!

Gao Sihai, his eighteen-year-old son Qingshan and Qiufen, newly come to their house as a bride of seventeen, all took part in the uprising. Because of his courage, Qingshan became one of the leaders.

But in no more than a matter of days the uprising was defeated. One sultry day the peasant insurgents were forced back to the dike where, planting their red flag on Five-dragon Temple, they put up a last desperate stand, in the course of which Qingshan was wounded. That evening Old Gao got a friend to hide his son in his sampan and carry him to safety along with Gao Xiang, a middle-school student from their village.

Because of the confusion after the fighting, only two people saw Qingshan off. His father called through the window of the sampan:

"So long! Once safely away, you'll make shift somehow. Let those devils wait!"

He shoved the boat off, then turned back to help the peasants who had struggled and lost with them and now must bury their comrades shot down in the fields.

The other person seeing Qingshan off was his seventeen-year-old wife Qiufen. While father and son were talking, she stood a little way up the dike embankment. Black clouds from

4

the western hills had covered half the stars in the sky, and she was almost invisible in the dark. The sampan was nosing out into the river before she ran down, snatched a package from her pocket and tossed it neatly under the awning. Qingshan picked it up and leaned out to call her name.

Qiufen said nothing, just walked level with the boat along the dike. The storm broke. Raindrops as large as copper coins pelted thick and fast on the water. A northwest wind was helping the sampan along. Lightning flashed and thunder rumbled. The lurid light illumined the girl distinctly as she rolled up her trouser legs, pulled a ragged length of sacking over her head, and followed the small boat for a good ten *li*.

Wind and rain beat down on the seeds of revolution, burying them deep in the earth to wait for spring, when storm clouds would gather again. . . .

For nearly ten years there was no news of Qingshan. They did not know whether he were alive or dead. Then the student who had escaped with him was arrested in a factory in Shanghai. On his way to prison in Beiping the previous year, he had managed to send word that Qingshan had gone to Jiangxi.

All the land Old Gao owned was four *mu** on the flats. In a good year this gave him some black soya beans. He built himself a hut on the dike near the ferry, fixed up an awning before it, and sold tea and noodles here.

Qiufen made the noodles, the old man plied the bellows. He fetched water all the way from the village wells and sold it to passers-by, getting boatmen to bring him back cheap coal from Zhengding. In this way the two of them managed to make a living.

---

* One *mu* is equal to one-fifteenth of a hectare or roughly one-sixth of an acre.

Qiufen grew vegetables round their hut. After dusk she put a lamp in the small window facing south to guide the boats. On a frame before the window she trained loofah gourds and the loofahs, when full grown, hung down through the thick leaves nearly to the ground. At the southwest corner, overlooking the river, she planted a row of sunflowers, ready to welcome wanderers far from home. . . .

In winter and spring each year the river dried up and the ferry service stopped. Then Qiufen begged her father-in-law to water her plants while she went back to Ziwuzhen to help her younger sister spin and weave.

2

Ziwuzhen, just across the river from Five-dragon Temple, was very rarely flooded. Most of the rich loam east and north of the village was given over to irrigated fields which produced at least two and sometimes three crops a year. It was just the reverse of Five-dragon Temple with its sandy, alkaline flats and harvests so often spoiled by flood or drought.

All the landlords in Ziwuzhen had the surname Tian. The village head, known as the "boss" or One-eyed Tian, had lost an eye the year of the uprising, when he helped the county militia to hunt down the peasants. He owned nearly four hundred *mu* of good irrigated land and employed half a dozen farm hands. His large compound at the north end of the village included a threshing-floor and several courtyards. The family's living quarters on the left, divided into three courtyards, were hideous grey, brick buildings of fairly recent construction. By the threshing-floor on the right were the farm hands' quarters, the stable, mill, pigsty and poultry house. Poplars, weeping willows, peach, apricot and sweet cedrela trees grew inside the mud wall, against which were stacked piles of wheat, millet and sorghum stalks accumulated over the years. Half a dozen large mules were tethered in the shade of the trees, and on the threshing-floor were several big stone rollers.

Young Mangzhong, one of the hired hands, was chopping up straw in the shade of a willow with Old Wen, the handyman. Fragments of straw were flying in all directions, and soon they had stacked quite a pile. A hen with feathered legs was pecking for food nearby. Suddenly her wattles flushed and with a few squawks she laid an egg, which was soon buried in the straw.

The cart lumbered through the gate and Old Chang, cracking his whip a couple of times, strode on to the threshing-floor. As he hooked his whip on to the cart, Tian Yaowu alighted and brushed off his clothes. Old Chang carried the young master's luggage into the inner courtyard while Mangzhong put down his chopper, ran over to unharness the mules and led them to the well outside to be watered. Old Wen started unhitching the harness.

"Don't put that away!" Mrs. Tian, dressed in white linen, had come out to make sure that nothing had been left on the cart. "Someone will have to fetch Peizhong back tomorrow. What other daughter-in-law gives herself such airs? She won't come back unless we send to fetch her."

She examined the nesting-boxes at the foot of the east wall and called to Mangzhong, who was leading back the mules:

"I told you to keep an eye on the hens. Where have they laid all their eggs?"

"It's too hot in those boxes," replied the lad promptly. "They look for somewhere cool. There's no keeping track of them."

"Always some excuse, haven't you! I want you to buy some meat now. When you come back you must search till you find all the eggs." With this parting thrust, she went back to the house.

A family reunion! Like a good son, Tian Yaowu gave his father and mother lengths of contraband Japanese silk bought in Beiping. He had other things, too, never seen before in these parts: a thermos flask, electric torch and safety razor. He spread out a whole set of law books on the table, having specialized in law at Chaoyang University in Beiping. In his very first year there he started apeing officials, wearing a long gown, short black jacket, silk socks and satin slippers, playing mahjong or bringing prostitutes into the hostel. The eve of his graduation coincided with the Japanese threat to North China, and the atmosphere in Beiping became tense. The December 9th Movement* made most students more realistic: some did propaganda work among the troops, others went home to the country to organize the peasants. Tian Yaowu took no interest in such activities, though, devoting all his energy to finding an official position. Failing in this, he had no choice after his graduation but to go home.

His father consoled him, saying:

"If you can land an official job, so much the better. If not, we can afford to keep you at home. I put you through college to learn how to draw up petitions and charges. As long as we can hold on to our property, we'll be all right."

That evening saw a small celebration too in the outhouse.

---

* This refers to the patriotic demonstration held by students in Beiping under the leadership of the Communist Party on December 9, 1935 with the slogans, "End the civil war and unite to resist foreign aggression!" and "Down with Japanese imperialism!" After this, the Anti-Japanese United Front proposed by the Communist Party became the openly advocated policy of all patriotic people.

Old Chang and Old Wen were sitting on the stable *kang**
while Mangzhong lit the paraffin lamp over the manger,
brought in fodder and fed the mules.

"Mangzhong," said Old Chang. "Go and make sure the
gate to the inner yard's locked. Then bring us the bottle you'll
find in the tool box underneath the cart."

Dumping the fodder, Mangzhong hurried out to return
very soon with a bottle. Having opened it, he tilted back
his head and took a good swig before passing the spirits on to
Old Wen.

"How does it taste?" asked Old Chang. "That's strong
stuff."

"Wait a bit," said Mangzhong softly. "I'll fix something to
go with it."

He grabbed a ladle used for mixing mash, washed it in the
water bucket and emptied into it the dark oil from the cart's
two lamps. Then he rummaged in the straw for some eggs,
and fried them on the stove for heating the *kang*. Last of all
he broke up some stalks to serve as chopsticks.

"You drink a lot for a young 'un!" remarked Old Chang.
"Don't overdo it."

But each time the bottle came round to him, Mangzhong
did it full justice. Before very long he flopped down on the
kang.

"What a lad!" Old Chang sighed.

"Are things lively in Baoding now, Brother Chang?" asked
Old Wen.

"The place is seething. People are worried."

"Looks as if we'll have to fight the Japanese, does it?"

"The station is full of army officers, all seeing off their
families to the south."

----
* A brick platform used as a bed and for other purposes.

"So they don't mean to fight!" Old Wen pulled a long face. "How far have the Japanese got? Are they heading this way? What does the young master say?"

"What does he know?" Old Chang laughed. "He spent his night in Baoding at a bawdy-house. Seems to me young Mr. Tian will never amount to much." Once more Old Chang sighed. "He's been through university but he talks less sense than his wife. Here they've all been working themselves to the bone to feed such a useless clod."

"Working themselves to the bone? Not them!" scoffed Old Wen. "They've cartfuls of grain in the fields, piles of interest on the money they've invested in shops, not to mention an oil press and a cotton gin. Enough for him to fritter away! It's easy come, easy go for the likes of them. But we three and the poor devils pressing oil and ginning cotton for them have to keep our noses to the grindstone the whole year round. Look at him!" Old Wen laid a hand on Mangzhong's head. "He's never even been to primary school, let alone university."

Mangzhong sat up and patted him on the back.

"And Elder Brother Wen here is getting on for fifty, but has he married?"

"Let me ask you a riddle, Mangzhong," said Old Wen with a chuckle. "A fish bone between a pair of chopsticks — what's that?"

"Search me!"

"Two old bachelors and a young one! We ought to call this shack of ours 'Bachelors' Hall'. Or put up a placard saying, 'The Last of Their Line'. Oh, to hell with it. Time to sleep now." He swung his legs off the *kang*.

Mangzhong slept out on the threshing-floor on a mat. The night was fine with a breeze from the northwest, and there were no mosquitoes. The Milky Way slanted over the lad's head and in the utter silence his thoughts wandered.

He was at the age for day-dreams. Just turned eighteen, he had worked six years for the landlord. It was Chun'er's father Wu Dayin, then overseer on the farm, who had got him the job. But during the autumn harvest One-eyed Tian flew into a rage because Wu gave the young hands an extra meal of thin gruel. He kept twitting him with having a communist son-in-law, until Wu Dayin quit in disgust and set off in a tattered gown for the Northeast. Before leaving he entrusted his daughters to Old Gao's care and Mangzhong to his work-mate Old Chang. He told the girls to do Mangzhong's sewing and mending and make shoes and socks for him. The boy, for his part, rose early and slept late so as to have time to fetch water and do other heavy work for the two sisters.

If a poor country lad helps a girl with her work and she takes an interest in his food and clothing, they are likely to fall in love.

Today, when Mangzhong took his mules out to be watered, Chun'er was bending over her distaff on the dike, swaying lightly as she spun. He stood staring till one of his mules upset the empty bucket with a clatter and it nearly fell into the well. At that Chun'er had looked round and laughed.

Now Mangzhong scanned the Milky Way for the Weaving Maid. Then he located the halter thrown down beside her by her Cowherd husband, and the shuttle she had tossed to him.*

---

* The Cowherd and the Weaving Maid are the constellations Aquila and Lyra. According to Chinese legend, these were lovers parted by the Queen Mother of the West, who set them on opposite sides of the Milky Way and only allowed them to meet once a year, on the seventh day of the seventh month, when magpies formed a bridge over which they could cross.

11

In fancy he could see the Cowherd rushing frantically along the Milky Way, terrified that she might escape him. Would he, Mangzhong, ever save up enough to get married and hire a sedan-chair to fetch his bride home, he wondered? Would he ever have two or three *mu* of land or a little house of his own?

At that hour Chun'er was sound asleep on her *kang,* unaware that a young man was thinking about her. She did not hear her sister tossing and turning or murmuring endearments in her dreams. A green grasshopper on the trellis outside the window drank its fill of dew and set up a joyful shrilling. The gourds heavy with moisture drooped, and dew-drops rolled down the tender bloom on their skins. A large white flower on a long stem was reaching up from the trellis to the sky. Chirping away, the grasshopper crawled slowly up it.

Late in the night, dew fell. It fell on the sorghum thrusting up in the fields, on the russet dates splitting open as they ripened on the wall, on the spacious threshing-floor, on sturdy young Mangzhong and the stone roller beside him.

3

In spite of his assurances, One-eyed Tian now started pulling strings for his son. He was connected with Commissioner Zhang Yinwu of Boye and Yangcun, to whom he sent Yaowu with a letter. Zhang Yinwu was in charge of several adjoining counties, responsible for organizing militia and "electing" district heads. He told Tian Yaowu to go home and help in his own district.

One-eyed Tian's next move was to invite all the village heads and deputy heads of their district to a banquet. At the height of the feasting, his son's visiting cards were passed round and Tian Yaowu offered a toast. Then his father made clear the reason for this invitation.

"Brothers, I want you to do what you can for your nephew!"

The guests, mostly counterparts of their host, replied:

"That goes without saying. On one understanding: When Tian Yaowu is district head he must do what he can for us."

"Of course," agreed One-eyed Tian. "You may be sure he'll keep your interests at heart in all matters, large and small. Commissioner Zhang says the Japanese troops may be here any day. There's nothing any of us can do about that. If all the soldiers the government's been feeding can't stop them, what can we civilians do? But we must be on our guard. Because when that time comes there's bound to be trouble here, and we may take a beating — it won't be the first. With Yaowu in the district office, things won't be so bad. Commissioner Zhang wants to organize militia too. The order will soon be coming down for the well-to-do families in each village to buy guns and supply men. This is playing with fire! Without a reliable man in the district office, we'd have trouble on our hands."

"This drought has spoiled the harvest. Where's the money for guns to come from?" The village heads were worried. "Even a gun made in Hubei costs between seventy and eighty silver dollars."

"Well, it can't be helped. Those are the commissioner's orders. But that needn't worry us. When you get back to your villages, do your best. Make those who are flush fork out, and divide the remaining cost among the small fry. One thing, though: The people must pay, but once the guns are bought they must stay in our hands!"

So the feast ended, all the village heads and their deputies having promised to vote for Yaowu as district head.

It was very close. After seeing off his guests, One-eyed Tian had a wicker couch put in the porch and flopped down on it to cool off.

East of the village lived a certain Old Jiang who had never done an honest stroke of work in his life, but lived on the scraps he picked up from rich men's tables. Other people's misfortunes were meat and drink to him, for a wedding or funeral in the village, a trial on a capital charge, a fire or the ceremonies to invoke rain, meant pickings for Old Jiang. Now that the weather was so dry, some peasants could always be found at dawn and dusk staring up from the dike at the clouds and wondering when it would rain. Old Jiang would accost them, saying:

"Old Man Heaven is waiting for Ziwuzhen to put on a fine show!"

Few made any reply. They knew well enough that no amount of rain now could save the harvest. Nor could they afford the cost of putting on an opera to beg for rain.

Old Jiang was at a loose end when Tian's guests left. At once he slipped in, flourishing his fan, and padded softly over to One-eyed Tian.

"Old Man Heaven must be blind, I swear!" he exclaimed. "He won't send a shower of rain to cool you off in this confounded heat."

Tian did not raise his eyes, simply wagged the slipper dangling from his big toe.

"Get out!" he growled, half angry, half amused. "Have you come to lap up the dregs of my wine again?"

"Seems to me you've no idea how to live," said Old Jiang. "In the big cities they have electric fans. Why not get Yaowu to buy you one? We could stand beside you and enjoy the breeze."

14

When One-eyed Tian made no reply, Old Jiang started fanning him.

"All right," declared the landlord, sitting up. "Go and fetch my steward. The two of you can eat what's left of the feast."

Old Jiang lost no time in calling the steward, and the landlord told them his plan for raising funds to buy guns.

The steward and Old Jiang, one with a large abacus and the other with a wallet, started their round at Chun'er's cottage in the west end of the village.

Qiufen and Chun'er were just wondering where their padded clothes for the winter were to come from. They rose every day at cock-crow to spin while the moon was still in the sky. In the heat of the day they moved into the shade, spinning for all they were worth, to get enough yarn to sell at the next fair. When they heard of this new levy, Qiufen exclaimed:

"The crop's failed. We've no money to pay the usual levies. How can you ask for all these extras?"

"That's a wicked way to talk," replied Old Jiang. "Our village will have quite a decent harvest."

"Who in our village?" demanded Qiufen.

"If One-eyed Tian doesn't get eight bushels a *mu*, you can cut off my head!"

"He doesn't count," retorted Chun'er. "He's got those big water wheels. But we poor folk — don't talk about eight bushels — you can cut off my head if we get as much as eight pecks!"

"How much land have you, may I ask?" sneered Old Jiang.

"He's the one with all the land, let him pay the whole lot."

"Why should he bear the brunt?"

"If he won't, neither will we!"

"This concerns the whole village," persisted Old Jiang. "I'm not going to waste my breath arguing with you. If you refuse to pay, you'll have to give your reason to the public."

"Call yourselves the public?" Chun'er snorted. "Grubs from the same cesspool, more like. Apes from the same valley."

"You watch your tongue, my girl," warned the steward. "This fund's for buying guns to fight the Japanese. Once they get here, they'll make five households share one chopper and forbid you to bolt your door at night — would you like that?"

"To fight the Japanese I'll pay!" Chun'er drew some notes from her pocket. "This is what I got for my cloth at the last fair. For one *mu* and a half, seventy-two cents and a half — there." She handed Old Jiang the money.

"What a tongue that little bitch has!" grumbled Old Jiang as he and the steward moved on.

Since guns and bullets were said to be cheaper in the hills, Old Jiang wrote a letter to one of his shady friends there and One-eyed Tian told Mangzhong to handle the transaction. It was over a hundred *li* to the western hills, and the journey both ways would take two days and a night. But the boy was strong and could rough it.

It was seldom that Mangzhong had a chance like this. As soon as he received his orders, he put on a tattered straw hat and set out with nothing but two flapjacks to eat on the way.

The sun had already risen and peasants with hoes on their shoulders were heading for the fields. At the outskirts of the village, Mangzhong looked through Chun'er's wicker gate and saw her and her sister fastening the warp on a loom under the gourd trellis. Chun'er, holding a hank of yarn, had

16

fixed up half the warp. Mangzhong's jacket was torn — a good excuse to go in. At the sound of his step, Chun'er faced him without a word. Qiufen looked up to ask:

"Aren't you working yet, after sunrise?"

"Do me a favour!" He grinned. "Mend this jacket for me." He put down his flapjacks and took off his jacket.

"What's the big hurry?" asked Chun'er, stopping work.

"I'm taking a letter to the hills."

"Trust them to send *you* on an errand like that!"

"I eat his rice, I have to carry out orders." Mangzhong hung his head.

"Chun'er will mend it for you," said Qiufen. "She's got her thimble on."

Chun'er went inside to rummage in her work-basket and came out with a needle stuck into the breast of her jacket, the long strand of white cotton threaded through it reaching nearly to the ground. Taking the jacket she exclaimed:

"It's so far gone, what it really needs is a patch."

"Just cobble it up and that will do," said Mangzhong.

Paying not the least attention, Chun'er went inside again for a piece of white cloth which she measured against the rent and sewed firmly into place on the reverse side. Then she bit off the thread, smoothed out the material and said:

"Well, that place should hold now, whatever else gets torn."

Mangzhong pulled on his jacket and went to look at their vat.

"Empty again!" he cried. "I'll get you some water."

"We'll do it ourselves presently," said Qiufen. "If your master sees you, you'll catch it."

"This is none of his business, he can't stop me," countered the boy. "I shan't be back again for two or three days."

17

He took their buckets and pole and fetched them two loads, filling the vat to the brim. Then he fetched another two bucketfuls to water the gourds.

Behind his back, Chun'er smiled. The jacket she had just mended was gaping again.

"Here! That needs a few more stitches." She beckoned him over.

They stood face to face, the girl half a head shorter than the boy. On tiptoe, she moved his arm to where she wanted it and set about her mending. Mangzhong lowered his head and kept his lips clamped together. Chun'er's proximity and her warm scent set his blood racing, made his breath come faster. And when she met his eyes, a wave of colour swept over her neck and cheeks, suffusing her whole face. Hastily making a knot, she broke off the thread then turned away, telling him over her shoulder:

"You must make do with that for a couple of days. When our weaving's finished, I'll make you a new jacket."

4

Mangzhong picked up his flapjacks and bounded off down the dike. Never before had the birds in the Ziwuzhen willows sung so sweetly. A breeze blew over his shoulder, he felt as if on wings. He overtook an ox cart taking a young wife to visit relatives, then passed a hawker carrying a great load of musk-melons to the fair. He outdistanced everybody going his way. Some wheat had been knocked down by the side of the road. "Fine big ears, it's too bad to let them be spoiled," he thought, and propped the plants up again. There was a large pot-hole in the rutted road where a cart might easily upset, and he filled it in. On the slope leading up to a village an old man was sweating and straining behind a barrow of grain, which kept sliding back till Mangzhong lent a helping hand. In the village he found a child who had fallen down. He picked it up and comforted the toddler, then told it to run home to its mother.

That evening he crossed the Beiping-Hankou Railway. He saw grey water-towers and red and green lights at the station and heard the whistle of engines. Coach after coach of soldiers and horses were rolling south. On the roofs, stacked with baggage, there huddled women and children.

Now he struck into the mountains up a stone path, climbing one hill after another. Each time he asked the way of a countryman, he was directed to the hill in front. "Just keep going that way. Straight ahead."

Summers here were short. The grass on the south side of the hills was green, but on the north it was silvered over with frost. Dates were spread out on white roof tops, black goats were leaping from one rock to another. There were many wayside springs whose slow upwelling of water reminded him of a crab blowing bubbles. Never had Mangzhong tasted such pure water. He kept kneeling down to cup his hands and drink.

He forged ahead, kicking up pebbles, till the soles of his shoes were in holes and pebbles got in. "I'll have to ask Chun'er's help again when I get back!" he thought. He picked up some smooth purple stones and slipped them into his pocket, for these were treasures to children on the plain, who occasionally found one in the fields and maintained that it was dropped by a crow carrying it back from the hills to serve as a pillow. He would give these stones to the little girls for their games.

At noon he reached Chengnanzhuang, a sizable market. Under a clump of willows on the river bank a middle-aged

19

woman was sitting making cloth shoes by a barrow of dates and beancurd. Mangzhong sat down on a rock and took off his shoes.

The large stream in front was called the River of Rouge. Sunlight glinted on clear water as it rippled over the red sandstone bed. From the opposite bank sounded singing and cheerful shouting.

Presently troops rounded the hill, not in formation but in twos and threes. They wore broad-brimmed straw hats and had shabby padded jackets over their shoulders. Coming to the river, they took off their shoes and rolled up their trouser legs to wade swiftly across, talking and laughing together. They stopped to rest under the willows.

"What troops are those, sister?" Mangzhong asked the woman.

"Red Army men," she told him. "One lot passed through here a few days ago. They don't look much, but they can fight! I've heard they fought their way up here from Jiangxi. Over twenty thousand *li*."

"From Jiangxi, eh?" said Mangzhong. "Any men from these parts among them?"

"Not that I've seen," she answered. "They talk in an out-landish way. But they don't try to cheat you. They're good to us ordinary folk."

"The troops on the train were going south. Why are these marching north?"

"They're two different sorts, that's why. The ones going south are Chiang Kai-shek's men. They eat the people's grain but don't fight, they're good for nothing but bullying honest people. These soldiers are really out to fight the Japanese. Just listen to what they're singing."

Mangzhong listened and heard a song calling on the people to get organized and resist the invaders. The Red Army men

20

had scattered, some to sleep in the shade of the trees, others to wash their faces in the stream. A dark, gaunt man walked up to Mangzhong and asked:

"Where are you from, young fellow? You don't look like one of the hill people."

"I'm from the plain," said Mangzhong. "Shenze County."

"Shenze?" The soldier's face lit up and he went on in the local dialect, "Which village in Shenze?"

"Ziwuzhen. You speak like a man from hereabouts, sergeant."

"Come on, we two must have a talk." The soldier led Mangzhong under a nearby tree and rolled a cigarette for each of them.

"Let me ask you something." He eyed Mangzhong eagerly. "Do you know a man called Wu Dayin in your village?"

"I should say I do! We used to work for the same boss. In fact, he found me that job. But he's left home now and is growing vegetables in Mudanjiang."

"He has a daughter. . . ."

"Two daughters, Qiufen and Chun'er," Mangzhong put in. "Which village are *you* from? Do you know Gao Qingshan?"

The Red Army man's eyes shone but he paused before answering:

"I know him. Are his folk alive and well?"

"They certainly are! Times are hard, of course, but they manage. They're just longing for Qingshan to come back. Have you any news of him?"

"He may be coming this way." The soldier smiled. "I wouldn't be surprised if he went home for a look."

"That would be grand," cried Mangzhong. "Qiufen's eating her heart out for him. If you see him, be sure to tell him to go home and see them."

"Where are you off to now?"

"I'm delivering a message for my boss."

"What's his name?"

"One-eyed Tian."

"Who's he?"

"The landlord at the north end of our village. That year of the uprising the Red Army shot him in the eye."

"Him!" The soldier's eyes glinted coldly and his thick eyebrows contracted. "What's become of those who took part in the uprising?"

"Some are dead, some have left home."

"How's the people's morale?"

"What's that?"

"Are they keen to resist Japan?"

"I'll say they are! I'm on my way to buy guns so that we can train to fight the Japanese."

"Who's taking the lead in this?"

"One-eyed Tian."

"Bah!" growled the soldier. "He won't use the weapons against the Japanese. You must get organized and take over the guns yourselves."

He explained to Mangzhong the need to resist Japan. But it was late, the boy had to be going on, and the soldier saw him on his way. As they parted, Mangzhong asked:

"Will you honestly be seeing Qingshan, comrade?"

"Yes. You tell his folk not to worry. He's doing fine. He'll surely be over to see them before long." With that, he lowered his head and turned away.

Mangzhong went on more cheerfully than ever now that he had reliable news of Qingshan. How pleased this was going to make the two sisters! He delivered the letter, transacted his business, and started quickly home the next day. But the troops had already left the River of Rouge. The woman selling beancurd told him they had marched north the previous night.

Back in Ziwuzhen, Mangzhong found Qiufen and Chun-er finishing off a length of cloth. From a distance he started grinning. Striding up to them, he said softly:

"Sister Qiufen, come on inside. I've news for you."

"What's the mystery now?" Chun'er looked up.

"Come on in, both of you." He strode to their cottage.

There, sitting on the edge of the *kang*, he told them:

"I've grand news! Brother Qingshan will soon be home."

Qiufen in the doorway bombarded him with questions. Mangzhong had to tell his story again and again. When finally he had given a detailed description of the Red Army man's appearance and way of talking, Qiufen burst into tears.

"Why, what's the matter?" asked Mangzhong in dismay.

"It was him you saw, I'm sure," sobbed Qiufen. "Has he no heart, to hide the truth from one of his own folk?"

Chun'er, who had brought in an armful of yarn, started scolding Mangzhong too.

"Hadn't you enough sense to question him properly? What were his clothes like?"

"Very old and patched."

"And his shoes and socks?"

"He wasn't wearing socks. And I wouldn't call those shoes either — just a few rags bound together." He gestured to show what he meant.

"Why ask such questions?" demanded Qiufen. "I'm sure it was him. Who else would know so much about us?"

"Did he have a beard?" persisted Chun'er.

"Hair all over his face," replied Mangzhong.

"Doesn't sound like him," said Chun'er.

"He's been away for ten years, why shouldn't he grow a beard?" retorted Qiufen, laughing. Too excited to keep still, she set off for Five-dragon Temple. Chun'er watched her with a smile. Her sister's step was as light as if she had just got over a serious illness.

5

Back in Five-dragon Temple, Qiufen told her father-in-law Mangzhong's news coupled with her own reading of it.

"It must have been him," agreed Old Gao. "He couldn't speak openly because these parts are still under the same old gang."

He threw a jacket over his shoulders and picked up his pipe.

"You stay and keep an eye on things here while I take a turn in the village."

"Don't tell anyone!" she cautioned him. "Wait till he's really back."

"I know. What do you take me for, a fool? I'm only going to tell a few close friends, folk we can trust. After all, they think as much of Qingshan as we do."

He was still not back by nightfall, when Qiufen locked the door and went to the village herself.

She called at the home of Gao Xiang, who had run away at the same time as Qingshan and was now in prison in Beiping. The household consisted of Gao Xiang's father and mother, a wife about Qiufen's age, and a little girl. Qiufen often dropped in to chat with Gao Xiang's wife. They did not see eye to eye on everything, for young Mrs. Gao had been rather spoiled as a child and, much as she loved her husband, she could not understand him and thought his conduct foolish. Because his family was fairly well-to-do, she had not supported the uprising but been badly frightened by it. Still, she always enjoyed a talk with Qiufen and would say, "Qiufen,

we're in the same boat. . . . I'm even worse off than you."
For at that time there was simply no word from Qingshan
while Gao Xiang was in prison as a Communist and that, as
even his small daughter knew, meant he might lose his head.

Gao Xiang's parents had travelled up to Beiping to see
him, but when his wife wanted to take the child to the prison
the old folk said he was against it. Instead they told her to
make him a padded gown. It had to be cut to fit over the
chains round his waist, with a curious bulge in the middle
like the gown of a child unable to fasten a belt. Since she
could not bear to work on it for long at a stretch, it took her
several nights to finish. At each stitch she let fall a tear, till
the cotton was soaked.

They had been a loving couple from the day of their
wedding. When Gao Xiang escorted her on her first visit
home and they crossed the Hutuo which was swollen in summer, the rocking of the ferry-boat made the timid young bride
feel faint. Then in front of everyone her husband put his arm
round her and covered her eyes. The villagers with their
feudal ideas had a good laugh at that and the story spread
far and wide.

Recalling the past only made Gao Xiang's wife more
wretched. She had never smiled again since her husband's
imprisonment, never worn any new clothes. The family hung
up no red lanterns at New Year, bought no moon cakes at
the Mid-autumn Festival. When night fe'l they closed their
door and went to bed.

This evening Qiufen reached their house just as lamps
were being lit in the village. She saw light through the window paper and for the first time in ten years heard Gao
Xiang's wife laughing.

She found the family seated round the table so absorbed
in a letter that her entry went unnoticed.

"What are you all so pleased about?" she asked.

"We've had good news."

"My dad's out of prison!" cried the girl, who was leaning over the table.

"Yours is a dad in a thousand!" Her mother patted her, and told Qiufen, "Gao Xiang's come out. He asks after you all in his letter. You've arrived just at the right time. Sit down, quick, and listen."

So Qiufen had to keep back her own good news and sit down on the *kang* to hear theirs.

The letter had in fact been read out earlier that day, but after supper the little girl begged her grandfather to read it out again. He spread it flat on the table while he polished his glasses, then picked up the letter and held it this way and that as if to find the best light. These preliminaries lasted so long that his wife, sitting by the quilts on the *kang*, lost patience.

"You're slower, I do declare, than an actor dressing up!"

"If you're so smart, you take over." He put the letter down on the table again, took off his glasses and weighed them in his hand. "Can't you see I'm old and my eyes are failing, woman? And your son's writing is mighty hard to read. I can't abide these new-fangled fountain pens."

"All right. Get a move on! Read!" His wife shut her eyes to listen. The child strained forward, tugging at her ears.

Although Gao Xiang's letter was addressed to his parents, even his ten-year-old daughter, not to say Qiufen, could tell that many passages were meant for her mother. As her grandfather read, she saw her mother's face turn a deeper and deeper crimson.

The letter said:

After my release I came straight to Yan'an. Now I'm studying in Wayaobao under the direction of Chairman

26

Mao himself. Soon we shall be marching north to resist Japan. This makes up for all my wanderings and troubles of the last ten years.

His father broke off at this point to say:

"Yan'an. That's a familiar name. I can't just rightly remember where it is. Go and get me a map from his case."

Gao Xiang's wife promptly fetched and opened her husband's dusty case of books, not touched for years. After hunting in it for a while, she passed a volume to her father-in-law, who said:

"This is a dictionary. Let *me* have a look."

He found his son's old geography book and pored over the map of China. After quite a search he located the name Yan-an in brackets under Fushi County in the province of Shaanxi. Measuring the distance with two fingers, he declared:

"Look, here's Shenze where we are, and here's Yan'an where Gao Xiang and his friends are. Only about an inch apart, but to cover that distance on foot would take some days."

Gao Xiang's mother sighed.

"Ten years he's been away, keeping us on pins and needles all the time. When at last they let him go, why didn't he come home to see his mother before running off like this to the back of beyond?"

"You're a foolish old woman," said her husband. "There's someone there your son cares for more, that's why."

The letter mentioned Qingshan and the likelihood that he had joined the Long March and had come north from Jiangxi to resist Japan. At this, Qiufen told them the news Mangzhong had brought and they shared in her happiness. The old man put the letter back in its envelope and gave it to his daughter-in-law. Handling it as if it were gold or jade, Gao

27

Xiang's wife passed it to old Mrs. Gao, who tucked it carefully under the pile of quilts.

Cupping her chin in her hands, the little girl looked at her mother and cried:

"Mum, let's go and find my dad."

"You're ready to leave home?" her mother asked.

"Of course I am. Will you come too? If you won't, I'll go alone."

"You go alone." Her mother laughed.

If only she could send the child to her husband! It would be like making a coat, with her child as the needle to carry the long thread from her mother's heart to him, binding them together; or like a canal bearing water from one pool to the next, a small bird flitting from bough to bough, from one tree to another. . . .

That night at least two women in the little village of Five-dragon Temple were too excited to sleep.

It was oppressively hot. Old Gao was not yet back when Qiufen reached home. As soon as she lit the paraffin lamp, insects flew in through the window to flutter round it. The *kang* was so hot that she picked up a tattered rush fan and stepped out on to the dike. The sunflowers shedding golden pollen in the dark were giving off a cloying scent. A speck of light was approaching from the village; she recognized the sparks of Old Gao's pipe.

After supper Chun'er had come to find her sister. She was pleased for Qiufen's sake and looking forward herself to Qingshan's return. As Qiufen was out she went back, crossing the river under a pitch black sky. Then the moon came up, turning both banks white and disclosing the upturned ferry-boat, grounded and waiting for the river to rise.

Now she had to cross a white sand dune and clump of willows.

Smooth, lissom willow branches stroked her hands and face, while a grasshopper that had just cast its skin set up a cheerful din. Chun'er stopped and, gently parting the willow branches, tiptoed forward to catch the grasshopper.

Suddenly a black figure jumped up from the ground at her feet. The girl gave a cry.

It was Mangzhong. Chuckling, he said:

"After supper I fed the cattle and washed my feet by the well in the kitchen garden. From there I saw something white flitting through the willows. I thought it was a big bird come here to roost. When I slipped out to catch it, I found it was your white jacket."

"After scaring me stiff, you spin a yarn like that!"

"All right, so I came to meet you. Is Uncle Sihai pleased?"

"Who wouldn't be pleased when his son's coming back? Tomorrow he may treat you."

"Treat me to what?"

"To a big bowl of noodles with all the trimmings." She smiled. "You've gone and frightened my grasshopper away. Let's go home."

"What's the rush? Let's stay and have a little fun here."

"What fun? This place gives me the creeps." Chun'er started off.

"Wait for me!" called Mangzhong softly. "Wait while I catch that grasshopper. It's chirping again." He slipped in between the willows, following the sound, and Chun'er tagged at his heels.

Suddenly he gripped her hand. With a choking feeling she pulled away, lost her balance and fell down.

The willows above made a thick canopy. Late as it was, the sandy soil was soft and warm after a day of fierce sun. Anthills sprinkled the ground and brown ants were still milling

29

around in the dark. One crawled up Chun'er's flushed, moist cheek.

Unaccountably, the girl burst into tears.

"What are we doing here?" she asked. "If you've something to say, go on and say it."

"They're all tickled pink because Qingshan's coming back. Tell me, why shouldn't the two of us get married?"

Chun'er hung her head and scooped up a handful of sand. The damp earth below felt cool to her burning fingers.

"It's no use," she answered at last. "You couldn't keep me."

"But if Qingshan comes back? And if I get a chance to make good?"

"I only hope you will!" she assured him. "But I'm not an old woman yet. What's all the hurry?"

6

When Chun'er reached home the courtyard was flooded with moonlight. She opened the door, went in and sat on the *kang*, staring dreamily out of the window.... Her white jacket, wet through, smelled of soil and the crushed grass under the willows. Moonlight streaming in through the vine leaves and lattice window fell on her firmly rounded, youthful breasts.

Her heart was beating fast. She felt rather frightened, rather frustrated too. She pricked up her ears. The wind was rising out there in the fields.

She went out. Black clouds were gathering swiftly in the northwest. Soon all stars and trees there were blotted out from sight. Mist veiled the parched fields. Crops, trees, grass and flowers were trembling in joyful anticipation of a storm.

30

At midnight the storm broke. Torrential rain merged earth and sky in one. A faint roar like the bellowing of an old bull sounded in the distance upstream.

Mangzhong had not repaired their roof this year and it started leaking. Water came dripping through a dozen cracks. Chun'er put all her bowls and basins on the *kang* to keep it dry and, holding the lid of a pan over her head, paced up and down the room.

Hundreds of frogs seemed to have sprung up from nowhere. The din of their chorus of croaking was enough to split the sky. Chun'er was a little afraid, all on her own, but she ran out through the pelting rain to the dike. All around was a swirl of white. A hare dashed wildly on to the embankment, turned a somersault at her feet and streaked towards the village.

"The river will soon be in spate!" she thought, hurrying back.

The next day the weather cleared and the flood swept down, breaching the north side of the dike and surrounding Ziwuzhen. Day and night, sounding gongs and drums, the villagers mounted guard over the dike. They heard a distant rumbling, but did not learn till later that Japanese troops had occupied Baoding. Water could not stop the homeless refugees from coming over like swarm after swarm of locusts. Every day after their meals, the people of Ziwuzhen gathered on the embankment to watch the pitiful sight.

Some of the refugees came from nearby Baoding or Gao-yang, others all the way from the Northeast. You could gauge the distance and the time spent on the road from their faces, foot-gear and the possessions they carried, which dwindled from day to day. Those from far away had blistered feet swollen from immersion in the muddy water. Sounding the water with a green stalk of sorghum, they made their way

31

slowly and painfully towards the dike. Their haggard faces were blackened by the sun, sorghum flowers sprinkled their hair, and because their strength was spent they had to ask watchers on the dike to help them up.

One young woman with a baby on her back was leading a child who kept slipping and falling in the turgid water. When at last they reached the embankment, she appealed to Chun'er:

"Will you help my kiddy up, lass?"

When she had pulled them all up, they sat down on the dike and a group of women flocked round. Chun'er ran home to fetch some steamed buns for the children.

"Thank you, lass!" cried the woman. "We had a home of our own and a trade too. But now the Japanese have taken over there."

"Where are you from?" asked Chun'er.

"The Northeast. We thought this side of the Great Wall we'd be all right. But the Japanese have raced us here. They push on faster than we can run away. Heaven knows if we'll ever reach a place of safety."

"Have you no husband?" asked Chun'er.

"It was too much for him — he died near Beiping. . . ." She wiped her eyes.

"How far have the Japanese got now?" asked another woman.

"There's no telling," was the reply. "Yesterday when we stopped for the night there, Gaoyang was just as quiet as you are here. But when we got up this morning the people of Gaoyang started running too."

This news was received in silence. After nursing her baby, the woman limped off down the dike with the other refugees.

The day was clear and bright. The flood lapped round the village and flowed east. The peasants, knee-deep in water, reaped the crops which had ripened and piled them on the dike or spread them out over the roof tops to dry.

A drone like that of a gadfly was heard in the sky. As it grew in volume, they saw something like a hawk. Drawing nearer, this proved to be planes flying in formation towards the village.

"Look!" The peasants pointed upwards. "Three airships. No, five of 'em!"

For them this was a rare sight. Those indoors rushed out into the yard, those in the yard climbed the roof. Bands of children scampered along the dike, clapping their hands.

One of the refugees called over her shoulder:

"Don't stand there watching, folks! Take cover! Those Japanese planes are coming to bomb you."

No one paid the least attention. Some women urged others to put down their sewing and come out.

"Hurry! Hurry! They'll soon have passed."

But instead of passing, the planes circled overhead.

"Like hens with wings!" cried one woman. "Looking for somewhere to lay their eggs."

Crash! Not till the bombs fell and the planes started strafing did the villagers scatter in confusion or fall flat. Two were killed on the dike. A mule was blown to pieces.

Following the curve of the bay, the planes kept up their strafing. A boatload of refugees was crossing the river. The water was so high, the current so strong, that when the passengers panicked the ferry-boat overturned, plunging old and young into the swirling waves. They rose to the surface, screaming for help, then sank. . . .

The planes went on strafing and bombing, raising blood-red jets of water.

All the swimmers in Five-dragon Temple jumped into the river to save the refugees. Old Gao tore off his clothes and struck out through the waves to rescue a baby who was being swept downstream. Swimming over a *li* in one spurt, he caught the child by the leg and carried him ashore. Walking through the dripping refugees who had been rescued, he shouted:

"Where's this boy's mother? Whose is this child?"

Unable to find the boy's mother, he laid the child face down on the dike and jumped into the water again. He made a point of rescuing women, and to each of them he said:

"Don't cry! Hurry up and cough up that water you've swallowed. I've saved your little boy for you."

When the woman shook her head at sight of the child, he jumped into the river again.

So it went on till dusk, by which time the flood had claimed a great many victims. When bonfires had been lit to dry the survivors, Old Gao made another search for the little boy's mother. Told that she was the dark young woman from the Northeast, who had been wounded and drowned with her elder boy, Old Gao called Qiufen over.

"Take this baby to someone who has milk," he said. "His own mother's dead, so we'll keep him."

"Keep a baby, in times like these!"

"If you won't take him, I will." Hot tears welled up in his eyes. "Times like these, indeed! Don't talk rubbish!"

That night, the refugees slept sprawled out by the embers of the bonfires. The river ran fast and savagely pounded the bay, sucking away clods of earth. Moonlight fell on a boundless expanse of misty water, on ruined crops lashed by the waves. All the villagers far and near were gripped by panic. Many were sleepless that night in their despair. A child's ear-splitting cries filled Old Gao's hut.

"Damned Japanese!" Curses drifted through every small village window, muttered even by those tossing restlessly in their dreams.

7

Before this, Ziwuzhen had bought guns. One-eyed Tian appropriated a revolver, gave a mauser to his son, and handed over two rifles to some landlords' sons in the village. They agreed to drill each morning at the cross-roads under Tian Yaowu's direction. Since these fellows had no interest in drilling and dreaded the possibility of actually being called upon to fight, they never showed up punctually or in force, and generally scattered as soon as the roll had been called. And their instructor, although a university graduate who had gone through military training in the summer vacation, had no idea how to drill them. One day he drew his men up in two lines.

"First rank, attention!" he shouted. "Second rank, forward march five steps!"

When the second rank butted the backsides of the first, Tian Yaowu turned scarlet in front of the whole village, after which he never mustered his men again.

But these youngsters did take an interest in their guns. They slung these rifles over their shoulders at night to go whoring, and boasted that they would soon be officers. Tian Yaowu, whose wife had not come back, was having an affair with Old Jiang's daughter Su'er, with whom he spent most nights.

Su'er was Old Jiang's third daughter. Her two elder sisters, both married now, were not particularly good-looking. But Su'er was the village beauty. By fifteen she already had so

35

many lovers that she never had to pay for a meal at a fair, or buy herself a length of material. She was nineteen this year and her spotless room had snowy white paper on the windows, a red silk quilt on the *kang*. Tian Yaowu, arriving towards midnight, dumped his gun on the *kang* to frighten her.

"You'd better look out! If you mess around with anyone else, I'll get you with this."

"Think you're scaring me?" She chuckled. "I've handled more guns than you've seen. You lug it around, but can you use it? Can you do this?" Planting one foot on the *kang*, she laid the gun across her red-trousered knee, cocked it and pointed it at him. Tian Yaowu ducked quickly behind the *kang*, protesting:

"Stop fooling! You might hit me!"

Su'er clicked back the safety-catch and put the gun on the table.

"Don't try to frighten me with that," she said. "If you threatened to stop my allowance if I went with another fellow, I might sit up and take notice."

"Rubbish. You can hitch up with anyone you please. Soon I'll be leaving."

"Where are you going?" She trimmed the lamp and plumped down on the *kang*.

"South, to get an official post."

"Taking that with you?" She indicated the gun.

"Yes. The roads are none too safe."

"You people with money can go wherever you like. Will you take me along to wash and clean for you?" When he simply grinned, she went on, "I was only joking. Why should I go with you? I was born unlucky, hard knocks are all I expect. I'll wait and see what it's like when the Japanese come; if you're fated to die, there's no getting away. Why worry? If the sky falls the earth will prop it up. Still, it'll cost you a pretty sum travelling south."

"We aren't short of cash," said Tian. "But my old man's buried it all. I'll have to go to our shop in town to get money."

"Even a poor man takes money for the road, and you're rich. When are you leaving? Is the date fixed yet? I must give you a good send-off."

"There's no need for that. Get undressed now and let's sleep. I'll tell you before I go."

Undressing slowly, Su'er said:

"The roads aren't safe. Is anyone going with you?"

"No. The Beiping-Hankou Railway's cut. Old Chang will see me to Puyang and from there I'll go by train."

"Will you cross the river at Five-dragon Temple?"

"That's it." He blew out the light.

That night the arrival of troops threw the village into confusion, and One-eyed Tian sent Mangzhong to rout Tian Yaowu out of his warm quilt. Barely had Su'er closed her eyes again when she heard a tapping on her window.

"Has he gone?" a man called softly.

"Yes, he's gone."

"Did you find out?"

"Yes, he'll have a gun and money. Old Chang will be with him. They'll cross at Five-dragon Temple."

"When?"

"That isn't fixed yet. Just keep a watch on the ferry. And if you pull it off, don't forget to thank me."

"You've done a good deed!" The man outside chuckled softly. "I'll buy you a new coloured jacket."

"Are you coming in to sleep?" she asked coaxingly.

"What, take another man's leavings? To hell with you!" He climbed the roof and left.

A cavalry unit had galloped into the village. At first they were taken for Japanese and the villagers bolted their doors. When the soldiers broke the doors down, it was seen that these were men of the 53rd Army. Sweat was pouring off their horses which lay down, saddles and all, in the road to rest. At once the village office prepared food, drink and fodde·, while the soldiers ransacked the place, firing at random. If a dog ran across the street, they shot it dead. One-eyed Tian asked the commander to his house and was giving him a feast when some soldiers burst in. He went to the gate to say:

"Take it easy, fellows! Your commander is here."

"Devil of a commander!" They prodded One-eyed Tian with the butt of their rifles. "Fetch him out! We want to see him. If he had any guts he'd lead us against the Japanese. All this bastard does is to lead a retreat. He's nearly ridden our horses to death, the swine!"

Before cock-crow, after some looting, these troops were ordered to start south again. Cursing and swearing, they swung into their saddles and rode off helter-skelter.

"Looks bad." One-eyed Tian had called in his son. "You must cut that long hair of yours."

"What difference will that make?" asked Tian Yaowu glumly.

"What difference?" bellowed his father. "Does it make no difference to you if you live or die? The Japanese come down hard upon students. I'm not afraid for myself."

His mother pleaded with him too and called Old Chang to shave her son's head, round which she wrapped a new towel.

"That towel's too conspicuous," grumbled One-eyed Tian. "You'd better eat early and make a trip to town."

Tian Yaowu's appearance with a shaven head greatly increased the villagers' consternation.

"Why has the district head given up that foreign hair style?"

"For fear of the Japanese."

"Does a shaved head mean you're all right? We've all got shaved heads."

"Why should the Japanese care how much hair a man has?"

After collecting several hundred dollars from the shop in town, Tian Yaowu went to the county government. The placard above it had been taken down, the front door to the main building was barred, there was no one responsible on the premises. He searched for quite a time before he found a messenger he knew, who told him that the county head and section chiefs had commandeered eight carts and left for the south in the middle of the previous night, taking guns, money and provisions. Tian promptly went home and lost no time in packing.

"Take our title-deeds with you," urged his mother.

"No one's going to move the land away," scoffed One-eyed Tian. "What good would it do to take away the deeds? We'll just bury them. Don't forget I'll be guarding the house."

He sent for Old Chang and gave him certain instructions. Old Chang went back to his quarters to fetch some shoes and found Old Wen and Mangzhong on tenterhooks.

"Brother Chang," said Old Wen. "Ask the young master if he won't take me too."

"What would you do down south?"

"Earn my rice the same as up here. I don't want to stay here to be killed by the Japanese."

"Ask him to take me too," begged young Mangzhong.

"What a hope!" said Old Chang. "Don't worry, things will work out. I'm starting off with him, but the moment he doesn't need me he'll send me back. That's why I'm taking an extra pair of shoes. While it suits their book they'll use us, then kick us out on to the rubbish heap. Why should you want to go with him? You could starve for all he cares."

Not till dusk did Tian Yaowu set off with Old Chang. To avoid attracting attention, his father and mother did not see him off. The travellers took a muddy path round the village, and met not a soul on their way. When they neared Five-dragon Temple, Old Chang went ahead to call the ferry-boat which was moored unattended by the opposite bank. Old Chang made a megaphone of his hands to hail it. Some minutes passed before an answering shout came back across the misty river.

"Coming!"

Tian Yaowu and Old Chang waited on the shore. The water was beginning to subside but the current was swift and the boat heading downstream was tossing like a leaf. It drew alongside with only three people aboard. In the darkness a girl jumped down, calling mockingly to the ferrymen:

"Thanks for the ride! I know you won't take my money."

"Anything to oblige!" retorted one boatman, laughing. "Next time we'll ask you for a ride."

"Get along with you! Dirty dogs!" Just then the girl caught sight of Tian and said:

"Isn't it the district head?"

Tian had recognized Su'er's voice and answered coolly:

"I've some business in Five-dragon Temple."

"Business?" She laughed. "Even the county head has skedaddled. It's time for the district heads to hand over too."

Not troubling to answer, Tian made Old Chang go aboard.

"Who is it?" asked Old Chang. "I don't know your voices."

The boatmen cast off in silence. The helmsman kept his back to them, looking out across the swirling water to where

Su'er was being swallowed up in the darkness. The crossing did not take long. As Tian Yaowu jumped ashore and took out some money, the helmsman finally spoke.

"We're not asking any fare. Leave us your gun!"

"Why should I?" demanded Tian apprehensively.

"The villagers stumped up for that gun to fight the Japanese. Where are you taking it?" The helmsman leapt ashore and seized Tian's arm.

"You robbers!" cried Tian Yaowu, struggling.

"Are we robbers, or you? We've stopped eight carts belonging to the county government. There's nothing you can do. If you don't want to travel by land, there's always the river." He heaved Tian over his shoulder.

"All right, you win." The district head threw down his gun.

"Fifty bullets too!" said the helmsman.

"What use are bullets to me without a gun?" He handed them meekly over.

"And your money."

"I need that for my journey," protested Tian. "How am I to travel if you take it away?"

"You've more than you need. We'll leave you enough to take you to Puyang."

Some other men materialized to search him. Heaving taken his money they left. Out on the river the helmsman tried the new gun, firing a round from it.

"The bandits!" spluttered Tian. "Where are they from?"

"One sounded like Gao Ba, who's so thick with Su'er," said Old Chang. "Well, do we go on?"

"What else can we do?" replied Tian. "I can't stay here. But they've left me so short of money, after seeing me one stage you'll have to go back."

41

8

After the army's retreat and the county head's flight, the villagers of Ziwuzhen resigned themselves to fate, not troubling to harvest the crops in the water-logged fields. Small groups of gamblers sprang up everywhere. A Taoist from Changshi Temple in Anguo moved in to live with Old Jiang and set up a shrine where he invoked ghosts and spirits. Women flocked day and night to kowtow there.

Word came that the Japanese had reached Dingxian. One of the local gentry, a salt merchant and a pharmacist had formed a committee for the maintenance of order to which all the village heads were affiliated, and they intended to welcome the Japanese into the town on August the fifteenth. One-eyed Tian returned from the county seat with some red and white cloth and ordered Old Jiang to see to the making of Japanese flags and the collection of money to pay for the cloth.

Once more Old Jiang started his round from the west of the village. He handed Chun'er two strips of cloth, white and red.

"Cut out a round red sun and sew it in the middle of the white cloth," he told her.

"Not I!" cried Chun'er. "If you want to welcome them, get Su'er to make you a flag."

"Of course we'll make one too. A handsome flag to hang over our door. If the Japanese find no flag, they kill everyone in the house, even chickens and dogs! So think again."

"I don't need to think," flung back Chun'er. "I won't do it." She picked up a small hoe and a handful of rape seeds and went to her plot of land.

A fortnight earlier the county authorities had conscripted peasants to dig a long trench here, saying this was where the army would fight the Japanese. It had been a big job. The trench was over ten feet deep, covered with branches, mats and a thick layer of earth. Every few dozen yards or so was a dug-out.

It was raining steadily and the crops were waiting to be harvested, but the peasants soaked to the skin worked with a will, standing up to their knees in water to dig that trench. It ran in a straight line, through the ripening crops. The grain on Chun'er's one and a half *mu* was growing well, but now the greater part was dug up, while the pretty willow at the end of her field was taken for the roofing of a dug-out. The villagers felt sorry for her, but when Mangzhong came back from digging to break the news, she simply said:

"Go ahead and dig. I'd gladly give all I have to beat the Japanese."

Now the branches spread over the trench were still green, the earth above was still loose. Chun'er levelled it with her hoe and sowed her rape seeds while a hawk wheeled over her head.

Her work done, she sat down by the trench and wondered: "If they'd really put up a hard fight here, would we be so scared today of the Japanese coming?"

Near by, the crops higher than the water had been reaped but the shorter were rotting in the mud. Further off, the red ears of some late-ripening sorghum were swaying in the breeze. A man was limping towards her. When she saw that he was a deserter, his rifle slung round his neck, walking with a stick, Chun'er dodged behind a tree. But the man had already seen her and he hurried towards her. She nervously gripped her hoe tight, until his exhausted, famished look emboldened her to straighten up and ask:

43

"What do you want?"

"Don't be afraid, lass!" He sank painfully to the ground to rest his puffed, swollen feet. "Can you give me a bite to eat and a drink of water?"

"Why not ask in the village?"

"I daren't. The peasants hate our guts. They hate us because we don't fight the Japanese, just loot. If they caught me alone they'd bury me alive."

"Well, and why don't you fight the Japanese?"

"You think we don't want to, lass? Little you know! We're all from the Northeast and the Japanese have taken our homes — just give us a chance to hit back! But it's not up to us to decide. We were holding the front when the order came to fall back. No one cared what became of us, so we had to retreat."

"You talk big!" Chun'er's lip curled. "I'm giving no food to a man with a gun who won't fight."

"Go on, get me a bite." He unslung his gun. "I'll leave this with you. It would fetch me a few dozen silver dollars, but it belongs to the state. I'll leave it to you to use against the Japanese."

"You expect a girl like me to fight?" She laughed.

"Well, someone will use it. There's a united anti-Japanese army over our way. That's where I'm heading."

Chun'er looked at his gun and thought it over.

"You wait here," she said presently. "I'll get you something to eat."

"We're all Chinese," declared the deserter. "While you're about it, do something else for me. If you've some worn-out men's clothes at home, bring me a jacket and pants. I don't want to travel in this uniform." When she nodded, he went on, "But don't tell a soul. This is a tricky stretch of country. If anyone finds out who I am, I'm done for."

"Don't you worry," she reassured him, and went off to tell Mangzhong and ask his advice.

"Go ahead!" said the lad. "In times like these a gun gives a fellow courage. You go back with the things while I keep an eye on him. I'll stay out of sight so that he doesn't get the wind up."

Chun'er found an old jacket and trousers belonging to her father, wrapped up some unleavened cakes and pickles, and took these to the soldier. When he had handed over the gun and changed his clothes he limped off, skirting the village. She did not risk carrying the gun home until nightfall.

"There's not going to be much work this winter," said Mangzhong. "While everything's at sixes and sevens, One-eyed Tian's putting on a show of being poor. He's hinted that he won't be needing me. Besides, I've had enough of slaving for him. With this gun, I can join Gao Ba's outfit."

"Don't be in such a hurry," retorted Chun'er. "Gao Ba's not straight. How can you trust him? If my brother-in-law were back, that would be different. I'd let you have the gun."

She hid the rifle carefully away.

9

Gao Ba had made his name in these parts as a horse thief who could spirit away a fine mule without a sound. Now that he had intercepted eight government carts south of the county town, taken over the guns of the absconding officials and stopped several groups of deserters by Five-dragon Temple ford, he styled himself a regiment commander. He sent his company commanders round the villages to bully the village heads and rich families into handing over their weapons. Some, rather than part with their guns, made their sons join

45

his outfit. Central Hebei had plenty of soldiers who "joined the colours" in this way. Gao Ba swilled and gorged himself every day at the biggest eating-house in Ziwuzhen, and spent every night with Su'er. As time went by his force grew, his power increased, and he made Su'er a formal offer of marriage.

Congratulatory messages from the villages all around covered the walls of Old Jiang's house and overflowed on to the street walls outside. On August the fifteenth, the day of the wedding, Gao Ba ordered two official sedan-chairs and two bridal chairs, and called out an escort of scores of cavalrymen in front and a battalion of infantry behind. For the customary fire-crackers they substituted bursts of rifle fire, with the result that no one dared to watch this brilliant procession. The people in every village they passed locked their doors and kept off the streets, which were strewn with spent cartridges.

Old Jiang, dressed in style, had his work cut out greeting the bearers of gifts. Several tables of food were ordered from the restaurant. But the gift bringers, finding the atmosphere very tense, left immediately after putting down their presents. That suited Old Jiang, who got happily befuddled.

His sole companion was the village accountant. After the newly-weds had retired to bed, the two men went on drinking and Old Jiang remarked:

"Must be lucky influences at work on my land to get me a regiment commander as son-in-law."

"Luck changes with the times," replied the accountant. "And this is just a beginning. He'll rise from a regiment commander to be a brigadier and division commander. You'll be going up in the world."

"That Su'er has her head screwed on the right way." Old Jiang spoke as if she were someone else's daughter. "Go-

46

betweens have been on our doorstep ever since she was fifteen, but she turned down every offer. It was Regiment Commander Gao took her fancy. What do you suppose makes the regiment commander so lucky?"

"That scar of his. Summer or winter, rain or shine, it's always bright red. On top of that he has nerve and brain. At a time like this such a man is bound to rise to the top."

As they were chatting, in stumped One-eyed Tian. Old Jiang made haste to offer him a seat.

"Sit here, village head. Take the seat of honour. You've always treated me before. Today I can repay your hospitality."

"I'm not here to drink." The landlord's face was glum. "I've come to ask you a favour. When you've a chance, tell Regiment Commander Gao I'd like to invite him to a simple meal."

"There's no need for that," said Old Jiang. "We're all old friends. Why should you go to such trouble?"

"No, I want him to come. You two must be my guests as well. Since Commissioner Zhang went south, we've had no one to rely on. Now luckily we have Regiment Commander Gao. We hope he'll see to things here."

"That goes without saying," Old Jiang promptly assured him. "My son-in-law will do whatever I tell him."

Two days later a notice bearing a large official seal was posted up at the cross-roads in Ziwuzhen. Since it was three or four months since the appearance of the last official notice, all who could read crowded round.

The notice, issued by the Political Department of the People's Defence Corps, called on the people to unite and take up arms to resist Japan. The commander of the corps was Lu Zhengcao.

A man back from Gaoyang reported that he had seen some genuine Red Army troops with a red star on their armlets. Mangzhong bounded off to share this news with Qiufen.

"They've come at last!" he cried. "Gaoyang's not far from here. You ought to go and have a look. Don't miss your chance again."

Qiufen made ready to go, wishing she could find a companion for the road.

Gao Ba was rather down in the mouth these days. He had sent one of his men to make inquiries in Gaoyang and learned that Lu Zhengcao had appointed commanders to reorganize the different local units. Red Army discipline was strict, it seemed. Officers ate millet like their men, it was forbidden to take so much as a needle or thread from the people, the leaders had to undergo training too, and each regiment had a political commissar. Because of his shady past and dislike of discipline, he could not decide what to do.

One night he confided his fears to Su'er, who laughed.

"What's worrying you? Just go and ask them to confirm your command."

"Who knows if they will or not? I've not kept in with them. They may march in one day and order us to hand over all our guns."

"I've a way to get on their right side." She pursed her lips.

"You know Commander Lu?" He brightened up.

"Not Commander Lu, but someone fairly high-ranking. They say he's quite a big shot in the Red Army."

"Out with it — who is the fellow?" cried Gao Ba.

"Gao Qingshan of Five-dragon Temple. You go to the Red Army in Gaoyang and tell them you fought with Gao Qingshan that year during the uprising. In other words, you helped the Red Army. That's your trump card. They're bound to give you a command."

This struck Gao Ba as feasible, still he protested:

"We've never had much truck with his folk. They may not believe what I say."

"That's easily fixed."

Su'er jumped up from the *kang* and went to find Chun'er, from whom she learned of Qiufen's plan to go and look for her husband.

"Sister Qiufen!" cried Su'er, overjoyed. "The roads aren't safe and it's a long way to Gaoyang. That's no easy journey. But my husband's going to see Commander Lu. Why don't you go with him? You'll have an escort and can travel in style. I tell you what: I'll ask them to give you a horse so that you needn't trail through the mud and dirt. When you find Brother Qingshan in Gaoyang, what a happy reunion you'll have — just like in a play! It's been hard for you all these years without your husband. Others may not have noticed that but I saw it all right. The first thing you should do when you see Brother Qingshan is to ask for some decent clothes. He's a big official now, what he says goes, you can have whatever you like."

Before Qiufen had recovered from her surprise at this speech, Chun'er put in:

"If I were you, I'd go on my own two feet. It's not as if you'd never left home before."

"What way is that to talk, sister?" Su'er clapped Chun'er on the shoulder. "You're too young to understand these things. Qiufen will be a lady there. People will be crowding round to stare at her. Invitations will come pouring in. It wouldn't look well for her to go on foot. I know plenty of wives beg their way a thousand *li* to find their husbands, but here's a horse ready waiting for her to ride. Go on! It's as safe as

49

riding in a bridal sedan-chair. I've ridden one myself and I know."

Refusing to take no for an answer, she caught up Qiufen's bundle and ran off.

"See here," she told Gao Ba. "It's worked out even better than I dared hope. She was just setting off to find her husband. You can go with her."

Gao Ba had a piebald horse saddled for Qiufen and ordered one of his men to act as her groom.

"You'd better change your clothes," Su'er advised him. "That fancy get-up of yours won't go down well with the Red Army."

So Gao Ba changed his silk suit for a khaki uniform and removed the red silk tassel from his gun. He also made his men dress less garishly. Then he put on the rush sandals Su'er had made him. Snowy white with red pompons in front, these were said to be the rage in the Red Army.

So he set off with a company of soldiers to Gaoyang.

At the cross-roads in all the villages they passed, the village heads and their deputies stood beside tables laden with fruit and tea and bowed respectfully to welcome the regiment commander and his men.

"You fools!" swore Gao Ba in exasperation. "Who told you to put up this show? Don't do it again."

The village heads, not quite knowing what this portended, quickly had the tables removed. Seeing a woman riding among Gao Ba's men, they jumped to the conclusion that he had kidnapped someone else's wife.

10

Qiufen had never ridden a horse before. Soon her legs were aching and sweat was dripping off her. They proceeded at a brisk pace, not stopping to rest, and she reflected wryly, "If I'd known how uncomfortable this was going to be, I'd have walked, as Chun'er suggested." She even wondered if Gao Ba might be trying to kidnap her.

It was a long, tiring journey, but at last as dusk was falling they sighted Gaoyang. They were still some distance from the gate when out came a squad of soldiers, neatly equipped, with the red star she had heard about on their armlets. Their officer greeted Gao Ba and told him to leave his men outside and go into the city alone.

"This young woman has come to find her husband," said Gao Ba. "You must let her in too."

The Red Army men took some persuading, but eventually they agreed and escorted them through the gate. The streets were lively, the shops brightly lit, and brisk business was being done in the restaurants. The town was full of soldiers, some in uniform, some in civilian dress, some in civilian dress and an army cap with a pistol at the belt. All around Qiufen saw slogans and notices calling on people to resist Japanese aggression. All around she heard singing.

They took Gao Ba to army headquarters, then escorted Qiufen to the Political Department. This was housed in a large compound, and Qiufen's feet kept slipping on the stone steps. There were several square tables in the main hall, the walls of which were plastered with slogans and maps and hung with rifles and cartridge-belts. Some men in grey uniform were seated round the tables holding a meeting. They offered Qiufen a seat and one soldier asked with a smile:

"Are you from Shenze?"

"That's right," she said. "I'm looking for Gao Qingshan of Five-dragon Temple."

"Gao Qingshan?" repeated the soldier thoughtfully.

"Didn't he take part in the uprising that year? What relation is he to you?"

"My husband." Qiufen lowered her head. "We both joined in that year."

"There's someone here from your village named Gao." The soldier smiled. "I'll send for him." He turned to a boy. "Fetch Section Chief Gao of the mass work section. Then bring a basin of hot water and ask the cook to serve a meal for a guest."

After Qiufen had washed her face, someone brought in a big bowl of millet and another of cabbage and pork. They urged her to eat but, hungry as she was, she was too excited to swallow many mouthfuls. She was straining her ears to catch every sound from the courtyard.

"You have a mass base in your village," said one of the men. "Are you fully mobilized yet? What are Gao Ba's troops like?"

Qiufen, hardly knowing how to answer, replied:

"Little better than a bunch of bandits."

The Red Army men laughed.

"Never mind," said one. "Spring rain makes weeds and crops shoot up together. But the people as a whole are dead keen to resist Japan. Tomorrow Section Chief Gao will be going out your way to straighten things out."

Footsteps were heard outside and someone said, "Here he is." Qiufen sprang to her feet to stare eagerly at the man who now walked in. Short, with glasses on, he had the look of a student.

"Where's the visitor from Five-dragon Temple?" he asked.

Qiufen smiled and exclaimed:

"Why, Gao Xiang! When did you come back?"

Gao Xiang walked over to peer short-sightedly at her. "Sister Qiufen!" He clapped his hands. "I guessed it was you." He told his comrades, "Let me introduce you to Gao Qingshan's wife — a woman fighter in the peasant uprising."

"How did you know it was me, not your wife?" demanded Qiufen.

"It comes to much the same thing." Gao Xiang chuckled. "You mustn't be too disappointed. Count seeing me the same as seeing Qingshan."

"Have you any news of him?"

"Yes, he's come north. I heard that in Yan'an. He went to the border region and I saw his name on a military communiqué. I've asked the organization section to put him in touch with me. Before long we should know where he is."

Just then in walked a girl in a blue gown with a grey army jacket over her shoulders.

"Are you ready, Section Chief Gao?" She had an attractive voice. "They're all waiting for you to talk."

Then she turned round, smiling, and Qiufen saw it was One-eyed Tian's daughter-in-law, Li Peizhong.

"All right, I'm coming," said Gao Xiang. "You come too, Sister Qiufen, and have a look. This is a meeting for the women of Gaoyang. Much bigger and livelier than those meetings we used to hold ten years ago."

It was nearly midnight before the meeting ended, but Qiufen could not close her eyes all night. She was re-living so many scenes from the past, all she had felt and heard ten years ago. It looked as if what had happened then was being repeated now all over the country, yet with a big difference too. It was the same short Gao Xiang who had led the meeting, addressed it and shouted slogans. Like a bird winging through the air, he seemed to be urging others to fly with him. Ten years in prison had not crushed the young man's spirit, only made him more experienced and capable. In that

53

case, ten years of fighting could surely not have destroyed her Qingshan's youth or damped his ardour!

But what was One-eyed Tian's daughter-in-law doing here? She and Gao Xiang seemed to be on the best of terms. Did these men away from home find new girl friends and forget their own wives?

The next morning she got on a truck with Gao Xiang and Peizhong, and together they set off for Shenze. They passed three county towns, Lixian, Boye and Anguo, and dozens of villages. The peasants' heartfelt desire to fight the Japanese aggressors and save their country was obvious all over the Hebei plain, in every town, village and field, for everywhere Gao Xiang received the warmest of welcomes.

The truck jolted over the road, which badly needed repairing, and Peizhong sang in the teeth of the wind all the way. Qiufen felt that after ten difficult years she was sharing today in the glory of the struggle. She had no idea of the further hardships and tests in store for her in the long War of Resistance Against Japan.

They reached Ziwuzhen towards dusk. As soon as Qiufen alighted, someone took her aside and whispered:

"Qingshan's back, in Five-dragon Temple. You came home by truck, he drove home a herd of goats!"

Without stopping for a second, Qiufen rushed down to the river. The people on the ferry-boat teased her:

"When you waited day and night, he never came. When at last he does come, nobody knows where you are."

From the boat, Qiufen saw a crowd round the door of their hut. The rosy light of the setting sun picked out a tall man dressed in light blue homespun. He was standing there talking and laughing with the neighbours. With a wife's sure instinct she recognized the husband she had not seen for ten years.

As she jumped ashore her legs very nearly gave way. Her heart contracted. She felt an urge to sink down on the bank and have a good long cry.

But people were waving to her, calling her name. Her husband, too, had turned to look at her. With scarlet cheeks, Qiufen climbed the embankment.

They had come home at a time when the central Hebei plain, undefended, was in desperate case and the people at a loss what to do.

II

When Qiufen reached the top of the embankment the neighbours left, smiling and talking. Qingshan smiled at her too before stepping inside the cottage. His father had cut an armful of grass on the flats to feed the goats tethered under their south window. At sight of them Qiufen laughed.

"Is this the fortune he's made all these years he's been away?"

Scratching the horns of a large billy-goat, Old Gao said:

"I haven't asked whether he's made a fortune or not. But this lot he's brought back will keep me busy all winter. Have you eaten anything? Go in and get a meal with him."

Qiufen stepped over the threshold with the same sensation as ten years before when she alighted from the bridal sedan-chair. The cottage struck her as suddenly brighter and warmer than usual. Her tall husband, seated on the edge of the *kang*, was looking searchingly at her. Hot tears sprang to her eyes and she hurriedly turned to the stove to make up the fire. The embers below the ashes were still red and, as soon as she worked the bellows, the coal started smoking and red flames leapt up. The sight of the blazing fire had a steadying effect. Qiufen emptied out all the flour from their earthen pot, energetically kneaded the dough and carefully rolled and chopped noodles, not sparing salt, oil, soya sauce or vinegar for the seasoning. When the water boiled she took the lid off the pan and with both hands put in the long, fine noodles.

Suddenly, on the far corner of the *kang*, a baby started crying. Gao Qingshan whirled round in astonishment, and saw that a child of less than two had woken up and was clenching its little fists, lustily kicking and crying.

"Well! Where did this come from?" He stood up and looked at Qiufen.

"Where did it come from?" She giggled. "A long way away. Don't you start getting ideas! This summer a refugee from the Northeast was killed at the ferry by Japanese planes, and your dad decided we'd bring up her child. That's how you've a ready-made son here waiting for you."

Qingshan chuckled and dandled the baby as if holding his tortured motherland to his heart. His eyes were moist.

They were having supper when Gao Xiang dropped in. The two old comrades-in-arms gripped hands silently for a while. Then Qingshan took a letter from his pocket and passed it over.

"That's my letter of introduction," he explained. "The Party told me to hand it over to you. To avoid trouble on the road, they advised me to dress like a peasant and bring a flock of goats. I had an easy journey, but didn't expect to find you at my journey's end."

After reading the letter, Gao Xiang said:

"You've come in the nick of time. I've no army experience, and it's a ticklish situation here. Don't go to Gaoyang yet awhile. Help me with a job here first."

Before Qingshan could ask what job this was, Gao Xiang's father and daughter arrived.

"Who've you come to see?" asked Qiufen, taking the girl's hand.

"My dad!" was the reply.

Qiufen pointed him out, but the child hung back shyly from this stranger. Gao Xiang strode over and hugged her.

"Who sent you to find your dad?" teased Qiufen.

"My mum!" The little girl laughed.

The whole room joined in her laughter.

"I don't think I ever saw her," remarked Qingshan to Gao Xiang. "How tall she's grown!"

"Of course you haven't seen her," said Qiufen. "Her mother was lying in when you went away."

"It shows how quickly we're growing old," observed Gao Sihai with a smile. "Here are these children catching up with us."

"I don't think Sister Qiufen has aged," said Gao Xiang. "She looks the same as the day we left the village."

"Shows how short-sighted you are!" retorted Qiufen. "You just don't see how I've changed. Stop making fun of me. If you'd waited a few more years before coming home, you'd have found me a white-haired old woman."

"Spoken like a heroine!" mocked Gao Xiang, patting his daughter's head. "The fact is, it's no good for revolutionaries to come home too often. Leaving again is too much of a wrench."

"Do you call this coming home too often?" demanded Qiufen.

"I won't argue with you." He grinned. "I want to have a talk now with Brother Qingshan, so that we can get things moving. Do the rest of you mind leaving us for a while?"

Old Gao left with Gao Xiang's father and the little girl.

"Can't I listen?" asked Qiufen, pouting.

"I'm afraid not," said Gao Xiang. "You haven't made contact with the Party yet. After all, we've been separated for ten years. In a day or two I'll have to go over your history."

"You're welcome to." Qiufen lit the lamp for them and left.

While the two young men talked, Qiufen and the others sat on the dike outside. One by one, stars appeared in the sky and the little girl pointed up at them.

"There's another, grandad. And another over there!"

Even after the whole sky was studded with stars, the two young men were still deep in their discussion. Gao Xiang's father said to Old Gao:

"Were we fools, longing for our boys to come back? Now they're back they just drive us out to sit in the fields."

Old Gao puffed at his pipe and made no reply. Sparks from the bowl of his pipe flew over the bank. His son's return made him happy but recalled sad memories too. They were back, the two of them, planning some new uprising together again. The enthusiasm, struggles and bloodshed of ten years ago rose before his eyes once more, and the faces of friends who had fallen seemed to have encircled him in the late autumn fields. The old man was stirred, yet he felt a pang of sadness. It had been a hard life for the last ten years since his son left home and the uprising was defeated. They had taken some living through for him and Qiufen, those long days and weary nights. And now the youngsters were looking for trouble again. Last time they had fought the landlords and local despots, this time they were going to pit themselves against the Japanese. This enemy had a strong army and had already swallowed up whole provinces of China, driving the government troops headlong before them.

How could simple country folk with their crude rifles and guns get the better of such an opponent? As he cogitated, the grass by his side was wet by the night dew. Gao Xiang's daughter yawned and fell asleep nestled in her grandfather's arms.

At last Qiufen lost patience and swept into the house.

"Go on home, Gao Xiang!" she cried. "You'll soon have used up all our lamp oil. It's nearly dawn. Your wife's asking for you and a comfortable quilt is waiting for you at home."

"When will you women learn to put first things first?" With a laugh Gao Xiang rose to his feet. "All right, we'll finish our talk tomorrow, Qingshan. You've driven those goats several dozen *li* today, you'd better turn in. I must clear off before Sister Qiufen drives me out with her rolling-pin."

After Gao Xiang's family had disappeared into the night, Old Gao brought the goats inside, then put on his tattered padded gown.

"I'm off to find somewhere in the village to sleep," he said.

"Don't go yet, dad." Qingshan stood up. "Let's have a talk."

"Plenty of time for that later, now you're home. I can hardly keep my eyes open. Mind you lock up."

12

Excitement over her brother-in-law's return kept Chun'er awake half the night. She rose early the next day and asked Mangzhong, who was drawing water at the well, to leave his buckets and come over to her house. Having heated water to wash her face, she sat down by the window and combed her hair before a small cracked mirror her mother had left.

Then she took out a new print jacket and put it on. When Mangzhong arrived she told him:

"My brother-in-law's come back. Let's go and see him."

With a chuckle, Mangzhong retorted:

"The morning star and the evening star never meet, and neither should brother-in-law and sister-in-law. You ought to be keeping out of his way, not running over to see him."

"Mine isn't the usual run of brother-in-law. A Red Army man doesn't worry about all those old-fangled rules. Anyway, I'm doing this for you."

"Doing what for me?"

"You put on that rifle of ours, and I'll take you to sign on to serve under him. To give me face, he'll have to treat you right."

"Just listen to you!" Mangzhong grinned. "He's been gone ten years and more, and you bragged enough about what a fine fellow he was; but he comes back without a single bodyguard, driving a flock of goats. Don't you blush for him? Gao Xiang now, he rides back on a truck with a bunch of bodyguards. And when he stands in the streets of Ziwuzhen, the people crowd round seven or eight deep to watch. That's the man for me! I'll go and sign on as a soldier under Gao Xiang. After working half my life as a farm-hand, I don't want to spend the other half herding goats."

"What's come over you?" cried Chun'er. "Are you ashamed to be poor? So keen to get rich? The firmer a man's roots, the less he cares about appearances."

"Which of us is ashamed to be poor?" flung back Mangzhong. "Remember what you said to me that evening under the willows? Well, have it your own way. Get me the gun."

Chun'er took the deserter's rifle from the flue below the *kang* and, having dusted it carefully, put it down. Mangzhong reached out to pick it up.

"Wait a bit!" she cried and opened her battered chest to whisk out a new jacket. "I've made you this coat. Try it on."

Mangzhong cheerfully did as he was told and Chun'er surveyed him critically from all sides.

"It'll do," she decided. "Now take the gun."

He slung it over his shoulder and drew himself up proudly for her inspection. Chun'er tied a red ribbon round the barrel of the rifle. Then she locked up the house and the two of them set off.

"I must take the buckets back," said Mangzhong, "and tell my boss I'm off to be a soldier."

"Don't be in such a hurry," advised Chun'er. "Leave the buckets where they are. If he has no water, let him miss a meal. You'd better not give notice till you've joined up."

They walked on, one in front of the other, with children hopping and skipping after them, tugging at Mangzhong's new jacket, stroking his gun.

"Are you going to join up, Mangzhong?" asked some peasants who saw him.

"I'm going to fight the Japanese!" he replied with a grin.

"Why are you all dressed up, Chun'er?" some women asked her.

"I'm seeing him off to the army," she answered, smiling.

"Well, wonders will never cease!" There was general laughter.

Soon they reached Five-dragon Temple. Gao Qingshan and Mangzhong had already met in the hills, and now Qiufen explained the lad's background and his relationship to their family, while Chun'er explained how she had come by the gun. Gao Xiang said they needed someone they could trust and Mangzhong could act as Qingshan's orderly. He sent for two new uniforms, wanting them to make a good impression at the meeting that day, the rally at which Gao Ba's outfit was to be reorganized.

This rally to reorganize all the local units was to take place on the sand banks by the Hutuo. The county government had held a mobilization meeting and sent representatives. They had also got the best carpenters in the neighbourhood to bring timber, bamboos and matting to fix up an impressive review stand facing the river. A high wind had been blowing since morning, swirling sand into people's faces and flapping the bunting on which were the two slogans: "Strengthen the national united front to resist Japan! Wage guerrilla warfare in the enemy rear!"

Three regiments, led by Gao Ba, Li Suo of Jiaoqiuzhen and Zhang Daqiu of Madianzhen, were to be incorporated. The three commanders, neatly turned out, took their places on the stand to regroup their men.

But the ranks were so crowded and ragged that they could not straighten them out. The more orders were shouted, the greater the confusion, till finally fighting started and shots were fired. The three commanders on the stand stamped and swore, threatening to shoot the men who had opened fire, but they could not find the offenders. It was getting on for noon when Gao Xiang, in charge of the rally, asked Qingshan to help restore order. Qingshan conferred with the three regiment commanders, then summoned their battalion commanders and told them first to lead their men off, then march them back to the positions assigned. So at long last some order was achieved.

This motley assembly of soldiers had barely squatted down holding their rifles when they were surrounded by pedlars and snack-vendors. The formation of troops in all the villages had resulted in a mushroom growth of stalls and portable kitchens to sell the soldiers flapjacks, dumplings, smoked chicken or beancurd, for the villagers could make easy money this way. News of this rally of three regiments before a grand review stand had brought vendors rushing to the spot, jostling for the best position and raising pandemonium as they cried their wares. And the appetizing sights and smells set the troops milling about again to buy titbits. Qingshan sent Mangzhong to reason with the vendors, and finally they were persuaded to leave.

Then Gao Ba, straddling on the stand, introduced Gao Xiang.

"Brothers, this is Commander Lu's representative, Commissioner Gao. Let's clap him!"

Applause burst out down below.

"Comrades!" cried Gao Xiang. "The Japanese imperialists have invaded our land and killed our countrymen. Now they are shoving their way to our doorstep. The Japanese want to destroy our country. They want to enslave us! What do you say to that?"

"Down with the bastards!" yelled the troops.

"Down with Japanese imperialism!" shouted Gao Xiang.

His cry was taken up by the ranks and carried off by the wild wind over the racing waves.

"We want to defend our motherland and protect our homes," said Gao Xiang. "We must drive Japanese imperialism out of China. Comrades, you stout fellows want to resist Japan. When you saw the enemy approaching, you didn't run away and you didn't surrender. Instead you took up arms to fight the invaders. That was a fine thing to do, our country and our people honour you for it. On behalf of the People's Defence Corps headquarters and its Political Department, I salute you all."

Laughter and shouts of approval sounded below. The men were listening intently now. Gao Xiang went on:

"You comrades here have joined the resistance for different reasons. Some of you were so ground down that you formed robber bands to operate at night and scatter at dawn. Some are the sons of rich families who joined up rather than part with their guns. Some have joined because it's been a bad year, this winter is going to be very hard, and as soldiers you can eat at the army mess. Well, the fighting that's coming will test us. Time-servers will soon be shown up. We must reform ourselves and our way of thinking. We must turn ourselves into a well-organized resistance force, well led and disciplined."

Then he proclaimed the Three Main Rules of Discipline and the Eight Points for Attention,* as well as the chief principles governing relations between officers and men, between the army and the people. He continued:

"It's a just, honourable war we're fighting, and we shall certainly win. We're not afraid of Japan's superior weapons, only of lack of unity in our own ranks. Never mind if the Japanese have taken some of our towns, we'll fight guerrilla warfare in their rear and set up bases to resist Japan. Let those who have guns give guns, those who have money give money, and those who have labour power give labour power. Let everybody join in, men and women, young and old, to cut the enemy lines of communication, to give him not a mo-

---

* The Three Main Rules of Discipline and the Eight Points for Attention were the rules of discipline laid down by Comrade Mao Zedong for the Chinese Workers' and Peasants' Red Army during the Second Revolutionary Civil War (1927-37). The Three Main Rules are: (1) Obey orders in all your actions; (2) Don't take a single needle or piece of thread from the masses; and (3) Turn in everything captured. The Eight Points for Attention are as follows: (1) Speak politely; (2) Pay fairly for what you buy; (3) Return everything you borrow; (4) Pay for anything you damage; (5) Don't hit or swear at people; (6) Don't damage crops; (7) Don't take liberties with women and (8) Don't ill-treat captives.

ment's peace in his rear. Comrades, our country relies on us, the people are counting on us. We must bravely take up the task of liberating our motherland. The aim of our fighting is to drive out the Japanese invaders and build up a new China independent, rich and strong!"

Finally he read out the order from headquarters. The three regiments were to be reorganized into the Seventh Detachment of the People's Defence Corps under the command of Gao Qingshan and with Gao Xiang as political commissar.

13

For the last few days One-eyed Tian had been lying on his *kang* with no relish for his rice or tea. Taking the truck's honking that day to mean the arrival of the Japanese, he snatched up his white flag with the red sun and dashed out to the street, afraid he might be late to welcome the conquerors. But the sight that met his eyes was his daughter-in-law in army uniform, returned with that notorious Red, Gao Xiang! Hastily rolling up his flag, the landlord tucked it under one arm and slunk home. Since then he had not left his *kang*. His wife, afraid his depression would end in a break-down, urged him to take a turn outside and call on his friends.

"Leave me alone, woman!" snapped One-eyed Tian. "Where could I go? My own daughter-in-law has joined that gang. I'm ashamed to show my face."

"Don't mention that bitch to me," ground out his wife.

"Act as if she were dead. Soon as Yaowu comes back, we'll get him to divorce her."

"Don't worry!" retorted her husband. "Long before your son comes back she'll have broken with us."

The wind was swirling dust against their newly papered windows. Shouting from the great rally by the river was carried in gusts to their ears.

"They're out to make trouble again!" swore One-eyed Tian. "Go and bolt the gate. That din gets on my nerves."

His wife left the *kang* to do as she was told, when in came their hired-hand Mangzhong wearing a new army uniform with a gun slung over his shoulder. As he drew himself up in the middle of the room, Mrs. Tian scuttled back to the *kang*.

"What does this mean?" One-eyed Tian sat bolt upright, scowling.

"I'm leaving you, boss." Mangzhong smiled. "I've joined the army."

"What!" The landlord gave a start. "You should have got my permission first, you young fool."

"I don't see as how you can blame me. You told me some time back that there wouldn't be work for all of us this winter and I'd better find myself some other job."

"I meant a decent, honest job." One-eyed Tian screwed up his sightless eye. "What possessed you to join that lawless gang? Don't you know what riff-raff they are? They'll come to no good. The day the Japanese soldiers arrive, it's likely the whole lot will lose their heads. You listen to me, there's a good lad, and take off that uniform. Give them back their gun. No matter how badly things go, I'll make shift to feed you. Because we've been master and man so long and I know you're a decent young fellow, I'm talking to you like this for your own good. If it were anyone else, I'd let him go to his ruin."

Mrs. Tian added her voice to her husband's persuasion, putting on such a show of concern that Mangzhong, who had been walking on air, hardly knew what to do. He answered stolidly:

"It's no use, I've already joined up. They've all seen me with this gun."

"Never mind that," said One-eyed Tian. "Just tell them your boss won't have it." He caught himself up. "No. Just say you thought better of it."

"But I haven't," answered Mangzhong decidedly. "It's no use your arguing. It's my own life I'm risking, so why should you worry? I'll trouble you to pay me my wages."

One-eyed Tian's face darkened.

"You dare defy me!" he thundered. "If you won't do as I say, not a copper shall you have."

It was Mangzhong's turn to flare up.

"Stop throwing your weight about!" he cried. "Just try to stop my wages!"

Shifting the rifle on his back, he flung out.

Mrs. Tian gaped. "Why," she faltered, "they've started a rebellion again!"

"Have you only just discovered that?" sneered her husband.

Mangzhong went from the inner courtyard to the stable. Old Chang, just back from ploughing, was squatting in the doorway cleaning the plough. Old Wen inside was mixing fodder for the cattle. Catching sight of Mangzhong's uniform, he smiled.

"That's the boy!" they cried. "You've been as good as your word."

"I've come to say good-bye." Mangzhong beamed on them both. "I want to thank you for all you've done for me and taught me these years we've worked together."

"What have we taught you?" demanded Old Chang. "To work like an ox and to put up with hardships. Well, just don't forget us, that's all, now that you've bettered yourself and found a way out."

"Look here, Mangzhong," said Old Wen. "We've been together, day and night, all these years and had no big rows but plenty of little squabbles. Don't hold those tiffs against me! I'm not saying this because you're going, but we brothers ought to drink a few cups together."

"Don't ask him to drink," said Old Chang. "A family has family rules, a shop has shop rules, an army has army rules. He must put his whole heart now into soldiering and learn good habits, not bad ones. Hardships for yourself, enjoyment for others, Mangzhong! Be honest and work steadily. Keep a watch on your eyes and your tongue. Don't try to take any mean advantages and don't bully the common people. Will you remember this, lad?"

"Those old household maxims of yours may be no use in the army," scoffed Old Wen.

"Yes, they will," said Mangzhong. "And I shall remember them."

His eyes pricked and two tears rolled down his cheeks.

"Go along then," said Old Chang. "We mustn't keep you."

Mangzhong picked up the broom and swept the *kang* and the floor, then took the buckets to fetch water from the well. But Old Wen stopped him, protesting:

"Hurry up and go! You can leave these chores to me."

Mangzhong paced irresolutely round his old quarters and the stable, then lingered for a few moments on the threshing-floor looking at the door to the house, now bolted and barred. At last he took a warm leave of his old mates and shook the dust of the landlord's house off his feet.

It was early in the grim winter of '37 when this eighteen-year-old peasant lad took his first step towards freedom. The life he left was one long round of back-breaking toil. A farm-hand went cold and hungry year after year, growing old without house or field of his own, only to be driven away in the end like an old worn-out ox. But now he had become one of the people's fighters and, with his motherland, was to win through hard times to glory.

With these thoughts in mind, Mangzhong walked to Chun-er's cottage. The wicker gate was ajar. He pushed it gently open and latched it behind him. In the courtyard flooded with sunshine, plump, shiny gourds had ripened, but their yellow leaves were withering. A large white rooster with a scarlet comb was flapping dazzling wings and crowing at the foot of the trellis. At this sound, a speckled hen some distance away started preening her feathers with her pointed beak.

A rosy face pressed for a second against the small windowpane, and Mangzhong knew that Chun'er was at home. Opening the door and stepping inside, he found her by the window, her head bent over some work.

"What are you making?" he asked.

"Another pair of shoes for you." She looked up. "Well, in that uniform you look a real soldier! What did you do with the jacket I made for you?"

"I'm wearing it underneath. But why trouble with those shoes? They issue everything we need in the army."

"Do they?" said Chun'er. "Anyway, I'll make these for you to wear first. It looks bad, your toes showing through, when you've got that smart uniform on."

"Why are you looking so put out?" Mangzhong sat on the edge of the *kang*, his back against the door.

Chun'er said nothing. The rims of her eyes were red.

"What's wrong?" asked Mangzhong. "Sorry you gave me your gun? You can have it back and put it away again. Now that I'm in the army, I don't have to worry about getting a gun."

69

"You idiot!" Chun'er laughed. "You'll be leaving now, and I may never see you again."

"Why not? I'm not going far, just a stone's throw from home."

"I'm not so sure. Each step will take you further away from me. Look at Qingshan, away for ten years."

"How can I compare with him?" retorted Mangzhong. "I'll die happy if I'm ever half the man he is. You should have seen him at that rally today. Was he hot stuff!"

"You must learn from him and do even better," said Chun'er. "Don't give my sister a chance to laugh at us."

"I'll remember what you've said," Mangzhong assured her.

"You'll be gone a long time." Chun'er lowered her head. "Don't forget me. Not even if you become an officer."

Mangzhong did not know how to answer. His cheeks burning, he protested:

"What nonsense you talk! As if I could ever forget you!"

"Prove it then!" Chun'er raised her flushed face, a radiance in her eyes that would have melted even a heart of stone.

"Prove it?" repeated Mangzhong. "Want me to put it in writing?"

"No!" She gave a breathless laugh. "But why did you tease me so that day under the willows?" Hiding her face in her hands, she burst into tears.

Mangzhong sat nonplussed for several minutes before he grasped what she meant. He took Chun'er gently in his arms and pressed his lips to her cheek.

"All right." She pushed him away. "That'll do. You must go. Whatever happens, I'll be waiting for you."

Mangzhong hurried back to his unit. No ties had held the lad before, but now his sweetheart's love had fired his blood and made him determined to show himself worthy of her.

In the days to come, steeled by warfare and revolution, little by little this village boy increased in mental stature. For years he owned nothing but the shoes on his feet, a coarse cotton uniform, a stub of pencil and a little notebook, but his insight into life grew steadily richer and stronger. For ten years and more he fought doggedly on with no respite day or night. Battling over the mountains and plains of his great homeland, he was exposed to wind and frost, to rain and dew, to hunger, cold and illness. But whether wounded in action, opening up waste land for the villagers, working or studying, this former farm-hand kept a strict watch on himself and proved a worthy member of the Chinese Communist Party. One flag only fluttered before his eyes, one voice only called to him. His country's honour and independence, the contribution he might make to the revolution, and the love of a village girl, these were the sole concern of young Mangzhong's heart.

14

As a matter of fact, Gao Xiang was political commissar in name only, for the day after the rally he returned to Gao-yang, handing over the newly formed detachment to Gao Qingshan, whom he also made responsible for that county. He left Li Peizhong as Gao Qingshan's assistant, mainly to run the Mobilization Committee.

They set up detachment headquarters in the county town, in a large compound which had housed the Security Bureau. Since the flight of the Kuomintang officials and police, nothing remained of this once imposing bureau but a vast, empty building. The rooms had been stripped of furniture, some doors and windows were missing, and the courtyard was

71

littered with rubble. Gao Qingshan and Mangzhong, arriving there after a tour of inspection of the three regiments, found not a room fit to live in. Not until the evening did the Mobilization Committee send over a man with two quilts. He stuffed up the broken windows for them with straw.

Gao Qingshan had too much on his mind to worry about this, but young Mangzhong was dismayed. He blamed himself for listening to Chun'er instead of going by truck to Gaoyang with Gao Xiang. Now he had landed himself in this barracks of a place, with nothing but a tumbledown *kang* to sleep on. It was no better than working for the landlord, simply no improvement at all! Wrapped in a damp, musty quilt, he could not sleep.

Late as it was, Qingshan did not turn in but sat on the edge of the *kang* by the dim oil lamp, and after some moments' thought jotted down a few notes in his diary. Mangzhong leaned towards him to say:

"Winter will soon be here, Detachment Commander. This place will be too cold to sleep in at night. Why not go back to Five-dragon Temple, where we've thick quilts and warm *kangs*?"

"What's this?" Qingshan grinned at him. "Homesick the very first day?"

"Not a bit of it! What home do I have? But why put up with this? You saw today the style that Gao Ba and that lot live in: fine houses, fancy quilts and plenty of bedding. Yet he's only a regiment commander. Our detachment headquarters should have better bedding."

"Let's not compare ourselves with him," said Qingshan. "The first thing a revolutionary must learn is to put up with hardships. We're not fighting now, but on the Long March what wouldn't we have given for a big, smooth *kang* like this?"

Mangzhong, unconvinced by this, turned his face to the wall. When Qingshan spread the other quilt over him, he blinked.

"Aren't you going to cover yourself?"

"I don't feel the cold. I've slept without a quilt for the last ten years. And don't leave your gun lying about like that. Here, lift your head and stick it there as a pillow. Tomorrow, if there's time, I'll teach you to shoot."

Half asleep, Mangzhong grumbled to himself:

"Call this hard, uncomfortable thing a pillow? I shouldered this rifle so as to better myself. If I'd known what the life was like, I'd have stuck to my hoe in the fields."

The next moment he was dreaming. Qingshan paced up and down in the yard for a while, bringing back two bricks to serve as his own pillow. He was just about to blow out the light when steps approached and a girl called through the window:

"Are you still up, Detachment Commander Gao?"

Li Peizhong's pretty face could be glimpsed through a hole in the window.

"Yes, come on in, Comrade Li," he said. "What brings you here?"

"I came to see how you're getting on." Smiling, she slipped into the room. She was wearing a new uniform but no cap, and her glossy black hair hung neatly to her shoulders. She carried a new holster swinging from a strap, like a schoolgirl with a satchel. Glancing round, she asked:

"Who's that on the *kang*?"

"My orderly. I can't offer you a seat."

"This isn't like my place," she cried with a laugh. "Your headquarters reminds me of a big, dilapidated temple, while our Mobilization Committee is like a playhouse, with people streaming in and out all the time. I can't understand why the work here is so backward compared with Gaoyang. Comrade Gao Xiang has left us in the lurch with all these problems on our hands. Let's go to the telegraph office and ring him up. Tell him we haven't even anywhere to sit. How does he expect us to work in these conditions?"

"Better not disturb him at this time of night. He's busy enough as it is."

"He's busy all right." She smiled. "We think the world of him here. Before he came the rest of us had no idea how to mobilize the masses or organize a militia. No one gave us directives or sent us any instructions. The first few days and evenings after his arrival, he passed on to us what he'd learned in Yan'an, his own experience, and particularly Chairman Mao's most recent talks. That explained our policy and aims in resisting Japan, our strategy and tactics. Being able to see our way clearly boosted our morale and gave us much more strength. But he's terribly busy. He's in great demand as a speaker and wherever he goes people tag after him, begging him to solve their problems. I just can't tell you how much we admire Gao Xiang for his energy and eloquence, his fine record all these years in the revolution, and the fact that he's fresh from Chairman Mao's side in Yan'an! He's told us stories too of the Red Army on the Long March. And he mentioned you, Detachment Commander Gao. You have an even more glorious record. I'm longing to hear some of your experiences on the Long March."

Qingshan said with a chuckle:

"For ten years we've been fighting or marching all over the country, and been in plenty of tight corners too. I wouldn't know what to start telling you about. The main thing for a revolutionary is not to lose faith in the revolution, no matter how great the difficulties and dangers. Be firm

74

and stick to your guns till victory is won. That's the spirit we need."

"Why won't you tell me properly?" Peizhong pouted. "At least tell me some of the most interesting titbits."

Just then Mangzhong called Old Wen and Old Chang in his sleep, asking them to feed the horses and hitch them to the cart.

"Why, I know that lad!" cried Peizhong. "He used to work for us."

"How did you come to join the resistance," asked Qingshan. "That family of yours in Ziwuzhen. . . ."

"It's not my family!" The girl flushed. "The marriage was arranged by my father."

"I hear your husband's run off to the south. You showed pluck, deciding to stay in the enemy's rear."

"Don't talk to me about him, Detachment Commander Gao. You're my chief now, let me tell you about my background. I belong to the Li family in Rear Street here."

"Another of the biggest families in this county."

"Yes, but I'm not in the direct line." Her face was scarlet. "My father used to keep a company of players, and my mother was one of the young actresses. He made her his concubine and so I was born. Because he and old Tian are friends, they fixed up this match. But at last I've broken with both those families."

"And quite right too. Plenty of students from feudal families have joined the revolution. Did you take part in any action before the Lugouqiao Incident*?"

---

* On July 7, 1937, the Japanese aggressors attacked the Chinese troops stationed at Lugouqiao, about fifteen kilometres southwest of Beijing. Spurred on by the anti-Japanese upsurge of the whole nation, the Chinese troops resisted the Japanese. Thus began the heroic eight-year War of Resistance of the Chinese people.

"No, I didn't. When I entered normal college the Chinese teacher gave me good marks for an essay, and that made me take an interest in literature. I learned something about revolution from the novels I read. But I was scared to join in any action. The movement to resist Japan was a great challenge and stimulus to me, because people just as weak as myself were caught up in it. First I joined the National Salvation Association. Then I went through a course of political training at Gaoyang."

"The resistance movement marks a high tide in the revolution," said Qingshan. "Together we must stand up to all tests in this war, to prove our ideals and our courage."

"I'm sure I shall learn a lot working with a veteran revolutionary like you. Gao Xiang was ever so good about helping me. I hope you'll be the same."

"Tomorrow I'll go through the work of the Mobilization Committee with you," said Qingshan with a smile. "We mustn't refer every little problem to Gao Xiang. Since he gave us this job, we must do it."

The oil lamp on the *kang* sputtered and went out, leaving the room in darkness except for the moonlight filtering through the torn paper of the window. A cock started crowing by the city wall.

"You must get some sleep," said Peizhong. "I see you've no quilt. I'll fetch you a couple from home."

"You said just now you'd broken with your family. How can you take their quilts?" asked Qingshan with a grin.

"It's my mother's family." Peizhong smiled. "It's quite in order for the Mobilization Committee to ask them to contribute two quilts. Nothing wrong with that!"

When he insisted that there was no need, she left, singing softly to herself.

15

The next day Gao Qingshan was up very early. He pottered about for a while in the yard, stacking the broken bricks up at one side, then called to Mangzhong through the window. The lad put on his clothes and hurried out.

"Where's your gun?" asked Qingshan.

"Blessed if I haven't forgotten it again!" Mangzhong ran back to fetch it, saying on his return, "I'm not used to carrying this. Back at home now, getting up early to go to the fields, I'd never have forgotten my sickle or hoe. They'd be tucked into my belt."

Qingshan scooped up some lime from the rubble and drew a few circles on the opposite wall. He showed Mangzhong how to hold his rifle, explained the purpose of the sights, then taught him how to load the gun and fire.

"I want you to practise aiming first thing each morning and to study in the evening," he said. "Concentrate on these two things, and stop thinking about feeding cattle or drawing water."

"Drawing water?" echoed Mangzhong, who had practised for a while. "I've no idea where the well is here. We can't even wash our faces when we get up."

"Let's go over to the Mobilization Committee."

Qingshan led the way and Mangzhong with his rifle followed behind. It was market day and the streets were already crowded. Qingshan sauntered casually along, squeezing his way through the press and stopping now and then to make way for others. Mangzhong was disappointed that his commander cut such an unimpressive figure. If it were Gao Ba now, people would have spotted him a long way off and drawn aside to let him pass. He hoped no one from Ziwuzhen was here to witness this sorry sight.

The Mobilization Committee was in the former Bureau of Education. Early as it was, a meal had already been served.

The yard was full of benches and square tables covered with thick, blue-patterned bowls and new red bamboo chopsticks. In the middle of the yard were two piping-hot stacks of steamed buns, and men with bowls were squeezing in and out of the kitchen. Peizhong, up betimes and neatly dressed, was standing with a thoughtful frown on the steps of the main office. At sight of Qingshan, she hurried down with a smile.

"Doesn't this remind you of a soup-kitchen?" she asked softly. "We've no idea which villages they're from, all these people who come to us for a free meal."

"Good for them!" remarked Qingshan. "If they come to eat our rice, that shows they want to join the resistance. The thing now is to lead them and find them work."

"Work? When they've finished they just wipe their mouths and go. See what I mean?"

Qingshan watched a group of men who had finished eating push their bowls aside, brush themselves off and stroll away towards the market, talking and laughing.

"That's because we've no system of work yet," he said. "Let's go inside and make plans."

She took him into the main office, calling back with a smile to Mangzhong:

"Help yourself to a hot steamed bun! You're used to three meals a day at home, you must be hungry."

Mangzhong took three steamed buns and squatted on the warm, sunlit steps to eat. Looking up, he caught a glimpse of a girl outside. He ran to the gate and found it was Chun'er, holding a little bundle, hiding behind a stone lion at the entrance. She was wearing new clothes but was dusty from the road.

"Have you come to the market?" he asked.

"I've brought you your shoes," she whispered. "Things must be lively in town with the resistance. I wanted to have a look."

"Had any breakfast?" He handed her a bun. "Come on in and have something to eat."

"Am I allowed to?" she asked with a smile.

"Everybody's welcome. Our Mobilization Committee stands treat."

He started to lead her in.

"Wait a moment," said Chun'er. "There's someone else. Here, Brother Bian Ji!"

A tall, thin middle-aged man in a long gown which gave him a scholarly air was standing not far away.

"Don't you know him?" asked Chun'er. "He's from Five-dragon Temple. He can play the flute and paint pictures, and he's come to see my brother-in-law."

Mangzhong took them in and made them sit down at a long rectangular table. Chun'er hung her head in confusion at the sight of so many people, while Mangzhong went to the kitchen and told the cook:

"Give us two more bowls of vegetable soup, will you? Two guests have come to see the detachment commander."

The cook, his head glistening with sweat, took one look at Mangzhong's uniform and replied:

"Help yourself, comrade, there's plenty in the pot. Makes no difference whether it's for the commander or not — we serve everybody who comes."

Mangzhong filled two bowls with vegetables and grabbed half a dozen steamed buns, happy to play host. Chun'er said approvingly:

"Well, how about it? Aren't you glad you joined the resistance? Where else could you get such good steamed buns every day?"

"The grub here's not bad," admitted the lad with a chuckle. "But the *kang*'s rather cold at night."

"You must ask my brother-in-law to find Brother Bian Ji a job too."

"That's easy." Mangzhong assured them. "We're looking for helpers."

"That's why I'm here," said Bian Ji slowly. "If a man has any special knack, it seems a pity not to use it. Now the country needs men, I ought to do my bit."

He stood up, drew a roll of papers from his pocket and spread them out on the table. They were four paintings in ink and watercolours which he held flat for Mangzhong's inspection. Asked his opinion, the young soldier examined them carefully and said:

"They're fine paintings, carefully done. A little more colour would make them even better. But can you use pictures to resist Japan?"

"Of course you can!" Bian Ji flushed. "In propaganda."

"This is over my head," Mangzhong made haste to explain. "But here comes our detachment commander. Show them to him."

Gao Qingshan came down the office steps, followed by a smiling Peizhong with a red notebook.

"Isn't that One-eyed Tian's daughter-in-law?" whispered Chun'er to Mangzhong. "I thought she was with Gao Xiang. What's she doing here?"

Before Mangzhong could answer, Bian Ji stepped forward with his paintings and asked:

"Remember me, Qingshan?"

After one glance at him Qingshan cried with a laugh:

"Of course I do, Brother Bian Ji!"

"I was sure you'd have forgotten me." Bian Ji was obviously most gratified. "You've a good memory for faces."

"Are you here for the fair or on business?" Qingshan made him sit down.

"Catch me coming eighteen *li* just for a fair! I wanted to talk to you." He unrolled his paintings again. "Would this knack of mine be any use to you?"

Qingshan scrutinized the four paintings in turn and declared:

"You paint even better than you used to, and the resistance needs artists. But paint us some pictures about resisting Japan instead of these insects and birds."

"Of course. I showed you these just to give you some idea. I can paint other things too. Cartoons, for instance. I'm having a dab at them now."

He produced another rolled-up sheet from his pocket. A wizened little old fellow squatting on the ground was peering up at a fat man, blind in one eye, whose backside was sticking out.

Mangzhong clapped his hands and leapt into the air. "I like that one!" he cried. "That's One-eyed Tian and Old Jiang drawn to the life. This was posted up on the sly this summer in Ziwuzhen. So you were the one who did it."

After one glance at the cartoon, Peizhong drew Chun'er aside to discuss how to get the women to join the National Salvation Association.

"How have you been managing all these years?" asked Qingshan, carefully rolling up the picture and returning it to Bian Ji.

"After you left I went back to being a painter. There aren't many temples built nowadays, so I've been painting spirit screens and woodwork, or lanterns for New Year. It's beggar's life. The day I heard you were back I went to the dike, but you'd already left. I was afraid, now you'd become a big official, you'd have nothing to do with the poor likes of us."

"Don't talk nonsense!" protested Qingshan with a grin. "How could I forget the comrades who went through the struggle and risked their lives with me?"

"So you didn't forget us?" cried Bian Ji, jumping up. "Hold on a bit, there are some others outside."

"What others?"

"Some of the old fellows and their sons from our parts. I came first to sound you out. The rest of them are still by Gao Family Inn at the West Gate. I'll go and fetch them."

"They've walked far enough. I'll go and see them there." Qingshan was beaming.

They went out followed by Mangzhong, with Chun'er at his heels. The market was now so busy that it took them some time to thread their way through the crowds to the inn by the West Gate. Standing in the sun outside the matting door was a group of peasants wearing dark blue homespun.

Qingshan recognized some of the older men but could not remember the names of the younger ones. Ten years ago, he recalled, they had gathered to plan their revolt in some hired hands' quarters. He strode eagerly forward to greet them.

As they crowded round him, one said:

"We were afraid to go into your big *yamen*, but it seems you haven't changed one bit, coming all this way to meet us."

"Why are you still so shabby now you're detachment commander?" asked another. "You haven't even an overcoat, and no more than one soldier with you. Just give the word and we'll form a bodyguard for you. We'll keep you safe no matter where you go."

"We're not out for show, any more than ten years ago,"

said Qingshan. "We're out to fight Japan. I hope you've still as much grit as you showed then. Hurry up and get organized!"

"That's what we're here for!" they shouted. "But you must be our leader. We won't follow anyone else."

"I'll lead you, don't you worry." Qingshan laughed.

"Good. You're the man for us."

"We must organize all the workers, peasants, women and young folk to resist Japan and save the nation. You go on back to the village and make a start by setting up a peasants' union."

"We've already got one, for everyone with less than thirty *mu* of land."

"Don't limit it to thirty *mu*. We want as many people as possible. Get in everybody who's willing to join the resistance. We need a united front."

"We wanted your father to be chairman," someone told him. "But he refused. He used to be so keen, what's come over him now? We're hoping you'll go back and give us a talk. You can explain things clearly to us all and win your old man round."

Qingshan promised to do this as soon as he was free. Then the villagers left, escorted for quite a distance by the detachment commander and Mangzhong.

16

While preparations for a peasants' union went ahead in Five-dragon Temple, in Ziwuzhen they first set up a women's association. Li Peizhong, representing the county administration, called a meeting of all the women at the crossroads to explain the purpose of the association and the urgent need for shoes and socks for the army. Then she called Chun'er forward and asked her to say a few words, but the girl, blushing furiously, refused to speak. Gao Ba's bride, Su'er, had been squeezing her way to the front and now she took the place of tongue-tied Chun'er.

"The lass is shy, so let me speak instead," she offered.

She modelled her remarks on what Peizhong had said, and the village women clapped her, commenting:

"She's got what it takes. In times like these we need her sort to get things done. She's thick-skinned and has the gift of the gab. Let's elect her."

So Su'er was elected chairman of the Women's Salvation Association, with Chun'er as one of the committee members.

Su'er lost no time in getting down to work. That same afternoon she and Chun'er set out to tell every household how many shoes to make. They were accompanied by the village accountant, an abacus under his arm.

Su'er, leading the way, asked:

"Where shall we begin?"

The accountant said:

"In the old days, when we collected grain or funds, we started with that cottage in the west end where Chun'er lives."

"We're not bound by those old rules any more," protested Chun'er. "Make a clean sweep, I say, from bottom up."

"Hear, hear!" agreed the accountant with a smile. "In the past it was always us folk in a small way that bore the brunt, but now times have changed. Where do you suggest we start?"

"With One-eyed Tian," cried Chun'er. "He's the richest man in the village, it's only right he should take the biggest share. Are you game to tackle him?"

"Why not?" said Su'er. "He's not a tiger or a monster, is

84

he? Come on." She set briskly off.

Su'er led the way, Chun'er came next, and the accountant shuffled along behind. But once in sight of One-eyed Tian's gate, he stopped at the corner of the wall.

"Come on. What's up?" asked Su'er, looking round.

"You go on in while I smoke a pipe," he mumbled, as if he had a hot egg in his mouth. "This flint is no good — it sparks but the tinder won't catch."

Her lips firmly clamped together, Su'er marched in. As they passed through that tall gateway Chun'er's heart fluttered. She had only been here a few times before, to borrow a tool from the Tians or to use their mill, and they had always made such a favour of it that she hardly dared to open her mouth. When festivals came round she looked on from a distance as red lanterns were hung up before the imposing house and men dressed in silk and brocade passed in or out. Keeping close behind Su'er, she asked:

"Think that dog of theirs is tied up?"

"I don't care if it isn't. If it bites me, Tian will just have to keep me for a year." Su'er had come by now to the inner courtyard. Catching sight of a huge black hound at the foot of the spirit screen there, she pulled the double gate shut with a bang and kept a firm grip on the copper door-rings. Chun'er fell back in dismay.

"Open the door!" yelled Su'er.

The black dog leapt up, barking, with a great clatter of its chain, while a large gander in the back yard started hissing and cackling. Some minutes passed before Mrs. Tian came padding slowly along the passageway to ask in offended tones:

"Who's there? Really!"

"It's us!" cried Su'er.

"What do you want?"

85

"Keep hold of that dog of yours and we'll come in and tell you."

"Come on in. He doesn't bite."

Su'er pushed open the door and there stood Mrs. Tian, short and pudgy as a ball of dough. Her small out-thrust hands looked like a duck's webbed feet. Without budging an inch, she glared at Chun'er and snapped:

"Well, what do you want?"

"We'll tell you inside," replied Su'er. "Don't keep us standing out here in the cold."

"My husband is poorly today. He's just covered himself with a quilt and started to sweat. Whatever your business is, you can tell me here."

"We've just come to tell you to make some shoes," said Chun'er.

"Shoes for whom, pray? Will you provide the labour for it? We've no sewing women here."

"They're for the anti-Japanese fighters. If you can't make them, hire someone else to do it."

"What do you mean by anti-Japanese fighters?" Mrs. Tian sniggered. "I never stir from home, that's the first I've heard of them. What are the anti-Japanese fighters to you, that they get great bouncing girls and young brides to find people to make them shoes?"

"That's no way to talk," cried Su'er. "This is public business."

"I'm not going to lower myself to argue with you," declared Mrs. Tian. "How many pairs do you want?"

"It's shared out fairly," said Chun'er, then called to the accountant, "How much land do they have?"

The accountant, who had been smoking with his back to them in the gateway, now hurried over and smiled at Mrs. Tian.

"Goodday, ma'am! Is Mr. Tian any better? Well now, they have 320 *mu* of land." He flicked the beads of his abacus. "They'll have to contribute seven pairs. That does sound rather a large number, doesn't it?"

"Seven pairs!" Mrs. Tian's eyes nearly popped out of her head. "Are you crazy? Is this a shoe shop? You'd better start making inquiries. What money has our family put by these last few generations? Do you take us for suckers?"

"Why farm so much land then?" retorted Chun'er. "I'm planning to do more than I'm asked. This is to resist Japan, so no one's allowed to wriggle out of it."

"To resist Japan?" She had mastered this new term now. "Well, our family has people resisting Japan. Isn't my daughter-in-law on the county committee? Wasn't she the one who got you organized? I haven't asked you for shoes for her, have I? What right have you to demand so many from me?"

"Don't give us that talk!" snapped Su'er. "Having someone in the resistance doesn't exempt you. My husband's commander of a regiment — does that mean I won't do my share?"

"You!" Mrs. Tian drummed her fists together. "Don't make me sick!"

"Shit on you!" swore Su'er, stamping.

"Shit on you, dirty slut, leading that son of mine into bad ways! Aren't you ashamed of the money you've cost our family, you filthy prostitute? Get out of here! You're making the courtyard stink."

"I'll knock you dead, you old bitch!" Su'er stepped back and lowered her head, then charged. Mrs. Tian staggered, toppled backwards over the threshold, and rolled into the passageway. Su'er bounded after her and butted her fat, flabby stomach.

One-eyed Tian could no longer sham ill. A long gown over his shoulders, he hurried out, bellowing:

"You rebels! This is assault and battery! We'll lodge a complaint against you in the county court. Don't forget the Tians have a daughter-in-law there."

He unleashed the black dog as Su'er jumped up, her hair tousled, and raced out with Chun'er at her heels. The dog chased them into the street, snapping at their legs.

"Come on!" screamed Su'er outside, shaking her fist. "Let's go hand in hand to the county court, One-eyed Tian! I'll charge you with obstructing the war effort."

The street was full of curious spectators.

"This should be worth watching," they said. "Let's see which charges the other. It'll be a case of the pot calling the kettle black."

17

In the end, after all the commotion, neither party charged the other. When Old Jiang heard the uproar in the street, he set down his wine jug and rushed out to swear at his daughter, who instead of subsiding gave back as good as she got. All her father could do then was hurry over to reason with One-eyed Tian.

"Don't lower yourself to her level, village head. For the sake of our old friendship."

"Who are you calling village head?" Tian stamped his foot. "They treat me worse than a dog."

"The day will come when you'll be village head again." Old Jiang steered the landlord away. "They may not respect you, sir, but I certainly do."

With a sigh One-eyed Tian calmed down and staggered home, aware that he might well lose out if he took the matter to court. For although his daughter-in-law was on the county committee, it was far from certain that she would take his side. The power to reckon with in the county was Gao Qing-shan, his bitter enemy of ten years ago. Worse still, Su'er's scoundrelly husband Gao Ba was a regiment commander, capable of any bastardly trick if you crossed him. His thoughts turned wistfully back to the days when his relative Zhang Yinwu was in the saddle and he had been able to lord it over the village. He had no idea what post, if any, his son had managed to get down in the south. Could it really be that their power had gone for good? The landlord lowered his head.

Old Jiang helped him into the house and, sitting on the *kang*, advised him:

"Don't let this worry you, village head. I'll go home and give that hussy a piece of my mind. She doesn't pay much attention to me now she's married, but once her husband comes back I'll get him to control her."

"That's right." Tian looked up abruptly. "I asked you to invite Regiment Commander Gao over here for a chat. Did you pass on my invitation?"

"Of course I did. He would have come, but then Gao Qingshan turned up out of the blue and became detachment commander over him. He was drafted to town and now he's not his own master."

"It's very strange," remarked the landlord, blinking. "Regiment Commander Gao has a will of his own — why did he knuckle under to them like that? He was the one who got that regiment together. Who's Gao Qingshan anyway? A young beggar from Five-dragon Temple who ran away after making trouble that year. Now he comes back after scrounging a living outside all these years and passes himself off as one of the Red Army. He didn't light the fire or provide the rice — how could your son-in-law cook the meal and hand him a heaped-up bowl like that? If I'd been in his shoes, they could never have tempted me into joining that detachment. With guns and men he could afford to be tough. It's not as if this were the only place where official jobs are going. Why truckle to this beggarly crew? You listen to me, Old Jiang. We've hit it off all these years, we're as close as brothers. If things go well with you, I gain by it too. When Regiment Commander Gao comes back, try to get this across to him. But don't tell him it's my idea — if word leaked out, there'd be trouble!"

After thanking the landlord profusely and addressing some soothing remarks to his wife, Old Jiang prepared to leave.

One-eyed Tian saw him off and said:

"Go easy with Su'er when you get home. We had words because she's been taken in by that lot. Wu Dayin's daughter Chun'er at the west of the village is no better than she should be, I've known that for some time. A great girl of seventeen or eighteen, she's been leading my farm-hand Mangzhong astray and got him to join the army."

Su'er, too, proved unable to lodge a complaint. As she approached the outskirts of the village Gao Ba came riding towards her on a big roan horse with an escort of seven or eight riders, like a swarm of hornets. Gao Ba's face was black, and instead of greeting his wife he cracked his whip as he passed her. One of his bodyguards leapt to the ground, lifted Su'er into his saddle and, holding the reins, raced after his master back into the village.

All Ziwuzhen was astounded by Gao Ba's return. Did Su'er have magic powers that she could summon him back so speedily? One-eyed Tian had better look out!

Gao Ba dismounted in Old Jiang's yard, and Su'er led him in to the *kang*. His bodyguards, having handed their horses over to the villagers to water, went to Erfeng Tavern for a drink, while all women and children hid themselves indoors.

Gao Ba sat with his back against a pile of crimson quilts and flicked the dust from his trousers with his riding crop, maintaining a sullen silence.

"What's the matter?" ventured Su'er. "What brings you home today?"

"Aren't I allowed to come home?" He scowled at her.

"Get away with you!" She gave him a playful shove. "Who's trying to stop you?"

Having heard his son-in-law return, Old Jiang hurried in. But finding the atmosphere stormy, he sat down on a stool and smoked his pipe in silence. Presently Gao Ba demanded:

"Has that Taoist from Changshi Temple left or not?"

"Not yet," said Old Jiang. "He's treating a sick woman in that west room of mine."

"What's wrong with her?" asked Gao Ba casually.

"Colic," said Old Jiang. "He's rubbing her belly for her. Why do you want him?"

"Fetch him in!" ordered Gao Ba. "I want my fortune told."

Old Jiang brought in the Taoist, a man of over fifty, with a large head and plump, rosy cheeks. The priest bowed to Gao Ba, who said:

"I hear you've uncanny powers. Cast lots and tell me what luck I'll have this year."

"I don't cast lots," replied the Taoist. "You must write two characters."

"Don't you know that I can't write?" bellowed Gao Ba.

"Oh, well then, just choose some word," was the hasty reply with a mollifying smile.

"Training!" spat out Gao Ba, as if the term were distasteful.

"Training, eh?" The priest closed his eyes. "The training you're given, you mean?"

"Who the hell's to give me a training?" Gao Ba was livid. "I train my men. Who dares train me?"

"You've chosen a good word, Regiment Commander Gao." The priest opened his eyes and laughed. "You're due for promotion. Before the year's out you'll be a division commander."

Old Jiang smiled ingratiatingly, but his son-in-law rounded on him and yelled:

"Get the hell out of here!"

As the Taoist was leaving Gao Ba turned to him to ask:

"What will be the upshot here do you suppose?"

The priest reflected for a moment, then said:

"These are troubled times. We can't look for any peace."

"Will these troops be able to hold their own?"

"With you among them, of course."

"I'm not one of them. How do you think the Japanese will make out?"

With a searching glance at Gao Ba, the Taoist said:

"The subjugation of China by the Japanese is a disaster that cannot be averted. I foresee plenty of bloodshed in these parts. What do men like Lu Zhengcao and Gao Qingshan amount to? They can only bring people big trouble. Those with level heads will find their own way out."

Gao Ba stared at the ground and said nothing. Old Jiang seized this chance to repeat One-eyed Tian's advice.

"Don't give me that talk!" cried Su'er. "Fancy repeating dirty rubbish like that! So now you're taking orders from

92

One-eyed Tian. That bastard's just waiting for a chance to turn traitor. Get out now. It's time for us to go to bed."

Gao Ba stopped the Taoist again to ask:

"How do you keep so fit at your age? What's the secret of those ruddy cheeks of yours?"

"It's no secret. I've led a good life since I was a boy."

"You're telling me!" scoffed Su'er. "You spend your whole day rubbing women's bellies — that's your idea of a good life."

The Taoist turned purple and left, followed by Old Jiang, feebly expostulating.

Su'er lit the lamp and spread out a quilt for Gao Ba. In her pink jacket and capacious black padded pants, she crouched on the *kang* to pull off her husband's socks.

"You must be tired after that long ride." She smiled. "But what's really troubling you?"

"Headquarters has ordered me off to a training camp. Isn't that enough to make you livid?"

"What sort of training is it?"

"Oh, it sounds very fine: military science, politics and so forth. Now the river's crossed they're going to break the bridge, that's how I see it."

"Is it just you, or others too?"

"A whole bunch of us. They're forming one military and one political unit. They say we'll still rank as officers during our training, and those who do well will be promoted."

"What's wrong with that? Why don't you want to go?"

"Don't you see what they're after? Once they've got me there without a gun, they'll shoot me. A bandit chief was shot not long ago at Gaoyang."

"I don't believe it." Su'er laughed. "I liked the way Gao Xiang talked that day."

"You can't trust everything they say. I've a shady past,

let's face it, and people must have carried tales to Gao Qing-shan. Even if it doesn't come to the worst, they'll send us up to the hills to eat rice full of grit and sleep on a cold *kang*. We'll have to drill, climb mountains and stand sentry duty. Why should I put up with that after being regiment commander?"

"If you can't take more than others, how can you lead your men?" retorted Su'er. "It's not as if you hadn't roughed it since you were a boy. Look at Gao Qingshan, the tough time he's had of it."

"I can't make up my mind about Gao Qingshan. He doesn't treat us too badly, but he's an odd fellow. We've been attending meetings every day, and I always took a dozen bodyguards with me. So did Li Suo and Zhang Daqiu. But all he had was one young orderly with an old rifle. We three regiment commanders talked it over and decided it didn't look dignified for a detachment commander to go around like that. It didn't seem right, either, for us to have so many guards and him so few. We agreed we'd each send him two horses, two guards and two Mauser pistols. Would you believe it, the fellow wouldn't take them! He advised us to cut down on our orderlies and to take on our complement of political workers. These Communists just don't know how to live. They go out of their way to find hardships. I don't see much future with them."

"What are you thinking of doing then?" Su'er frowned.

"When that order came today and the secretary started reading it out, I galloped off before he'd a chance to finish. I'm not going to study. If they press me too hard, I may take my men over to the other side."

"Don't you do that!" She slapped his leg. "If others can study, why shouldn't you? You only need a little patience. It won't be a bad thing if you learn to read and write."

"What the hell is the use? If I'd been cut out for study, I'd have made a start long ago. I've the guts to fight Japan and that's enough. What else do I need to learn?"

"Well, don't study then," said Su'er. "But talk it over with the others properly. Don't go getting silly ideas. Those men joined you so as to fight Japan and win a good name for themselves. How can you take them over to the other side? Do you mean to run south like Chiang Kai-shek, or turn traitor and go over to Japan? Neither's any good."

"Well, take off your clothes and let's sleep," replied Gao Ba. "I can think it over tomorrow."

18

Gao Xiang rang up Gao Qingshan to urge him to keep his troops well in hand, educating them while he prepared them for combat.

When Qingshan called another meeting of his regiment commanders and cadres, Gao Ba failed to appear, and Li Suo said he had gone home without leave the previous day, probably because he was unwilling to study. Qingshan thought the matter over, and after the meeting set out with Mangzhong by bicycle for Ziwuzhen.

It was pleasant cycling over the white sandy track bordered by vegetable plots. All the cabbages had been cut, leaving nothing but a few rotting leaves in the fields. The wells were deserted, frost had withered the vines, and some plump orange pumpkins, coated with rime, were lying on the sunlit ridges of the fields.

Soon the south end of Five-dragon Temple came into sight. At one end of the tall dike in front of the village sat a woman spinning yarn, at the other end stood a woman making shoe-soles. They belonged to the newly organized defence corps.

They were both young, these women who were working as they stood guard in the sunshine. When the one making shoes caught sight of two men in uniform some way off, she cried out:

"Hey! Here come two soldiers!"

The spinner did not raise her head but replied:

"No need to shout. Just check up on them when they come."

"How can I? Soldiers may flare up if they're challenged."

"They'll have to like it or lump it." The spinner smiled. "It's an order from higher up."

"If they flare up, I'll point you out and say, 'That's the detachment commander's wife, so keep quiet!'"

"Don't do that. Just mention Gao Xiang — that's a name to conjure with."

As they were teasing each other the cyclists drew nearer, and the woman making shoes recognized Qingshan.

"Talk of the devil!" She giggled. "Go home quick and get a meal ready."

The spinner, who was none other than Qiufen, looked up for a second at her husband and Mangzhong, then bent over her work again, protesting:

"I like that! Am I to leave my post just because he comes?"

"A strong-minded woman!" retorted Gao Xiang's wife.

At sight of them, Qingshan dismounted and asked:

"Keeping each other company on sentry duty?"

"That's right," said Gao Xiang's wife. "Hand it over!"

"Hand what over?"

"Your travel pass." She pulled a stern face. "A man of your rank should be able to carry out orders."

"Oh!" Qingshan turned quickly to Mangzhong. "Did we bring a travel permit?"

"No." Mangzhong burst out laughing.

"We'll remember it next time," promised Qingshan. "We left in such a hurry today that we forgot."

"If you haven't one next time, we won't let you into the village. These are your own orders, yet you don't obey them. Someone who knows you will have to vouch for you." With a smile she pointed at Qiufen.

Grinning, Qingshan wheeled his bicycle on, while Mangzhong turned back to shout:

"That's all you know!"

"What do you mean?" asked Gao Xiang's wife.

"Fine sentries you are, just checking up on us, not on anyone else. You see men in uniform with army packs and check up on them strictly. If someone dressed like a peasant comes along, you don't even bother to look at him, for fear of holding up your work."

"How can you say such a thing?"

"You're afraid of catching it for neglecting your duty as sentries. But no matter what paper people produce, so long as there's a red chop on it, they can fool you. You turn it round this way and that as if you understood, when really you're like me — can't read a word. You ought to be ashamed!"

"Get away! Only grannies do that." Qiufen laughed and called after her husband, "Want me to go home and boil some water for you?"

"No need," he called back. "Stick to your post. If you can't read, you'd better hurry up and start a literacy class."

Five-dragon Temple is such a small village that as soon as Qingshan entered from the south he was visible to people at the north. It was time for the midday meal and the whole

97

village, young and old, ran out to the street carrying a bowl of sweet potatoes and greens in one hand and in the other a large flat sorghum cake — favourite winter fare in these parts. Qingshan called out greetings to the old folk.

"Good day, uncle! Are you keeping well, aunty?"

"We're still alive and kicking." The old people smiled. "See that, the rest of you! He minds his manners, does young Qingshan. If he hadn't spoken first, we'd have held our tongues. Why is the lad still so thin? Got too much on his mind."

The village boys beamed at Qingshan, who had a question for each: Have you joined the defence corps? Learned to shoot yet? The young wives tiptoed up behind the older women to stare. Qingshan gave the children rides in turn on his bicycle until their delighted mothers called out:

"Get down now! Let uncle rest."

The old people sighed approvingly and declared:

"The Communists teach people right. See the way he talks and behaves? Qingshan was full of mischief as a lad. Used to climb a tree and piss on you, he did! Tell us, Qingshan, are the Japanese coming this way?"

"Don't you worry," he assured them. "If they come we'll fight. We'll throw them out."

"Mind you put up a good fight," urged one old woman. "All our old lives depend on you, boy."

"Everyone must join forces to fight," replied Qingshan. He explained the situation to them as he went, so that all the villagers felt they knew where they stood and their spirits rose.

Climbing the dike at the north end of the village brought him in sight of his home. The cottage glowed a mellow gold in the winter sunlight. Gao Sihai was just setting off somewhere with his goats, but when he saw his son he struck a light for his pipe and waited by the door.

Mangzhong, leaning his bicycle against the cottage, bounded forward to feel one of the goats and cried:

"They're much fatter. What fodder have you been giving them, uncle?"

"Fodder indeed! I've just been letting them graze. I know where all the best grass is in these parts. There's no work in winter, so I take them out all day long."

"Have you got a peasants' union going here yet, dad?" asked Qingshan.

"We're signing on now," said his father. "They wanted me to be chairman, but I said someone else had better have the job."

"If they want you, why don't you do it?" Qingshan laughed.

"And have folk said I'm cashing in on your position? I'm not so certain, either, that your lot will succeed."

"Why not?"

"You're too badly fitted out. As I see it, the Japanese have aeroplanes and big guns, while all you've got are cranky homemade rifles."

"Once the fighting starts we'll get everything we need," Qingshan assured him. "That's how it was with the Red Army. They started off with nothing. But the longer they fought, the more men, the better weapons, and the bigger territory they got. Fighting's the way to speed up the revolution. Don't just look at the Japanese aeroplanes and guns — apart from those, they've nothing. They're invading China. And there's not a single case in history of invaders who've been able to stick for long in someone else's country. They charge in like lions but slink out like beaten curs, because aggression is a fearful crime. For the moment Japan is dreaming a sweet dream, but they'll wake up when we start fighting and

99

wish they'd never been born. Our troops are defending their own land, driving out the brigands who've broken into their homes. Our soldiers have spunk, they'll seize the enemy's weapons to arm themselves."

"All right, leave weapons out of it, but your people are no good either," insisted the old man. "Ten years ago, remember what a fine set of people we had? Your troops now are a bunch of riffraff, and here in the very next village the chairman of the women's association is Gao Ba's wife Su'er! Chun'er's working under her. I've told Qiufen to stop her from mixing with that rotten crew. If Su'er's in, count me out. If things go on this way, you won't be able to tell good folk from bad."

"Don't be so narrow, dad," protested Qingshan. "Revolution can change people for the better. Nobody's bad by nature."

"If you don't want to join in, uncle, just take it easy." Mangzhong sniggered. "You're too old and rickety to do a good job, even if you wanted to."

"What's that, Mangzhong?" The old fellow flushed and bristled. "An old dodderer, am I? Not a bit of it! I'll take you on any time you like, my lad. At farming or soldiering. When it comes to handling a sickle or hoe, I won't yield first place to you. As for shooting, you've only just started carrying a gun — I could make rings round you any time, with my eyes shut."

"Why this funk then, each time someone mentions Japan?" Mangzhong turned away to hide a smile. "You're scared to be chairman of the peasants' union."

"Who's afraid of Japan? Just wait till they come! Who's scared to be chairman of the peasants' union? I'd like to see anyone else take the lead in Five-dragon Temple!"

Qiufen was climbing the dike now, her spindle in her arms.

"Why don't you go in?" she asked. "What's all the noise about?"

"We were only joking," said Qingshan. "Have you left your post?"

"I've done my stint." She smiled.

"What stint?"

"Each person does sentry duty for the time it takes the shadow of the west room to lengthen two feet." Qiufen opened the door. "Come on in."

"I must go on to Ziwuzhen." Qingshan started wheeling his bicycle off again, while Mangzhong swiftly mounted and shot down the bank. Qiufen saw her husband a little way and asked softly.

"Will you be home to sleep tonight?"

"No, I won't. Things are warming up, I've a lot of work waiting for me."

19

Presently Qingshan and Mangzhong reached Ziwuzhen, a sleepy village except on market days. Gao Ba's bodyguards were raising a din outside Erfeng Tavern, but at sight of Qingshan one cried, "Here comes the detachment commander!" He blew a whistle and they all slipped inside. As soon as Qingshan had ridden past they darted out again and called softly to Mangzhong:

"You come back later, mate. We've wine and grub."

Mangzhong grinned, then showed Qingshan the way to Su'er's home in a lane at the west end of the village. The unvarnished wooden gate was standing open. Mangzhong walked towards the window and shouted:

"Is Regiment Commander Gao at home?"

Su'er's window was a fine sight, newly pasted with snow-white paper inset with a bright pane of glass bordered with red. After one peep through the glass, Su'er came flying out, her pink jacket unbuttoned at the neck, having only just slipped on her embroidered slippers. She stared at Qingshan for some seconds, then parted her red lips in a welcoming smile.

"Why, it's the detachment commander! You're a rare visitor. Come in, quick. Just leave your bicycles there, no one will touch them."

"Is Regiment Commander Gao in?" asked Qingshan, not budging from where he stood.

"Not just now," said Su'er. "But come on in and sit down. I've hot water for you to have a wash, and tea for you to drink. Just look how dusty you are!" She darted in to fetch a red silk whisk, and vigorously dusted off Mangzhong's clothes.

"Are those the shoes Chun'er made you?" she asked with a chuckle. "They look fine. She's done a good job. Are you going to see her?"

Mangzhong's cheeks burned but he said nothing.

Qingshan was prevailed upon at last to go in. Su'er's room did not match the exterior of the cottage with its mud walls and thatched roof. It was bright and warm, reeking of scent and powder. Qingshan, who had come through the Long March, was stunned. He could hardly keep his seat and felt he was choking.

Su'er bustled about hospitably to get them tea and hot water. When she offered to make some flapjacks and fry some eggs, Qingshan said:

"Don't trouble. Just find Regiment Commander Gao, will you? I've something to talk over with him before we go back."

"If he were anywhere else, I'd have gone like a shot," answered Su'er. "I'm in and out of every house in Ziwuzhen. But I've just had a row with that particular family."

"Which family?" asked Mangzhong.

"Why, of course, *you* can go!" she cried. "He's with your old boss One-eyed Tian."

"What's he doing there?"

"How would I know?" Su'er struck her fists together. "That old devil One-eyed Tian kept inviting Gao Ba right and left, but I wouldn't let him accept. Today they've a visitor, and my fool of a father insisted on dragging him over."

"Who's the visitor? Where's he from?" Qingshan, who had followed this closely, raised his head.

"I was too fed up to ask. You go and call him, Mangzhong."

Mangzhong looked at Qingshan, who answered after reflection:

"No, don't go. We'll have a stroll and come back presently."

"You must come back at noon, please," said Su'er.

The lane took them out to the fields north of the village. Qingshan strode along thoughtfully with lowered head in the teeth of a north wind. When they had covered some distance he turned to say:

"Let me test you, Mangzhong. Why d'you suppose One-eyed Tian sent for Gao Ba?"

"He's up to no good, you can be sure of that."

"There are people here out to down us on the sly. One-eyed Tian wants to win Gao Ba over. At this meal today, he'll try to set him against us. He may even persuade Gao Ba to turn deserter."

"What shall we do?" asked Mangzhong.

"We must be prepared, that's all. I didn't send you to

find Gao Ba, because that would just have made things worse. It's still up to us to win him and educate him. If he stays here in Ziwuzhen he'll go to the bad. Don't you agree?"

"Sure." Mangzhong laughed. "Lying all day in that snug little nest of Su'er's, with counter-revolutionaries getting at him all the time, who'd want to join the revolution?"

Qingshan smiled, very drawn in that moment to Mangzhong. The Party's training and his own experience were turning the lad into a lieutenant he could love and trust.

"Let's go into the fields and talk with some of the men," he said.

"What about Old Chang?" suggested Mangzhong. "That's him ploughing with the two big mules over there."

Not far to their north was a peasant, well on in years, in blue homespun with a girdle round his middle. He was leaning sideways to steer the plough and encouraging his mules, who pulled steadily forward. The bright ploughshare turned up the damp loam in furrows clean as the ripples of a stream in spring or the lines chiselled by a sculptor.

"He's a first-rate farmer, is Old Chang," remarked Mangzhong. "His furrows are as straight as a die."

"Too bad he's working for a landlord," said Qingshan.

"Old Chang!" yelled Mangzhong. "We'll wait for you up here."

Loosening his grasp on the reins, Old Chang halted for a second before driving his team to the end of the field and back. Then, having set down the plough, he pulled Mangzhong over to sit beneath a willow.

"That's our detachment commander," said the lad, pointing.

"I remember him from way back." Old Chang smiled. "Everybody in these parts knows him."

Qingshan had sauntered over to the plough.

"Can I have a go at this, Old Chang?" he asked.

"I know you're country born, but these mules are skittish. They don't take kindly to strangers."

"Never mind." With a grin Qingshan picked up the reins, righted the plough and shouted to the team. Recognizing a peasant's voice, the mules started meekly off. Qingshan threw a triumphant smile over his shoulder.

"He's got good stuff in him," commented Old Chang. "No wonder he can lead the troops and fight."

After ploughing two furrows, Qingshan came back to sit with them and asked:

"How many hired hands are there in Ziwuzhen?"

"A matter of sixteen or seventeen," replied Old Chang, puffing at his pipe.

"You ought to start a workers' union."

"I dare say. But we've nobody to give a lead."

"You can take the lead."

"Me?" The old peasant guffawed. "What time do I have? You eat another man's rice and your time isn't your own — not even at night. Besides, the boss would never let us join."

"This is none of his business. He's no say in the matter," replied Qingshan. "With a union, it's easier for workers to stick together. We can study and see our way better. We're the backbone of the resistance to Japan, so we must help to run the village affairs. Those with gumption may become village heads."

"Village heads!" Old Chang crowed with laughter. "Not likely. I never heard of a hired hand becoming a village head. Just give us better grub, a bit more pay, fewer dirty jobs, and I'll be satisfied."

"We learn through working and fighting." insisted Qingshan. "Once we've driven out the Japanese, we'll forge ahead in a big way. Our folk will have to head provinces and counties."

"Right, then. I'll go back and get hold of some others," said Old Chang, standing up. "I mustn't sit here with you any longer. If my boss saw me, there'd be trouble."

Back in Su'er's cottage, they found Gao Ba sprawled out tipsily on the *kang,* in no state to have a serious discussion. Qingshan urged him to go back quickly to headquarters and assured him they could come to some understanding. Then he and Mangzhong wheeled their bicycles off.

Su'er, unable to stop them, saw them to the gate. There she grabbed hold of Qingshan's handle-bars.

"Tell me, detachment commander," she begged, "why are you so set on sending Gao Ba to study?"

"It's a fine thing to have a chance to study," he explained. "In our army, officers and men alike, we all study. If he doesn't take this chance, before long some of those below him who've studied well will come to the top, and he'll drop behind them. Study's for the sake of work, but it's to his own advantage as well."

"He can't see that," said Su'er. "You're his chief. When he goes back, do teach him some sense."

"You'd better teach him some sense yourself tonight," put in Mangzhong. "I fancy one word from you carries more weight with Regiment Commander Gao than anything his commanding officer says."

"Cheeky devil!" Smiling, Su'er let them go.

As they neared the river, Chun'er raced after them, calling: "Wait for me, brother-in-law!"

Qingshan dismounted and turned back to ask:

"What's all the hurry about?"

"I've come to see you off," she panted. "How could you come to Ziwuzhen and not look in to see me?"

106

"It's not me you came to see off." Qingshan chuckled.

"Get away with you! Who else would I come to see? I want your advice on a problem. Our women's association asked One-eyed Tian for seven pairs of shoes, but he refused and set his dog on us. That's not all either. That wife of his is boasting now that they're on good terms with Gao Ba, they've a daughter at court and a friend in the army, so she's not afraid of a pack of beggar-girls like us. Tell me, what shall we do if he won't produce those shoes when the time comes?"

"Report him to the county court," replied Qingshan firmly. "I can see how it is: If we don't take that feudal diehard down a peg or two, we'll get nowhere with resistance work in this village."

"You're absolutely right," Chun'er agreed. "People are watching to see how the wind blows, and whether that brute One-eyed Tian really knuckles under or not. If we charge him, brother-in-law, you must back us up."

"It won't be me backing you up," retorted Qingshan. "You'll have the revolution behind you."

20

Things were tenser these days on the central Hebei plain. The Japanese had swept unopposed across the Yellow River but now they found a force dogging their steps, a knife pointed at their heart. They did not take Lu Zhengcao seriously at the start, when the whole Kuomintang army fled south but this young regiment commander on the banks of the Daqing struck back against Japanese imperialism. His courageous fight dispelled the fear of Japan that had filled so many soldiers and civilians. Even the loss of half his troops did not make the young commander lose heart. He joined forces with the local armed units organized by the Communist Party and stood his ground, setting up a glorious base of resistance. As soon as the Japanese realized that Lu Zhengcao was a Communist, they started to worry. Now, in order to thrust across the Hebei plain, they had set up additional strong points along the Beijing-Hankou Railway and occupied Hejian in the north, the better to advance against Gaoyang.

Part of the whole-hearted support for the resistance given by the people of the plain was the peasants' drive to make shoes for the troops. Chun'er inspected those brought to her, pair by pair. Some were of good material, carefully made. Others were of old cloth dyed black with soot from the bottom of the pan, the soles padded out with paper. But most young peasant women were glad of this chance to do something for the men defending the country. Never before had they made anything for others than members of their own families, and the soldiers would wear these shoes to fight the enemy threatening their homes. At night, after their husbands and children were asleep, they lit the lamps and worked until cockcrow. They brought the stoutest cloth uppers they could from the pedlar, taking care to tell him that these were not for their own families but for the resistance fighters. And they carried these materials triumphantly home like small resistance flags, aware that all eyes were on them and that everyone honoured them for what they were doing.

When the shoes were finished they took them to Chun'er's cottage or, if ashamed of their poor handiwork, got their mothers-in-law to deliver them instead. Chun'er praised these young co-workers and produced the shoes she had made for their inspection. Hers, of course, were the strongest and best pair of the lot.

"The soldier who gets these shoes will be in luck," said one woman. "You ought to put your name on them."

"I have — on the sole!" said Chun'er. "It'll leave a print at each step." She turned over one of the shoes and there, in the middle of the sole, her name stood out embroidered in stout thread. Yes, Chun'er's name would leave a clear imprint on China's soil wherever a battle was fought.

When all the shoes were delivered but the seven pairs due from One-eyed Tian, Chun'er asked Su'er to go with her and collect them. Su'er, however, had lost her previous keenness. Although capable sometimes of tackling an opponent with no thought of the consequences, she had no staying power. Gao Ba was now back in town, but after his meal with One-eyed Tian he had told Su'er:

"Quit working for these women. The Japanese have taken Hejian, and Gaoyang may not be able to hold out. We're not like Chun'er, who shares a *kang* with Gao Qingshan. Of course she's going all out to save the country. But we must leave ourselves a loop-hole and not offend One-eyed Tian."

This morning the boom of big Japanese guns had frightened Su'er too. And she was no longer on good terms with Chun'er. It had not escaped her notice how the other young village women respected Chun'er while for her they had nothing but contempt, although afraid to offend her. When Chun'er suggested tackling One-eyed Tian, she retorted:

"I've had enough of being chairman. I did the dirty work last time; this time it's your turn. I don't get all the credit, so neither should I be the only one to offend folk."

Then Old Jiang joined in, a vicious look in his eye.

"You gad about all day by yourself — why not go alone? Why keep on butting in here? I won't have Su'er mixed up in this foolish business. Since that women's association of yours was set up, we've had no peace at home. You've worn out my doorstep between you."

"We've worn out your doorstep?" retorted Chun'er hotly. "Those rich, important friends of yours, more likely!"

"See here, sister!" cried Su'er. "That's a mean thing to say. We're treated like dirt, cold-shouldered by everyone as if we weren't fit to associate with you. Well, let me tell you this: I've never skimped and scraped to find the time and cloth to make clothes and shoes for a young hired hand, or slipped into town to see him on the sly. We live in the same village and I don't wear blinkers — I know what I'm talking about. So don't put on that virtuous act with me."

This was too much for Chun'er. Her bundle of shoes in her arms, she fled, sobbing with rage. But she stuck to her guns, much as the unjust taunt rankled, for like the whole nation she was working for a splendid cause. Straightening her shoulders she marched off alone to the house of One-eyed Tian.

Old Wen in the outer courtyard was cleaning out the pigsties. The whole place stank. He saw from Chun'er's expression that something was wrong and put down his spade to ask:

"What do you want, lass?"

"I've come to collect their shoes."

"Where's your chairman, Su'er?" Old Wen sniggered. "Why isn't she leading the attack today?"

"She's caved in. Next time not even the blind will elect her. She's hardly worked for more than three days when the rustling of leaves scares the daylight out of her. She refused to come, so I've come on my own."

"Take my advice and go home." He lowered his voice. "They haven't done a thing about those shoes. You'll only get into trouble asking for them."

110

"They've got to make them. Our soldiers have left their homes and jobs to go to the front. We've all got to do our bit. We can't expect the men to fight barefoot."

"Go back home, I tell you!" He leant over the edge of the sty. "You're not a brazen baggage like Su'er. She's not afraid of anyone, that shrew. But you're a girl from a decent family, you don't know how to swear or fight — all you can do is cry. Our boss is a tiger, his wife's a tigress. Look out!"

"I'm not afraid. They can't eat me." Chun'er had reached the gate to the inner courtyard.

That same moment out came One-eyed Tian, speeding a parting guest who looked a cross between a retired official and a merchant. He came from Baoding, now occupied by the Japanese, and was the visitor who had been invited to keep Gao Ba company a few days earlier. One-eyed Tian glared at Chun'er and snapped:

"What do you want now?"

"I've come for the shoes."

"What shoes?" asked the stranger.

"Shoes for the resistance fighters."

"Well, well!" The visitor smiled at One-eyed Tian. "A great girl who doesn't sit spinning on the *kang* or go out to pick up firewood, but wants to join the resistance! Is Japan so easy to resist? Can you resist aeroplanes and heavy artillery? The Japanese will be here any day now."

"If they come, our men will fight them," said Chun'er stoutly. "What do you mean by such talk? Aren't you for the resistance?"

"I'm advising you for your own good." The fellow sniggered. "No matter who comes, the peasants have to till the fields, eat and pay taxes. Don't you listen to that nonsense the students talk. Wasting their parents' good money,

111

they refuse to study, just hold forth about resisting Japan. It's their fault, I tell you, that Japan's attacked China."

"You talk like a traitor!" cried Chun'er.

"Dirty bitch!" One-eyed Tian knocked her off her feet. "How dare you insult my guest?"

"If you don't want to be called a traitor, stop farting like one!" yelled Chun'er as she picked herself up.

One-eyed Tian charged towards her, but before he could strike her again Old Wen with his pitchfork vaulted out of the sty. Thinly clad, his shoes caked with dung, he rushed over to intervene.

"Don't you hit her, sir!" he growled. "She's only a girl. What would folk say?"

"Are you telling me what to do, you stinking lout? Go back to your muck raking, and be quick about it!"

"We sweat for you and go hungry and cold, yet you say we stink?" shouted Old Wen. "Just ask the villagers who stinks worse — you or me."

"Are you defying me too, you dog?" roared the landlord. "Don't put too much faith in your friends in town. Listen to the artillery!"

"Not I!" cried Old Wen. "We're not waiting to welcome in those foreign devils. You won't catch us turning traitor."

"Get out!" One-eyed Tian kicked him savagely in the belly. Old Wen collapsed, groaning and clutching at his stomach.

"Chun'er," he panted. "Go to town and report him."

As Chun'er scurried off, One-eyed Tian bellowed:

"Yes, go and tell those fine officials of yours. We'll have it out in court. Old Chang! Get out the carriage!"

Old Chang had been ploughing not far off, just north of the village, but hearing this commotion had run back to find

Old Wen rolling on the ground. Having helped his friend up, he answered One-eyed Tian:

"We're through with you. Get the carriage out yourself."

"Fine!" cried Tian. "Hired hands are dirt cheap. Clear off my premises, both of you, this instant!"

Old Chang supported Old Wen to the home of a friend, while One-eyed Tian led out one of his mules and tried in vain to harness it to the carriage. At last with the help of the visitor he succeeded in pushing the mule between the shafts, but forgot to fasten the traces. When he cracked his whip the mule bolted, rocking the carriage so that it nearly upset. It crashed through the gate, knocking off a chunk of mud wall, and the mule raced off to the fields.

"I'll walk," declared One-eyed Tian, hurling his whip to the ground.

It was the Japanese gunfire that had given the landlord the courage to go to court. That combined with the fact that Gao Ba had accepted his invitation to a meal, and his daughter-in-law had risen to the rank of superintendent of the county administration. One-eyed Tian put on this act in front of his guest because he hoped to recover his power and lord it over the villagers again.

One-eyed Tian's kick succeeded, where all else had failed, in establishing a workers' union to resist Japan and save the country. As soon as word of his action reached the seventeen hired hands in Ziwuzhen, they rushed to Old Wen's bedside, had themselves enrolled, put a thumb-print beside their names, and elected Old Chang as their chairman. They urged him to hurry after Chun'er and accompany her to the county town.

So now the three of them, Chun'er in the lead, were making their way to town. It was an early winter day and the hoar-frost on the trees by the road, melted by the noonday sun, dripped on to her head. Today the troops from all around and the People's Defence Corps were moving up to the front. To the northwest rose a cloud of swirling dust. Their breath steaming in the frosty air, the people's troops advanced in good order across the Hebei plain. Peasants working in the fields or walking down the highway stopped to watch them, men and women clustered in front of their villages, and the cocks on the haystacks beside the cottages kept up a lusty crowing. As the great battle to repulse the invaders started, the nation surged forward in fury, all its sons and daughters fired with the determination to make what contribution they could to the war.

21

Old Chang, covering the distance in great strides, soon passed One-eyed Tian and came within sight of Chun'er.

The girl, in a glow from walking, her back moist, was gazing eagerly at all around her. The countryside was spilling over with our troops. She saw the long trail of footprints left by the soldiers, who were wearing the shoes and socks that she and the other village women had made. Her own step was light and she fairly overflowed with energy as she advanced with the men. Her heart flew to join them on their march towards the front, and she wondered if Mangzhong were among them.

Old Chang hailed her.

"You girls deserve all the praise you're getting. You walk like the wind. I'd a hard time catching up."

"What are you doing here?" Chun'er turned to him. "Are you going ahead to sound a gong and clear the way for your master?"

"Not I!" Old Chang laughed derisively. "I'm through with him. We're on the same errand, lass. I'm chairman of the Ziwuzhen workers' union and come to help you have the law on him."

Chun'er brightened at that and asked:

"When were you elected?"

"I've just this moment taken up office. I came after you as soon as the meeting was over, without so much as stopping to change my clothes. They said a tongue-tied, timid young girl like you would be no match for that old wolf."

"If you're with me, so much the better. But even on my own I'd have managed."

"I'll stand by you and back you up." Old Chang sighed. "Why, lass, not even your father, let alone you, has ever given anybody a rough answer, much less gone to court. It's the big landlords who keep making trips to town. My old man dinned this into me when I was a nipper. Starve sooner than steal, and put up with anything rather than go to court. Yes, we've steered clear of *yamens*. But tell me, Chun'er, how much money have you brought?"

"Why bring money? I'm not doing any shopping."

"For the lawsuit. It costs money just to get into the court."

"There's no need. I'll go straight to my brother-in-law."

"That's right." Old Chang smiled. "My head was so full of money, I clean forgot him. We've nothing to worry about. With him on our side, we're sure to win." He pulled his tobacco pouch out of his wallet and extracted his tinder-box.

"What d'you mean — with him on our side?" retorted Chun'er. "We've the right on our side."

"Yes, of course." Old Chang bent his head to strike a light. His tinder-box was so old that the flint had long since worn away, and now looked like a child's marble. Clasping it between gnarled fingers, he struck the old steel against it

115

repeatedly but produced not a single spark. He persevered in his efforts while chatting with Chun'er and so they covered more than ten *li*, passing several villages, without his managing to strike a light. Not until they reached the West Gate of the town did he put his tinder-box back in his pouch and stow that away inside his shabby wallet. This had to stand him instead of smoking a pipe.

Chun'er went straight to the Mobilization Committee, only to be met with the news that Detachment Commander Gao was talking to the troops. Assuming that Mangzhong was busy too, she said:

"We're here to go to law."

Having ascertained which village she came from, the man in the Mobilization Committee said:

"The Party, government, army and mass organizations each deals with its own affairs. Take your case to the county government. The superintendent comes from your parts and she's a woman too — her name's Li Peizhong."

When Chun'er went out and relayed this news to Old Chang, his face fell.

"That's torn it! She's One-eyed Tian's daughter-in-law, bound to take his side against us. We're wasting our time."

"Since we're here we may as well try. We'd be cowards to turn back now," protested Chun'er. "What if he *is* her father-in-law? It's the truth that counts. A cadre, eating the people's millet, can't twist the law."

Having asked the way to the county government, they followed a lane past the race track and, turning right, saw the town hall before them.

Rubble littered the ground in front, for since the flight of the Kuomintang officials no one had cleaned the place up. After the establishment of local defence corps, the cadres had been so busy mobilizing the people that the new county government had only just been formed. When Peizhong was asked to head it, she sulked for several days. She had barely learned the ropes in the Mobilization Committee, yet here they were transferring her to this difficult new post! The leadership told her: "The fundamental question in the revolution is that of political power. . . . We've struggled all these years for women to take part in the government, so how can you refuse? Besides, the superintendent of the county government ranks equal to a county head. No woman has ever been county head in China. You'll be the first in the resistance base, Comrade Li." Then, laughing, she promised to have a try, on condition that they transferred her if she proved unequal to the task. She had moved into the large empty town hall the previous day.

A stickler for cleanliness, the first thing she did was to sweep out her living quarters. The old runner hurried over when he saw this.

"Give me that broom. Let me do it," he cried. "What will people think if they see you sweeping the floor?"

With a laugh, Peizhong went out to the yard, where she discovered a pot of nandina which was dying of neglect. She carried it inside, put it on her window-sill, and told the runner to water it.

"Anyone can see you come from a good family," he remarked. "Your husband was only a district head, and now you're the head of a county. Women have certainly risen in the world."

Frowning slightly, Peizhong said:

"Fetch me a big sheet of red paper, a brush and some ink."

"I knew you had book-learning. They say our detachment commander started life with a hoe in his hand. You're the best educated of all the county cadres."

"Hurry up and get those things!"

"Will you give me a chit for the general affairs department?"

"What general affairs department?" She stamped her foot. "Can't you see I'm the only one here? Go and borrow the things from the Mobilization Committee."

When he returned with the ink, brush and paper, it was already midday and very warm. The runner ground the ink and smoothed out the paper while Peizhong paced up and down the room. Her pale face faintly flushed, she stopped by the window and the bright sunlight fell on her rounded breasts. An unhappy marriage had left its mark on her, but now her heart was filled with concern for the people and determination to realize her ideals by working for the revolution. She snipped the dead leaves off her plant with a small pair of scissors, glad to find fresh sap in the stems. If carefully tended, it should put out new shoots before spring.

Then, bending over the sheet of red paper, she wrote in bold, clear characters: "The People's Government."

The runner chuckled and said:

"I know what that means. The government is our county government. People's means it's father and mother of the people* — right?"

"No, it's just the other way round. The people's government is a government that manages affairs for the people."

"Every government does that. If they didn't manage people's affairs, how would all those officials get rich?"

"Ah, but there's a big difference." Peizhong carried the paper over to dry in the sun. "The old feudal rulers were like a millstone round the necks of the people. Our government

---

* In feudal China a magistrate was often referred to as "father and mother of the people".

118

today is against all feudal oppression. The people have risen up to take power themselves."

"I don't quite get it," said the runner.

"Wait till I try a case and you'll understand. Now make me some paste and we'll post this up."

The old man went back to the Mobilization Committee for some flour and mixed a large bowl of paste. The two of them carried the red paper out to the front. The runner, impressed and puzzled by this inscription, was wondering what new regulations this county head would introduce.

Great was his astonishment when Peizhong climbed nimbly on to a desk and brushed a thick layer of paste over the town hall's old signboard. A flock of sparrows flew out from their nets behind, and the old man urged her to be careful. Then, while he held the desk steady with one hand, signing with the other to help her get the paper straight, she carefully posted it up. This done, she stood there surveying her handiwork and hot tears sprang to her eyes.

It seemed to her as if the bright red placard had lit up the whole town hall and was shining out across the race track to the fields where Gao Qingshan was addressing four thousand soldiers, who could be heard thundering slogans. The inscription was visible to all passers-by. It was to set up a government of their own that so many people had worked and fought for long years. For this they had given their young lives, and their dear ones had wept till they had no more tears to shed.

22

"What's wrong?" asked the old runner, shocked to see the county head in tears. "It's a red-letter day for you, taking up this new post. Has someone been treating you badly? This is only a little place, but you'd hardly credit the number of good people here who've been hounded to death. I've worked in this office most of my life and seen some shocking things, I can tell you. But that's over and done with. I know what you meant just now."

"That's right." She jumped down from the desk.

"Ten years ago," he went on, "they arrested plenty of Communists in this county, mostly peasants who'd made trouble in your parts. Quite a few were killed, among them a young school boy. Each time I took his father and mother in with food for him, they nearly cried their eyes out, but I never saw that boy so much as frown. Plucky young fellow, he was. And when he'd half a chance he told me how good the Communist Party was. The day he was killed I asked for leave — I just couldn't bear to see it. It made me sick."

"I was crying for him and others like him." Peizhong straightened her clothes and smoothed her hair. "Well, let's go in."

"There's someone coming, county head," he whispered. "You go in and wait till I sound the drum to show the court's in session."

Peizhong turned and saw a girl coming through the gate followed by a middle-aged peasant. She recognized Chun'er at once, as well as her father-in-law's hired hand Old Chang.

Running over to take Chun'er by the hand, she asked:

"What are you doing in town? Have you come about the women's association?"

"No, to go to law. It's your father-in-law we're charging."

Peizhong flushed as she shook her head at the old man, who had brought in a shabby chair and was putting it behind the magistrate's table.

"What's he done?" she asked.

120

"Refused to make his share of shoes for the army. Knocked me down when I went to ask for them. And kicked a worker, Old Wen. How will you punish him?"

"I'm the witness," put in Old Chang.

"He's chairman of the new workers' union in our village and he saw it all," Chun'er explained. "Your father-in-law's coming too. He's somewhere behind."

"See here, my girl," said the old runner to Chun'er, "You're in a court of law, not gossiping on the *kang*. What's all this about 'your father-in-law'? Has the accused no name?"

"We don't know his official name — there he is!" Chun'er pointed outside.

One-eyed Tian had at last arrived. Never having walked eighteen *li* before in his life, he was sweating profusely. His thick fur-lined gown and padded shoes were covered with dust. Panting, he looked round at the gate for someone to announce him. Finding no one, he walked in and discovered his daughter-in-law with the two plaintiffs.

"Do we still have to hand in a written indictment for a lawsuit?" he called out.

Peizhong, flustered by her father-in-law's arrival, recoiled a step and sat down on the chair. Getting out her notebook, she replied:

"There's no need for a written indictment. Both parties can put their cases here."

"Both parties? What two parties?" asked One-eyed Tian.

"Plaintiff and defendant," she answered.

"Who's the defendant?"

"You are. Why did you knock down a cadre working for the resistance and assault a worker?" Her cheeks were burning.

"Ha! Cross-examining your own father-in-law, are you?" He snorted indignantly.

121

"This is the government and I'm doing my job," she retorted. "Keep personal relations out of it."

"Government? I've been here more times than I could count, but I've never seen a government like this of yours — it's more like a tumbledown temple."

"None of us has seen a government like this." Peizhong spoke as if refuting someone in a study group. "Didn't you see the inscription over the door? This is the age of people's political power."

One-eyed Tian was such a diehard that he no longer read the newspapers and consequently knew none of the new terms. He was at a loss for an answer. Meanwhile word of this case must have spread, for the hall was rapidly filling up with interested spectators. Among them was Gao Qingshan, who had finished his talk. And Mangzhong squeezed his way to the front of the crowd, his eyes fixed on Chun'er, who stood stockstill blushing furiously, not knowing which way to look. Still, encouraged by his presence, she now asked:

"What's your decision on this case, Comrade Li?"

One-eyed Tian, fearful of losing face for his ancestors in front of so many people, was turning red and white by turns. But presenting a bold front, he blustered:

"Wait a bit! I haven't had my say yet."

"Very well," said Peizhong. "Did you or didn't you hand in the shoes the village authorities told you to make for the army?"

"I didn't. They wanted too many."

"It was your fair share," put in Chun'er. "According to instructions from above."

"Fair?" cried One-eyed Tian. "You may call it fair — I don't!"

Peizhong nearly had to laugh at this frank reply. She stole

122

a glance at Qingshan, who was standing there gravely and listening quietly. Composing herself, she demanded:

"Did you kick and injure the hired hand, Old Wen?"

"He asked for it! A hired hand has no right to interfere in his master's business."

"He was right to interfere to stop you from hitting someone. A hired hand is as good a man as his master. Did you knock Chun'er over?"

"Only because she insulted a guest of mine."

"What guest? Where from? Had he a travel pass?"

One-eyed Tian was speechless for a moment. Then he protested:

"Call this a cross-examination? It's propaganda! You're obviously taking their side. Treating them as your own folk and me as a rank outsider."

All eyes were on Peizhong as she stood up and declared:

"Since these are the facts of the case and you admit them, I'll pass judgement. For refusing to obey the laws of the resistance and contribute your fair share, you will have to hand in double the number of shoes. Knocking down a cadre and kicking a worker are serious offences. You will go back to the village and make a public apology to Chun'er and the worker you assaulted. You will be responsible for all his medical expenses. When he is better, it is up to him to decide whether to go on working for you or not — you are not allowed to dismiss him. And you must promise never to do such things again." This sentence delivered, Peizhong turned to Chun'er to ask:

"Does that satisfy you?"

"It's all right so far as it goes," said Chun'er. "But what about food for the worker he assaulted? He needs special invalid food and we haven't any. When the defendant goes back to the village, it's only fair he should buy some cakes, eggs and noodles at the market for Old Wen. That's all I can think of. I don't know if the chairman of our workers' union has anything to add?" She turned to Old Chang, who promptly shook his head.

"The idea!" spluttered One-eyed Tian. "Want me to buy cakes, fruit and sugar, do you? We don't have a spread like that even when there's a wedding in the family."

"Oh, don't you!" exploded Old Chang, unable to contain himself any longer. "You treat your hired hands like dirt while you gorge yourselves. If you want to give him fruit and sugar too, I'm all for it."

"You will do as Chun'er said." With this Peizhong dismissed the case.

The crowd scattered, discussing the affair at the top of their voices. One lad had a difference of opinion with an old man.

"She went too far for my liking, this woman county head," said the old man. "Dressing down her father-in-law like that, she loses face herself."

"That's no way to look at it," rejoined the boy. "You don't make allowances even for your father in court. A prince who does wrong should be punished like anyone else. The main thing for an official is to be absolutely impartial."

23

Having seen Chun'er off, Peizhong went back to her room and started singing, too elated to sit still. Qingshan's arrival made her break off abruptly, and she asked him with a smile:

"How about my stand, Comrade Gao, in that case today? Please tell me frankly."

"You handled it all right," replied Qingshan cheerfully. "Folk seemed pretty pleased, and that goes for Chun'er and the rest as well. A decision like yours does well enough today. As for your class stand, you'll have other chances to steel yourself. Do you honestly think it's enough to make One-eyed Tian apologize and pay expenses after kicking a hired hand? Under the old regime, a hired hand who kicked One-eyed Tian wouldn't have got off so lightly."

Looking stunned, Peizhong cried in dismay:

"You mean I shielded him?"

"You didn't shield him. I know you tried to lean left. It's a long business changing the old way of thinking. Your sentence has had a useful effect already in helping working people to hold up their heads. Word of it will spread through the villages in no time and make our mobilization drive much easier. Let's not talk about that. I've other business on hand."

"I'm tired," said Peizhong despondently. "But go on."

"I'm leaving with the troops tonight for the front. We're hoping to wipe out a few enemy units to give people more faith in the resistance and raise their morale. It will cover the move of our head offices too. Headquarters may be moving here. Your job's to get the roads destroyed and, more important still, to pull down the city wall."

"The roads are easy, but why pull down the wall?"

"We can't fight if we stick to these towns. We need to be a scattered, mobile force. The enemy may take the county town, but if we pull down the wall he'll be exposed and it'll be easier for us to hit back."

"Before a shot's fired you talk of giving up this town! Have we been working all these months for nothing?"

"Of course not," retorted Qingshan. "We've finished the first stage of mobilization. Folk are keen to resist and organized too. It's the town we're giving up, not the people. Once fighting starts, we'll be as close to the people as fish to water, able to organize them even better. It's pluck and confidence we need. We mustn't lose our heads. We must bring the people's strength into play, make them more determined to fight, and accustom them little by little to guerrilla warfare."

"Destroying roads is simple," said Peizhong. "But how are we to pull down such a big wall? What shall we do with the bricks? Where shall we dump the earth? Heavens, three years wouldn't be long enough! And where am I to find the labour?"

"I dare say it was even harder to build the wall, but they managed it. Why shouldn't we be able to pull it down? You must go about it the right way and explain the reason, or you'll have the whole town against you, for fear this brings bad luck. Once people understand the need, they'll know how to deal with the bricks and earth. When the work starts, see that each village does its fair share and that there's food, drink and a lodging in town for each work team."

"You're leaving us too big a job!" protested Peizhong, half in fun and half in earnest. "When I think of that huge wall that's stood for hundreds of years, my head starts to reel."

"If you won't use your brain or talk it over with the people, of course you'll be swamped by difficulties. This is part of the war effort — it's got to be done. You work it out while I go and have a meal."

"Don't go!" She darted forward to bar his way. "If you're leaving this evening, let me treat you to a meal."

"Treat me to what?"

"To the mutton dumplings they make north of the crossroad. That suit you? I know you don't like going to restaurants, so we'll ask them to send the dumplings here. The old runner can fetch them. You mustn't go."

With that she slipped out and Qingshan, pottering round the room, was struck by the plant on her window-sill. When Peizhong came back he remarked:

"So you've time to grow flowers, comrade. How ladified!"

"I brought that in when I was feeling pleased. Now that you've snowed me under with work, I can't think about anything else."

"There's a war on, guns are booming; this is no time for gardening." said Qingshan. "I'm not against culture, mind you. It's good to sing sometimes or play the mouth-organ, and I know how musical you are, Comrade Li."

"Me musical! I have an ear-splitting voice."

Then the dumplings were brought in. She sat down opposite Qingshan to help him to food and insisted that he make a good meal.

"After word came down that we shouldn't eat steamed buns and pork, the canteen has gone to the other extreme," she said with a smile. "Now it's millet for every meal, and if it's not overcooked then it's underdone. But just show any distaste when you fill your bowl, and the cooks say you're soft and decadent, with a backward mentality. It's enough to burn you up! They don't even bother to put salt in their cabbage soup. Try stirring it and whole leaves float to the top. It's more like fishing than eating."

She herself had a small appetite and ate slowly. It took her several bites to finish one dumpling, whereas Qingshan popped them in whole and was soon flushed and sweating. But when she passed him her scented towel, he did not like to wipe his face properly. After simply dabbing his lips he put it down.

The meal at an end, Peizhong cleared the table gravely

as if she had something on her mind. Then she sat on the *kang* in silence, resting her head on the thick, soft pile of clean, flower-patterned quilts.

"Time's getting on," said Qingshan, rising to his feet. "I must be off. Those dumplings were very good. Thank you for treating me."

"I don't want your thanks, it's enough if you don't scold me!" countered Peizhong. "Wait a bit, I've something to ask you. Do you old cadres despise intellectuals?"

"What an idea! Education's a fine thing. An educated person can do very useful work for the revolution. I've had lots of trouble myself because I never went to school. It's a big drawback. When I meet intellectuals I'm filled with respect for them. We certainly don't despise them. Of course, intellectuals have their faults and they should try to overcome them, so as to put their knowledge to the best use."

"There's another thing, Comrade Gao."

"What is it?"

"The question of my marriage." Peizhong sat up. "I want to get a divorce. What do you advise?"

"That's up to you. It's hard for me to advise you. Now you've joined the revolution I'm sure you'll get rid of that millstone round your neck and find what happiness means. It's a problem that should be solved, not allowed to drag on."

"You'd approve of my getting a divorce?"

Qingshan nodded and walked into the yard, where he took a deep breath of cold air and straightened his uniform.

Peizhong saw him to the main hall, then stopped him again.

"What d'you think of the inscription up there, Comrade Gao?"

Qingshan turned to look.

"You write a good hand," he declared. "I didn't know you

128

were a calligrapher. But until we get instructions from above, we'd better stick to calling it the County Government of the Resistance."

24

At dusk Peizhong stood by the cross-road to see the troops off to the front. Most of them had never been into action before, and they waved to the county head as they filed swiftly past. Qingshan brought up the rear, gravely leading his horse. Peizhong watched him all the way out of the East Gate before returning to the county government. That night, alone in the large compound, she lit a red candle on her window-sill. She seemed to hear the troops marching through the cold night wind, snow whirling into their faces. Their commander on horseback would hardly be thinking of love. . . . She pulled herself together and started planning the demolition work.

As she worked there on her own, she was very conscious of the mothers lulling their children to sleep this cold night, the wives nestling close to their husbands. For a while she found it hard to concentrate and kept laying down her pencil. An old locust tree in the courtyard rustled in the wintry wind, turning her thoughts again to the men on the march, whom she determined to take as her example. But as she eyed the candle flame her heart was flooded with the bitterness of her unhappy marriage. With an effort she brushed her unhappiness aside.

On a sheet of drawing paper brought from school she drew a chart for the road demolition, plying her well-sharpened pencil as carefully as a girl embroidering in the school dormitory.

Mid-winter had locked the plain in ice and snow. Each coming winter for the young women of her generation would be a season of cruel fighting. She could picture the enthusiasm with which the peasants in a few days' time would be wielding their pickaxes and shovels to destroy the roads and city wall, doing all in their power to halt the enemy. This was a historic task that she was planning. The work helped her to forget her personal troubles and filled her with exaltation.

A brick wall five feet high separated the county government on its east side from a small printing press. At midnight the hand-operated press clattered as the workers printed the *Resistance News* put out by the Mobilization Committee. It occurred to Peizhong that once her chart was finished and an explanation added, it could be published in the newspaper.

The clatter of machinery stopped and the printers could be heard discussing something. Presently the head of the press, lanky, bald-headed Cui, climbed over the wall and came to Peizhong's room.

"What's the matter?" she asked, turning round. "What brings you here at midnight?"

"You ought to have a guard here, Comrade Li. Aren't you scared, all alone in a compound this size?"

"I'm too busy to be scared." She laughed.

"I've come to see if you can help us." He sketched a gesture with one hand. "The felt on our press has worn out. Without it the rollers won't turn, the paper can't come out, and we'll fall down on our job of propaganda, which would be bad for the resistance. If this were Beijing or Tianjin now, felt would be as easy to find as waste paper; but in this small county town it's like searching for diamonds — there isn't any to be had for love or money. It finally struck me that you're the one person who might be able to help, because you've attended a foreign-style school."

"Did you say felt?" Peizhong still did not know what he wanted.

"Yes, the sort of felt tailors use."

"Is a felt coat any good to you?" She stood up to pull a bundle from under the bed and, opening it, produced a red felt jacket.

"I'm in luck!" exulted Old Cui, rubbing his hands. "This beats conjuring or magic. Marvellous! What a pity, though, to spoil a coat like this. You're very generous, but I haven't the heart to cut off a strip for that greasy black roller of ours. Can't you find some scraps instead?"

"This is all I have," said Peizhong. "Don't make such a song about it. If it's useful it won't be wasted, so why be sorry? I never wear this jacket anyway. It's just put away there for the moths to get at. Go on, take it without all this fuss!" She threw the coat into his arms.

Bald-headed Cui caught it and stroked it admiringly.

"The resistance comes first and that's a fact," he said. "You could get five sacks of good white flour for this in Beijing."

"Is this a time to think of flour?" retorted Peizhong. "Don't let flour blind you. I had this made for my wedding, but the marriage turned out badly and I never wore it. Now it's wartime we all wear cotton or padded clothes — who'd want to be seen in this? I brought it as an extra cover for cold nights."

"I'll fetch you another quilt presently," promised Old Cui. "We don't need all this. One sleeve would be enough. Too bad!"

"If you took one sleeve, what would I do with the rest?

131

Take the whole thing. It may come in useful later." Peizhong resumed work on her chart.

"I just don't know how to thank you." Old Cui tucked the coat respectfully under one arm. "Thank you on behalf of our press and all the readers of the *Resistance News*. Thanks to Comrade Li's exemplary conduct, our press can start up again."

After Bald-headed Cui had gone Peizhong finished her chart and decided that trenches five feet long, three feet wide and three feet deep should be dug at five-foot intervals across all the county highways. That should make it virtually impossible for the enemy's transport to advance.

As she laid down her pencil to examine her work, the candle which had burned low flickered fitfully. She shut her eyes for a while and a sense of satisfaction stole over her. When she next opened her eyes, a huge shooting star was streaking down like a flare of mercury outside her window, filling the whole courtyard with light.

25

It was nearly New Year when the road demolition chart was distributed. This year's festival was unlike any the people of the plain had known before. After the tenth of the twelfth month, crackers exploded all round to celebrate weddings, for to set their parents' minds at rest many girls consented to be married early. Go-betweens were kept busy, and some long debated matches were settled in a few words now that the brides' families made no awkward conditions. In certain houses where the bridegroom was away, his sister deputized for him at the wedding ceremony.

Enemy atrocities — fire, murder and rape — threatened

the plain-dwellers. Shortly before New Year, on both sides of the railway, many girls of sixteen or seventeen changed into clean clothes and were taken by their fathers to their new husbands' homes. Parents in the resistance base still insisted on bridal sedan-chairs, and the music of wedding processions sounded all through the night until dawn. But the proximity of Japanese cavalry and tanks set the frozen fields shuddering and cast a certain gloom over the carts bowling down the highways to meet the brides, the crackers let off when they entered the village, and the singing at the head of the street.

In these conditions, the call for demolition met with an immediate, overwhelming response. All families with land by the highway set to work digging trenches of the specified size in the hard, frozen soil. Each morning when the sun lit up the rime on the wheat, peasants with picks and shovels thronged the roads.

Old Wen, once he recovered, had gone back to work for One-eyed Tian. So had Old Chang, on condition that time was allowed for his duties as chairman of the village workers' union. The Tians' daughter had a baby this month and, as soon as the news reached her parents, Mrs. Tian prepared four hampers of noodles and dumplings, which she told Old Chang to deliver.

"Our chiefs want us to dig trenches today. I can't go," said Old Chang.

"Any excuse to scamp work!" Her face darkened. "Who pays you, us or those chiefs of yours? You get all your food and pay from our family. I haven't seen them give you so much as four ounces of tobacco. Why should you do everything they say? Don't you know which *kang* is warmer?"

"Digging trenches is for the country, for everyone. Of course that must come first. Or will you dig trenches for me by all those wheat fields of yours near the highway?"

133

"When did you see me handle a pick or shovel?" retorted Mrs. Tian, frowning. "I couldn't even tell you what shape they are. Will trenches stop the Japanese? You just don't know what's best for you. Take these hampers and they'll offer you a drink. Or would you rather swing a pick in a biting wind like this?"

"Let the master go. We've got to dig trenches."

"Since when has he been a porter? You want him to lose face before our in-laws?"

"Does carrying a load make a man lose face? If that's so, lots of us lost all our face years ago. Let him dig the trenches then."

"The idea!" spluttered Mrs. Tian. "A hired hand giving orders to his master!"

"I may be your hired hand," retorted Old Chang, "but I'm one of the village cadres too. When you're given a little work for the resistance, don't try to wriggle out of it. Just decide which you'll do — take the hampers or dig the ditches?"

Mrs. Tian went inside to discuss this with her husband and, enraged as One-eyed Tian was, he chose to take the hampers, for after all that was the lighter work. Old Chang went off with his tools to round up his fellow workers.

Mrs. Tian tied up the hampers for her husband and fastened them to the two ends of the pole. The load was not too heavy. But having walked down the steps and along the corridor, One-eyed Tian came back, unwilling to be seen like this in the street. He paced the yard as if rehearsing a play.

"What are you doing?" asked his wife. "Time's getting on. It wouldn't look well to take gifts in the afternoon."

"Why should I make a show of myself?" he fumed. "Why must she choose this time to have a baby? I'm not going. She's *your* daughter. *You* go."

He dropped the pole so abruptly that the badly-tied ropes came off, the hampers fell open, and white dumplings started rolling all over the yard.

His wife hastily picked them up, blew off the dust, and put them back again.

"Go on, do!" she pleaded. "I'll slip out and have a look, and when there's no one about you can leave the village."

"They're digging ditches all over the place," he grumbled. "Can I fly over their heads? I'll go and fetch that fellow back."

One-eyed Tian went to the fields, where he found Old Wen working away. Going up to him, the landlord roared:

"What d'you mean by digging up my wheat? Want us to go short of flour?"

"We're working to specifications," said Old Wen.

"All you have to do is put up a show. No one's going to examine these trenches carefully."

"That's not true. The county head's coming to inspect them. If they're not just right, we'll be told off."

"You go home and deliver the presents." One-eyed Tian took the shovel from Old Wen and proceeded to fill in the half of the trenches in his fields and to extend the other side. By this means he could save his land and push the trenches into his neighbour's field. Old Tian was an adept at encroaching on his neighbours. The custom in these parts was to plant a mulberry tree to mark the boundary between two properties. Each spring when ploughing time came round, he ordered his men to push the mulberry back and stood there to supervise the operation. He made the oxen tug with all their might, not even worrying when the ploughshare broke on the tree's roots, happy to have grabbed a furrow or two of someone else's land. So the mulberry trees bordering One-eyed Tian's land never flourished, for the half on his side always withered. The neighbouring children had no mulberry leaves for their silkworms, but had to pick elm leaves instead.

An old man was digging trenches opposite. Although his hair was grey he worked with a will. He owned a long, narrow strip of land not more than five furrows wide, but since it lay alongside the road he had to dig twelve trenches, and this involved sacrificing much of his wheat. His trenches were deep and level, with high banks on either side like city walls. As he jumped into the last one and bent to dig up the moist black soil, he was sweating so hard that the vapour round his head was like mist round a peak.

It was old Gao Sihai.

At the sound of One-eyed Tian's voice, he straightened up and caught his breath. When he saw the landlord fill in a trench, he did not show his anger but called out:

"Mr. Tian, you're a scholar and you've held public office for years. Tell me, what's meant by conscience?"

Leaning on his shovel, One-eyed Tian glared at him.

"Why ask such a question?"

"The Japanese want to grab our land. We're going to all this trouble to destroy the roads in the hope of keeping them out. Yet here you are filling up trenches as if to welcome them in. As if you want to make it easy for them."

"Isn't it much better to dig up the road?" protested Tian craftily.

Along came two bridal sedan-chairs just then, followed by several big carts. The first carter cracked his whip and nearly upset his passengers when he reached the ditch by Tian's land. The musicians told Gao Sihai that there was bad news. Someone further north had sighted Japanese cavalry.

"See!" cried Old Gao to One-eyed Tian. "You're not stopping the enemy, only holding up our own folk. You're leaving a way in your fields for the Japanese to pass. You'll be to blame if we have trouble here."

"Why should I be to blame?" Tian took his tools home.

"A man who's such a miser can only be a traitor in times like these," commented Gao Sihai as he deepened his trench. "Once he turns traitor he'll sell anything, even the last shreds of his conscience."

26

Chun'er, a bright, long-handled spade over one shoulder, came up laughing to Gao Sihai and wiped her perspiring face and dusty hair on her sleeve.

"Aren't you through yet, uncle?"

"Just a minute!" Old Gao heaved up one last spadeful of earth and clambered out of the trench. It was midday and the peasants had left their digging to go home for a meal. All the villages around shimmered in the sunlight. The distant honking of enemy trucks reminded both the old man and the girl of the roar of the Hutuo each summer when it was in spate.

Old Gao headed for the village, Chun'er at his heels. Most of the trenches on both sides were finished.

"How old are you this year, Chun'er?" asked Old Gao.

"I'll be nineteen at New Year."

"High time you were married," he remarked without looking round.

Chun'er made no reply to this but presently said:

"Think the wheat will do well next year, uncle?"

"We've had plenty of rain, it's coming up thick and sturdy. If it stays free from rust the harvest should be fair. You counting on a good harvest to get yourself a dowry?"

"Not I!" She laughed at the idea.

"I must talk it over with your sister when I get home. We'll find somebody suitable. Noticed the number of bridal-chairs passing these days?"

"I don't want to get married. Why should I?"

"A girl needs someone to look after her. You lost your mother early and your dad's so far away, in troubled times like these your sister and I can't help worrying about you."

"You think I'm too old to live on my own." She chuckled.

"Yes, you've nobody to turn to. You need someone near and dear to care for you. When you dig trenches all morning, say, then go home, the mat on your *kang* is cold and your pan is empty. No matter how fagged out you are, you have to fetch water and light the fire yourself. If you had a husband, there'd be someone waiting at home to welcome you. Then you'd soon stop feeling tired and forget all your troubles. In sickness or danger you need someone still more, even in normal times. And in days like these no girl should live on her own. Just find a husband and, suppose you have to run away or go into hiding, you'll have him to look after you."

"I don't see it that way," replied Chun'er with a twinkle. "If the Japanese come and all we do is run, what use would a husband be? Could he look after me with his bare hands? We'd just get in each other's way, I'd do better alone. Unless I find one with a gun...."

"You mean one of the Eighth Route Army men?" The old man looked round with a grin. "I'm against that, lass."

"Why, uncle? Isn't my brother-in-law a soldier?"

"Folk like the Eighth Route Army men because they fight Japan. But I wouldn't look there for a husband."

"Why not?"

"They're too busy with the revolution to think of their

138

homes." Old Gao sighed. "Look at your sister. Married all these years, yet what time has she had with Qingshan? Less than twenty days at most. She doesn't complain, but I know how hard it is for her. I don't want you to have to put up with that. Has she ever talked about it to you?"

"No, she hasn't. But I'm not too young to understand. You can't have everything in this world. If all the men put their families first and wouldn't stir away from the *kang*, who would protect us? What hope would we have? Remember the flood last July, uncle, and that woman refugee from the Northeast? She had a home, husband and children, but what became of them? Her husband died running away, she was killed by a Japanese bomb here in our river, and her child's being brought up by strangers. That happened because none of them fought. Now we have troops — they're the ones who'll keep us safe."

"I see you're set on an Eighth Route Army man." Old Gao smiled to himself. "Have you anyone in mind?"

Before Chun'er could answer they reached the cross-road. The highway to the south led to Five-dragon Temple, the smaller track running southeast to Ziwuzhen. Chun'er stopped.

"Come home with me, uncle, and I'll get you a meal."

"No need. Your sister's expecting me. We must talk this over. You've more sense, lass, than I thought."

Flushing, Chun'er ran down the track past some vegetable plots and a couple of wells to her cottage. As she pushed open the wicker gate, her hens rushed towards her, clucking.

"Laid any eggs for me? Not dropped them outside, I hope," she said softly to her speckled hen as she went to the nesting box outside the window. When she found a big pinky egg, still warm, she laughed and scattered some sorghum for the fowls.

She lit a fire and cooked her food, then took it to the small table on the *kang* and ate her solitary meal. The recollection of what Old Gao had said made her wish there were someone sitting opposite — but he was on the battlefield. "Yes," she thought, "there should be someone to fetch firewood for the stove. When he milled flour, I'd sieve it. When he hoed the fields, I'd take him food. But with the Japanese here, that's just not possible." Her sweetheart had gone to the front, and it was up to her to help him. "He's right to fight, and I'll dig trenches. That's how husbands and wives ought to help each other today."

Both she and Mangzhong should do their bit for the country, besides urging other folk to take the same path.

After Chun'er had eaten and cleared away, she got out an old spear her father had used when he minded the melon fields. The red tassel was dingy now and the point had rusted. Having washed the tassel, she took a grindstone into the yard and, humming softly to herself, whetted the spear till it was bright and sharp.

The spear over her shoulder, she went out to the street and blew her whistle to summon the women's defence corps. This was the first time the people of Ziwuzhen had heard women summoned to defend the country, and the signal was blown by a village girl of eighteen!

The men smiled at first at the ragged way the girls marched, but the thought of their common duty and all this meant made them hurry to fall in themselves in order not to be outdone by the girls. In general it was the men who took the lead, but sometimes the women were ahead of them.

The girls formed ranks and marched briskly off, arms swinging. They passed One-eyed Tian's gate just as Su'er's father, Old Jiang, finished drawing water from the well there. He tagged after them, muttering:

140

"A fine exhibition this is disgusting, I call it!"

"What's that?" The last girl in the troop overheard this remark.

"Nothing." Old Jiang sniggered. "I was only joking."

"How dare you!" The young women surrounded him.

"Here, now, what's all this?" Old Jiang swung his pails. "Don't put on that act with me. Save it for the Japanese."

"We're drilling so as to fight the Japanese. What dirty crack was that you made? Out with it!" They refused to let him go.

"They're waiting for this water, girls, to cook rice at home." He doubled back and broke away. "If I spoke out of turn I take it back."

When Chun'er led her contingent off again, they were followed by a crowd of old women and children.

"A landlord's toady is just the type to turn traitor when the Japanese come," called out the girl at the rear.

"You keep a civil tongue in your head!" Old Jiang stopped and turned round. "That's the ugliest name you can call anyone today. Don't pin that label on me! I'd rather you cursed eight generations of my ancestors."

"Sister Chun'er!" called the girl. "Let's go and search his house on our way back. That stinking Taoist priest who's hanging out there can't be up to any good. Now the fighting's so fierce, their place is crowded day and night with people kowtowing and burning incense. If they're not traitors you can gouge out my eyes!"

Ziwuzhen's two defence corps, the men's and the women's, drilled on two large threshing-floors on opposite sides of the road. The men were unwilling to make a poor showing before their wives and sisters. They formed orderly lines and marched smartly, while their leader yelled commands at the

141

top of his voice. But they were ignored by the spectators, old and young, who had crowded round the women.

Only when the men started throwing hand-grenades and offered to take on the other corps, did the children scamper over to their side, then swarm back to relay this challenge.

The girls hung their heads, never having handled grenades. Then Chun'er straightened her shoulders and walked over.

"This is new to us. But let me try throwing a couple."

She pitched two grenades towards the willows lining the field. And her third shot beat the men's record.

Before dismissing her corps, Chun'er addressed them.

"This morning, north of the village they heard Japanese trucks. It's no use us girls going into hiding or getting married in a hurry — no matter where you hide you're not safe from the Japanese. We must take arms and defend ourselves. Our troops have gone to the front to fight, our husbands and brothers are there. It's up to us to help them as best we can, just as we'd help them in the fields at home."

A wind rising in the countryside swayed the willows. The trees knew that this boisterous wind was spring's harbinger, for already they felt the spring warmth of the earth. And the sap rising through their slender branches was like the blood coursing through the veins of the girls on the plain as they braced themselves to do battle.

27

The next day, the twenty-seventh of the twelfth month, was the day of the big fair before New Year. Generally pedlars would arrive before it was light to find a place for their goods, and the street was lined with crystallized persimmons, walnuts and black dates, crammed with barrows of kelp, bean vermicelli and dried mushrooms. Villagers flocked in with children from all around until you could hardly move for the crowd and it took hours squeezing from one end of Ziwuzhen to the other.

Vendors of New Year pictures hung their wares in the entrance of the inn, while the West Square was taken up by fireworks and crackers. Five-dragon Temple was noted for its fireworks and the salesmen dressed up like travelling showmen with red cloths round their heads. Dangling their crackers from spears, they stood on big carts to let them off, shouting their wares and trying to outdo each other, as if this were a competition rather than business.

This year was very different, however, for the Japanese occupation of the railway meant that no goods had come from the mountains to the west and no marine delicacies from the east. The market was unusually quiet, and there were fewer fireworks from Five-dragon Temple.

In the past, Bian Ji of Five-dragon Temple had always had a fireworks stall outside Chun'er's gate. Chun'er would sweep the place clean the day before, and when he was busy serving customers at noon she would take him out a meal. Bian Ji's rockets went up straight and high with a loud bang and were a fine sight to watch as five balls of fire cascaded down like falling petals. When he packed up at dusk he would leave her a few of these rockets as "stall-money".

This year, instead of rockets Bian Ji brought a crate of lanterns, beautifully made and painted in bright colours. Among them there were some revolving lanterns, and when he had lit a candle inside one the paper figures round it started turning. A few Japanese soldiers were being chased by the Eighth Route Army, and some peasants were digging trenches with picks and shovels. When the Japanese fell into the trenches they were caught.

143

Children crowded round to look and used their fireworks money to buy these lanterns. Bian Ji warned them not to tear the paper and explained how to light them.

Chun'er coming out from her cottage with a hank of yarn, asked with a smile:

"Why haven't you made any rockets?"

"You may not have been to the district meeting, but didn't your Defence Committee relay its instructions?"

"What instructions?"

"Ziwuzhen's a big place, yet how backward your work is here!" explained Bian Ji. "Isn't there a Defence Committee in every village? This year they've decided not to make fireworks but keep all the saltpetre and gunpowder for land mines and hand-grenades to fight Japan."

"Oh, that's stale news." Chun'er laughed.

"Then why ask why I didn't make rockets? Should we let instructions from above go in at one ear and out at the other? Or should we carry them out seriously?"

"Well, what have you made these toys for? To exchange for bread?" Chun'er had covered her mouth to hide a smile.

"They're not as silly as you seem to think." Bian Ji was quite red in the face. "This is good propaganda. You take one of these home to hang over your door on New Year's Eve, and everybody going in or out will learn a lesson from it. What better things could I sell?"

"You're a clever man, brother." Chun'er laughed. "And you've clever hands."

"In my own small way I'm a cadre of the resistance. I don't for a moment forget where my duty lies." He picked up a large handsome lantern. "I'll give you this to hang on your wicker gate over New Year."

"What sort of cadre are you, brother?" inquired the girl.

144

"Propaganda chief of the Peasants' Resistance Association in Five-dragon Temple," was the solemn reply.

"Oh, that reminds me. We're going to start a literacy class. Will you be our teacher?"

"Why ask me when your village is swarming with university graduates? Only a fool shows off in front of sages."

"These rich men's sons are difficult customers. If you don't ask them, they complain. If you ask them nicely, they try to take advantage. They gossip behind your back and made fun of you. Those who are any good are already working outside, and this trashy lot left wouldn't be much good at teaching — they might even teach us bad ways. In any case, what self-respecting woman would want to learn from them? Even with no encouragement, that low, vicious bunch keep making eyes at the girls. They're bad enough already. Give them a chance to teach and there'd be no holding them. No, we won't ask them. You're our local sage, it's you we want. Our two villages are so close. Couldn't you give us a lesson every evening?"

"There's something in what you say," replied Bian Ji. "I won't claim to know more about the resistance than anyone else, but you'll find no one keener or with a firmer stand. I'll talk it over with our chairman when I get back and see if my organization agrees. It's not for me to decide."

"All right. I must go and sell my yarn. Drop in, will you, after the fair? I've something else to ask you." With that, Chun'er bounded off to the cotton market.

Having sold her thread, she went to a cloth stall and bought seven feet of calico. By the time she came back it was late afternoon and Bian Ji had packed up and brought his crate into her yard. Chun'er swept the *kang* and dusted the low table on it, then offered Bian Ji a seat. She boiled water and poured him a drink.

"Why go to all this trouble?" he asked. "I'm no stranger."

"I want you to write a letter for me," said Chun'er. "I'll go and buy paper and borrow a brush and ink."

"I've got all you need. Just bring in my crate. I supply the stationery when I write a letter for anyone."

He sat cross-legged by the low table and spread out the paper while Chun'er, standing by the *kang*, ground the ink.

"Well, who's it to?" he asked. "Your father?"

"No. Someone else."

"How shall I start?" He picked up the brush.

"It's like this." Chun'er's cheeks were burning as she pointed at the paper. "You write it to my brother-in-law, but what I'm saying is meant for someone else."

"I've never written a letter like that, pointing to the mulberry but scolding the elm! How can you do that in writing?" Bian Ji put down his brush. "It's all right when you're talking — you look at the one you mean. But that won't work in a letter."

"Go on, it's not hard. Start with my brother-in-law's name."

"I've got that. What next?"

"Next ask what victories they've won. Is he wearing that pair of shoes I made for him? I'm not sitting idle at home. I've helped dig trenches and after New Year I'm going off to pull down the city wall. My sister and her father-in-law are well. It's awkward not being able to read or write. He ought to learn some characters."

"Well!" declared Bian Ji, writing rapidly. "This isn't a letter so much as the minutes of a meeting! But what you say doesn't make sense. You tell Gao Qingshan to learn some characters, when he writes pretty well as it is."

"That's meant for someone else. Just you write it the way I said and that'll do. Go on: I'm now head of the women's defence corps, and we've been drilling. Next month we're

146

starting a literacy class and I shall begin to study. There's been plenty of rain for the wheat, next year's crop should be good. Just fight well and stop the Japanese from coming. That's all."

"That's all," repeated Bian Ji. "This isn't a letter, lass, it's a conundrum!"

28

Chun'er took the letter to her sister's home, meaning to find someone to deliver it and to ask Qiufen's advice about something that was on her mind.

Her sister's cottage on the dike at Five-dragon Temple was bathed in sunlight and the goats were basking in the sun by the wall.

The cottage door was shut tight, but Chun'er heard voices inside. As she tried the door, the conversation stopped. She heard Qiufen get down from the *kang* to ask:

"Who's there?"

"It's me!" called Chun'er. "Why keep your door shut in broad daylight?"

"It's my sister," Qiufen said.

"Is she one of us?" another woman asked softly.

"Not yet," replied Qiufen in the same low voice. "D'you mind waiting a second while I go and see what she wants?"

She came out slowly, pulling the door shut behind her.

"What brings you here now?" she asked.

"Must I look up the almanac and choose a lucky time before I come?" retorted Chun'er crossly.

"We're having a meeting." Qiufen smiled.

"What's so wonderful about that? I've been to meetings

in the district town, I've been to meetings in the county town, but I've never seen a meeting like this in your little Five-dragon Temple where you shut the doors. Afraid someone will rush in to grab your house?"

"Go and amuse yourself for a while by the river, sis. I'll call you when we're through."

"I'm going in to see who these fine people are." Chun'er pouted. "Not fit to look at them, am I?" She started forward.

"Listen, child, it's a secret meeting." Qiufen barred the way. "A meeting of our Party cell."

Chun'er stopped at that, her cheeks burning.

"All right, then. I'll wait by the river."

"There's a good girl." Qiufen brushed the dust off her clothes. "Don't go away. We'll soon have finished."

As Qiufen went back inside Chun'er called to the goats, who got up and trotted after her to find grass.

Sunlight lay all over the banks, but Chun'er's mood was glum. Every mention of the Party filled her with a sense of wonder and excitement. A poor girl, who had never known a parent's care, it was as natural as spring sunshine or flowers that she should be attracted by the Party.

She knew that her sister and brother-in-law were both Party members, and possibly Mangzhong too. All her dear ones had joined — she was the only exception. It is hard to say just what communism meant to Chun'er. She could remember that the revolt ten years previously had been for the sake of the poor, and just when she dreaded that the country would be ruined the Party had come back to organize troops to resist, had mobilized the people, established political power and helped her to win her case against One-eyed Tian. To her, the Communist Party meant the guarantee of a better life. It would make her dreams come true.

Chun'er needed no urging to join the Party and work for

it. When she joined the Women's National Salvation Association and the defence corps, it was clear to her that she belonged to the Party. But apparently a gap still remained — she had been shut out by her sister.

She must join the Party, must apply through Qiufen. This decision reached, she stroked the big nanny-goat's thick clean coat and raised her head towards the sun.

Soon Qiufen saw the others off and returned to the dike to beckon to her sister. Chun'er ran back with the goats.

"Don't sulk now!" cried Qiufen with a smile. "We can't let outsiders in — not even our own fathers, mothers or husbands."

"Stop lecturing me," protested Chun'er. "Do you still take me for a silly child?"

"I was afraid you wouldn't understand. New Year will soon be here. Why aren't you at home getting ready some good things to eat? What's up?"

"That's it, of course!" Chun'er laughed. "I've come because I've nothing to eat at home. If I mind your goats for you, will you give me a bowl of noodles?"

"Come off it. How is your defence corps shaping?"

"Not badly. We're making quite a go of it." With a smile she produced her letter. "Find someone safe to deliver this for me, will you?"

"Who's it to?"

"Your husband. With a message for Mangzhong." Chun'er turned away to play with the child from the Northeast who was crawling over the *kang*.

"Yesterday when my father-in-law came back, he talked about finding a husband for you," said Qiufen. "You'll soon be nineteen. What's your own feeling about it?"

"My feeling?" Chun'er laid her cheek against the child's. "My, how chubby he's grown! I'm in no hurry."

149

"Are you just saying that, or do you really mean it?"

"I mean it." Chun'er straightened up to look her sister squarely in the face. "It's something else I'm in a hurry to settle."

"What's that?"

"You introduce me to join the Party, sis." She spoke in eager earnest. "I want to be a Communist."

Qiufen assented gladly.

Home again, Chun'er heated up some left-over rice. As dusk fell she closed her wicket gate, stopped up the hen coop, lit her small paraffin lamp and sat down on the *kang* to spin.

She worked cheerfully, busy with her thoughts.

She was pondering what it meant to be a woman, but her experience was limited to stories she had heard or plays she had seen. In the dim light she looked at the old pictures on the wall which showed a man setting off to the wars, while his wife remained wretchedly at home and stayed true to him. She understood the feeling behind each picture and could guess what the woman was saying, what she was thinking. "We're luckier than they were," she thought. "Apart from spinning and weaving, we're learning to fight."

The window paper rustled and she heard distant gunfire. Stopping her spinning wheel, Chun'er jumped down from the *kang* and hurried into the yard to mount the short ladder to the roof.

Standing by the chimney flue, with the sky full of stars overhead, she noticed that the roof was covered with frost. A fire had broken out in the northeast and the sound of artillery was booming over the dark countryside. Our troops had engaged the enemy there, and Chun'er's heart beat fast as she longed for their victory. On that bitter cold night of battle, the village girl's thoughts winged through her mother-

150

land's sky, across the galaxies of the Milky Way, to join the fighters at the front.

29

No matter how early or late the lunar New Year fell, the plain-dwellers took the first day of the first month to mark the arrival of spring. Only then did they lay aside the worn padded jackets that had served them all through the winter.

On New Year's Eve, having made sure that there was no wind, Chun'er hung the lantern Bian Ji had given her above her wicket gate. Then she went inside to put her new clothes by her pillow, but she could not go to sleep. In troubled times like these everyone was up before dawn, and as soon as she heard one of the neighbours' children start letting off firecrackers, she scrambled up.

She opened her gate and lit the lantern, thinking gleefully that she was now a year older. By the lantern's light she discovered that the road was full of troops. Soldiers were sitting in a row with their backs to her mud wall, rifles on their knees.

They were illumined by the lanterns outside every cottage. The whole of the village office had turned out and, as Chun'er was talking to the men, Old Chang hurried up.

"Let's get going, Chun'er! We must find billets for the troops."

"You don't need me for that," she cried. "This isn't sharing work out among the women."

"No job can be done without the help of the women."

Chun'er made the rounds of several households with him to urge the villagers to make room for the troops.

"Clear a warm room for them and sweep the *kang* clean,"

said Old Chang to one householder. "Never mind doubling up for a couple of days, we must let our troops have a good rest. They've been fighting for ten days and more, and last night they marched over a hundred *li*. Not a bite or sup has passed their lips yet, and there they are sitting in the road in this perishing cold."

"Just leave it to me," replied the villager. "Here, mother! Clear all that junk of the *kang* and take away that piss pot."

"Don't bother to move anything that's not in the way," said Old Chang. "These soldiers won't take a needle or thread from our people."

At One-eyed Tian's house they found Mrs. Tian supervising the cook, who had scores of dumplings set out on the stove. As soon as she heard that some soldiers wanted billets, she whisked all the dumplings inside, reappearing to complain:

"This is the limit! Can't we even spend New Year in peace? We don't want outsiders here on New Year's Day when we eat dumplings. How can we put up troops? It's really too bad!"

"The soldiers have homes too," retorted Old Chang. "They've left their families to fight for us all. This is no time to be fussy."

"You know very well our rooms are too cluttered up to put anyone in," groused Mrs. Tian. "Now you're a cadre you have no consideration at all for your master."

"You've more space than anyone else, so why grumble? Clear out the whole east and west wings. I should think you could sleep a company on those four big *kangs*."

Old Chang went on from here to Su'er's home but found the gate closed tight. He knocked and shouted for some time before Old Jiang came out, whining:

"What's all this banging on doors before dawn, Old

152

Chang? That din will drive away all my luck for the year."

"Troops have come!" bellowed Old Chang. "Clear a room for them."

"This isn't an inn. What extra room do we have?"

"There's only two of you. Move in with Su'er."

"You've come at the wrong time. Su'er's just had a baby." Old Chang was dumbfounded but Chun'er said:

"First I've heard of it. Why didn't we know about it?"

"Do we have to report everything to a chit like you?" demanded Old Jiang.

"I don't believe it." Chun'er marched into the yard.

Su'er's room in the wing facing south had a thick quilt over the window. Chun'er standing outside heard groaning on the *kang*.

"Well?" Old Jiang grinned. "What did I say? If you'd come at any other time, I'd have thought nothing of giving you a room."

"I'll believe it when I see it," retorted Chun'er, and made to open the door. Old Jiang stopped her, protesting:

"What way is this for a girl to carry on? You can't go in there. A new-born baby mustn't be exposed to strangers. Besides, the place stinks!"

Chun'er paid no attention but pushed her way in, took matches from her pocket and lit the lamp on the dressing-table which had just been blown out. When she starting fumbling under Su'er's crimson quilt, Su'er threw it off and sat up, fully dressed in all her New Year's finery. At the same time she burst out laughing.

"Fine goings on!" cried Old Chang. "So your daughter had a baby, did she? You old liar!"

Aggravated by Su'er's laughter, her father flushed red.

"Well, bring your soldiers in. Our family's always glad to accommodate them."

By the time all the billets were found the sun had risen. And Chun'er, going home, saw a big black horse tethered to her window bars.

"Whose horse is that?" she asked.

"Mine!" A soldier ran out of the cottage, young Mangzhong.

Chun'er blushed up to her ears.

"Don't you lock the door when you go out?" asked Mangzhong.

"Who's afraid of thieves with all these soldiers outside?" She beamed at him. "You've got a horse, does that mean you're an officer now?"

"I don't rightly know. I'm squad leader of the mounted orderlies."

"I'll fetch a bucket of water for your horse. It's all in a lather."

"Don't water him. Just let him rest a while. I must be off to deliver another message."

"Let me cook you some dumplings first." Chun'er fetched fuel from the yard. "Don't tell me you've eaten."

Mangzhong followed her in, protesting:

"We've orders not to eat the villagers' dumpling."

"If you're blamed for it, say I invited you."

When the food was ready she handed him a heaped bowl.

"How did the fighting go this time?" she asked.

"We won a battle at Yellow Earth Slope and captured quite a few rifles. Then the enemy brought up reinforcements and we played hide-and-seek with him. Our headquarters' moving into your village. After you've eaten you must go and see Commander Lu."

"How can I do that? Where's my brother-in-law?"

"Still stationed in the county town."

"And Gao Ba?"

154

"He's with our unit. He fought very bravely this time. We'll see how he shapes."

Having finished now, Mangzhong put down his bowl to leave.

"Wait a minute!" cried Chun'er. "Don't rush off just after a meal."

"Soldiers aren't so soft." The young man untethered his horse, led it out of the wicket gate and jumped on to its back. The horse wheeled round before Chun'er's admiring eyes.

"What's the hurry?" she called. "I've something else to ask you."

"Go on!" He reined in his mount.

"How old are you this year?" She looked up at him.

"Nineteen. The same age as you, don't you remember?"

"You're like a grown man now." She hung her head.

"In the army they still call me a 'little devil'." Mangzhong chuckled. "We're young, we ought to study hard."

"Could I join the army, do you think?"

"Why not? Best thing you could do." With that Mangzhong twiched his reins and galloped off down the dike.

30

Chun'er decided to take a stroll outside, for the streets this year were a novel sight with so many soldiers in grey padded uniforms among the women and children in green and red. The soldiers divided up to sweep the streets, while the peasants tried to snatch their brooms away and urged them to rest. When this proved useless, the villagers went home to fetch brushes and help. Ziwuzhen had never looked so spruce before.

Some soldiers at the cross-roads had a bucket of lime with which they were writing anti-Japanese slogans on the brown mud walls. Gao Xiang had gathered a troop of children to sing. Normally these boys and girls would not play together, but today they lined up neatly before this Eighth Route Army man and sang a chorus together.

Not far away another tall soldier with flashing eyes and a ringing voice was talking to some peasants. Rather more neatly dressed than most, he had on an overcoat with a fur collar and an old pair of leather shoes.

One young woman whispered to Chun'er:

"That's Lu Zhengcao!"

Chun'er, standing at a distance, scrutinized this commander of the people's defence forces. He was her superior officer too, but never had she expected to see such an important personage in Ziwuzhen.

Commander Lu was telling the villagers that the road demolition had not been properly done. Their little trenches were only good enough to stop farm carts, not the enemy's trucks and tanks. All highways must be dug into deep trenches so that the plain became impassable. When he asked about the villagers' defence corps, they told him:

"We've made a start and we've plenty of men and horses, Commander Lu. Only thing we're short of is rifles. Can't you give us some army rifles? Doesn't matter how old and battered they are."

When Commander Lu agreed to this, Chun'er was so pleased that she felt the time had come for her to say something. She walked slowly up behind the commander.

"What do you want, Chun'er?" asked one old peasant. "Have you some favour to ask?"

Commander Lu turned at that and saw the girl. He had

met many like her in the central Hebei plain, girls who would not take "No" for an answer.

"I'm the head of our women's defence corps."   Chun'er stood to attention and smiled.

"When I send those rifles to the village, of course you'll get your share," said Commander Lu.

"There's something else I'd like to ask.   We're no good at fighting in formation.   Will you show us how to do it, Commander Lu? I'll assemble my corps right away."

"I'll send a company commander to drill you tomorrow," he replied with a smile.

"Do you want women soldiers in the army?"

"You'd like to fight, would you?"   The commander chuckled.   "We're not recruiting women just now, but our political department has started a concert group.   If you like singing and acting, you can join that."

"Not I!" Chun'er scampered back to where all the women were standing, while the other girls laughed at her discomfiture.

That evening a celebration for soldiers and civilians was held on the big threshing-floor west of the village. The folk from Five-dragon Temple came over too.   After Commander Lu and Gao Xiang had addressed the meeting on how to help the war effort, the Frontline Drama Group put on a show.   Chun'er and Qiufen sat on the same bench to watch, while Gao Qingshan and Mangzhong, just returned from town, stood at the back of the audience holding their horses. The short plays were very simple, but this was the first time Chun'er had seen what a Japanese soldier looked like.   Then Ziwuzhen's gongs and drums raised a cheerful din on the stage, after which army dependent Gao Sihai was pushed up to give them some tunes on his flute.   He gazed down in delight at the soldiers and peasants in the audience below, then played so enchantingly on his flute that it seemed as if the clouds rolled away from the sky, moon and stars grew brighter, plants started to put forth shoots, and the River Hutuo flowed gently and peacefully. At the end, all cried, "Bravo!" Old Gāo then made a speech about resisting Japan, concluding with the words, "The world belongs to us now."

Chun'er and Qiufen also felt that this was really *their* meeting, for beside them stood their own folk and all they had seen and heard delighted their hearts.

31

Now a democratic base for the resistance, starting from Mount Wutai and centred round Fuping, was taking shape in the border area of Shanxi, Chahaer and Hebei. In the chief counties of the central Hebei plain the political power of the resistance gained in strength while the volunteer units formed to resist Japan became better organized. Rapid progress was made in setting up an administration for central Hebei, and the headquarters of the people's defence forces moved with the political department to Ziwuzhen, so that the nearby villages became the core of the resistance in central Hebei, infusing fresh energy and vitality into all the regions around. Every day cadres came some distance to report on their work, others set out to inspect outlying areas and orders were transmitted from the border. The streets of Ziwuzhen were thronged with resistance fighters. Carts and horses streamed through, loaded with rifles, bullets and supplies. The village had become a key place, brimming over with life.

A good rain fell one night that spring and the next day dawned clear and fine. Catkins drifted from willows putting forth fresh leaves, the fields were one moist expanse of golden-green, and tender willow shoots swayed in the breeze as if eager to show their colours off to the sky. The soldiers had changed into thin uniforms of the same yellowish green. Mounted orderlies cantered out from Ziwuzhen along the soft, muddy highways, and singing could be heard from the threshing-floors and river flats where troops were being drilled.

All the villages were preparing to pull down the city wall. The previous evening Chun'er had put a little brush on her mill and made ready the upper stone. She rose at dawn, fixed a new elm-wood handle to the mill and ground herself a two-weeks' supply of meal, which she poured into a bag. The two work corps from Five-dragon Temple and Ziwuzhen had combined to form one brigade, and she had agreed to go into town with her sister.

The first of the third lunar month was the day to start. The night before, Chun'er slung her rations over her shoulder and, a change of clothes under her arm, hurried to Qiufen's cottage as excited as if she were going to a temple fair. Early the next morning on the dike Gao Sihai loaded a small wheelbarrow with the tools and food they would need in town, and fastened the child from the Northeast on top. He told Chun'er and Qiufen to take turns pulling the long rope tied to the front and, having slipped a harness round his shoulders, he started pushing the creaking barrow towards the town.

People and carts from every village were streaming to the county town and the creaking of wheelbarrows on the narrow track swelled into a deafening din as they raced each other along. Gao Sihai was wearing padded trousers, and the back of his thin tattered jacket was wet with sweat. Chun'er, her face scarlet, had a towel draped over her shoulders. When the road lay uphill she had to pull hard on the rope, but going downhill Old Gao told her to slacken it.

Once through the West Gate of the town, they found all the shopkeepers and townspeople out in the streets to watch the fun. The county government had arranged billets for all the work corps. Both Chun'er and Qiufen were assigned to a small inn at the foot of the wall.

After the midday meal they took their tools and hurried up the wall to see the section allotted to their brigade. Ziwuzhen and Five-dragon Temple had been given the northwestern corner of the wall. Outside was a moat, inside stood the Temple of the Goddess. Some county cadres were talking to the workers on the wall and Peizhong came over to Chun'er's brigade, climbing on to an earthen platform to address them.

"Fellow villagers!" she cried. "We're going to pull down the wall. You don't need me to explain why this has to be done. This fine solid city wall was built over a thousand years ago, and a wood has grown up around it. When you come into town on market days, you can see the high battlements quite a distance away, and the dense mist rising from the trees looks like an auspicious aura over the town. No one liked the idea of pulling down this grand old wall, which isn't the property of any one person but was left to our whole county by our forefathers. Still, we've got to harden our hearts and pull it down, just as we must harden our hearts to destroy the young wheat in our trim, well-tilled fields by digging trenches over ten feet deep. This is because Japan has invaded us, plunging us into a bitter war, and we shall fight on as long as need be till the final victory is won! We're determined to defeat Japan, to win glory for our ancestors and happiness for our children. When we start on the demolition, each time we prize loose a brick or dig up a spadeful of earth, we'll curse

Japan! Once we've driven away the enemy we'll begin to build again. We'll fill in the trenches across the roads and put up a new city wall."

"By that time there'll be peace, we won't need a wall," put in Bian Ji. "Why not turn it into a tramway, or plant flowers to make a park all round the town?"

"Stick to the present!" cried Old Chang, chief of the Ziwuzhen work corps, who had squeezed his way to the front. "Once we've pulled this down and levelled the ground, we could plant enough sesame here to keep both our villages in oil. But what are we to do with the bricks?"

"The village that dismantles them can have them," said Peizhong. "You can take them back and sell them cheap to families in the resistance who are hard up. Then your village can use the proceeds to buy more rifles."

"That's the idea!" cried the peasants. "Let's get cracking. Everything for the resistance!"

They were splitting up to start work when along came three men in long gowns and short black jackets, headed by Peizhong's tall, burly father Li Juren. Each had something in his hands. Li Juren was playing with two highly-polished walnuts, the second man had a red-wood bauble shaped like a kidney, and the third a string of black beads. Hurrying forward, all three of them raised clasped hands in greeting.

"Wait a bit!" they cried to the crowd. "We have a message for the county head."

Peizhong made no move as the three men approached her and said:

"We represent the local gentry and merchants, who have a proposal to make to the county head."

"Let's discuss it later in the town hall," said Peizhong. "I'm busy now."

161

"It's an urgent matter," insisted the man with the red-wood kidney. "We want you to cancel the order to demolish the city wall."

"What! You're against pulling it down?"

Li Juren stepped forward to explain:

"Since ancient times armies must either defend or attack. As our weapons are inferior to Japan's, naturally we must take the defensive. According to the county chronicles, this city wall dates back to the Song Dynasty and it's massive enough to make an excellent bulwark. But instead of leading troops and civilians to defend it, you have ordered them to pull it down. What is to become of our townsfolk the day that Japan attacks?"

Li Juren had headed a troop of actors for so many years that his views were derived from old plays and he often talked and behaved like an actor on the stage. He was known to nearly all theatre-goers in town, and the villagers gathered round with their picks and shovels.

"Didn't we hold several mass meetings to explain the need for this?" demanded Peizhong. "Weren't you at the last meeting?"

"A cold kept me at home," he replied apologetically.

"We're going to keep the initiative by fighting guerrilla warfare," his daughter told him. "We don't want to stay on the defensive. The wall is being razed to make it difficult for the Japanese to entrench themselves here."

"Fight in the open country," urged Li Juren. "In days gone by, the Yellow Emperor defeated Chi Yu in one battle on the Zhuolu Plain. You can read that in the histories. But I've never heard of demolishing city walls."

"Our war to resist Japan is harder than any in history," retorted Peizhong. "It will decide the fate of our whole nation. It's a war led by a revolutionary party and the entire

162

population's been mobilized to take part. Naturally there are many things about it that you wouldn't find in old books."

"Once the wall's pulled down where are all the townsfolk to go?" Black Beads nerved himself to ask.

"If the enemy occupies this town, we'll get them to move to the villages around and find them food and somewhere to stay. No self-respecting Chinese would want to live in the same town with the enemy."

"Is it so easy?" demanded Li Juren. "Do you think the shopowners and innkeepers are willing to give up all their property?"

"The enemy's forced us to, like it or not. Look at our fighters. They've given up everything to take up arms. There's only one honourable course open to us now, and that's out-and-out resistance to Japan, without counting the cost."

"I'm thinking of you too," murmured Li Juren. "As county head you're responsible for demolishing the wall. How is that going to be recorded in history?"

"History will record that we led the people to put up a hard fight and defeat the Japanese invaders. That's all the histories will say. You're right, every one of us should think of the verdict of history."

The three old men would have argued the matter further had not the villagers lost patience and started grumbling.

"It's plain enough for us peasants to understand," said one. "How is it you gentlemen in long gowns can't see it? Don't waste our precious time. Get out of the way."

They rushed back to their places and laid about so energetically with picks and shovels that the dust flew in all directions and hung in a thick cloud over the town. The three men in long gowns beat a hasty retreat. Li Juren made straight off, but his two companions stepped back to bow in farewell to

163

the county head before returning by the way they had come. As they shuffled along, Black Beads sighed and said:

"We'll have nowhere to stroll in the mornings now. Nowhere to give our birds an airing."

Kidney-bean added glumly:

"The platform where Old Li used to rehearse is being knocked down too."

Li Juren simply flapped his long sleeves and burst into a song.

32

From the city wall the men returned to Li's house. As soon as they stepped inside the yard they heard his wife singing an air from *Su San the Courtesan*.

The place looked not unlike the house of a ruined landlord. The black varnish had peeled off the massive gate and the tub meant for goldfish in front of the spirit screen was planted with scallions which had withered for lack of water. Of the two large pomegranate trees before the house, one had been allowed to die of exposure during the winter. A smell of rancid mutton greeted them at the threshold, and when they lifted the door curtain there on the *kang* making dumplings was Li Juren's concubine and Peizhong's mother, who had started life as an actress with the stage name Guo Yansheng.

Yansheng's hands were floury and the board in front of her was heaped with dough, chopped meat, garlic and scallion. Barely forty and young for her age, she had a fine white complexion. She sat with her legs tucked under her, the tips of her embroidered red satin shoes just visible on each side.

"You're back early!" she greeted them with a smile. "I haven't even stuffed the first lot of dumplings."

"Never mind that," said Li Juren. "Get us some water to wash in. We're all over dust and dirt."

"There's hot water in that brass kettle on the stove. You can pour it yourself. Did you see Peizhong?"

"We did," replied Kidney-bean. "She snubbed us properly."

"What did I tell you?" Yansheng laughed as she dusted the flour from her hands. "She's got a stubborn streak in her, that girl."

"We ought to have taken you along," said Kidney-bean. "She might have listened to her mother."

"It wouldn't have made any difference. A girl married off is like water poured on the ground — gone beyond recall. Take my case: Sold to a troupe when I was nine, with no word from my father or mother ever since." Tears started to her eyes.

"That's ancient history — forget it!" said her husband wiping his face. "Next month we'll make arrangements to go to Beijing. That's the only thing to do, damn it."

"Hasn't Japan taken over there?" asked Yansheng. "We want to get away, surely, not go sticking our heads into the tiger's mouth."

"Japan's taken over there and the Eighth Route Army's taken over here," retorted Li. "Between them we'll have no peace. But I figure that up in Beijing things would be easier. We'll fold up the business here, sell our things and try our luck in Beijing for a couple of years. There are plenty of rich people there, not like this place where every single levy falls on us — why, what they call a 'fair burden' is killing me. We'll find somewhere to live in Beijing, and if the worst comes to the worst you can always go back to the stage."

"At my age? So long in the tooth! Who'd come to hear me? Why throw away a property like this? Trim your sails to suit the wind."

"I shouldn't say this when Peizhong is one of them," put in Kidney-bean. "But how long can they last, the crazy way they're carrying on?"

"Don't mention that name, she's no daughter of mine!" cried Li. "I wash my hands of her. They're in the saddle now but a day of reckoning will come. You're right about that."

"Don't worry," said Yansheng. "Help me stuff these dumplings."

"We have better things to do," said Black Beads. "Go on singing your *Su San the Courtesan* while we sit here and pass judgement."

"To hell with you! Go home and pass judgement on that wife of yours — ask who she's carrying on with nowadays."

The three men reverted to the topic of the wall.

"It's clear they don't mean to defend this town," said Black Beads. "Those beggars with no homes or trades of their own can go off with the Reds to be guerrillas. But what are solid citizens like us to do? We can't take our property with us."

"That's simple," said Kidney-bean. "Stay put."

"Stay put and they'll call you a traitor. Who wants a label like that?" objected Black Beads.

"When that time comes, they'll be too busy running away to pay any attention to us," said Kidney-bean. "The thing now is to stop them from pulling down the wall, because pulling it down won't do us any good."

"It's too late," lamented Li. "They're going at it now ding-dong."

"Rig up some unlucky omem to scare them and they'll not dare go on," whispered Kidney-bean.

"Who's going to do that for us?" demanded Li.

"Between us we can fix it." Kidney-bean turned to Black Beads. "You go to the Temple of the Goddess and get that old nun to fake some sign tomorrow that will frighten these village women. Juren and I will call on the foreign priest at the church by the West Gate and ask him to put the fear of God into the young men of his flock. How about it, eh?"

"An excellent idea!" Li Juren promptly started off with them.

"You're stirring up trouble!" Yansheng shook her head as they left.

The Temple of the Goddess by the North Gate was a massive structure built on a hill, with a hundred and eight stone steps leading up to it. Because the temple was so magnificent, pilgrims came from near and far to offer incense. The statue of the goddess was a fine work of art which the simple villagers accepted as an exact likeness, and her kindly expressive eyes seemed to mark and comfort each one who prayed to her. The nun in charge of the temple embroidered on the legend of the goddess, supplying her and her husband with a pedigree. She made out that the goddess had been ill-treated by her mother-in-law and that her own folk were poor peasants from Lihe, north of the river. So every summer the villagers from Lihe used to take her effigy across the river to pass the worst of the heat there.

Their belief that the goddess came from a poor family and had been cruelly treated by her mother-in-law strengthened the village women's faith in her. In these dark years when this region was ravaged by flood, drought and fighting, the women from several counties around put all their trust in the goddess.

Another story, but not such a pretty one, was attached to the Catholic church at the West Gate. The year after the Yi He Tuan Uprising,* two foreign missionaries appeared in the county town, picked out a plot of land and beat up the owner, an old innkeeper who refused to sell it to them. The peasants in that neighbourhood were so justly incensed that they came with their muskets to the old man's rescue and opened fire on the troops with foreign rifles brought in by the missionaries. For three days and three nights they held the mud fort at the West Gate, while their wives and children kept them supplied with food and ammunition. But the county magistrate sold out and sent cavalry to attack them from the rear. So the peasants were defeated and the foreigners marched into town to kill the old innkeeper and seven young men who refused to leave the fort. Before the blood had dried, the missionaries forced the local people to build them a church, over which they erected a cross.

Of course, after that Catholicism spread and a good many peasants in that district joined the church. But they never forgot what had happened. Those over fifty still remembered the names and faces of those who had died, and could describe the battle and its tragic conclusion. In years of flood, when not a grain of wheat was harvested, the foreign priests brought in sorghum and distributed gruel along with several catties of yams to each Christian. The peasants joined the church not because they understood what they were taught — to them Christianity meant yams.

---

* The Yi He Tuan Uprising, known in the West as the Boxer Rebellion, refers to the spontaneous mass movement of peasants and handicraftsmen in North China in 1900. Forming themselves into secret societies based upon superstitious cults, they carried out an armed struggle against imperialism. After the joint forces of eight imperialist powers occupied Beijing and Tianjin, the movement was savagely suppressed.

At the start of the War of Resistance, some peasants had sought protection from both temple and church. The Catholic priests promised that if the Japanese came all converts could take refuge in the church; but soon after that word spread that the Japanese had broken into the Zhengding cathedral and raped the nuns there. The Taoist nun at the temple simply told the villagers that this was fate and the goddess had gone to Mount Emei for the duration of the war.

When heaven and earth refused to help, the peasants took the path of resistance, acquiring a new firmness and political faith.

33

Soon the battlements of the wall had disappeared. The Ziwuzhen work team made a chute of long poles lashed together and girls slid the dismantled bricks from the top of the wall to the level ground by the moat, where old men loaded them on carts to take home.

The thick coat of lime on the wall was hard to crack. Sparks flew from the young men's mattocks and the heavy blows jarred their wrists until they hit on the plan of dividing the lime into small squares and prizing these up one by one. Li Peizhong rolled up her sleeves to help carry off the lime, but two trips left her flushed and breathless, with a gashed hand.

"Take it easy, county head!" urged the villagers passing with heavy loads of bricks on their shoulder-poles. "You're not used to this work."

"I can learn," she retorted with a smile, bandaging her hand with a white handkerchief. Spotting Chun'er with two baskets on a shoulder-pole, she cried, "Find me a shoulder-pole too, Chun'er. Let's have a race!"

"Right you are." Chun'er chuckled. "I'm no match for you in book learning or settling problems, but you can't beat me when it comes to heavy work."

Joking, they set off together at a run. The men watching grinned till Brigade Leader Chang ticked them off.

"Don't just stand gaping. The county head's given us a lead — get cracking!"

The example set by the women was a powerful stimulus to the whole brigade. The men swung their mattocks higher, shovelled harder and put on a spurt.

Chun'er liked a bit of fun and in her eagerness to come first forget to show consideration. She dragged the county head along so fast that soon her padded jacket was wet with sweat.

"This is the age of air travel, county head," she teased. "You're lagging behind like a tortoise!"

Peizhong's hair was tousled, her lips were pale. Breaking into a cold sweat she staggered dizzily.

"Chun'er!" cried Old Chang. "Make the county head rest a while. She's got more important work than this to do — public affairs."

Then Chun'er put down her load and led Peizhong over to her sister to have a drink and rest.

Old Jiang in the same brigade looked on scornfully and whispered to his work mate:

"Tell me, is that your idea of a county head? You wouldn't think, to look at her, that she's a university graduate, daughter of the Li family in town and daughter-in-law of the Tians of Ziwuzhen. Messing about all day with those rough hoydens!"

"What's wrong with that?" asked the man carrying bricks

170

with him. "Do you have to be bastinadoed before you'll kowtow and respect the county head?"

"There's such a thing as propriety," insisted Old Jiang. "You've got to stand on your dignity to be respected and feared. She forgets what's due to her position."

"You don't understand the new set-up," replied the other. "This is the way of the whole Eighth Route Army. And the less airs they put on, the more people respect them. Don't talk about the county head, what section chief in the old days would have mucked in with us here? At most he'd send an overseer with a stick — that was their way of getting a job done. Nowadays it's all persuasion and 'mobilization'. After getting you ready and glad to do a job, they give the lead themselves. What's wrong with that?"

"I'm not saying there's anything wrong with it. It's just not grand enough. Compare her with a high official on the stage, who comes out in embroidered robes and a jade belt, with men before and behind to clear the way — that was impressive, that was. A magistrate should have runners to keep order in court and an escort when he goes out, that makes him worth watching. Imagine a shabby official like her on the stage. The audience would melt away."

"Your brain needs overhauling." The other stopped arguing with Old Jiang, simply urging him to work faster.

After drinking a bowl of boiled water, Peizhong felt better. Smoothing her hair, she took a closer look at Qiufen as, seated on the ground, she carefully sent brick after brick down the slide.

"Is this your elder sister?" she asked Chun'er.

"Yes," said Chun'er. "You won't have seen her many times. In the old days who liked to pass through that grand gate of yours?"

Peizhong asked Qiufen:

"Are you Comrade Gao Qingshan's . . . unh?"

Qiufen laughed as Chun'er put in:

"Yes, she's Comrade Gao Qingshan's 'unh'. What is an 'unh' exactly?"

"Is this your little boy?" Smiling, Peizhong picked up the child who was playing by Qiufen's side.

"Mind he doesn't dirty your clothes," said Qiufen. "We adopted him. His mother was killed by a Japanese bomb."

"So that's it!" exclaimed Peizhong. "I was thinking, Comrade Gao's not been back six months. Poor little fellow! You must look after him well. We'll avenge your mother, sonny. You'll grow up to the sound of gunfire." She playfully slapped his small behind as the little boy clung to her and nuzzled her knee.

"Doesn't Comrade Gao know you're here?" she asked Qiufen.

"No, we haven't seen him yet."

"He's at a meeting now. I'll go and tell him. Where are you staying?"

"In that little inn near the West Gate."

"Presently I'll find another room for you. It's not often you have a chance to be together. You must make the most of it."

Qiufen flushed and made no reply, while Chun'er cried:

"I call that thoughtful of the county head."

At this, Peizhong coloured up too.

The sun was sinking among rosy clouds when a whistle blew and the work brigade downed tools. Birds flew back from scouring the countryside for food and alighted, twittering, on the old locust trees.

After supper Peizhong found a room in town, but when she went to fetch Qiufen the latter protested that she ought not to take it.

"If the county head's good enough to find you a room, you

may as well move in," said her younger sister. "All the more room for me on this *kang*!"

Peizhong picked up the child and led the way to their new quarters, then sent a message to detachment headquarters. When Qingshan arrived and saw who was there, he said:

"They've come to pull down the wall. Won't this make a bad impression?"

"Why should it?" retorted Peizhong. "Everyone knows how long you've been separated, how seldom you see each other. In fact, if we didn't do this, folk would call us callous."

"You think of everything, county head." Qingshan grinned.

"Count this as a bit of mass work on my part! Well, I'll leave you now to rest. Good night." With a smile Peizhong slipped out and closed the door behind her.

Passing the big gate of her old home, she dropped in and found her mother alone, having just lit the lamp. Yansheng was overjoyed to see her daughter.

"What a girl you are!" she scolded. "I thought you'd forgotten your mother and home completely. Sure you haven't come to the wrong door?"

"Quite sure!" Peizhong laughed. "Where's my father?"

"Your father?" Yansheng sighed. "Out strolling with those no-good friends of his. I've made dumplings ready but he doesn't come home to eat them. You've arrived just at the right time. Wait till the water boils and the two of us can have supper together. Where have you been to get so covered with dust? Come here and I'll brush it off."

Peizhong turned round to let her mother brush her back.

"Tell me, Peizhong, are you going back to the Tians?"

"No, mother, I'm not."

"Going to run wild all your life like this? Where will it get a girl, running about with those soldiers?"

"It'll get me where I want to be." Peizhong smiled. "The

173

base is big, but wherever I go to work I feel quite free and happy. There are people to look after me and care for me, and others to teach and guide me. Don't you worry about me, mother."

"I know it's no use my talking." Yansheng sighed again. "Listen! Don't I hear someone at the gate? That'll be your father."

"If he's back I'm going," said Peizhong. "The two of us can never agree."

"Yes." Yansheng lowered her voice. "They're doing all they can to stop you pulling down the wall. You'd better watch your step."

34

As it happened, father and daughter met in the courtyard. Reeking of liquor, Li Juren called out:

"Is that Peizhong?"

"Yes, father. Where have you been?"

"To a sickening place," he answered furiously. "With every day that passes, those foreign devils are treating us more like dirt. We're lower in their eyes than swine or dogs. If the country really falls, those bastards will be trampling all over us."

"That's why we must go all out to resist Japan," responded Peizhong, mentally noting that only when her father was drunk could she agree with him. "Only if we fight for all we're worth can we hold up our heads as a nation. What foreigner did you go to see?"

"Ha!" Li began to sober up. "I went with a friend on a small matter of business to see that French Catholic priest. First time I've ever set foot inside a church. And there I saw

174

for myself how that old scoundrel treats Christians who want to see him. Some were simply ignored, others doused in a torrent of abuse. He practically made them kowtow to him, in front of the two of us, mind you!"

"What was your business with him?"

"Let's not go into that. I've been waiting for a chance to ask you something. What are you going to do about Tian Yaowu?"

"What am I going to do?" Peizhong lowered her head. "We'll go our separate ways. Don't try to butt in, father."

"Who's trying to butt in?" he retorted with a show of concern. "That old turtle-egg Chiang Kai-shek isn't going to get anywhere. I've no faith left in him. Those 'loyal subjects' who fled with him to the south will end up surrendering and paying tribute to Japan. I'm all for a clean break between you."

"You're becoming quite progressive, father." Peizhong smiled.

"Hardly that," replied Li. "I'm resigned to being a slave in a conquered land. If there's justice in heaven, China's bound to be defeated."

"Don't talk in that defeatist way!" she protested. "Are you blind that you can't see how eagerly the soldiers and civilians in our base are preparing to fight? Are you deaf that you haven't heard the brilliant, well-thought out instructions from Comrade Mao Zedong?"

"I've no faith in your lot. In the first place, you've no idea how to recruit local talent. You don't take able men like me seriously at all. Extraordinary, I call it."

"Who says we don't take you seriously? Have you ever offered to join our work?"

"Of course, I'm not interested in fiddling things," declared Li impressively. "I'd consider a post as adviser in your head-

175

quarters. You must suggest it some time to Commander Lu. On condition, though, that I don't eat millet like the rest of you and that he gives me three guns, two horses and a bodyguard."

Making some excuse, Peizhong left him in disgust. On her way back she passed the room where Qingshan and Qiufen were staying and, looking over the low wall, saw that their light was still on. A dog in the courtyard barked at the sound of her steps and Qiufen's shadow flashed across the window before she blew out the light.

Peizhong decided to make sure that the work brigades had settled down comfortably. She walked down the deserted road towards the West Gate. All the inns had locked up for the night and the only lights were the lanterns of two portable kitchens by the cross-roads. There she ran into Mangzhong.

"Up so late, Comrade Li?" Mangzhong saluted her.

"Yes. Where are you off to?"

"I just took our detachment commander another quilt," replied Mangzhong with a smile.

"If you've nothing to do, come with me to the West Gate. Let's see where the work teams are sleeping."

Mangzhong was only too glad to accompany her. He flashed his torch to light the way for her.

"I don't need that." Peizhong laughed softly. "I know this road well, I shan't fall. That light dazzles my eyes."

Although so many villagers were putting up near the West Gate, the streets were unusually quiet, for all were sleeping soundly after their labours. The only lighted building was a small lodging house near the Catholic church.

"That's where Chun'er is," whispered Peizhong. "Let's go and see what she's doing." She tiptoed to the window and on its paper saw the shadows of Chun'er and the old landlady, the two of them seated face to face on the *kang*.

"Feel it — the *kang*'s warming up," said the old woman. "I burned a bundle of firewood specially for you. A young girl catches cold easily on an unheated *kang*."

"You shouldn't have troubled, aunty," said Chun'er.

"We're like mother and daughter," the old woman went on. "I took a fancy to you the moment I set eyes on you. I'm getting on for seventy, mind, and living here by the city gate I've seen plenty of good girls and good young wives, but never one that measured up to you. You're the lass for me!"

"You're flattering me, aunty." Chun'er laughed.

"D'you think well enough of me to be my god-daughter?" The old woman looked up eagerly. "There's nothing I'd like better."

"If I'm not too clumsy for you. I'm afraid I'd make an awkward sort of daughter."

"That's settled then. Good!" cried the old woman in delight. "We were both born unlucky, you left an orphan and me widowed so early. But now each of us has someone near and dear."

"When did you lose your husband, mother?"

"That year they built the church." She pointed outside. "The foreign devils stole our big plot of land and killed my man, then drove me here, child. I'll never forgive them for it."

She broke down and sobbed. Chun'er soothed her. Presently the old woman dried her eyes and said:

"That's why I was so pleased to hear you talk of fighting back against Japan. You're too young to know how those foreigners have trampled on our country."

Peizhong and Mangzhong heard the old woman sobbing, but Chun'er was silent, lost in thought. Her mother had died when she was only a child, and just when she needed guidance

177

most her father had gone away to the Northeast. She knew very little, it was true, of the foreign aggression during the last century and the fearful memories in the hearts of the peasants on the Hebei plain. For that she should have had a mother who'd been through such disasters and would tell her the story in the quiet of the long winter nights, sitting over a small oil lamp. Now Chun'er, whose own mother was dead, was being schooled by another. Nor did the old woman's words fall on deaf ears, coming at a time when the girl was newly awakened and eager to fight for freedom and liberation. Her love for her country and people had become a powerful driving force in her heart. For a hundred years the peasants had shed their blood times without number to defend their homes from foreign invaders. Should they let defeat and oppression undermine their morale or store up experience and foster the spirit of revolt? Should they lose faith or bide their time and build up their strength? Both ways were open to them. But when the Communist Party gave the lead, the smouldering fire of resistance had burst into flame on the plain.

At last Chun'er broke the silence.

"That means, mother, we must go all out to fight Japan. How good it'll be when our country's strong again!"

"I'm longing for that day," agreed the old woman. "We're not far here from the Temple of the Goddess. I burn incense and kowtow to her on the first and fifteenth of each month, praying she'll protect our soldiers and help them to win. But just now the old nun told me the goddess is rather put out the last day or two."

"How's that?"

"She's appeared to people in dreams and says it's wrong

of the Eighth Route Army to pull down the wall. That's the wall of her palace, and pulling it down is a sin."

"Do you believe that, mother?"

"Yes, I do." The old woman clasped her hands. "When the goddess appears in a dream, you have to believe."

Smiling to herself, Peizhong was just about to go in when some crows roosting on the big elm by the city wall abruptly took flight and whirred around in the dark, cawing. Then came the thud of a brick falling from the tower above the city gate. Mangzhong raised his torch, but Peizhong quickly stopped him.

"Don't flash it! You'd scare them away. Run up and see who it is."

His rifle at the ready, Mangzhong went off while Chun-er came running out, alerted by the noise. She snatched up her pick and hurried after him.

They caught two men in the tower. One was digging a hole, the other holding a bottle of explosive.

"These traitors want to sabotage us!" gasped Chun'er. "If we hadn't discovered them, tomorrow when we pulled down this tower we'd all have been blown to smithereens."

With the help of a cane the old woman came panting up too.

"Why, I know who they are!" she cried. "That's Wang Ergui who grows vegetables for the Catholic priests. The other's the Taoist novice from the temple. Mercy on us! Why are you helping to do such a wicked thing?"

"I didn't want to," snivelled the boy, shaking with fright. "The old nun made me come."

Peizhong had them marched off to the county government and sent a messenger to inform Gao Qingshan, with the result that the principals were arrested that same night.

35

They decided to call a meeting the next day to announce this attempted sabotage and the punishment of those responsible, as well as to give a further explanation of the principles of guerrilla warfare. This would be a joint celebration for the villagers demolishing the wall and the troops quartered in the town.

Someone suggested that a play about the capture of the traitors should be staged at the meeting by the real people concerned. This task was entrusted to the Political Department's drama group.

Young Wang, who headed this group, had always loved the theatre and before the outbreak of the War of Resistance he had joined a drama group organized by Beijing students. Then, brimming over with enthusiasm, he took up propaganda work and marched with stage properties on his back from village to village, posting up red paper announcements appealing for actors, until soon he'd assembled a drama group for the army.

He set out at dawn today from Ziwuzhen with his rucksack full of make-up, and having found Mangzhong in the county town went with him to the lodging house where Chun-er was staying. Her landlady readily agreed to act, but Chun'er wouldn't hear of it.

"This is a glorious task, comrade," pleaded Wang. "Surely after such exemplary conduct you'd like to act out your heroism in an artistic form as a lesson for the masses?"

"Doing it was nothing." Chun'er flushed and stamped her foot. "But I can't act. I'd never get a word out on the stage."

"It's not so hard," coaxed the old woman. "We'll just repeat on the stage what we said in this room."

"Right!" cried Wang. "At least, not quite. There'll have to be some artistic processing."

"Who says it isn't hard?" protested Chun'er. "We're not acting yet, but already I can't understand what this comrade says." She reached for her pick. "I'm going back to the wall to carry bricks."

"That won't do!" Wang barred the way. "The show must go on this evening, and I've asked leave for you. Quick, let's start rehearsing. Take this as the stage." He grabbed Chun'er's pick and with it marked a square on the ground outside the door. Then he made Mangzhong borrow a wooden bed and set a tall lamp on it.

"I know the plot," he told them. "So go ahead. Aunty, you're sitting on the bed with Chun'er. Sit down. This is your *kang*. You stand here, Mangzhong. This is the window."

"What about the county head?" Mangzhong moved over.

"She's too busy. We must do without her. We'll have her in the trial scene. Art doesn't have to copy reality, an author's free to select or reject material as he sees fit."

"He's talking over my head again!" exclaimed Chun'er nervously, cross-legged on the bed.

"It's quite simple really," said Wang. "I'm the producer. Just do as I say. We'll begin with the two of you chatting by the lamp. You start, aunty."

"First I asked her to be my god-daughter," the old woman recollected.

"Don't narrate it but address the audience directly. And don't look at me. Talk the way you did last night."

So the old woman began:

"I don't know if you're willing, lass, but I'd like so much to have you as my god-daughter."

"Stop!" Wang shook the pick in his hand. "Put more feeling into that, aunty. Raise your voice at that point, like this. . . ."

He proceeded to demonstrate what he meant, until Chun'er burst out laughing. She had never heard declaiming like that in her life.

"Be serious, now!" protested Wang. "Go on."

What followed evidently satisfied him, for he thrust his hands into the pockets of his uniform and tapped the ground with one foot.

"I've seen plenty of girls and young wives," the old woman went on. "But not one I like as well as you."

"You're flattering me, aunty," said Chun'er with a laugh.

"Stop!" Wang stepped forward and asked, "Why laugh in that silly way? You should hang your head and look shy. Crumple the hem of your tunic between your thumb and first finger."

"What's that for?"

"Just do as I say. That heightens the effect of shyness."

"With this hand?" Chun'er raised her right hand.

The young man nodded.

When the landlady came to tell of the seizure of their property and her husband's murder, she started sobbing in good earnest, lowering her head to wipe away her tears while Chun'er and Mangzhong wept in sympathy.

"Aunty, this should be a climax," put in Wang loudly. "Your blood is boiling — you've got to get that across! Hold up your head, fix your eyes on the curtain, and raise your voice as high as you can. Shout if you like."

"Where's the curtain?" asked the old woman, drying her eyes.

The rehearsal was over by midday and that evening they performed to all the work brigades and the whole detachment. Young Wang by the light of an oil lamp backstage put so much make up on Chun'er's face that she felt as if covered with plaster. But she threw herself into her part and was soon so carried away by it that she forgot nearly all the stage directions; yet the effect was excellent, gripping the audience. This was valuable experience for Chun'er, who could speak in public after this without blushing. Mangzhong followed Wang's instructions so mechanically that his performance was the worst of all, he had no idea what to do with his hands and feet. For all its faults, however, this was a good first attempt at putting real people and events on the stage.

After the performance the detachment's mass movement officer mounted the stage and announced that, since the work brigades must be tired, the next day the troops would interrupt their drilling to help pull down the wall and give the women a rest.

Chun'er, her face still streaked with make- up, thanked the troops on behalf of the women for this kind offer, but said they hoped the armed forces would go ahead training, for that was the best guarantee of victory. The women would use their day off to wash and mend all the soldiers' dirty clothes.

The next day Chun'er and her friends decided to do their laundry at Clear Water Pool to the left of the Temple of the Goddess.

There was so much rock-salt around this pool that the earth seemed dusted with snow, the water of the pool was a limpid green, and clothes washed there emerged sweet and spotless. All the unmarried girls joined the laundry team.

They skipped round the pool looking for the best place to work and crouched on the bank to splash each other in fun before racing up to the temple with bubbles still on their faces.

From that height they could see the whole county town. Many households had just lit their kitchen fires, and the little northern town was wreathed in a faint haze of smoke. The main hall of the temple was locked, but they poked holes in the window paper and peeped inside.

"They say this is the real goddess herself. Is that true?" a girl from Five-dragon Temple asked Chun'er.

"How could it be?" said Chun'er. "It's a statue made of clay."

"Then why does it look so lifelike?"

"Shall I tell you? There's a story behind that."

"Oh, yes, do tell us!" The girls clustered eagerly round.

"It was Bian Ji who told me this," Chun'er began. "He says pretty girls should never go near a temple that's being built, because the craftsmen who do the statues and paintings are always on the look-out for a model. If you go, they steal your looks and mould them in clay — worse luck for you!"

Some of the girls believed this and looked dismayed. One of them said:

"That only happens to the pretty ones. A fright like me has nothing to be afraid of."

"It was a master craftsman who made this statue of the goddess," Chun'er continued. "He put all his skill into the job and soon produced a lovely figure, but he wasn't satisfied with the expression of the eyes. So he stood up here all day long, forgetting to eat and drink or shelter from the wind and rain, waiting for a really pretty girl to come along. All work on the temple stopped. The carpenters and masons downed tools to keep him company day after day, looking out for a pretty girl."

"You mean to say none passed this way? Wasn't there a single girl pretty enough for him in a county town this size?"

"He had no use for those dressed in silk or satin. Nor for

184

those who were painted and powdered, those who minced along, those who talked in soft, refined voices. He waited until the crops were ripe. Then one morning a girl came back from the fields bowed under the weight of a big sheaf of red sorghum. At the foot of these steps she put down her load to rest and wiping the sweat from her face she looked at the men. 'She'll do!' said the craftsman. 'The goddess has appeared.' And he copied that girl's face. You can see from her expression that the goddess knows what it means to be tired and hungry."

The girls were not too impressed by Chun'er's tale. One by one, with shouts of laughter, they slid down the white stone balustrade to the foot of the hill. For early that spring in the north, not even an immortal was happier than these village girls who had joined in the fight to defend their motherland.

36

Once the wall was down the work brigades packed up to leave, and at the farewell meeting held for them Ziwuzhen and Five-dragon Temple were cited as model villages. On the way home Chun'er helped Gao Sihai again with his barrow. When they left the West Gate they could hardly believe their eyes, for while they were demolishing the wall other work brigades had dug deep trenches where the roads had been. As carts trundled along these trenches, even the carters' heads were hidden from sight. Only the red tassels of the whips they flourished skimmed forward like dragon-flies along the road. Every half *li* there was a short drive leading out. Today traffic was brisk and carters' shouts kept floating through the air.

This transformation of the plain into "hilly terrain" was another historic event which testified to the strength of the people here and their confidence in the resistance. At the same time it showed their resourcefulness and courage. These trenches were like arteries running through the whole of the resistance base.

"We were proud enough of pulling down the wall," said Old Gao as he pushed his barrow. "But seems to me this job they've done beats everything."

Chun'er laughed. "Most people think their own work the best."

Soon Chun'er was back in her cottage, where dust had accumulated for two weeks. After cleaning the room she swilled out the vat, filled it with water from the well, fetched back the hens entrusted to her old neighbour and then lay down, exhausted, to sleep.

She was roused from a pleasant dream by someone calling her name. Sitting up and rubbing her eyes, she saw Old Chang.

"Our young master's back," he told her.

"Who's back?" she asked, quite bewildered.

"Wake up! Our young master — Tian Yaowu."

"So he's back. Well, what of it?" Chun'er yawned. "It has nothing to do with us."

"Use your brain, girl! Of course it has. He's in army uniform. He rode back on a big horse with a bodyguard."

"Has he joined the Eighth Route Army? I didn't think they took men like him."

"There you go again! If he'd joined the Eighth Route, I wouldn't be worrying. No, he's in Chiang Kai-shek's army. And Zhang Yinwu's come back too." Snorting, Old Chang plumped down on the *kang*, his back against the wall, and lit his pipe.

Chun'er was wondering why men who had fled helter-skelter to the south should choose this time to come back.

"Isn't Gao Xiang staying in your place?" she asked. "What does he say about it?"

"I don't know. As soon as I got back, Tian Yaowu showed up. He's wearing one of those grey uniforms and cuts an odd figure, I can tell you. Our men are all in green. So when this fellow turns up he sticks out a mile — like a wolf in a flock of sheep. The sentry in front of the village held him up."

"Had he no pass? He should be nabbed."

"Listen! When the sentry challenged him, he flared up. You know the vile temper he has. He fished out an envelope a good foot long and fumed: 'This is my home. What right have you to stop me? I've come as representative of Chairman Lu and General Zhang to negotiate with your Commander Lu.' After the sentry reported this, Gao Xiang had him fetched in."

"Chairman Lu, General Zhang? Who are they?"

"Zhang Yinwu and Lu Zhonglin. This Lu is another of those warlords, I've heard say. They're up to no good, you can be sure of that. There's more in this than meets the eye, don't you agree?"

"Go back and keep your eyes open. See how Gao Xiang handles him."

"Yes, I'll be off now." Old Chang rose to his feet. "I just came to tip you off. Better be on your guard. We don't want this young bastard stabbing us in the back."

"Don't worry. There's nothing they can do with all our troops here."

"I wouldn't be so sure of that. Let's not take any chances. Here we've just scrapped the wall and dug up the roads all ready to fight Japan, and this sneaky toad pops up again, confound him!" He tapped out his pipe on the sole of one shoe before trudging back, still in a huff.

It was midday and the village streets were deserted except for the old tobacconist who had a stall at the cross-roads and was selling cigarettes to Tian Yaowu's bodyguard.

The guard had a pistol hanging from his belt. His jacket was unbuttoned, disclosing the filthy collar of his shirt and some round red scars on his throat. He picked up a packet of cigarettes, lit one and stuck it in the corner of his mouth, then tossed a banknote over to the old man.

"Give me change!"

The tobacconist looked at the money in his hands and asked:

"What's this note, comrade? What's Chiang Kai-shek doing on it?"

"The Generalissimo!" bellowed the bodyguard.

"Generalissimo, eh? We don't use this money here. I can't take it." With a smile he handed it back. "D'you mind changing it?"

"You bastard!" The Kuomintang soldier rolled bloodshot eyes. "What do you use for money if not this? How dare you disobey the Central Government?"

"Don't call people names!" protested the old man. "Are you in the Eighth Route Army?"

"No, the Central Army."

"That explains it. They don't have your sort in the Eighth Route Army."

The guard caught hold of his pistol.

"Steady on!" cried the tobacconist, wide-eyed. "Don't you dare touch me!"

"I'll shoot you, you rat, for insulting the government."

"Brave, aren't you?" The old man slapped his chest. "Aim here!"

Before the other could carry out his threat, Old Chang rushed over. Two Eighth Route Army men just off sentry duty also hurried up to intervene.

"What are you doing, comrade?" they demanded.

"Threatened to shoot me, he did," declared the tobacconist. "He ought to have a look round. This village is full of troops, but not one of them bullies us ordinary folk."

"That's no way to behave," said one of the Eighth Route Army men to the guard. "You must treat people decently. Don't behave like a warlord."

"Why don't you accept our Central Government notes?" The guard made the most of his grievance.

"I'm not saying we don't, but this has to be talked over. At the start you carted off all the banknotes to the south, and the printing press fell into Japanese hands. Real notes got mixed up with false, and the people lost out so badly that we had to issue border currency. Now you're back, don't be surprised if they don't want your money. In any case, this old man hasn't much of a turnover. When you hand him a five-hundred dollar note for a packet of cigarettes, how on earth is he to change it?"

Unable to bluster it out, the guard stuffed the note into his pocket and turned away.

"Come back, you!" shouted the tobacconist. "Where are my cigarettes?"

The guard fished out the packet and tossed it on to the stall.

"I want pay for that one you're smoking," said the old man.

"Let it go, uncle," urged the soldiers. "He's from our brother army."

"What brother army? Why should I treat a bully like that to a cigarette?" With this parting shot at the guard, the old man opened a fresh packet and offered it to the soldiers.

"Our own troops now, they're welcome to a whole carton. Go ahead, comrades, take one."

"Thanks, uncle, but we don't smoke." Smiling, the Eighth Route Army men walked on.

Old Chang, reaching One-eyed Tian's inner gate, found the landlord standing there with his head in the air like a woodlouse just emerged from hibernation. At sight of Old Chang he yelled:

"After messing about in town the best part of a month, isn't it time you got down to work again? The earth in the pig-sty needs changing and the stables must be cleaned out. The Central Army will soon be here. We must grind some millet ready for them. You fix up the big millstone this afternoon."

Old Chang did not trouble to reply.

37

The situation certainly called for vigilance, and Old Chang was rather on edge as he filled two sacks with grain from his master's huge bin, carried these to the outer yard and yoked the grey mule to the mill. He tipped out the golden grain and spread it flat over the large, dark millstone. Then he leaned against the winnowing machine to smoke a pipe while he pondered his master's reluctance to contribute public grain for the Eighth Route Army and his eagerness to welcome the Central Army. It dawned on him why the two forces had different supporters as he realized the nature of the gap between One-eyed Tian's family and men like himself, and the relation of both armies to the country and people.

After mixing mash for Tian Yaowu's horse, Old Wen whacked it over the head and came out to the mill.

"Well, what's brewing, brother?" he asked.

"There's no knowing. We'll have to be ready for the worst."

"I smell something fishy."

"Never mind. There's always a way out. Doesn't matter if they plot and scheme so long as we stick to our colours."

"Here's Mangzhong!" Old Wen swung round at the clatter of hoofs and saw Gao Qingshan jump down from his horse, pat the dust off his clothes and make for the inner courtyard. He ran out to help Mangzhong with the horses, and asked in a whisper:

"You've heard the news?"

"Of course. That's why the detachment commander's come," answered Mangzhong equally softly.

The negotiations took place in One-eyed Tian's reception room, where four men seated themselves around a square table. They were Tian Yaowu representing Zhang Yinwu, Gao Xiang and Gao Qingshan representing the people's defence forces, and a lad to take the minutes.

"Isn't this a coincidence!" After ascertaining their names and place of origin, Tian Yaowu showed his discoloured teeth in a smile. "We're all three from this county, with only a river separating our villages."

"Being local people, we know the history of these parts," rejoined Gao Xiang. "We all feel keen concern over the fate of our homes and the people hereabouts. We are delighted to welcome you as your army's representative, and hope that at this meeting we can work out the most effective way of fighting the Japanese."

"Would you tell us your army's main policy in this northern expedition?" said Gao Qingshan.

"This is my home, it's up to me to play host." Tian Yaowu rose to his feet. "I'll get them to prepare some dishes and wine."

"Let's have our discussion first," interposed Gao Xiang. "We'll have plenty of chances later to enjoy your hospitality."

Forced to resume his seat, Tian asked:

"What did this gentleman say just now?"

"I hope you'll give us the gist of your army's plans and strategy," said Qingshan. "Then we can cooperate better."

"I've no instructions on this point from my superiors," was Tian's reply.

"What do we discuss in that case?" Gao Xiang raised his eyebrows.

"Well, if you insist," said Tian, "I can tell you this. Of course this question, or the main thing, actually, is.... This is quite immaterial...."

The young man taking notes had sharpened several pencils and prepared plenty of paper in readiness. As he listened intently to this speech, his pencil hovered uncertainly in mid-air, for he did not know what to write. Looking up in frustration at Tian, whose lips were still moving, he silently implored him, "Have a heart! Can't you say something to the point for me to put down?" But his wish was as difficult to realize as an old woman's hope to get eggs from a broody hen.

"What we want to know is this." Gao Xiang cut short Tian's maundering. "How do you mean to fight Japanese imperialism?"

"You must excuse me," replied Tian in some confusion. "That's a state secret which I'm not at liberty to divulge."

"We can tell you the strategy of our people's defence forces, if you'd like to hear it," put in Qingshan.

"I'd be only too delighted!" Tian clapped his hands.

"We make no secret of our resistance policy," said Gao Xiang. "In fact we keep announcing and explaining it to the masses. We have the same aims and same interests as the people. Even before the occupation of the Northeast we were going all out to organize the people to resist Japanese imperialism. Before the Lugouqiao Incident we organized armed resistance in the Northeast and in Chahaer and Suiyuan provinces, and called upon the rest of the country to unite to resist Japan. At that time it was the duty of your troops and government to defend this territory, but you abandoned the people to their fate and fled south by land, sea and air, taking all the valuables you could lay hands on. Then our troops marched north, deep into the enemy's rear. The honest peasants had the pluck to arm themselves, and countless small units combined to form a mighty resistance movement."

"The Generalissimo wants me to express his profound sympathy and concern for the troops and people in the enemy rear," announced Tian unctuously.

"We set out from Shaanxi with little equipment," resumed Gao Xiang. "But our men and officers pressed on regardless of danger. We advanced from northwest Shanxi to the Shanxi-Chahaer-Hebei area, from eastern Hebei to the Northeast, from Hebei to the Shandong coast. We repulsed all enemy attacks and with the support of the people set up a large number of democratic resistance bases. That changed the dangerous situation brought about by your army's retreat and refusal to fight. It guaranteed our advance to victory and gave you people in the interior a breathing space in which to prepare for action."

"I agree with you there," said Tian. "As soon as we had established ourselves in the interior, we started back in full force."

"We'd still like to know your reasons for marching north," said Gao Xiang.

"Put briefly, it's to recover lost territory," rejoined Tian with a smile.

"To recover lost territory," repeated Gao Xiang thoughtfully, as if weighing the words to see how much truth there was in them. "Although the time hasn't come yet to recover lost territory, according to Comrade Mao Zedong's instructions, that makes a fine-sounding slogan. We approve of your resolve to fight Japan and shall certainly do our best to cooperate. We only hope you won't use this grandiose slogan as a cover for disruptive activities which would weaken our resistance to Japan."

"I must confess I fail to understand you." Tian assumed a shocked expression.

"I wonder. According to reliable information, your army shows no sign of going to the front to fight Japan. You have marched in along the way we opened up to station yourselves in our rear, where you are sabotaging the resistance and undermining the morale of the people. You must be well aware how seriously this affects us. It is out and out perfidy."

"I assure you I can clear up this misunderstanding," cried Tian. "We have encamped behind you because, being fresh from the interior, we have no experience yet in fighting Japan. We shall rest for a while behind you and use that time to learn from our elder brothers."

"Your arms and equipment are ten times better than ours," continued Gao Xiang. "You have ample military supplies which we lack. We hope you will use this strength against Japan. For, true as it is that you lack experience in this field, you have very rich experience of another sort."

"You flatter us. What experience do you mean?" Tian looked blank.

"In civil war and attrition! We sincerely hope that slogan

you are shouting so loudly — Recover lost territory! — is not just aimed at us."

"Most certainly not!" Tian flushed and winced. "Most certainly not."

"If you have the honour of your army at heart, you must stop isolating yourselves from the people."

Tian Yaowu fidgeted at finding himself put on the defensive like this. He had as yet had no chance to broach an important proposal. Observing that Gao Xiang and Gao Qingshan were silent, he nerved himself to remark with a crafty smile:

"I forgot to pass on some most important instructions from the Generalissimo. The Generalissimo sets great store by men of outstanding ability. I am sure the capabilities of both you gentlemen would meet with his warm approval. I know how hard your life is, but if you were to transfer to the Central Army, I can assure you there would be no difficulty about finding you positions with handsome emoluments."

"We understand you much better than you seem to understand us!" exclaimed Qingshan, who had been silent all this time. "If you had looked up our records in advance, you wouldn't have made such a ridiculous proposal."

38

Tian Yaowu had no choice but to spend that night with his parents. They blew the lamp out early and conferred softly in the dark.

"With them billeted here, we have to be careful how we talk," said Mrs. Tian. "Those Eighth Route paupers preach at me too — as if I wanted to listen!"

"Has Peizhong been home?" Wide-eyed in the gloom, Yao-wu turned over restlessly.

"You're just back." His mother sighed. "I don't want to upset you. Let's not talk about her."

"Isn't she county head now?"

"Making a fool of herself. Setting tongues wagging. Take my advice, Yaowu, and break with her. We'll find you someone better. What she's done has made you lose face for all your ancestors."

"Cut your cackle. Why bring that bitch into it?" growled One-eyed Tian. "Yaowu, what were you discussing with Gao Qingshan and Gao Xiang? They're our enemies."

"General Zhang told me to get some troops to come over. But I found those two swine too stubborn to budge."

"You've got to pick your man," One-eyed Tian informed him. "Go and see Gao Ba tomorrow. He's not liking it much in the Eighth Route Army. I fancy he'll jump at the chance."

"Why go looking for trouble?" demanded Mrs. Tian. "Kao Ba's taken over Su'er and you can't drop in at her house any more."

"Never mind. That was private business, this is public," countered One-eyed Tian. "Yaowu, the Japanese are attacking in strength, are you a match for them?"

"We've no intention of fighting the Japanese. If we had, why should we have run off to the south? Our troops are coming to pin down the Communists and stop them from having it all their own way."

"I see," said his father. "A Mr. Bai, who works for the Japanese in Baoding, called the other day to ask when you'd be back. You should get in touch with him as soon as you can. You'll need to join forces with them against the Reds. The Generalissimo knows what he's doing."

There the conversation ended, and with One-eyed Tian's remarks in mind the three of them went to sleep.

Next day was a fair day at Ziwuzhen and Tian Yaowu strolled through the streets with his bodyguard at his heels. Just as his flight earlier on had increased the villagers' alarm, his sudden reappearance now gave rise to considerable panic and suspicion. At a butcher's stall he blundered upon Su'er, some leeks in her hand.

"So you're back?" She recoiled a step to size him up.

Tian nodded.

"I see you're an officer." Su'er smiled. "You've risen in the world."

"Aren't you the wife of an officer?" he retorted with a wry grin.

"A poor sort of officer's wife — with no money to spend. See, this is the time to eat pork-and-leek dumplings, but I can't afford even a few ounces of meat."

"Well, the man who'll foot the bill is back, isn't he?" Liu Fu the butcher pointed at Tian Yaowu. "I'll give you credit. Do you want fat or lean?"

"Who says he'll foot the bill?" Su'er glanced at Tian. "I'm no more to him than cast-off clothes or left-over food. Just see if he doesn't ignore me."

"An old flame cool off? Not likely!" Chuckling, Liu Fu cut her some rump.

"All right, score it up to him." Su'er took the meat, smiling. "Well, Mr. Tian, you must come and eat dumplings this evening. I'll be waiting for you, mind!"

After much hesitation, under cover of darkness when no one was about, Tian Yaowu went to Su'er's house. A squad of soldiers had been billeted there, but the squad leader had been so annoyed by the way Su'er kept bursting in on them day and night that he had moved his men elsewhere. Old

Jiang, who was waiting at the gate, greeted Tian Yaowu with a smile.

"The wine's already warmed," he cried. "And the water in the pan's boiling, just waiting for your arrival to cook the dumplings."

Ignoring him, Tian hurried inside. Su'er dressed in her best was standing by the stove.

"At last!" she exclaimed. "It's harder to get you here than to get a girl into the bridal sedan-chair. Come on, sit on the *kang*."

"Will Regiment Commander Gao be back?" inquired Tian anxiously. "Why don't you bolt the gate?"

"His headquarters is here in the village and the Eighth Route Army's very strict. He won't be back, don't worry. And if he does come, I'll take care of him. Do sit down."

Old Jiang brought them bowls and chopsticks while Tian Yaowu and Su'er sat opposite each other on the *kang* and drank two cups of wine.

"I've missed you," she declared. "I only married Gao Ba because I needed someone to support me. You ought to know what I'm like."

"Never mind," said Tian. "We weren't husband and wife. I couldn't expect you to stay chaste for me."

"You've still got the old ideas." Giggling, Su'er pointed her chopsticks at his nose. "Even if you're married, you can't stop your wife having lovers. Look at your Peizhong."

"What about her?" Tian laid down his chopsticks.

"What about her? Oh, she plays fast and loose, that's all. Why else should you come here when you arrive home after six months away?"

"Damn it!" swore Tian. "Wait till I get my hands on her, I'll kill her!"

"Could you get away with that? She's county head. By the way, what sort of cadre are you now?"

"Cadre? I'm an official. One order from me and all these Red county heads will be dismissed."

"What's your rank? How much do you make a month?"

"At very least, you can call me a commissioner."

"Which is higher, a commissioner or a regiment commander?" asked Old Jiang, who was sitting by the *kang* and listening intently.

Before Tian could answer, the door curtain was raised and in strode Gao Ba.

"Well!" cried Su'er. "When did you learn these sneaky ways, slipping in without a sound?"

At the sight of Tian, Gao Ba drew his pistol and shouted:

"I wondered why the gate was open and the room so bright at this time of night. So it's you, you bastard. Get out!"

As Tian ducked under the table, cups and dishes overturned and soup ran all over the *kang*. Su'er steadied the table with one hand, mopping up the soup with a handkerchief in the other.

"Call yourself a commissioner!" she scoffed, kicking Tian's head. "At the first show of force you cave in. Get out of here!" She turned with a smile to her husband. "You haven't learned much all this time in the Eighth Route Army if your temper is still so bad. He's Chairman Lu's representative, the commissioner for this district, comes to make contact with us and arranges about troops and fighting. No one ever kills an envoy — didn't you know that?"

"Why doesn't he make contact somewhere else? Why must it be on my *kang*?" Gao Ba banged his pistol on the table so hard that the dishes leapt two feet into the air while dumplings flew in all directions.

"You weren't at home," explained Su'er. "It was you he

came to see. He's a representative sent by General Zhang."

"To hell with General Zhang's representative!" Gao Ba jumped on to the *kang,* hurled the table aside and grabbed hold of Tian Yaowu.

It was some time before Tian calmed down again.

"How many of you have come?" inquired Gao Ba.

"Not many of us. But we've brought plenty of money."

"What post would a man like me rate on your side?"

"You could be a colonel," said Tian. "But you'd have to take over all your men, horses and weapons."

"Are you crazy? The way things are in the Eighth Route Army, who's able to go over to the enemy with all his men?"

"You'll have to wait for an opportunity — when things warm up and the Japanese attack."

"Join the Japanese against our own folk? Say, what are you, Central Government troops or traitors?"

"This is the indirect way to save the country. According to the Generalissimo's instructions."

"Why approach me instead of other people?" Gao Ba grinned. "Is it because you respect me most?"

"That's it!" At last Tian ventured a smile. "I know Regiment Commander Gao's reputation."

He went on to relay all the arguments for going over to the Kuomintang.

39

Lu Zhonglin notified the Shenze county government of his intention to come and inspect its work, and when Peizhong asked Qingshan what should be done he told her to organize a welcome rally.

The rally was held on the race track in front of the county government, on the wall of which the propaganda corps had written the slogan: Welcome Chairman Lu, Resist Japan to the End! Since each character was several feet high, now that the city wall had been pulled down they were plainly visible a good eight *li* south of the town.

Gao Xiang presided over the rally. It had started drizzling early in the morning, but the men and women of the defence corps of both the town and the villages around assembled on the race track and waited there with Gao Xiang in the rain.

Lu Zhonglin kept them waiting until nearly midday, when a small body of horsemen came into view.

Looking every inch a general, Lu Zhonglin was helped off his horse by four or five aides. He sat on the rostrum smoking cigarettes and drinking some beverage brought by his retinue. After he was thoroughly rested, he walked slowly forward to address the meeting, while four secretaries seated behind him took notes of his speech.

His delivery was so stilted and his voice so low that the peasants could hardly understand a word. They were fascinated, though, by the figure he cut. Old Jiang, who had walked eighteen *li* to watch the fun, whispered to his daughter beside him:

"Who's that speaking, Su'er?"

"Chairman Lu," she whispered back.

"What's he saying? How is it I can't understand a word?"

"He's a high official. If you could understand him, who'd respect him?"

"True enough." Old Jiang nodded. "That's how it is. He's not like Gao Xiang and the rest of them, who talk like clodhoppers counting cabbages. What was that he was drinking just now? Even from this distance you could see its orange colour."

"Fruit juice," replied Su'er. "And weren't they pretty bottles? I'd like to take one home to use for a lamp."

After Lu Zhonglin had finished, General Zhang Yinwu spoke. He advanced like a man practising Chinese boxing, and declaimed like an actor on the stage. Pointing at the county government wall he cried sternly:

"Whose idea was that? What's the meaning of the tail? What was the point of adding that rigmarole?"

"What tail?" asked one of the audience.

"That slogan!" shouted Zhang. " 'Welcome Chairman Lu' would have been enough. That's a complete sentence. Why add 'Resist Japan to the End'?"

"Aren't you going to resist Japan to the end?" asked others of the crowd. "Don't you intend to stay here? Are you going back after you've finished what's in those bottles?"

"Silence!" bellowed Zhang Yinwu. "How dare you interrupt me?"

"Silence yourself!" the peasants shouted back. "We know you, you scoundrel."

"Wipe out those words 'Resist Japan'!" Red in the face, Zhang Yinwu retired to the back of the rostrum.

Gao Xiang stepped forward then and said:

"We can't wipe out those words: they're too important. If we'd thought you didn't mean to resist Japan, or to resist to the end, our country folk wouldn't have come all this way through the rain to welcome you."

"Hear, hear!" Shouts and applause sounded from below.

"We welcome you to resist Japan," went on Gao Xiang. "Resisting Japan is glorious. Although you fled last July as soon as you heard Japanese artillery, we still welcome you back and still hope you'll resist to the end."

"Please, chairman, can I say a few words?" A girl in the crowd raised her hand, and Gao Xiang and the others clapped to welcome her.

She pushed her tattered straw hat to the back of her head so that tiny raindrops pearled her jet black hair and shoulders. Her damp lined jacket clung to her figure as she bounded up to the rostrum. Throwing back her shoulders, she said:

"My name's Chun'er, from Ziwuzhen. I'm a poor girl with no one to support me. Now I'm the instructor of our women's defence corps. I'd like to say a few words at this meeting."

Her earnest enthusiasm caused such a hush in that audience of several thousands that you could hear the spring rain pattering on the leaves.

"Little more than six months have passed," declared Chun'er. "We can remember all that's happened in that time. Last summer when there was that fearful flood and we heard the Japanese guns, the officials and troops fled south with all the rich, influential families. Those people had always treated us like dirt, and they took guns, money and grain with them when they left. What could we do? Just wait to die, we thought. But heaven always leaves men a way out. China can't be destroyed. Along came the Eighth Route Army led by the Communist Party. The Eighth Route Army explained things to us so that we took heart again. We saw our way out was in firmly resisting Japan. Then we country folk organized and armed ourselves. Our peasants and women set up salvation associations. We stood guard, wrecked the roads, tore down the city wall. We learned to read and write. We practised democracy. Since then I've been thinking: Better times lie ahead. Once we've driven out the Japanese, we won't let these swine trample on us any more. Down with Japanese imperialism! Down with traitors and the party of surrender!"

As she raised her small fist and shouted, the crowd followed suit. Then she leapt down from the rostrum, the hand-grenades at her waist clanking against her tin mug as she ran back to the Ziwuzhen defence corps.

After that Gao Qingshan reviewed all the defence corps on the race track and gave them a political quiz. Gao Xiang invited Lu Zhonglin and Zhang Yinwu to watch the review. But although a high standard was reached, these two officers stood glowering on the rostrum as stiff as the clay figures at the gate of a temple.

"In the last six months, the people have made great headway in their military drill and in their ideas," said Gao Xiang. "This is our best guarantee that China will defeat Japanese imperialism."

Neither of the Kuomintang officers replied.

"Before the outbreak of hostilities you used to train militia, didn't you, Mr. Zhang?" pursued Gao Xiang. "How did they compare with our defence corps today?"

"It was different," said Zhang Yinwu curtly. He signalled to Lu Zhonglin and ordered his aides to lead over their horses. In high dudgeon both men mounted and rode off.

"Excuse us if we don't see you off!" shouted some villagers, laughing. They went on with their review and quiz, and Chun'er's contingent did remarkably well.

After the review, as everyone was leaving, Peizhong ran over calling Chun'er's name.

"What is it?" asked the girl, smiling.

"I've something to ask you." Peizhong led her below a small locust tree in front of the square. "I've been thinking of you a lot all this time."

"Same here." Chun'er laughed and waved to her comrades, calling:

"Don't wait for me. I'll catch you up."

"What have you been doing at home these days?" asked Peizhong.

"We're busy making shoes for the army."

"Have you attended the literacy class?"

"Yes. We've troops billeted in our village, and one of the women comrades is teaching us. Everybody's very keen. There's no cutting classes."

"How many characters do you know?"

"That's hard to say. All the characters in our text book."

"Has Tian Yaowu gone back to your village?"

"Yes. Why call it *our* village? Isn't it your home too?"

"Take this, will you?" Peizhong fished a letter out of her pocket. "Give it to Tian Yaowu."

"What's in it?"

"You can read, can't you?" Peizhong smiled. "I haven't sealed it. Read it for yourself."

"I wouldn't read a private letter." Chun'er cheerfully stuffed the envelope into her wallet.

"It's not a private letter," said Peizhong gravely. "It's to let him know that I'm divorcing him."

Chun'er could not think what to say to this. After a brief silence she asked:

"Is there anything else, Comrade Li? I ought to catch up with the rest."

Peizhong saw her to the West Gate by way of the demolished wall. The day had cleared, clouds were scudding across the sky and raindrops clung to the small golden flowers at their feet.

As they parted at the West Gate, Chun'er made an attempt to comfort the county head.

"You'll be all right now, Comrade Li," she said awkwardly.

Then she turned and ran down the dike. Wheat stood tall in the fields and as Chun'er ran down the small path she looked as if she were floating in the sea. The sun was obscured by white clouds, but from behind them golden shafts of sunlight fell on the girl and the wheat nodding all around her.

Peizhong watched from a height. Only seven or eight years separated the two of them. She was thankful that girls of Chun'er's generation would not know the unhappiness she had undergone.

40

Spring, clothing the flowers and trees in fresh, bright colours, quickened girls' heart-beats too. Chun'er, hurrying home from the county town, slowed down when she found she could not catch up with her unit. Water-wheels were creaking on both sides of the path. A girl slightly younger than Chun'er had just made a gap in the low dike round a field and was leaning on her spade lost in a dream. When the irrigation ditch started overflowing, the donkey slyly stopped turning the wheel, waiting for the next word of command from its young mistress.

"Hey, there! Want to flood the place?" cried Chun'er, halting.

With a start the girl looked round and, smiling sheepishly, made haste to fill up the gap. As she called to the donkey she eyed Chun'er's rifle and hand-grenades and asked:

"So the review's over, is it? Which village came first?"

"Ours did. Ziwuzhen in the fourth district."

"Where did we come? Small Wang Village?" The girl indicated a cluster of houses behind her.

"Small Wang Village?" Chun'er tilted her head reflectively. "Can't remember exactly. Nowhere near the top, anyway."

"What a shame!" With a few swift, vigorous strokes the girl cut another channel for the water. "They set off gonging and drumming. But they'll slink home ashamed to show their faces."

"Why didn't you go?" asked Chun'er. "Haven't you joined the defence corps?"

"What d'you take me for? If I'd gone, they mightn't have done so badly. But dad wouldn't hear of it — nothing would do but I must water the fields. A real old die-hard he is, and everyone knows it."

"Well, you must go to the next review. It's grand!"

"I will," the girl assured her eagerly. "I'll be seeing you in a few days at the next big meeting. My, it's sweltering! Like a drink of water from our new well? Rest a bit before you go on."

"I could do with a drink." Chun'er made straight for the well and slaked her thirst with its cool refreshing water. Then she straightened up, wiped her mouth and slapped the donkey's rump before moving on.

The russet branches of date trees along the road were all in tender leaf, while gourd vines had just climbed their trellises and were putting out their first flowers. A hare lolloped a'ong the ridge of a wheat field, and a bird with blue plumage from the hills dipped up and down over a patch of golden rape.

A sudden drowsiness overwhelmed Chun'er, who sat down with her back against a roadside willow, hardly able to keep her eyes open.

This was not far from Huang Village, and some children in a nearby field were after a bird. They reckoned that it would alight on this willow, the only tree in the immediate vicinity, and a small stocky boy came panting up to the willow with a net, attached a large mole-cricket to it as a bait, then planted it in the earth almost on top of Chun'er.

"What d'you think you're doing?" She opened her eyes with a start and grabbed for her gun.

"Find somewhere else to sleep, will you?" said Stocky. "I'm fixing up a snare here."

"Am I stopping you?" she retorted, rubbing her eyes. "Waking people up and ordering them off like that — what's the idea?"

"This land belongs to our village. If you want to sleep, go home and sleep on your *kang*. Nobody will disturb you there."

"Just listen to the boy!" exclaimed Chun'er. "What way is that to talk? Aren't we all Chinese? All out to fight Japan?"

"Don't try to lecture me," said Stocky, wiping his nose. "Get a move on, won't you! That bird's coming down."

Chun'er struggled to her feet and hitched her gun over her shoulder just as the bird arrived. It would have alighted if not for her sudden movement, which made it spread its wings in fright and skim off like an arrow to Cui Family Graveyard. The boy stamped his foot while his friends, who had joined him, sighed.

"There's a war on," scolded Chun'er, "but instead of studying properly at school you run wild all over the place."

"Who says we're running wild?" demanded Stocky. "We're training to fight guerrilla warfare. We'd have hemmed in the enemy force and mopped it up here, if you hadn't spoiled everything. What village are you from? Where did you get that gun? Have you a pass?"

Smiling, Chun'er searched her satchel and pockets. "No."

"Come with us to headquarters then," ordered the boy calmly.

"What headquarters?"

"The headquarters of Huang Village Children's Brigade." Chun'er was surrounded now by boys and girls.

Amused and vexed, she made haste to explain that she was on her way home from the review.

"Why aren't you with your unit, then?" demanded Stocky. "You're a straggler or a slacker, one or the other."

Chun'er had just resigned herself to going with them to the village when they heard the thud of hoofs and a soldier came galloping along the highway, rising and falling in the saddle. As the children turned to look, Chun'er's face lit up, for she saw it was Mangzhong.

Mangzhong dismounted and soon grasped the situation.

"Don't you kids know who she is?" he asked. "She came first of all the women in the review of the defence corps this morning."

"How were we to know that?" retorted Stocky, looking at Chun'er with a new respect.

"I'll answer for her," cried Mangzhong. "Hand her over to me."

"That's all right," said Stocky. "We know you. But we'd like to say this to the woman comrade. Of course, coming first in the review is good, but judging by what's just happened, you've two faults."

"What two faults?" asked Chun'er.

"First, you left your unit to wander about alone: that shows you haven't much sense of discipline. Secondly, you slept by the road when you were carrying a gun: that shows you're not very alert. We're pointing these things out in a comradely way. Are you humble enough to take criticism?"

"I'm humble enough to take it." With a smile at them all, Chun'er left with Mangzhong.

As soon as they were out of earshot, he asked:

"Were you waiting there for me?"

"Don't be an idiot! How was I to know you were coming? I got held up talking to County Head Li, and then there was this mix-up with those kids. Where are you going?"

"I've a letter to deliver for army headquarters. You must be tired, have a ride!" He reined in the horse.

"Wait till we're past the village," said Chun'er, dimpling.

Once past Huang Village, at Cui Family Graveyard, Mangzhong helped Chun'er to mount from the back of a stone statue. But when she tried cantering, the jolting she got made her pull up short in dismay.

"You ought to learn riding," said Mangzhong, striding over to hold the reins. "You never can tell when it will come in useful. It's handy to know and not hard to pick up."

"That frightful jerking and jolting!" cried Chun'er, frowning. "I can hardly stick on."

"After a few rides you'll get the knack of it. Relax. Don't just expect the horse to adapt itself to you — some give and take is needed."

As they neared Ziwuzhen, Chun'er told him with a smile:

"I'll get down here. You ride on and deliver your letter."

She jumped down from the saddle and was limping towards the village when she was overtaken by an old neighbour with a basketful of herbs.

"Where did you get all those fine herbs, aunty?" asked Chun'er.

"By Cui Family Graveyard. And besides fine herbs, you can see fine sights there too."

"What did you see? Children snaring birds?"

"No, a pair of love-birds." The elder woman's eyes twinkled. "Flying along the road they were!"

"I didn't see them."

"Of course you didn't. You were too busy riding his big horse."

"Oh!" Chun'er blushed. "What a tease you are, aunty!"

"That shop in the West Village has scrapped all its bridal sedan-chairs. Did you know that?"

"No. Why should they do that?"

"Seems brides won't be fetched by sedan-chair any more. Now you've set the fashion, they'll be riding big horses to their husbands' homes."

"Let them ride whatever they please." Chun'er giggled. "I've nothing for supper, aunty. Will you let me have a handful of your herbs?"

"Take as much as you want." The old woman put her basket on the ground. "Well, the two of us always find something to laugh about, don't we? What would life be without a bit of fun?"

Chun'er hurried home clasping a bundle of herbs, their roots milky white, their leaves still wet with dew.

41

Chun'er slept badly that night, still dazzled by the stirring events of the day, her ears ringing with the orders shouted at the review. Her room seemed uncomfortably close, she felt pent in. For the urge to do battle had fired her blood and was making it race through her veins.

A dog barked in the street, hoofs clattered, bugles sounded the order to fall in. Chun'er sat up in bed.

There came a knock on her gate. Throwing on her clothes, Chun'er ran out to the fence and saw Mangzhong with his big horse, which was stamping one front hoof impatiently.

Hastily opening the gate, she asked:

"What d'you want, so late at night?"

"Headquarters is moving," said Mangzhong. "There's going to be fighting here tomorrow morning."

"What about us? How can our women's defence unit help?"

"The army's discussed that with the local government. The district office will take charge of you. Better get everything ready in good time. I'm off to the city."

"Off you go, then. See you tomorrow on the battlefield!"

Mangzhong vaulted on to his horse as shadowy figures filed out from every street to assemble in the big square west of the village.

Each unit had a local man to guide it. The peasants were coughing and clearing their throats as they always did when they set out from home before dawn. One produced a flint to strike a light for his pipe, but some soldiers stopped him with a quiet caution.

"Of course!" The man stuffed his pipe back into his belt. "Those swine have sharp eyes."

The commotion brought all the villagers from their beds. Children got up too when they saw their parents dress. Families who had put up troops turned out in force to see them off, chatting as they tagged along.

"You've had to rough it, comrades, in our poor lodgings," said one man. "But we're all one family, you won't hold it against us. Next time you pass this way, don't you forget us! Mind you drop in for a chat. You'll be welcome to a drink of water and a piece of sorghum bread, so long as you don't look down on our simple fare."

"Of course we'll come, uncle," the soldiers whispered back. "Go home now and sleep. It's still early."

"You go through all the hardships of war, can't I miss an hour's sleep for once?" replied the peasant. "You didn't have much peace with us, I reckon. My old woman's tongue never stops wagging, and that boy of ours is always up to some mischief."

"She's a heart of gold, hasn't aunty!" retorted the soldiers. "And your boy's a fine little chap. Mind you send him to school."

"We'll make shift to do that somehow." The peasant chuckled. "Yes, in times like these, of course he must have some schooling. When he's big enough, we'll send him to fight the Japanese with you."

"We'll have thrown them out long before that." The soldiers grinned.

Even after they had reached the square and formed ranks, the peasant kept lopping over for another brief whispered exchange before darting back to the side. His wife came panting up too and gave each soldier a piping hot egg.

"Take it!" she gasped. "Such a flurry as I was in for fear you'd be gone, I don't know whether it's boiled long enough or not. Eat it while it's hot."

The man in charge of mass work at the head of the column had just announced that any damage done to villagers' property must be made good.

"Aunty, we smashed that glass bowl of yours," said one soldier. "I'll go and get you money for a new one."

"The idea!" she retorted softly. "We'll pretend our young rascal broke it."

"Quiet now, folks!" called the operations chief. "When we moved on from any village before, we left without any warning; but that upset people and they started complaining.

213

I'll tell you briefly what the position is, so that you'll be prepared. The enemy's heading this way from Baoding and Hejian, and has moved reinforcements to the Cangzhou-Shijiazhuang Railway. The main thing is that the force from Baoding has occupied our three county towns, Boye, Lixian and Anguo, and means to strike south of the Shahe. The Shahe and Hutuo rivers are dry just now. We know we can repulse the enemy attack, but for the next day or two we've got to give them the slip and keep them on the move. You people do what the district office and self-defence corps say. They've made p'ans for hiding provisions, keeping you out of harm's way, and helping our men to fight. We'll say good-bye for the time being, folks. In a few days we'll celebrate our victory together."

The troops marched off by two different routes. All the villagers watched from the dike until the last soldier had vanished from sight before going home to make preparations for battle.

Chun'er's first action on reaching home was to add fresh oil to her lamp so that it burned up brightly. Then from her chest she took her clothes and a length of cloth she was weaving, wrapped them up and hid them in a hole long since dug in readiness. She concealed the loom in a haystack, put her grain in a sack and carried it out to a wheat field. Having finally assured herself that nothing of consequence was left in the room, she sat down on the *kang* to inspect her rifle and hand-grenades, then put some food in her rucksack and went off to assemble her unit.

The troops, in fine fighting spirit, were marching full speed ahead in order to reach the enemy rear before dawn. They poured along the winding paths over the plain like rivers in spate. Once out of the village, they took a different guide, skirting a grove of date trees and the big trench. Mist hung

214

heavy over the fields and the Dipper was so low in the sky it seemed you could reach up and grasp its handle.

Gao Qingshan's contingent had orders to march from the county town to Five-dragon Temple and prepare to do battle there.

He made his headquarters in his own home — their cottage had a militant history! His father and wife were both out doing jobs in the village when he called a meeting of the district Party committee. The district cadres hoped he would put up a tough fight here to raise the prestige of the anti-Japanese forces, for that would make their own work much easier.

Gao Qingshan explained that the enemy still had military superiority. Our tactics were to choose the most advantageous time to strike, to build up our strength in the course of the fighting. A series of small and then larger victories would keep up and steadily improve the morale of soldiers and civilians alike. He explained to them:

"We've a saying in these parts: A tiger eats locusts piecemeal. And that's our strategy in fighting the invaders."

42

That night the district Party committee called a meeting of branch Party secretaries and chairmen of defence committees in all nearby villages to arrange for co-ordinated action in the coming fight. Old Gao Sihai was made head of the scout team, and one of the scouts under him was Chun'er.

"What d'you want me to do?" she asked as they left the meeting. "Are you sorry I'm in your team?"

"Go home quick and dress up as a shepherdess, then we'll go out together and see how the land lies." He grinned. "You're a smart girl, I know."

Dawn was breaking as the old man and girl left the cottage on the dike. Old Gao, a crate for firewood and grass on his back, had a white wallet tied to the belt round his ragged jacket. Chun'er, herding her sister's goats with a red-tasselled whip, had two hand-grenades and some unleavened bread in a shabby patchwork pouch at her waist.

Expecting the enemy to approach from the county town, they made as fast as they could for Cui Family Graveyard. Chun'er drove the goats along the sunken roadway while the old man walked on the bank, keeping a sharp look-out.

It was early in the fourth month and the wheat was in flower. A chilly wind blew through the fields yet Chun'er was all of a glow.

"Can you see any movement ahead, uncle?" she asked.

"Not a thing. After last night's meeting there's not a soul about."

"How good are your eyes?" demanded Chun'er, smiling. "Don't let me walk smack into the enemy, will you?"

"If you mistrust my eyesight, go and get me some glasses," retorted the old man in a huff. "Young people have no call to laugh at us greybeards."

Presently he stopped at Cui Family Graveyard, saying:

"We'll make this our observation post. Up with your goats!"

The sunken way lay ten feet or more below ground level, so that not even mountain goats could climb out. Chun'er had to lift each one up in turn to the old man, who pulled them up by their horns. Shaking off the dust on their coats, the goats rushed into the graveyard to crop the grass.

Then Old Gao helped Chun'er up.

This was a sizable graveyard. Two stone tigers by the roadside, half buried in the earth, had their mouths smeared with axle grease and mud. There were some stone horses

216

half covered by earth too. The goats jumped skittishly on and off their backs, for it was nearly a year now since they had last enjoyed being among rocks and hills.

The lush grass in the graveyard grew as high as Chun'er's waist and rows of tall willows were rustling although the wind had dropped. A pair of eagles perched on the grave flew slowly off as the two of them approached. Cracking her whip, Chun'er drove the goats deep into the herbage.

Gao Sihai set down his crate at the side of the road and started cutting grass, straightening up from time to time to scan the highway.

Chun'er was rather on edge. When a breeze ruffled the grass, she pricked up her ears. She heard a thudding on a big poplar nearby and, looking up, saw a woodpecker spread its pied wings and fly away. Slipping off her shoes, she shinned up the tree and sat on a fork commanding a good view. The grenades from her pouch she stuck into the wood-pecker's nest.

"There's someone coming!" she called softly to Gao Sihai, flattening herself against the tree.

A cyclist was riding along by the road from the east, alighting from time to time to look around.

Once past the grave, he took a pistol from the bag attached to his handle-bars.

Gao Sihai was cutting reeds and laying them neatly in his crate.

"Hey, old fellow!" The cyclist dismounted to accost him. "Which village are you from?"

"You talking to mc?" Old Gao straightened up. "A small village, Five-dragon Temple. Where are you from?"

"Never you mind." The cyclist flourished him pistol.

Old Gao stooped once more to his work.

"Any troops in your village?" asked the other man.

Old Gao made no reply.

"Hey! You deaf?"

"No." The old man went on with his work. "I can hear cocks crow and dogs bark. If you won't answer my questions, I won't answer yours."

"Stubborn as an old ox!" The cyclist covered him with his pistol. "Aren't you afraid of this?"

"No. In our parts the only people with guns are the Eighth Route Army and cadres. No one but a traitor would try to frighten us, and you don't look like a traitor."

"I don't look like a traitor, eh?" The cyclist grinned as he put the pistol back in the bag and propped his bicycle against a stone tiger.

"Don't lean it there. It'll get greasy," said Old Gao.

"So it will. Thanks for the tip." He wheeled his bike forward and stood it against a small tree by Gao Sihai. Then, sitting down on a heap of reeds, he remarked, "You're a good old fellow. Who smeared all that grease on the tiger's mouth?"

"They're a couple of vicious brutes." Old Gao sat down too. "If you don't grease their mouths they'll make trouble for you and you may come a cropper."

"A queer lot you are in these parts," commented the cyclist. "You dig your roads so deep, no lorry or tank can pass. Are all the roads to your village as deep as this?"

"I reckon they are. We don't run to lorries here."

"You don't, but the Japanese do. They have to fill in the roads as they go — a damned nuisance!"

"If they find it a nuisance that's their look-out." Old Gao offered his pipe to the cyclist. "Who told them to barge in here? Have a smoke."

The other man took the pipe and bent his head to strike a

light, fumbling ineffectively for some time with the flint. Meanwhile Gao Sihai filched his pistol and sat on it.

"Here, I'll give you a light. I can see you're used to matches."

"You're right. I usually smoke cigarettes, but the last few days we haven't been able to buy any."

"It's clear you're no villager. Brought up in a big town, weren't you?"

"Yes, Baoding."

"You've come out to guide the Japanese, you must be a traitor." Gao Sihai stood up.

The cyclist jumped up too and grabbed for his pistol. But Old Gao waved it at him.

"Here it is!"

As the traitor lunged out for it, Old Gao jumped to one side and sent him sprawling over the stone tiger so that his face was covered with grease and mud. He pinioned the man's hands behind his back.

"Can't have you taking word to the Japanese," he said. "You can cool your heels here for a while."

He undid the traitor's belt, thrust the man's head down inside his baggy pants and trussed him up as if he were a bundle of straw. Then he dragged him to the mouth of a fox hole deep in the undergrowth.

"Don't bury me alive, sir!" The traitor's voice was muffled.

"Who wants a traitor buried in his family graveyard? Tell the truth now: what were you up to?"

"The Japanese sent me to see if there were any of the Eighth Route Army about and whether the roads were passable or not."

"Where are the Japanese? How big is their force?"

"At Xinying. Two lorries and twenty cavalrymen. They may have crossed the river by now."

"Which road are they taking and where are they heading?"

"They'll be coming down this road to Ziwuzhen."

"You keep a watch from the tree, Chun'er," called Old Gao, "while I take word of this to your brother-in-law. I'll ride this fellow's bike."

43

Old Gao lowered the bicycle into the sunken road and started off, zigzagging from side to side.

Chun'er strained her eyes towards the town. Apart from the sand and straw swirled across the road into the wheat fields by the wind, there was not so much as a bird in sight. The villages around looked completely deserted. No smoke was rising from a single cottage.

Her eyes on the road, Chun'er mused: If not for the enemy, this highway would be thronged with carts hauling dung and earth, carters shouting at their horses and cracking their whips, children scampering off to cut grass or herd goats. On a fine day like this, there'd probably be women dressed in their best on their way to a temple fair, traders with money and baggage whose wives would see them all the way to the highway. And a common sight, too, was colourful bridal sedan-chairs accompanied by old musicians blowing cheerful, stirring tunes on their flutes.

None of this would be left, she thought, if the enemy were to occupy our land.

Suddenly Chun'er caught sight of two Japanese trucks. This was her first glimpse of these strange machines filled with enemy soldiers lurching so savagely over her native soil.

The trucks were driving beside the sunken road through the flowering wheat, crushing the dense plants and leaving a long, cruel trail behind them.

Chun'er's heart missed a beat, she bit her lips and clung tightly to the tree. The enemy trucks and horses seemed to be lumbering and trampling over her heart.

Just then Gao Sihai came back.

"The Japanese soldiers are coming, uncle!" she called. "What shall we do?"

"Keep cool!" Gao Sihai tucked his pistol under his girdle and took off his shoes. Then he climbed up the slippery poplar as nimbly as a monkey, hand over hand, as if walking on the highway.

"There's no time to get word to our people." Chun'er was worried. "Shall we throw a hand-grenade to warn the village?"

"Wait while I count them." Gao leaned out, clinging with one hand to the tree. "There aren't too many of them. We'll let them pass."

"What if they go into the village and start burning houses?"

"Our troops are ready for them. We'll wait until they're in the bag before we pull the strings."

Now the Japanese trucks were lurching past the graveyard, escorted by several dozen horsemen on either side. The invaders were dust-stained and sweating. Each step they took was one step nearer to hell. Old Gao and Chun'er kept well out of sight. Not until the enemy was half way across the river flats did the old man fire three shots into the air.

There was no cover on the gleaming white sand and the Japanese in the sunlight looked like fish laid out on a high bank to dry. Our troops moved swiftly into action from the sunken roads all around.

The enemy contingent was just a scouting party. Gao Qingshan directed one of his battalions to wipe it out on the spot.

The fight took place just outside Five-dragon Temple, and the fighters were all sons of peasants. The whole village gathered behind the dike to cheer them. As our men darted past them, the old folk whispered messages of encouragement and advice.

The women's catering team, headed by Qiufen, stood in two rows facing each other behind the dike like the stage attendants in a theatre. One row held eggs wrapped in pancakes, the other jugs of drinking water. But the fighters had no time to eat, the women had to wait till the action was over.

Our forces had to occupy the high ridge planted with willows.

This task was carried out by Mangzhong's squad, who charged across the sand with a light machine-gun.

The enemy on the flats started milling about wildly. One truck overturned, while the other broke through our cordon and hurtled back towards Cui Family Graveyard. But Chun'er blew it up with her two hand-grenades.

Then all the villagers rushed out to help clean up the battlefield, while the soldiers, after a hasty meal in the village, marched off again to the north.

44

To the north, however, things were not going so smoothly. Gao Ba had orders to station his regiment in the vicinity of Stone Buddha Fair to hold up the enemy, but to withdraw quickly if the Japanese force proved too strong. For some time now Gao Ba had been jealous of the other regimental commanders. It bored and irritated him when Gao Qingshan talked about politics or policy. To his mind, a soldier proved himself in battle and he was waiting for a chance to show the others what a good fighter he was.

Because it was lively there and the food was good, he had taken up his position with one battalion on the main road of Stone Buddha Fair. At noon, news of the victory of a brother battalion at Five-dragon Temple made him all the more eager to prove his mettle. The Japanese were approaching now from Anguo by the side of the road which had been destroyed, taking no precautions against any Chinese troops there might be in the neighbourhood. This was because they had come out in force, but Gao Ba interpreted it as a sign of bad judgment. Swearing angrily at them for this mark of contempt, he could hardly be restrained from leaping on to a roof to shout defiance. He made two of his company commanders post men on the roof tops and as soon as the enemy came within range he gave away their position by opening fire.

Gao Ba's troops had hitherto fought several defensive actions on the roof tops. In fact, in Shulu County they had held a town for nearly a month that way. But that was in the period of general confusion when rival bands were fighting among themselves. The Japanese, only too pleased to discover a target, speedily set about surrounding our troops. Soon their big guns were reinforced by planes, many houses were destroyed by shells and bombs, and fires broke out all over the little town. Gao Ba's men could not stand up to such an onslaught. They cursed their commander for a reckless fool and had no faith in his orders. Some scurried off with the villagers to the fields. And the local people saw with dismay that, unable to beat off the attack, Gao Ba's soldiers were retreating in disorder, leaving the civilians to their

223

fate, even knocking down women and children in their headlong flight. Now the Japanese had reached the north street of Stone Buddha Fair. The whole village would soon be surrounded, with no escape for soldiers or civilians.

Gao Qingshan, as the chief commander, had to save the situation. He led a force under cover to the enemy's flank and sent a battalion to cut the Japanese cordon.

Mangzhong and his squad joined in this action. He was still buoyed up by the glorious success of their last operation, which had been well directed. The sight of terrified women and children, their faces streaked with mud and sweat, went to his heart and he felt it his duty to protect them.

Having marshalled his men in the swamps, he led them at a run down the sunken way and across the dike. They were to pass some fields and a graveyard and then skirt the bank of the Zhulong to occupy the big stone bridge at the south end of Stone Buddha Fair.

The spring wheat was growing well, but was not high enough to cover their advance completely. The Japanese converging on the bridge spotted them and were thrown into momentary confusion. Mangzhong seized this chance to dash, head down, behind a water-wheel and then charge through the graveyard.

An enemy tank had just passed this way, uprooting elm trees with trunks the size of bowls and luxuriant foliage. One of the ancestral grave mounds had been ploughed up. Crouching behind the stone tablet of the grave, Mangzhong opened fire on the enemy as he waited for his comrades to catch up.

Before them lay the River Zhulong, its banks so overgrown with reeds and grass that the water was hidden from sight. Heavy enemy fire forced Mangzhong and his men to advance on hands and knees. They fired as they went, taking advan-

224

tage of every tree, bush and ditch that could serve as cover. It seemed to them as if everything on their great country's soil, even the sun which was sinking now in the west and the turgid river water, was closely bound up with their lives and their combat mission.

They hugged the ground, their hearts pounding, and felt the earth tremble beneath them. The knowledge that their motherland was in deadly danger lent her children strength. In this hour of humiliation, she had the right to urge her bravest sons to advance!

In a last swift dash they gained the river bank and hurled their hand-grenades at the enemy. By capturing the bridge they succeeded in cutting the Japanese force into two. But Mangzhong had been wounded.

As dusk fell, artillery fire raked the plain. Not a village but was drawn into the turmoil of war. The young and able-bodied offered their services as guides, stretcher-bearers or porters. The villages along the highway set up communication posts and dimmed red lanterns hung in the streets that night. The moment they were lifted on to stretchers, casualties felt they had reached home, for the bearers would rather bruise or gash their own feet than jolt a wounded soldier, and they kept their charges well covered against the evening dew and the cold night air.

Women working in shifts waited at the ends of the streets to receive the stretchers and carry them in to the post, where warm drinking water and boiled eggs were ready.

All the way, in every village they passed, the soldiers heard the same words of encouragement. When a man aroused by a soft voice raised his head and was offered a raw egg or noodles wrapped round chopsticks, he felt himself back with his own sisters or mother.

Mangzhong, wounded in the leg, was entrusted by Gao Qingshan to the stretcher team headed by Gao Sihai, who carried the lad to Chun'er's cottage in Ziwuzhen.

Chun'er, shouldering two rifles, followed the stretcher as the sun dipped behind the hills and a wind sprang up in the fields. Worried as she was about her sweetheart's wound, her heart was sinking too.

She ran on ahead presently to clean up her room and spread a thick quilt on the *kang*. When she had settled Mangzhong comfortably and seen the stretcher-bearers off, she went to find the doctor.

Ziwuzhen had a Western-style doctor named Shen, an outsider who had married one of the village girls and opened a small pharmacy in his father-in-law's house by the well in the main street. Previously a dispenser in a Baoding hospital, he was naturally not a skilled physician, but he always did his best for patients. Living with his mother-in-law, he took pains to be on good terms with all the villagers. If anyone was ill they had only to send a child to fetch him and he would go without a murmur, at no matter what time of the day or night. So the doctor was a general favourite, and at New Year or other festivals he was always invited to a number of feasts.

Chun'er found him just back from a visit to another village. He was unstrapping his medicine case from his bicycle in the yard, while his young wife sat by the stove plying the bellows to cook supper. At Chun'er's approach, Mrs. Shen sprang up, patting the dust from her clothes, and went to greet her.

"Come inside and sit down, sister. So you won a victory! Let me cook you something good to celebrate."

"Thanks, but I can't wait," said Chun'er with a laugh. "I'm here to ask Dr. Shen if he'll come over."

"Who're you calling doctor?" The young woman giggled. "He may have a beard of sorts, but by country reckoning he's your brother-in-law, so why not call him by his name? You live all on your own — who's ill?"

"A squad leader from the army. My brother-in-law asked me to look after him because I'm close to your house, with a doctor handy."

"You mean Mangzhong? Hurry along then!" she ordered her husband, twinkling. "Stop unstrapping your kit. Go on and see this patient. I'll have supper ready for you when you come back."

The doctor fastened his case in place again and pushed his bicycle towards the gate.

"Don't treat us as strangers now, sister!" called Mrs. Shen from the steps. "Don't you go boiling water or cooking a meal for him."

"Right you are!" responded Chun'er.

Home again, Chun'er trod softly, and the doctor left his bicycle quietly under the window before following her inside.

"He must be asleep," whispered Chun'er, lighting her small oil lamp and going over to look. But Mangzhong's eyes were wide open.

"So you're awake. Does it hurt?" she asked. "I've brought the doctor to see you."

"Well, let's have a look." Shen gently raised the quilt and sat on the edge of the *kang* to examine the wound. "Hold that lamp closer, will you, Chun'er?"

The girl leaned forward with the lamp in one hand but hastily averted her eyes at the sight of the clotted blood on Mangzhong's leg. She gulped hard to hold back her tears.

When the doctor had cleaned and dressed the wound, she brought out her newly spun cloth from its hiding place and tore off a strip as a bandage.

45

When Chun'er saw the doctor home, she approached his mother-in-law, a woman of fifty whose husband had gone to the Northeast the same year as Chun'er's father, and asked her to keep her company.

The elder woman readily agreed, for she always gave unstinted help to those in trouble. She brought over her quilt that night and, pointing to the *kang*, asked in a whisper:

"Has he eaten anything?"

"Not yet," said Chun'er. "Everything's so topsy-turvy with the fighting, I've nothing good to give him."

"I've brought a packet of noodles and three eggs." She produced these from her quilt. "Boil them for him."

When the meal was ready, Chun'er took it to Mangzhong on the *kang*.

"You've been on the go all day, lass, you lie down too," said the elder woman from the *kang*. "I'll keep an eye on him for the first half of the night."

Chun'er moved the lamp to the window sill and lay down behind her neighbour. But although she closed her eyes tight she could not sleep. After turning over several times she suggested:

"Suppose we change over, aunty? Let me take the first watch."

"There's no need for that. I may be old, but I've plenty of energy. I can go without sleep for three or four nights and not feel it. You shut your eyes now. Young people need their rest."

"I can't sleep." Chun'er sat up.

"Well, then, let's have a little chat."

"Wouldn't that disturb him?" Chun'er pointed to Mangzhong. "Why keep two people up? You sleep first, aunty."

"Well, if that's the way you want it. But as soon as you start nodding, mind you call me."

The elder woman stretched out, closed her eyes and was soon snoring. She dreamed that Mangzhong's wound had healed, he had shouldered his rifle and was saying to her:

"Aunty, I'll never forget what you've done for me. You made sure I wasn't too hot or too cold, you gave me food and water, sat up all night by my bed, and didn't even mind emptying my dirty slops. From now on, I'm going to be like a son to you."

"Don't you worry about that," she told him. "Who are you fighting for anyway if not for me? Just tell me where you're off to now and when you'll be back."

"I'm going to the Northeast," he replied with a smile. "I shall fight all the way to the Yalu River till all the Japanese invaders are wiped out."

"Wait a bit then!" she cried eagerly. "Wait till I've changed my shoes. I'm coming with you."

"It's a long, long way across mountains and rivers, aunty. Why should you go?"

"I want to find my old man. When he left home I wore a red flower in my hair. Now my hair is white but still he isn't back. I'm going to tell him: Now that we've got the Party to lead us here and the Eighth Route Army to fight for us, all the poor have found a way out. Young men don't have to leave their wives and children in the lurch any more and go to the Northeast. Come home and we can have a good life together."

"Come along, then, aunty." Mangzhong took her arm and they followed the column of troops. A long way they travelled, across countless rivers, through the pass and across vast forests. At dusk one day, in a landlord's outhouse, they found her husband.

Tears started running down her cheeks.

"I wonder if our troops have found billets for the night," said Mangzhong, turning over.

"Are you awake or talking in your sleep?" Chun'er chuckled.

"I'm awake."

"Aunty keeps talking in her sleep."

"She's had a hard life," said Mangzhong. "Her husband worked as a hired hand like me when he was a boy, and at last he was forced to trek to the Northeast. We were born in much better times than their generation."

"My dad's in the Northeast too. Don't you forget him."

"How could I forget him? I'm going to fight my hardest till we've fought our way up to liberate the people there. We'll fetch back all the folk from these parts who've been scattered east and west because times were hard or they were hounded by the landlords and gentry. We'll give them land to till, houses to live in."

"Is that your ideal?" asked Chun'er, dimpling.

"The first one."

"And the second?"

"The second's too big to put into a few words. The Party will help me to carry it out. I want to keep in the vanguard all my life, and never fall out of the ranks."

"Are you a Party member?" Chun'er leaned forward eagerly.

"H'm. Do you have an ideal too?"

"Of course I do!" She straightened up. "Don't you look down on me."

"Let's hear it then."

"Wait while I collect my ideas." Chun'er threw back her head. "My sister says the village Party branch is going to admit me as a member. My ideal is to be a good Communist!"

She grasped Mangzhong's fevered hand as she spoke, and gently stroked his hair.

Moonlight illumined the *kang* as the enthusiasm and hopes of the three of them pervaded the little room, usually so quiet.

The next morning Chun'er's neighbour went home to have breakfast. The girl let her hens out of the coop, threw them a handful of grain and told them softly:

"Have a good feed and go out to play. Mind you don't squawk even when you lay an egg. Don't disturb him with your noise. Do you hear?"

The hens seemed to be nodding assent as they lost no time in pecking for the grain.

She cut out cloth soles the same size as Mangzhong's old shoes and sat down in the courtyard. A magpie alighted in the yard with a cry, but she quietly shooed it away. Then along came a lively girl with a bundle of washing and squatted down by the flat grey stone in front of Chun'er's eastern room to beat the clothes. Chun'er hastily dropped her sewing and hurried over.

"Go somewhere else to wash, sister. I've a patient in the house."

"Fancy me forgetting that overnight! What a scatter-brain I am! Is he any better?"

"He's better. Just now he's sleeping."

"When he wakes, tell him I asked after him." The girl rolled up her clothes and went off. At the threshold she turned to ask softly:

"Who are the shoes for, sister?"

"For the wounded soldier. He can wear them when he's well enough to join his unit again. Don't you want to see the invaders driven out as soon as possible?"

231

"What d'you think?" The girl smacked her lips. "My, aren't you pleased with yourself!"

46

Gao Ba's failure to carry out orders had resulted in serious losses. After the Japanese withdrawal Gao Qingshan summoned all the cadres of his detachment to the courtyard of a large salt shop in Stone Buddha Fair, where he criticized himself for this fiasco, recapitulated the principles of guerrilla warfare under the existing conditions, and sharply reprimanded Gao Ba, who was sitting to one side, red in the face.

"Spouting principles won't take the place of planes and big guns," protested Gao Ba sullenly. "I don't know what you're driving at. Just blame me for the defeat and have done with it."

"We've got to get to the bottom of your defeat," rejoined Qingshan. "What was the reason for it?"

"Poor troops, rotten weapons and a powerful enemy." Gao Ba flung out one arm. "I didn't turn tail on the battlefield, anyway."

"You're in command of a regiment, responsible for the lives of all your men, not a travelling showman displaying your swordsmanship. Your troops' casualties prove you're no hero."

"Have me shot or beheaded then." Gao Ba hung his head.

"I shall refer this higher up," said Qingshan. "For the time being I'm going to send you to west of the railway to study."

The meeting broke up, and while the rest had a meal Gao Ba slipped out on his own. Stone Buddha Fair stood at the junction of two highways and was a busy port on the River Zhulong. Its main street was lined with shops, and by the stone bridge stood a tavern with an old winepot hanging above its entrance. Gao Ba walked in and cried:

"Heat a pot of wine! Any dishes?"

"No dishes," said the tavern keeper. "If you want something to go with your wine, comrade, there are two pieces of beancurd left over from yesterday. They may be a little rancid."

"Bring them here." Gao Ba slapped the table and sat down.

His seat was just in front of the window looking south across the Zhulong, a clear, quiet flowing river with water weeds floating on it. For years the households on both banks had been emptying their rubbish into it, with the result that a musty stench rose from the water. The people on the boats moored under the bridge were washing rice for their supper.

By the opposite bank, on a newly painted houseboat, a girl in a red cotton jacket leaned out of the back cabin window, her glossy black braid flapping against the boat's side as she emptied slops into the river. Still holding the basin, she stared over at the tavern.

Gao Ba was drinking in a dispirited way when he caught sight of her.

"What are you staring at?" he shouted, frowning. "Want me to come over?"

"Aren't people allowed to look at you?" The girl withdrew, banging her basin.

"You watch your tongue, my girl!" A white-haired woman put her head through the window. "Who are you cheeking?"

"Me!" cried Gao Ba. "How old is your daughter?"

"Eighteen."

"Time you married her off." He grinned. "How can you keep a girl in red and green?"

"A grown girl can't be kept at home," agreed the old woman. "A daughter's always on her mother's mind. You win more battles, comrade, and drive the Japanese away. As soon as there's peace again, we'll send her off in style with horses and a bridal chair, and a merry din of gongs, drums and fire-crackers."

"A girl like that ought to marry an army officer," he said.

"Yes, a man who's won glory fighting the Japanese."

The girl stepped over to tug her mother away, then slammed the small window shut. Gao Ba heard the two of them bickering in the cabin.

"Are you blind?" demanded the girl. "Why gossip with him?"

Her mother asked, "Isn't he one of the Eighth Route Army?"

"One who gets defeated." The girl spat. "If Detachment Commander Gao hadn't come to the rescue, we'd not be here having supper this evening."

"Damn it!" Gao Ba pounded the table and jumped up. "Sucking up to those in power."

The waiter hurried over with a conciliatory smile.

"Don't take offence, comrade," he begged. "You've come at an awkward time. When the Japanese attacked today, Regiment Commander Gao blundered so badly that this street suffered heavy losses. The Japanese took all our oil and traitors seized all our salt. Is the taste not to your liking?"

"Tell me," said Gao Ba softly, "where a fellow can amuse himself here?"

"What's that?" The waiter's eyes widened.

"Somewhere with a bit of life."

"There's no such place. Since the Japanese left, everybody's been busy putting out fires or burying the dead. What life d'you expect now?"

"You know the quarter I mean," persisted Gao Ba.

"Oh, no." The waiter brushed this aside. "In the old days there were some brothels by the river; but after the Eighth Route Army took over here some of the girls reformed and those who wouldn't sneaked across to the enemy. You're in the revolutionary army, comrade. Why go looking for such trash?"

"I'm investigating," said Gao Ba, and walked out.

He wandered on to the big stone bridge. The small stone lions on the balustrade all seemed to be craning their heads to look at him. Foam bubbled on the water below and there were bloodstains at one end of the bridge where a squad of his men had given their lives.

In high dudgeon he entered a bath-house on the south bank, a countrified establishment where the water was only changed two or three times a month. The place smelt dank and mouldy, and the water in the common pool looked thoroughly murky. Gao Ba threw off his clothes and jumped in, landing on a corpulent bather whom he had failed to notice in the swirling steam.

"Who's that?" Sitting up like a startled toad, the other man wiped the water from his face.

"I'm Regiment Commander Gao! Why didn't you get out of the way when you saw me? Were you trying to trip me up? To make me drink this filthy water?"

"Oh, it's Regiment Commander Gao." The other smiled. "This is a lucky encounter."

"Who may you be?" asked Gao Ba.

"We met in Mr. Tian's house in Ziwuzhen. Feasted at the same table that day."

"Are you Mr. Bai?" Gao Ba spread out to float on the water. "I thought you worked in Baoding."

"My home's here. I came back to have a look."

"The owner of this bath-house has a nerve, keeping open today."

"We've the Japanese to thank for that," rejoined Bai with a smile. "This is water the Japanese have washed in. It's some time since we last met, Commander Gao. You must feel on top of the world."

"That's what you think!" Gao Ba rolled over like a child learning how to swim, not caring how he splashed the other man. Mr. Bai shrank back into a corner out of the way and with his face averted asked:

"Haven't you been promoted?"

"Promoted? Not much! I'm being sent to the hills for training."

"Things are rough in the Eighth Route Army." Bai sighed. "Have you been in touch with Yaowu since he came back?"

"I saw him once," panted Gao Ba, and stopped thrashing about to rest on the edge of the pool.

"I hear the Central Government troops have occupied your county town," whispered Bai, crawling closer to him. "My advice to you is: Join them. Over here you have to rough it, you're hemmed in by rules and regulations. Over there, just fasten on your cartridge belt and you can do as you please. What else do men take office for? Why ask for trouble? Here you've served all this time as regiment commander, and now they want you to train as a private again. You'll be tied down hand and foot."

"How did they take the county town?" This news was a shock to Gao Ba.

"How?" Bai gave a scornful laugh. "It's like playing

draughts. Soon as the Eighth Route Army leaves a space, they fill it. What could be simpler?"

"If they join the Japanese against us, won't we be done for?"

"Of course you will. You've had a taste of a Japanese attack. You've seen their equipment, how well they train their troops. That's not all either. I hear they're bringing up strong reinforcements on every front. This time they're determined to wipe out Lu Zhengcao. Now that the Central Government troops are helping them, the Eighth Route Army will be on the run. You'll all have to take to the hills and live on wild herbs. Won't you be sorry to leave? Won't you miss your wife?"

"I can't quite believe it," said Gao Ba after some thought.

"May I drown in this pool if I'm trying to trick you," declared Bai solemnly. "Just think it over. Which side gives you the better chance of promotion and making big money? Don't leave it too late, going over. If you're willing, we'll go together."

"I'm wearing the Eighth Route Army uniform. That would make things awkward on the way."

"So long as you're willing, I've got all you need at home."

47

Gao Ba changed into civilian clothes in Bai's house and, surveying himself in the mirror under the lamp, felt he was back where he'd been a year ago. His scarred face flushed and he sighed:

"A year's effort wasted — still the same old Gao Ba."

"Come on," said Bai standing beside him. "You'll soon make up for it there."

With Bai leading the way, they darted across the dike by Stone Buddha Fair without running into any sentries. Late as it was, the roads were deserted. Only a screech-owl hooted from an old elm tree on the dike.

"We must go to Ziwuzhen first," observed Bai. "While I drop in to see Mr. Tian, you can go home and tell your family."

"Something puzzles me, Mr. Bai," remarked Gao Ba. "Are you working for the Japanese or for the Central Government?"

"It comes to the same thing," was Bai's cheerful reply. "First I threw in my lot with Japan, not that I felt too happy about turning 'traitor'. However, once the Central Army came, Tian Yaowu told me I'd done right and shown great foresight, because now I can work for them as well. That's given me more scope and more confidence."

"I'm a rough fellow," said Gao Ba. "What's going on is beyond me. In future I hope you'll give me some tips, Mr. Bai."

"There's no mystery about it. Look at it this way. The Central Government and Japan are like the two legs of a pair of trousers — we need both. If you can't follow that, here's another comparison. Weren't you a brigand before, out to steal and make money? You didn't mind what people thought of you so long as the authorities didn't catch you. That's how it is with us. Whoever feeds you is your mother. Whoever pays you is your superior. If the wind blows from the north you bend to the south; if the east room's hot you cool off in the west. The worse mess the country's in, the better for us."

"You're a smart man, Mr. Bai."

"I've learned how to succeed as a turncoat." Bai sniggered. "Once you've mastered the art, you can always float to the top."

By now they had reached the outskirts of Ziwuzhen and it was Gao Ba's turn to lead the way. Avoiding the sentries posted by the defence corps, he saw Bai to One-eyed Tian's gate before going home to see Su'er.

Tian Yaowu had just slipped home too. His mother handed him Li Peizhong's summons to court to arrange a divorce.

"Don't worry!" exclaimed Yaowu. "She can't get the better of me."

"She's county head," his mother demurred. "She's the one sitting in the *yamen* and what she says goes. You'd never believe what she's done. First she condemns her father-in-law, next she has her own father arrested, and now she's summoned her husband to appear in court."

"She may summon me, but she can't make me go. We don't recognize their authority. As far as seniority is concerned, as a commissioner I rank above her. I was sent here by the Central Government, the proper authority. What is she? A piddling little bogus official."

"Right," agreed One-eyed Tian. "Just ignore the bitch."

"If you're an official, where's your *yamen*?" asked his mother doubtfully. "Here on our family *kang*?"

"We're going to drive them out of the county town any time now," asserted Yaowu. "Here's Mr. Bai. Are you in touch with the Japanese?"

"I am," was Bai's reply. "And I've got Gao Ba to come over. If you attacked openly, you'd have trouble getting in; but let him lead the way, pretending you're the Eighth Route Army, and the county town will fall into our hands."

"You must do your part in the village too," Tian Yaowu urged his parents. "Do your best to spoil the reputation of the Eighth Route Army. And slander those villagers active in the resistance. Make the others stop trusting them."

"It's no joke running down the Communist Party and spreading rumours about the Eighth Route Army," objected One-eyed Tian. "I've been thinking this over for a year and more without hitting on any good scheme. Times have changed since the Communists were underground and the Red Army was thousands of *li* away. You could get away with anything in those days. But now the Communist Party is in the village, there are men of the Eighth Route Army on every *kang*. Folk don't believe it if you say the Reds murder people and burn their homes. The village is full of paupers, and the poor are as close to the Reds as fish to water. There are only seven or eight families like ours in this district, and many of them have sons in the resistance who've influenced their opinions. Everybody's a politician nowadays. The moment you open your mouth they judge where you stand. That makes it hard to talk."

"Of course Mr. Tian is right," agreed Bai. "But we mustn't take this lying down. Sometimes the people are against them too. The old folk don't like to see women drilling, attending meetings, acting plays, doing *yangko* dances and mixing with men. Some of the husbands are against it as well. And when it comes to contributing grain and shoes for the army or conscripting new recruits, we can easily find a chance to stir up trouble."

"Mr. Bai is very experienced," Yaowu explained. "Up in the Northeast he sabotaged the work of the Anti-Japanese Amalgamated Armies."

"The proverb says 'Even an uncracked egg may turn rotten'," reasoned Bai. "If there's a crack and you don't take advantage of it, you're not even up to a fly! It's easy to attack the cadres. If a man is keen, complain he's domineer-

240

ing, giving orders right and left. If a woman's keen, accuse her of having affairs with men. Don't mind mixing black and white to stir up trouble. Sling mud at them whenever you can."

"That Chun'er's a good target," observed One-eyed Tian. "She was the one who got our young farm-hand Mangzhong to join the Eighth Route Army. He was wounded in the fighting the other day, and now he's convalescing in her cottage. That's a good peg to hang something on. Kill two birds with one stone. You'll be spoiling the Eighth Route Army's good name and attacking a village cadre at the same time."

"I can't take the first step," objected Mrs. Tian. "I must get Su'er to do that."

"By all means," approved Bai. "Now her husband's come over, she's bound to take our side."

48

When next the doctor came to change Mangzhong's dressing he found the wound nearly healed.

"Why don't you join the Eighth Route Army, doctor?" asked Chun'er, who was beaming with satisfaction. "Use your skill for the country."

"I'm not as young and spry as I was," he replied, packing his medicines away. "I don't suppose the Eighth Route Army would have me."

"They'd jump at the chance," Mangzhong assured him. "If you joined, doctor, I dare say they'd give you a horse to make your work easier."

"When you join your unit again you must speak to my brother-in-law about that," said Chun'er. "But the doctor can join up first."

"Don't be in such a hurry." The doctor smiled. "I must talk it over first with my family. They depend on me for a living."

"They won't starve if you go," rejoined Chun'er. "Your wife can spin and weave to provide food and clothes. Don't shilly-shally. Everyone ought to do his bit for the resistance and you, especially, shouldn't be backward. Let's count it as settled."

"Steady on," he protested warmly. "I'm working for the resistance by attending Comrade Mangzhong. You don't seem to realize, lass, that every family has its difficulties. And mine can't manage without me."

"Who says they can't? You seem to think us women very backward. But your wife managed for seventeen or eighteen years without starving before you married her."

"That won't do. I must talk it over with her first."

"What is there to talk over? Could she stop you resisting Japan? I'll speak to her."

The doctor said no more but picked up his kit and walked out.

"Why fly out like that?" asked Mangzhong when he had gone. "Why shouldn't he go home to talk it over and settle everything? You don't have to force him."

"Who was forcing him? It's a glorious thing to resist Japan. It's not right for him to take to his heels as soon as he's asked to join the resistance. I just don't see why he should be so difficult."

"You're expecting him to behave like a good Party member." Mangzhong chuckled. "You ought to go to his house and see what difficulties they actually have. If they've real problems, help to get round them. Don't just shout: It's glorious to resist Japan."

"I accept your criticism." Chun'er giggled. "I'll go and see his wife. He's a hen-pecked husband. One word from her is worth more than an imperial decree."

"That's more like it. Do more work among the women. Help them take a broader view and look further ahead. Our recruiting will be much easier if they back it."

"Don't you look down on us women," protested Chun'er. "You think we're all narrow-minded and petty, do you? Are great hulking men so unable to think for themselves that they need a curtain lecture from their wives before they'll join up?"

"That was your idea — don't put words in my mouth. The fact is, women can play a very important part if they help with the mobilization."

"What about your own case?" Smiling she looked away.

"I went of my own free will." He grinned. "Of course I haven't forgotten your encouragement and help. All I mean is you should do more work among the women. Tackle them from two sides."

"What two sides?"

"Get them to study politics and learn to read and write. Then they'll understand the reasons for the resistance, what we're fighting for, and how the struggle will end. At the same time get them to do productive work."

"There are no slackers among us," Chun'er assured him. "Up at crack of dawn to spin, we sit up half the night to weave. Our women mind the children, cook meals, mill grain, feed the pigs and dogs, and look after the old folk. They're too tired to comb their hair or wash their feet, on the go the whole day long."

"You must organize them to learn farming too. Then when the men have joined the army, we needn't worry that there'll be no food at home, no crops in the fields."

"No one asked you to worry. Even if there are only women left, we won't let the fields run to waste."

"That means a lot of hard work. It's not just a question of guaranteeing it here. You say there are no slackers, but that's a lie. What about Su'er?"

Chun'er stepped into the courtyard then because it was clouding over and she decided she'd better fetch in more fuel. As she approached the woodpile, she heard a rustling, which sounded like rats or sparrows. Going closer she noticed a green belt by the pile. When she picked this up out fell a heavy bundle. The new born baby inside it started wailing! Chun'er was completely dumbfounded.

Her old neighbour, happening to drop in just then, was horrified to see a hungry infant at its last gasp inside one of the green rucksacks used by the Eighth Route Army.

"What's this?" she exclaimed. "Throw it in the river quick!"

"How can you drown a littel living creature?" Chun'er carried it inside, laid it on the *kang* and fed it two mouthfuls of the noodle soup made for Mangzhong.

"Take my advice and don't be too kind-hearted," Granny warned her. "Some trouble-maker may have planted it here to do you a bad turn."

"What bad turn?"

"Don't be silly! Can't you understand? How is a great girl of nineteen to explain a baby on her *kang*?"

Chun'er flushed and made no reply.

"If you won't get rid of it, I will." The old woman picked up the infant.

"No!" protested Chun'er. "We can't do such a wicked

244

thing. If people are trying to harm me, they won't get away with it."

Mangzhong, too, was against abandoning the child. He sat up to peer at its little face and, chuckling, pushed a noodle into its mouth.

"See here!" he cried. "Who does this nipper look like?"

"No one that I know of," said Chun'er. "What does it matter?"

"It's the image of Old Wen. Just look at that nose."

"Don't talk nonsense," said Granny. "Where would a poor bachelor get a baby from?"

"There's no knowing," answered Mangzhong. "But why shouldn't the poor have babies?"

"Let's not waste time," urged the old woman. "If you won't get rid of the child, I'll take it home. Nobody can gossip about an old woman who's getting on for eighty."

She wrapped the baby up and carried it out. But as she reached the gate Su'er rounded the corner of One-eyed Tian's house, her neck craned like an egret on the look-out for fish. The old woman scuttled back into Chun'er's yard.

"Trying to avoid me, granny?" Su'er hurried up, smiling. "Afraid I might drive your good luck away?"

"What good luck?" The old woman hid the child with her sleeve.

"There's no hiding such a big bundle." Su'er reached out prying hands. "Mercy on us! Whose baby is this?"

"I picked it up. Now don't start talking nonsense." Granny walked away.

"Picked it up on Chun'er's *kang*?" Su'er followed her. "She's got an Eighth Route Army man on her *kang*, where does this little Eighth Router come from? In a rucksack too, I do declare! So small and already in army uniform."

"Keep a decent tongue in your head!" snapped the old

woman. "You'll be sorry if you throw mud at honest people."

"I'm going to let everyone know about this." Su'er headed for the main street. "Thick as thieves all day long, I knew they were up to no good. I'm not one to gossip, granny."

The old woman was too thin-skinned to scold or answer back. She returned to report this to Chun'er.

"Botheration! I *would* meet this gossip. Now she'll broadcast the news through the village."

"Let her," Chun'er retorted. "We must get to the bottom of this." With that she too hurried off.

49

Like a dung-beetle, Su'er buzzed her rumours abroad, and soon they had their effect. Women by the mill near the road left off gossiping at Chun'er's approach and slipped inside to make a great commotion, shouting at the donkey yoked to the mill. But the moment she'd passed they darted out again to stare after her.

Paying no attention to them, Chun'er went to the doctor's house. He was out visiting a patient, and his young wife examined Chun'er from head to foot.

"What's wrong?" asked the girl with a smile. "See something the matter?"

"No," was the reply. "But there's something I must tell you."

"Go ahead." Chun'er seated herself on the edge of the *kang*.

"My dear," said the doctor's wife affectionately, coming up to her and laying one hand on her knee. "Although we're not next-door neighbours, we've always been like sisters."

"Just say frankly what's on your mind. Why beat about the bush like Tian Yaowu?"

"As children we gleaned the Tians' wheat fields, going out when stars were still in the sky and coming home by moonlight. In the midday break we sat under the same willow and shared the same meal of husks. That old swine One-eyed Tian used to chase us with his stick and call us filthy names. Do you remember?"

"Of course I do." Chun'er nodded.

"We girls of poor families must hold our own and work hard. We must value our good name and be on our guard. Not give anyone a chance to find fault with us."

"Have I ever lost face for you, sister?" demanded Chun'er.

"You're the finest girl in our village. But just now I heard talk about you and Mangzhong having a little bastard."

"Have you learned nothing as a doctor's wife?" exclaimed Chun'er, pushing her away. "You should take a look at that baby: it can't have been born any earlier than last night. The day before yesterday I was out in the fighting and climbed the tallest poplar in Cui Family Graveyard. Look at me, do I look as if I'd just been lying in?"

"You don't. But that's what they're saying."

"And do you have to believe every word they say? We must clear this up. That dirt they're slinging at me will soon be rubbed on their own faces."

"I won't believe them again." The doctor's wife beamed.

"Well, I didn't come here to clear myself to you, but to discuss something important."

"Is it about my husband joining the army? He mentioned it just now when he came home."

"Our country's at war and men like him are needed at the front. If he goes, will you have any difficulties?"

"Of course we shall, sister. First, money. He's not a bad doctor and the folk hereabouts trust him. As long as he makes his rounds on that bike, we don't lack for food or clothing. Still, now that we're fighting Japan, I know we shouldn't just worry about ourselves. So that's really not a big problem."

Chun'er laughed, and her friend went on:

"We've three and a half *mu* of land. That takes half an able-bodied man's time. And then if it's raining and the road's slippery, he fetches the water for me. If the house leaks, he mends the roof. Once he's gone, who's going to help me?"

"The village will look after army dependents. When it's time to plough or reap there'll be people to help you. Your water vat will be kept full. You won't see a single weed growing on your roof."

"I can work in the fields myself and climb the roof if I have to. But it wouldn't be honest to hide these things from you, sister. And there's a third problem too."

"As for the third, just be patient." Chun'er giggled. "Once the Japanese are driven away, husband and wife can be together again."

"In that case I'll tell him to go."

Chun'er left the doctor's house to go and give a talk to the literacy class. Very few of the women had turned up today and those that had come were hanging about outside bickering among themselves. But seated side by side in the front row were Mrs. Tian, who had never crossed the threshold before, and Su'er, who seldom attended.

Chun'er mounted the platform and began:

"What I want to talk about today is something important to all of us women — I mean marriage and having babies."

When the women outside heard this they crowded in, some

covering their mouths as they giggled, some hiding their eyes.

Chun'er went on:

"We often say we were born girls because of some crime in our last existence, but of course that's a superstition. It's true, though, that a woman's life is harder than words can tell. Children are their mother's flesh, and there's no dirty work she won't do to bring them up. What mother is there that doesn't love her child?"

The room was full now. Many who couldn't get in had crowded outside the windows and were sticking their heads inside.

Chun'er continued:

"Today I found a baby in my woodpile. I was sorry for the little thing and sorry for its mother. Why should she throw her child away? Maybe her family's poor and she has so many other children she can't support it? Or maybe she was married against her will, then fell in love with someone else and this is his child. But if we're poor, the government will help. And those who were married against their will can ask help from the Women's Salvation Association. Why should anyone still behave in the old way and be cruel enough to abandon her own child? I'm sure the mother's so wretched she's sobbing her heart out at home."

In one corner of the classroom someone was crying. At first she tried to stifle her sobs but presently she gave way to a storm of weeping. Chun'er ran over and saw it was a widow whose face was haggard, her head wrapped in a blue cloth.

"I thought you were ill, sister," Chun'er cried. "Go on home."

"Dear sister!" The widow caught hold of Chun'er's hand. "That baby's mine."

249

50

This widow, a fine strapping woman in her early thirties, lived at the east end of the village in a tiled, two-roomed cottage with a little courtyard. The previous autumn she had salvaged what sorghum she could from her flooded fields, laid it out in the yard to dry and then chopped it up. She sat down to rest before winnowing it, for the day was oppressively hot. When she tossed up a trial handful, chaff and grain fell to earth together. The leaves on the tree in her yard were completely still. She sighed. The sky was clouding over. A storm was brewing.

Just then Old Wen came back from the fields, a hoe over one shoulder. He knew every soul in the village after all these years and often joked with the women. Passing the widow's yard he turned to call:

"Hurry up and get that sorghum in before the rain!"

"There's no wind," she answered. "Have you time to help toss it?"

"Won't take long, that little bit." Old Wen rested his hoe against the tree and strode over to pick up a dust-pan. After weighing some grain in his hand he got ready for action, and the widow stood beside him with her flail.

Old Wen tossed the sorghum vigorously into the air, and soon the whole lot was finished. Having brushed away the grass clinging to the grain, he scooped it into a heap. And the widow, beaming, shovelled it into a sack.

No sooner was this done than the storm broke. The widow whisked her tools inside while Old Wen carried the sack into her cottage.

"I don't know how to thank you," she declared. "Another moment and my harvest would have been ruined. Hurry up and sit down to cool off."

She spread a straw mat on the ground. It was pelting with rain and the sky was so black that the room was lost in gloom.

"It's hard for a woman on her own," remarked Old Wen loudly.

"You're telling me! But I'm lucky in a way. I can count on you and Brother Chang to lend a helping hand."

"Jobs like this are child's play to a man, but awkward for a woman."

"We all have our troubles, don't we? For you it's sewing and mending. If you want anything like that done, bring it here."

Several times Old Wen rose to go but she stopped him, saying:

"It won't do to get drenched after sweating."

That was when Old Wen and the widow fell in love. After she found herself pregnant, she bound her belly tightly with cloth and later on avoided going out. A few days before this, however, Su'er had burst in and discovered her secret.

"You know," said Su'er, "there's nothing the Eighth Route Army hates so much as men and women carrying on like this. They'll dash the baby's brains out and shoot the father."

The widow, taken in, asked her advice.

"When it's born, just give it to me," Su'er proposed.

Now Su'er and Mrs. Tian were pushed up to the platform and called on to confess. The landlord's wife feigned ignorance of the whole business and stood there with folded hands and lowered head refusing to answer all questions. It was Su'er who finally broke down and admitted:

"The other day Gao Ba came back with a traitor called Bai and they met in One-eyed Tian's house. They told us to undermine the resistance work in the village and spoil the reputation of those keen to resist Japan. Mrs. Tian and I thought up this plan between us. I'm sorry now. I'll never do such a thing again."

This incident convinced Chun'er of the need to do more work among the women and children. She asked Bian Ji to paint her two sets of pictures.

Only too pleased, Bian Ji said:

"Of course, armed resistance to Japan comes first; but it's our duty as well to sweep away backward customs. I can paint something about freedom of choice in marriage, but when it comes to childbirth I'm out of my depth."

"What's your trouble? Your wife will tell you all about it."

"Her ideas are just the sort we want to reform. No, I'll have to ask the doctor about the new methods of delivery."

That evening he propped up the rolling-board as easel, lit the oil lamp and fetched his paints from his wife's dressing-case.

His surroundings were hardly conducive to work, with his wife unwell and the children on the rampage. But he painted as if oblivious of all around him. And presently he turned to his wife, who was suckling their youngest on the *kang*.

"Do you sit down or stand to have a baby?"

"What a question!" she retorted with a smile. "You're never painting that mucky business, are you?"

"What do you expect me to paint?"

"As if you don't know. What did your master teach you? All these years what else have you painted but immortals, clouds, flowers, birds and beauties?"

"That was work I was paid to do, of no use to the people. It only spread superstition and prettified the rotten old set up."

"Please yourself then," said his wife. "Each time I had a baby I was sitting and standing by turns all through the night."

"How do women cope with illegitimate babies?"

"Try to bring on a miscarriage by taking drugs or beating the womb with a stick. Or they'll get an abortion done with a big hook or pressure on the belly. I don't know what you're painting, but don't ask me any more questions. I want to sleep."

"Don't sleep just yet. Listen to me. At thirteen I started carrying my master's baggage and learning how to paint. I've been at it now for nearly thirty years. In wind and rain I stuck it out high up on the mountains or in lonely temples, my eyes glued to a whitewashed wall, painting away. I studied hard and looked for teachers far and wide. Took great pains over every stroke. Cold, leftover rice was all I had to eat, cold water from a tin kettle all I had to drink. Bare-bottomed children swarmed round me, pointing and passing remarks. A polite name for me was 'a craftsman', but frankly speaking I wasn't up to a beggar. I often thought: Of all the trades in the world what possessed me to choose this one? My work is no use to the people. I used to fume at the money-bags and bullies in each village, but all I could do was stick cartoons on their doors on the sly. It's only recently that my work has begun to be worth anything. Now I post my pictures by the road or in a meeting hall, and they help the work in the village by showing what's backward and wrong and what's progressive. These two sets, when they're finished, will help to change village customs and encourage girls to find husbands after their own hearts and bring up bonny children. It's the thought of this, see, that is making me paint better than ever before."

With a smile his wife got up and watched over his shoulder while he painted late into the night.

The pictures were stuck on the earthen walls of the literacy classroom. The girls who saw the series on freedom of choice

253

in marriage shook their heads over the deceitful go-betweens and the parents with backward ideas who insisted on arranging matches for their children. When they moved to the other wall with the paintings on childbirth, and saw the picture of an expectant mother lying down to give birth, they rushed away with cries of horror. But presently, hand in hand to give themselves courage, they sidled back in threes or fours with crimson cheeks to look at this set of pictures. They learned a great deal too. It dawned on them that only by taking an active part in the resistance and the new democratic life of the village, only by working and studying hard and acquiring general knowledge, could women win emancipation.

51

Thanks to the village doctor's daily visits, Mangzhong's wound had now healed sufficiently for him to take a turn in Chun'er's courtyard. The doctor had neither the skill nor the instruments to remove a small piece of shrapnel from the lad's leg. Mangzhong had a splendid constitution, however, and being in the full vigour of youth he recovered fast.

A dust storm sprang up that morning, and the gusty early summer wind flung dust against the window. After supper the wind died down and stars filled the sky as Granny came round to keep them company. She sat with Chun'er on the *kang* sewing shoes for the army by lamplight, while Mangzhong leaned back restlessly against the folded quilts.

"Chun'er," he said presently. "Pass me my gun, will you?"

"What for?" she asked, raising her head.

"Won't you and granny move a bit to give me some light?" Mangzhong sat up grinning. "I want to clean my gun."

"Here's your sweetheart." Chun'er fetched his rifle from

254

the wall. "You can't live without her. Mind you don't shoot us by accident."

Granny shrank back against the window, protesting:

"Why fool about with that at this time of night? It scares me when people play with guns and axes. Be careful you don't fire that off at us, Mangzhong. I may be old but I want to live to see the Japanese driven out."

"How can we drive them out, granny, if you won't let us have guns?" asked Mangzhong, laughing.

From the rickety cupboard facing the door Chun'er produced a small bottle of hair oil. After shaking it she handed it to him, saying, "Here's the oil our defence corps uses to clean guns. But use it sparingly. We're not like the regular army. These few drops at the bottom are all we have left."

As Mangzhong cleaned his gun at one end of the *kang*, Granny sat uneasily at the other, looking anxiously over her shoulder every few minutes.

"Hurry up and finish," said Chun'er. "You'll have granny pricking her finger and you'll be cross when she can't make shoes for you."

Just then, to the north, One-eyed Tian's dog started barking. It went on yelping loudly until every dog in the village had joined in and there was pandemonium.

"Listen!" Mangzhong pricked up his ears.

Chun'er and her old neighbour had stopped sewing. The street was in an uproar. Troops had marched in. They heard shouts, curses, rifle shots and pounding on doors. Mangzhong grinned from ear to ear.

"Fine! Our troops are back." He got up and groped for his shoes.

"Wait a bit," whispered Chun'er. "Suppose it's the Japanese?"

"Nonsense. They're talking Chinese."

255

"They may be traitors, using such foul language. Have you ever heard the Eighth Route Army pound on people's doors in that way? Like regular brigands! We must be on our guard. Let me take a look."

"You be careful too," urged Granny. "Mercy on us!"

Chun'er put on her shoes and softly opened the door. Slipping over to the fence, she saw men and horses milling about in One-eyed Tian's outer yard which was brightly lit.

No sign of Old Chang and Old Wen. But Tian Yaowu was standing with a few men on the steps to the inner yard, and she heard him shout:

"Surround the village, quick!"

Her heart missed a beat. What had become of their sentries?

She darted back inside and told Mangzhong, who decided that these must be Zhang Yinfu's men, in which case he must leave the village at once.

"Can you walk with that game leg?" she asked doubtfully. "There may not be any danger. Don't we have a united front with them?"

Mangzhong shouldered his rifle and answered impatiently:

"That gang isn't to be trusted. The dirty, double-faced lot want to stab us in the back. I'm off."

"I'll come with you."

"If that's who they are, you must both go into hiding," cried Granny. "I'll keep an eye on things for you. I'm not afraid. Don't imagine I'm a coward. If someone holds a knife to my throat, I'll fight!"

They opened the wicker gate and tiptoed out, Mangzhong followed by Chun'er, both carrying their guns. Using the dike as cover, they headed southwest past a grove of elms till they reached a patch of reeds outside the village.

In a clearing where bricks were made they found Old

Chang, peering from behind a pile of bricks at the village. When he saw who it was he exclaimed:

"Thank goodness! I was worried about you, Mangzhong."

"What happened to our sentries?" Chun'er stamped her foot.

"They're new to the job. They let themselves be fooled. That lot came in pretending to be the Eighth Route Army."

"But couldn't the fools see the grey uniforms?"

"Those in front wore green and Eighth Route badges," Old Chang explained. "Do you know who answered the sentries?"

"How should I know?" retorted Chun'er.

"Gao Ba. Seems that swine has sold out. We mustn't hang about here. Let's go straight to Five-dragon Temple to tell the district head."

As they hurried off, Mangzhong asked:

"How did you get out, Old Chang? Pick up any information?"

"It's a bad business. When they pounded on the gate, Old Wen and I were squatting in the cowshed learning characters. Soon as Tian Yaowu and Gao Ba burst in, Old Wen threw me a glance as if to say — Clear out! But I thought I'd try to see what they were up to, so I found an excuse to slip into the inner courtyard. I heard Tian Yaowu say they're out to take the county town. Then One-eyed Tian saw me and gave an ugly laugh. 'Chairman Old Chang!' he said. 'You keep out of this. Go and rest outside. We'll talk to you presently.' And knowing there'd be the devil to pay, I bolted."

"What about Old Wen?" asked Mangzhong. "He ought to leave too."

"It was hard enough me slipping out," explained Old Chang. "He told me to go first. Said he'd risk his neck to keep the coast clear. Come on. We must hurry up to warn the district."

In Gao Sihai's cottage in Five-dragon Temple, Old Chang reported this news to the district Party secretary.

"We're in a tough spot," said the latter. "The Kuomintang is playing a dirty game. We've only a small force in the county town and it's not prepared. We must lose no time in warning County Head Li and in calling out all the militia round here to fight."

Old Chang, Mangzhong and Chun'er set off at once to take a message to town, while the district head and Gao Sihai went to summon the militia.

Chun'er rushed down the dike crying frantically to Mangzhong:

"Hurry! It will be dreadful if we don't get there first. How's your leg? Does it hurt?"

"It's all right." Mangzhong hurried after her. "Keep your voice down on the way."

Gritting his teeth, he forged ahead of her, for at a time like this what young man is willing to be left behind by a girl? Old Chang caught up with them too.

Instead of taking the highway to town they hurried down a shorter path through the fields. Their legs brushed against heavy ears of ripening wheat covered with the evening dew. Mangzhong, still leading the way, put all his weight on one leg as he ran.

They must get there before the enemy to protect their liberated soil. And they had passed Huang Village before they heard the first cock crow and the sleepy twittering of birds. Villages, woods, paths and wheat fields were not passive spectators but breathed encouragement. By degrees the dark path grew clear and smooth for them. The countryside was spoiling for a fight. The plain urged her sons and daughters to make haste to resist the traitors who had betrayed their land.

They heard Tian Yaowu's troops set out from Ziwuzhen. Horses thundered down the highway.

If Tian Yaowu reached the town first, the villagers hereabouts would be plunged into all the horrors of night again. But if Mangzhong and Chun'er outstripped him, their folk could continue down the road to happiness and realize the young people's lofty ideal.

Ahead of them now the county town, its wall demolished, lay glimmering in the starlight.

The sight struck a chill into the hearts of all three. Had it been a wasted effort, after all, pulling down the city wall? How were they to defend the place now and repulse the enemy's surprise attack?

52

Mangzhong's party reached town first. Barely had he warned the militiamen on guard and sent Chun'er and Old Chang to alert the county head, when up galloped Tian Yaowu's cavalry.

"Halt! Give the password," shouted the militiamen from behind the mound where the West Gate had stood.

"Are your ears stuffed with wax? Don't you know your own people's voices? I'm Regiment Commander Gao." Gao Ba had already ridden up the slope.

"What have you come back for?" asked a militiaman.

"The enemy's on the march," was Gao Ba's reply. "We've come to defend the town."

"Who are those men behind you?"

"Detachment Commander Gao's troops."

"You renegade!" Mangzhong fired. Gao Ba's horse reared up, then fell to the ground.

Gao Ba picked himself up unwounded from the dust and ran back to join Tian Yaowu. Mangzhong gave the order to fire. But the militiamen's rifles and bullets were old, their marksmanship poor. And the size of the enemy force demoralized them, for they knew they could not hold up such a troop. As the cavalry charged the town from different sides, Mangzhong ran as fast as he could to the county office.

Li Peizhong had rung up army headquarters the previous day and learned that things were tense: the Japanese might launch an assault from the east. She had no inkling, however, of Gao Ba's desertion and Zhang Yinwu's surprise attack. The other members of the county committee had gone out to mobilize the villagers, leaving her to prepare for evacuation. She had the public grain carted out of the city and the chief criminals escorted by guards to different villages. She sent most of the cadres off, too, on various missions. That evening she gathered important documents into the white embroidered satchel which she kept by her, ready to go to the district the next morning. She was having a short rest on her plank bed when shots sounded at the West Gate. The next moment Chun'er and Old Chang rushed in and, snatching up her satchel and pistol, she followed them out. They were confronted by Tian Yaowu and Gao Ba. Tian flashed his torch on them, then raised his sub-machine gun and opened fire. Peizhong tossed her satchel at Chun'er before crumpling up on the race track. The other girl hastily threw a hand-grenade which sent Tian and Gao scuttling away.

"Carry her off!" Chun'er shouted to Old Chang as she groped on the ground for the satchel.

Old Chang lifted the county head on to his back. Chun'er

led the way and soon they ran into Mangzhong with some functionaries and townsfolk. Together they dashed out of the city where Tian Yaowu's troops were looting shops and houses and starting fires. Chun'er wept as they retreated and, keeping close behind Old Chang, kept asking:

"Is she very bad?"

"She'll be all right."

Actually Old Chang feared that Peizhong's wound might prove fatal, for his hands were soaked with her blood. But when he listened intently he could just hear her breathing. At least she was still alive.

Old Chang raged inwardly. With his own eyes he had seen that swine Tian Yaowu try to kill her. A useless weakling so vicious to his own wife! Never again would he work for One-eyed Tian.

They carried Peizhong to a small village and fetched a doctor for her.

"We fell down on the job," said Chun'er remorsefully. "Going, one was limping; coming back, we had to carry a casualty. One wounded by the Japanese, one by Zhang Yinwu."

They waited for their main force to retake the county town.

But they waited in vain. That afternoon, without firing a single shot, the Japanese entered the city and Tian Yaowu respectfully handed over its "defence" before withdrawing to Ziwuzhen to act as the enemy's right wing.

Traitors' rule was quickly restored in Ziwuzhen. Every democratic organization was searched, many villagers were arrested; resistance signboards were smashed, documents and newspapers burned, and the night school closed. Tian Yaowu sent two guards to stand in front of his father while One-eyed Tian addressed the people at the cross-roads, calling on them to elect a village head. Although a fair crowd had assembled, no one spoke. One-eyed Tian, suddenly modest, declared:

"Don't imagine I want to take office again. I don't. While the Eighth Route Army was here, you know very well how all of you treated me, but I don't hold it against you. We'll wait and see. I'm not standing for office again. But if there's no one else, what about Old Jiang? It was thanks to his son-in-law Gao Ba that they drove out the Reds this time and rescued our village."

Meanwhile Tian Yaowu at home had trussed Old Wen up by his ankles in the stable above a pile of cow-dung. A whip in his hand, Tian sat down on the edge of the *kang* on Old Wen's shabby quilt, and set about a cross-examination.

"You're a Communist!" he hissed through clenched teeth.

"Not I."

"What about Old Chang?" Tian showed the whites of his eyes.

"I wouldn't know about him."

"Tell me, do you support the Kuomintang?" Tian gave a crafty smile.

"I haven't seen what they're like. You'd better tell me."

"I'm one." Tian nodded his head.

"Oh, are you?" Old Wen gritted his teeth and was silent.

"Why don't you speak?" bellowed Tian. "Do you support the Reds?"

"I'd never seen Communists a year ago. Now I've seen them, heard their ideas and watched how they put them into practice. When Japan invaded China all of us panicked; but when the Communist Party came and led us to resist Japan, folk like me stopped feeling lost. Most of the Eighth Route Army cadres come from poor families and the soldiers are village boys too. Their officers don't bully you but explain things — they're not out for money like the old officials. Since they came the poor in our village have had hope. Old and weak, widows and orphans, have all been looked after. The women have gone to school and learned a whole lot. Nobody falls dead of hunger on the road any more; thieves don't break in at night; doors don't have to be bolted. There are no more money-landers out to ruin you, no swindlers, no kidnappers. I don't know what the Communist Party will do in future, but I'm all for what they've done so far."

"And you still say you're not a Red?" roared Tian Yaowu. "You've as good as admitted you are."

"Can I ask you something, sir?" gasped Old Wen. "Aren't we uniting to fight Japan? Why stab the resistance troops in the back and open up the way for the Japanese?"

"You bastard, it's not for you to question me. You'll hang there until you recant."

"I'll never recant as long as I live." Old Wen closed his bloodshot eyes.

One-eyed Tian, coming home just then, disapproved very strongly of his son's behaviour. Snatching the whip away from him, he protested:

"This won't do — he's worked here for years. Old Wen has let us down badly, I admit, but you can't do this to him. You're used to flogging your men in the army, but army discipline won't do at home. The wheat will soon be ripe and we'll need Old Wen to harvest it. It's true he's a pig-headed old fool, but that's all. He's been led astray by Old Chang. Hurry up and untie him."

Zhang Yinwu came to the village too, and One-eyed Tian nearly went down on his knees to ask whether the Central troops could hold out this time or not. But Zhang Yinwu's face was black. Although they had worsted the Eighth Route Army today, he was well aware that this district had undergone a thoroughgoing change since he had lorded it here this time last year. In his view, the villagers had been corrupted.

He ordered the peasants to kill pigs and chickens to entertain his men. Once more Old Jiang's work was cut out for him.

"How can you say I'm robbing your coop?" he asked one family. "I'm the new village head, I'd have you know."

"Haha, if you hadn't told us we wouldn't have known," said the woman of the house. "You'd better have your rank and title published in the newspaper, or hang a sign on your back. I've just finished a bowl of porridge, don't make me throw up."

"There's no call to talk like that," said Old Jiang sternly. "I'm warning you: the power has changed hands and General Zhang's here in our village. This isn't like under the Eighth Route when trash like you could talk any nonsense you pleased. You'll have to watch your tongue."

"We're not afraid of you." She saw him out scornfully.

In one day and one night Zhang Yinwu's troops transformed Ziwuzhen out of all recognition. That evening some villagers cursed bitterly as they picked up torn and trampled clothes from the ground, others wept in their empty pigsties. The streets were deserted as if curfew had been imposed. Every gate was closed tight. Children wept for fright in their parents' arms, and mothers whispered as they suckled their babes, "The wild cats have come!"

Goods were secretly hidden away, for everyone knew that these Kuomintang troops were only the forerunners of the Japanese. Ziwuzhen was rehearsing for the Japanese entry. Everything of use must be cleared out of the way.

It seemed to the villagers that they were back in July of the previous year. Only then the Japanese were still far away, now the brigands were at their gate.

That evening the only lively households in the whole of Ziwuzhen were those of One-eyed Tian and Old Jiang.

53

As soon as the young folk had gone, Chun'er's old neighbour closed the wicker gate tight, then bolted and locked it. Instead of letting the hens out the next morning, she scattered a handful of grain inside their coop. But the silly creatures knew nothing of the trouble in the village, and at noon the big speckled rooster crowed lustily.

Granny hurried out from the cottage, scolding softly:

"Hush! Zhang Yinwu's soldiers are outside. They'll come in if you're not quiet. You'll be plucked and put in the pan."

Presently the stupid rooster crowed again. The old woman kicked the coop hard.

The next moment strangers were clamouring at the gate. Before she could reach it, two of Zhang Yinwu's men had climbed the fence and jumped into the yard. The older of the two had a Northeastern accent, the lad with him spoke the Henan dialect.

"Why lock your gate in broad daylight, old woman?" asked the older man.

"I heard you'd come," was her reply.

"We aren't Japanese devils, what are you afraid of? When the Eighth Route Army was here, you fed them well and made them sleep on your *kang*. When we come, before you've even set eyes on us, you lock your gates. We're all Chinese troops, why treat us so differently? Have you any hens? Give us one."

"I've an old rooster, I can't stop you from taking that.

It's his fault anyway for crowing. But don't say I've given it to you."

"Haven't we had a rough time of it?" demanded the older soldier. "We made a forced march from the Northeast to the interior, from the interior to your village here. Are you telling me we haven't had a rough time?"

"What have you been rushing about like that for?" she asked.

"To resist Japan and recover lost land!" they reeled off in unison.

"Have you fought the Japanese?"

"Not yet." The young fellow grinned.

"How much land have you recovered?"

"Yesterday we took back your county town," said the lad. "But then the Japanese moved in. That wasn't our fault, we were ordered to withdraw."

They turned to each other then, ignoring her.

"What the hell is it all about anyway?" the young soldier asked his companion. "We marched up from the rear to resist Japan, so we were told. Why did we give the Japanese the first place we captured?"

"I know why," replied the other. "Ever since the loss of the Northeast, the higher-ups have been cheating us like this. Resist Japan, they say. Well, now that I've been in the army for ten years they can't fool me about fighting Japan. It's the Reds they want to fight."

"Why fight the Reds? What quarrel do we have with them?"

"The Reds are fighting Japan. Didn't you see the way, soon as we'd taken the county town from them, we offered it with both hands to the Japanese?"

"But doesn't that make us traitors?" asked the lad.

"I'm not saying it doesn't. Confound it! You can't blame folk for looking down on us."

Granny had followed this exchange with great interest. It struck her that these men were open to reason.

"What we country folk hate worst is traitors," she said with a smile. "And what we like best is resisting Japan. That's why we like the Eighth Route Army so much, because they're going all out for the resistance. I don't mind telling you, I've had Eighth Route men in and out of this little yard and I think the world of them. They're not only good to me, calling me aunty and sweeping the yard, fetching firewood or turning the mill, but the officers are just as good to their men — you never saw anything like it. Their regiment and company commanders treat the men under them like brothers. They eat and dress alike, have meetings and study together, and if a soldier is the least bit poorly his officer rushes round to look after him — he couldn't do more for one of his own family. He takes the sick man the best there is to eat, brings him the thickest quilt and goes out of his way to make sure he's comfortable. If relatives come they're welcomed by everyone, a man's parents become 'uncle' and 'aunt' to his whole platoon, and the same goes for brothers and sisters. These troops are one big family, I do declare. That's why I'm sure they'll win the war. Yes, the Eighth Route Army is bound to beat Japan and save us all. But is it like that in your army?"

"Ours? Huh!" exclaimed the young soldier. "Our officer's the king of hell, we soldiers are dirt to him. If you're ill he can hardly wait for you to die so as to draw your ration and pay. You won't get decent treatment unless you're his cousin."

"What I say is this," confided the old woman. "Either don't join up, or join the Eighth Route Army. They have a good name, decent treatment, and the people welcome them — what more could you ask?"

"Why, aunty," replied the old soldier, "you talk better sense than that braggart political instructor of ours. Don't treat us as strangers, aunty. I know someone in your village."

"Tian Yaowu or Gao Ba, I suppose. If that's who, I don't care what you do, we shan't hit it off."

"It's not them I mean but a girl."

Granny said nothing.

"A slip of a girl," he persisted. "It's too bad her name's slipped my mind. Last July, when our unit broke up and was legging it south, I got left behind. For fear someone would do me in on the road, I hid in a sorghum field with nothing to eat for days. That girl saw me, fetched me some clothes to change into, and brought me food so that I could go on my way. Before leaving I gave her my rifle."

"Then I know who you mean. That's my niece, Chun'er. That gun of yours joined the resistance long ago."

"I've been grateful to her ever since." The old soldier beamed. "Do call her and let me thank her."

"She's run away."

"Why should she run away?"

"Because she's in the resistance. When your lot marched in to arrest and kill all the villagers in the resistance, she upped and left."

"Well, isn't that too bad!" he exclaimed. "I've really let her down. I told her I was going to the Northeast to join the Anti-Japanese Amalgamated Army, but on the road the Kuomintang nabbed me again. Then they spun this tale about going north to fight Japan. When we arrived here I thought I'd be able to see the girl who saved me. Now it seems we're in different camps. We soldiers have no quarrel at all with the Eighth Route Army, aunty. When she comes back, tell her I asked after her. We'll go now."

"All right." The old woman opened the gate for them. "Do you want that rooster or not?"

"Have a heart! Don't rub it in." The two men grinned.

Meanwhile Tian Yaowu was conducting a propaganda campaign in Ziwuzhen. He ordered Old Jiang to assemble the villagers in the primary school. A long time went by, but the only ones to arrive were a dozen or so old men, some of them deaf. Tian Yaowu went up to the platform to harangue them.

"We've come to wipe out the Communists because they're wicked people," he declared. "You've all seen their wickedness for yourselves. Since their arrival they've turned our village upside down, stopping sons from respecting their fathers, daughters-in-law from obeying their mothers-in-law, the poor from fearing the rich, and hired hands from fearing their masters. Labourers have been holding meetings, making speeches, learning to read and write and trying to run the village. This is unheard of, quite impermissible. Resist Japan, indeed! Resisting Japan is up to our government and army, not something for peasants to raise a shindy about. It's not for you to meddle in affairs of state. In future you're all forbidden to resist. The poor are not to have guns. From now on, hired hands are forbidden to hold meetings and women are not to go to school or sing and dance the *yangko*. Rich and poor, men and women, must keep their proper places. No changes are allowed, everybody must obey orders. As from today we've abolished the levies you paid the Reds and you'll pay land tax instead. Do you understand? I'm passing on the orders of Generalissimo Chiang."

He left after making this speech and the old men dispersed with heavy, fearful hearts. For their sons had not turned against them, nor had their daughters-in-law been disobedient. They employed no hired hands, their own sons were working for others. Now fair levies were being abolished, and the millstone that had been lifted from their necks threatened to crush them once more.

54

At this critical time the wheat ripened. There had been ample rain the previous year on either side of the Hutuo to produce a fine crop of wheat on the white sandy soil as well as on the black loam. The heavy ears were swelling visibly and if you picked one and opened it, you found eighty plump grains inside. The wheat had grown as lusty and even as if hewn with an axe. A shove against one end of the crop set the whole golden mass swaying like a lake ruffled by the wind.

There's an old saying: Snatch your wheat in autumn. Even in normal times harvesting is rush work. A sudden storm may flatten the crops, a few days of rain may rot the grain, while unless the fields are cleared in time that holds up the autumn sowing. None of these things were what worried them this year. No, they were afraid of the Japanese in town and Zhang Yinwu's men posted round Ziwuzhen, wolves who prowled at dusk, who were out to rob the people of the fruit of their toil.

The villagers said, no need to hire patrols to watch our wheat this year: four pairs of eyes are fixed on it. On one side the Japanese and Kuomintang, on the other the peasants themselves and the Eighth Route Army. The Japanese in town had started bringing in truckloads of empty sacks from Anguo and seizing draught animals and threshing-fields near the town. Old Jiang, as head of Ziwuzhen, was searching for the old census and property records in order to replace the fair levy with a land tax.

It was for the wheat that the enemy had come.

The county government of the resistance base told all districts to organize armed guards for the crops.

The instructions were that neighbouring villages should join forces to get in the harvest. Mangzhong and Chun'er joined the militia and stood guard every day on the river bank. Gao Sihai was put in charge of the harvesters of Ziwuzhen and Five-dragon Temple, and his cottage became a headquarters once again.

Today they were to reap the wheat south of the river. Old Gao had prepared every family in advance, while Qiufen had approached the women separately. The peasants got up at cockcrow and assembled with their sickles on the dike in old, patched clothes and tattered straw hats, hats that had come through countless wheat harvests and weathered countless storms. Gao Sihai stepped out of his cottage with a rifle on his back, a sickle at his belt. This was a sickle he had used for years, its blade razor-sharp, curved and bright as the crescent moon now sinking towards the horizon. After only a few words to his brigade, the old man led them off to the fields.

The peasants, already divided into teams, set to work as soon as they reached their appointed places. They made a clean job of the reaping and bound their sheaves tight, each working at top speed. This was not the usual contest among themselves but a race with their two enemies. On the loamy soil they reaped with sickles, on the sandy river flats they used their hands, whirling the wheat high and slapping it against the soles of their bare feet as they surged forward through the dust.

271

By sunrise half the reaping was done. Whips cracked as carts bowled along the roads both east and west of the village. Forks flashed in the sunlight as they loaded the wheat. A team of women headed by Qiufen carried out food in earthen pots and reed baskets, while others brought along buckets of fresh well water. The children, too, were organized to follow behind as gleaners.

Five-dragon Temple had threshing-floors prepared with trestles set beside them, where lusty young men, stripped to the waist, stood ready with choppers. As soon as the carts unloaded the sheaves, women carried them to the trestles.

At noon they started spreading the wheat out to dry. From time to time they turned it and raked it flat. In the afternoon they yoked donkeys to stone-rollers and whipped them into a trot. They carried off the wheat stalks with pitchforks, heaped the grain together, tossed and winnowed it, and stowed it away in sacks.

That evening the militia and the reapers crossed to the north bank of the river. In three days and three nights they cleared the land and harvested all the wheat, which filled the bins of each household to overflowing. The fields looked like a shaved head with nothing but the tender green leaves of spring crops rustling in between the stubble.

Our troops were now attacking the Japanese on the outskirts of the plain. Since this was a new detachment, for the first few days they had dodged the main enemy force, marching at full speed day and night. For new recruits this was excellent training for battle, as the strict rules on the march taught them discipline and each man learned to size up the situation, decide on a course of action, and get to know the enemy's ways and his weaknesses.

First they harried the Japanese on the highway from Gaoyang to Baoding. And when the enemy withdrew his depleted forces from Shenze and Anguo, our men cut them off, destroyed the road near Tanghe and wiped out two whole contingents. Finally the Japanese fell back from Gaoyang to Baoding.

The day of the Japanese retreat from Shenze, the militia attacked Zhang Yinwu's men in Ziwuzhen. Gao Ba and Tian Yaowu fled to southern Hebei.

When this danger was past, Li Peizhong was still laid up. Mangzhong returned to his army post in town, while Chun'er and Old Chang went back to Ziwuzhen.

The days were scorching during the wheat harvest, but the night air was cool when stars clustered overhead and a fresh breeze blew. After supper the villagers of Five-dragon Temple took low stools or hassocks plaited of new wheat stalks to the flat clean threshing-floor, in the centre of which a huge rick of wheat stalks glimmered silver in the dark and scented the air.

There the peasants cooled off and recovered from the day's exertions, glad because they had successfully safeguarded their wheat. After the women had washed the pots and bowls, they latched their gates and came too, a child on one arm, a big mat over the other. They spread these mats behind the men and crooned lullabies to the children on their laps until the little ones closed their eyes and could be laid down to sleep.

This was a time of rejoicing in the village. The women listened quietly as the men chatted. The evening breeze ruffled their hair, stars twinkled above, at their feet was the soil won back from their enemies. Many were the tales of bygone wars and stratagems they had heard here. Times past counting they had listened with tears or low laughter to the adventures of high-hearted men and women who won through misfortunes to happiness in the end.

There's a saying, "The mind learns from stories, the heart is stirred by plays." In fact there had long been a clear class distinction in the recreations of the villagers. One-eyed Tian, when he had eaten and drunk his fill, would take a seat to his threshing-floor and tell episodes from the *Romance of the Three Kingdoms*, a book he swore by, from which he had drawn all his knowledge. But his audience consisted of the few rich men in the village, a couple of merchants who had made money outside, and the old, retired school teacher. The peasants had no inclination to join them. They all hurried to Five-dragon Temple to listen to stories that were more to their liking.

These last few days on the threshing-floor there, Bian Ji had performed a new ballad about the resistance. For the singing parts he insisted that Gao Sihai should accompany him. At first Old Gao declined. He was too busy. But enthusiasts set ready a table and stools for them as soon as dusk fell, and brought a big jug of boiled water from the canteen. Some even brought clappers and fiddles. So in the end the old man was forced to play at least one or two tunes each day.

Bian Ji needed no urging, however. He saw it this way: his hands soon ached if he reaped, he couldn't carry sacks, and he wasn't up to much as carter or ploughman, but at least he could do his best as a propagandist.

After he'd finished one story today he said it was time to rest — he had to get up early to hoe his late maize. At once some youngsters protested:

"What's the hurry, Brother Bian Ji? Give us another. We'll hoe your fields for you first thing tomorrow, without even asking for a meal. How about that?"

Then Bian Ji moistened his throat with water from the pitcher, picked up his clapper made from a broken plough-

274

share, and started a new recitation. If the truth be told, he'd have gladly gone on all night.

The peasants listened entranced, in absolute silence. Even when clouds darkened the sky in the northwest and rain began to fall, they were reluctant to leave. They took shelter under the trees.

"Go on, finish it," they urged. "We'll leave when it starts to rain hard."

Actually, there was nothing sensational in the story Bian Ji was telling. He had simply embroidered a little on their struggle to protect the wheat in Five-dragon Temple. In the main, however, he had stuck to the facts.

55

Soon it was raining harder, just the rain they needed for the late autumn sowing. When Bian Ji's story ended, his audience hurried home, the women bending forward to shelter the babes in their arms, the men holding hassocks over their heads for protection. Bian Ji slipped his clapper into his pocket and strode off bareheaded, as if impervious to the wind and rain. Alarmed for the safety of his fiddle, Gao Sihai wrapped the precious instrument in the skirt of his worn padded gown rather put out, but this slowed him up.

As he turned off from the village to the dike, he heard someone call his name.

"Wait a bit, Uncle Sihai!" Old Wen came running up. "I've something I'd like to ask you."

"Come back with me, then, to my cottage out of this rain."

"Rain at this time of year won't hurt you. No amount of Buddhist canons or sacrifices would get us a good downpour like this before. Funny, isn't it? The Kuomintang brought us flood, drought and hailstorms, but the Eighth Route Army's brought us good weather. As soon as the wheat is in, we can sow the next crop. What I wanted to ask you was this: Shall I go on working for One-eyed Tian or not?"

"Where will you go in times like these if you throw up your job?"

"I'm fed up with that family. They darn near did for me the other day, why wait to be trussed up like that again? I reckon I'm not too old or weak to earn my keep as an odd job man. Why must I stick with the Tians?"

"I don't like your being there either," said Old Gao. "But why not take a broader view? Right now, our main enemy is Japan and our tussle with One-eyed Tian is part of the resistance. If you take off, it'll make things harder for us."

"So long as I eat his rice, he's the master and I'm his man. Living under his roof, walking on his land, I have to do as he says. Once I leave, things will be different. I'll be as good a man as he is."

"Our job in the villages is to grow all the grain we can to help the front. One-eyed Tian is against the resistance, but he can't stop it. He hates handing over public grain, but if we work hard on the land and get in more grain, he can't refuse to pay up. Nothing would suit him better than your quitting. If you must go, though, join the army like Mangzhong. Old Chang and the rest can handle the work in the village. Building up our army will pay off in the long run. Go back and talk it over with Old Chang."

They parted at the foot of the dike, and as Old Gao climbed up towards his house he met a woman running down.

"Who's that?" he asked, stepping aside and looking round.

"It's me. Don't you know my voice?"

"Can't say I do. Where are you off to in this pouring rain?"

"I've just been to see your Qiufen." The woman slithered down to the level ground.

Old Wen, who had just reached the river, had recognized her voice immediately. He'd have heard it distinctly from even further away, even if she'd spoken more softly. This was the widow from the east end of the village who had lost her heart to him.

She had seen him too. She hurried over, calling softly: "Hey, wait for me!"

When she caught him up, Old Wen asked:

"What are you doing out in this heavy rain?"

"I went to hear Bian Ji's stories," she said with a chuckle.

"How come I didn't see you?"

"I was sitting right at the back."

The rain, still pattering down steadily, was soaked up by the parched soil. The earth was thirsty after the harvest. The spring crops thrust up curled shoots to catch the rain. This sudden warm shower refreshed them and hastened their growth.

Late as it was and hard as it was raining, Old Wen and the widow sauntered slowly along, glad of this chance to be together. When they reached the river shore, she sat down with her back to the ferry boat, repaired since the Japanese artillery had wrecked it.

"I'm tired," she said. "Let's rest a while."

Old Wen squatted down in front of her and fumbled for his pipe but on second thoughts decided not to smoke.

"What did you go to see Qiufen about?" he asked.

"About us. We can hardly leave things like this, can we? As it is, I can't take the baby outside the house. Will he have to grow up in that poky room and never see the sun?"

"Why shouldn't you take him out?"

"Just think! I'm his mum, but who's his dad?"

277

"Doesn't everybody know?"

"Even if they know, there's something we ought to do."

"What's that?"

"You must marry me!" She twisted away and started crying, her tears mingling with the rain falling on the boat. Soaked as he was with rain, Old Wen felt as if her tears were drenching his heart.

"I want to do the right thing by you and the little fellow," he said. "There's nothing I'd like better than to marry you. But I've no home of my own. I can't ask you to sleep under the trees while I look for odd jobs."

"I don't care if you've nothing," she sobbed. "I'd be happy begging in the streets with you. Besides, nobody has to go begging nowadays."

"What did Qiufen say?" Old Wen looked up.

"She said what we did wasn't really right. We should have got married first. But it wasn't all our fault either, because in the old society women had no free choice in marriage. Now she advises me to marry you. Says that will be better all round."

"The trouble is I've nowhere to live."

"I've worked that out. Haven't I got a two-roomed cottage and a few *mu* of brackish land? I need you to plough and sow it for me."

"That won't do. How can I move into *your* house? Your in-laws would have something to say about that too."

"What can they do? Qiufen says women can inherit property too nowadays. You're more old-fangled in your notions than I am. Why bother with those old rules?"

"I'm taking a broader view," retorted Old Wen. "The main thing right now is to resist Japan and stop the Japanese and Zhang Yinwu's troops from coming back. If they came, what hope would we have? It's not marriage I'm thinking

278

of now, but of quitting my job and joining the Eighth Route Army."

"Better still if you join the army. So long as Zhang Yinwu was here, Su'er kept pestering me till I hardly dared leave the house. If you go to fight Japan that'll give us face, baby and me. But aren't you too old?"

"It's grit that counts. This isn't like looking for a husband, when you ask the fellow's age. Of course I'm on the old side compared with Mangzhong, but I'm as good a man as he is when it comes to working. Better, maybe, as a stockman and farmer."

"You're going to be a soldier," she protested, chuckling. "Not a hired hand."

"They've cavalry in the Eighth Route Army too. So let's settle it that way."

"That's all right with me. But let's get married first. We'll have the wedding the evening before, and the next day I'll see you off to join the army. It's not that I'm backward, mind, but I'm thinking of my good name and of our child. We must be able to look people in the face."

"Well, there's truth in what you say." Old Wen stood up.

Out there in the open country, happiness and hope had dried the tears on her face when Old Wen planted a parting kiss on her cheek.

56

Old Wen went back and told Old Chang his decision to quit work, marry the widow, and join the army.

"Of course, I'll miss you," said Old Chang. "Fellows like us live off the land, but right now we've none of our own. And I certainly won't stop you from joining the Eighth Route

Army. The war comes first. We've no future unless we fight. So don't hesitate about going. When will you turn the job in?"

"Tomorrow morning. I'll ask Chun'er to put me up for a couple of days."

"Good," said Old Chang. "You're getting on for forty. Poor we may be, but we only get married once. We must do this thing properly. The two of us have been mates all these years, but I can't help you with presents for the bride. Any running about you want done, I'll do for you."

The next morning, as soon as Old Wen had fed the cattle, he bundled together his few old clothes and shoes and went to see One-eyed Tian. The landlord said:

"Now see here, Old Wen, you're quitting, I'm not sacking you. Make that clear to the Peasants' Union. The rule is, if the master sacks a man he pays him a year's wages; but if a hired hand quits the job, he's paid for the time he's worked. As it happens, this is a busy spell in the fields and you're letting me down by going without giving notice. But in times like these what can I say? I'll look up my books and work out how much I owe you."

"Old Chang will collect it for me," said Old Wen, walking out.

"We've been master and man for more than ten years and played fair by each other," said One-eyed Tian, following him. "It wasn't right, I admit, trussing you up like that the other day; but that was Yaowu's fault, not mine. We must take the long view, not hold grudges because of trifles. Well, I won't see you off. If things don't work out well, you can always come back."

"Don't worry, I'd sooner starve to death on the road than set foot in this house again."

"What's that you're saying, Old Wen? Are we such enemies? Don't let your temper get the better of you. I tell you frankly, this confounded land is more trouble than it's worth. I'm going to sell it off cheap and stop wearing the foul label 'rich man'. Then I'll join the Peasants' Union and we'll all be one family."

Old Wen was already out of earshot. This last speech was aimed at Old Chang, who was standing by the gate to watch his friend leave. But Old Chang made no reply.

Meantime Old Wen had entered Chun'er's cottage and dropped his little bundle on her *kang*.

"Chun'er, I've quit my job," he said. "Can you put me up for a couple of days?"

"Only too glad to. I'll cook you a meal."

"I can't eat here for nothing." Old Wen grinned. "Let me fetch you some water."

He took the buckets and filled her small vat to the brim, then brought in firewood and sat down to light the stove. Chun'er, mixing dough, laughed at him.

"I got in some wheat, so I'm treating you to steamed buns. That'll be a good day when I've a hefty hired hand like you."

"Don't say that. Hiring hands turns a man's heart black."

"I was only joking. With you here I've much less to do."

"Not for long." He drew a brand from the stove and lit his pipe. "I'm going to put you to a lot of trouble."

He told Chun'er his plan of marrying the widow. She was delighted but said anxiously:

"This is a big thing, I'm not sure I can handle it. I'll ask granny next door to help."

"Yes, ask her over."

Her hands covered with flour, Chun'er stepped outside and called out to her old neighbour that she wanted her advice on something important. Granny promptly came round, and as soon as she knew the business in hand she asked:

"Have you checked your horoscopes? Fixed a lucky day?"

"No need for that," said Old Wen. "Our horoscopes show we're both poor and have had a hard life. No need to choose a lucky day. The double fifth will do."

"Have you hired a sedan-chair? And musicians?" Granny wanted to know. "Maybe we can't afford a big official chair but a small one we must have. And it will look very shabby if you don't have at least four musicians."

"Cut the lot, I say," was Old Wen's reply. "This is war-time, we'll make shift without all that."

"I'm not for making a splash, but not for too quite an affair either," put in Chun'er. "This isn't like last year: now we're a resistance base. Why not ask some young fellows in our village band to play, and offer them a couple of drinks afterwards? That wouldn't cost very much."

"Old Wen doesn't know how to choose good cloth," said Granny. "You go to the fair tomorrow, Chun'er, and get a length to make him a new suit."

"All right," agreed Chun'er. "I'll make a pair of shoes too."

"I feel like a shop-manager who doesn't have to lift a finger." Old Wen chuckled.

The fifth of the fifth month was the Dragon-boat Festival. The day before, some children went to the marsh west of the village to pick rush leaves for their mothers to wrap round sticky rice dumplings. The poorer families couldn't afford these dumplings — not more than a dozen households in Zi-wuzhen made them. Chun'er stayed up hard at work all night, until Old Chang brought along two big carts and Old Wen, dressed in his new clothes, set off for the east end of the village to fetch his bride. Then at last she lay down to rest.

They had thought of having four musicians, but the village

282

band sent eight. And when Old Chang told the Workers' Union that Old Wen was getting married, all the other hired hands were eager to turn out and drive him and his bride round and round the village.

It was not yet light when the bride mounted the cart and was driven off to south of Five-dragon Temple.

At sunrise flutes piped up a march, and Chun'er and her old neighbour made haste to get up. There had been quite an argument about the way to receive the bride, because this was a second marriage and, according to the old custom, after she got down from the cart two young men should carry in big bundles of lighted millet stalks behind her to frighten away the ghost of her former husband. Chun'er said this was simply making mock of women, this cruel way the feudal powers treated widows. Now that there was free choice in marriage and women had a higher status, this wouldn't do. They must show her the same respect as to a new bride. So Granny agreed to dispensing with this ritual.

The courtyard was crowded by the time the bride arrived. Granny and Chun'er made haste to help her inside, then bolted the door. While children hammered on the door and clambered up to tear holes in the window paper, the musicians in the yard raised a cheerful din, playing their flutes and gongs for all they were worth till their faces turned scarlet, the muscles stood out on their necks and their eyes nearly started from their heads.

The old woman and Chun'er were hard at work inside, Chun'er clumsier than usual in her confusion. To show how experienced she was and also to prepare Chun'er for her own wedding, Granny insisted on going through the whole complicated wedding procedure. The bride was quite exhausted by the time the old woman opened the door and the musicians stopped playing.

Tables had been set in the yard, but on each there was only a catty of wine, a dish of bean sprouts and another of fried beancurd. Still everyone made merry as Old Chang and Old Wen went round from table to table offering a toast of thanks. Old Chang announced:

"This is a very simple affair, but you won't hold that against him. You must drink up, everyone, because this is a farewell party too. Tomorrow Old Wen's going off to join the army."

"Good for him!" they cried. "But don't forget, volunteers have to report in within twenty-four hours. Mustn't let his bride hold him back."

"She won't." Old Wen promised, smiling broadly.

That evening Old Chang brought round the cart again and drove Old Wen and his bride to the east of the village. Granny and Chun'er went with them and, after chatting for a bit, carried the lamp outside and closed the door to let the newly-weds have a good rest.

So now Old Wen had a wife and child of his own. A night passes quickly and a peasant who has worked most of his life on the land can tell from the colour of the window paper when it is nearly dawn. From boyhood he had done nothing but toil in the fields, handling green shoots and yellow grain, grubbing for roots in the dirt, working with whip, sickle, plough or hoe under a sweltering sun. Now his rough hands were fondling the wife beside him. From boyhood the sounds most familiar to him were the clatter of horse and cart on the road, the creak of the pulley by the well, and One-eyed Tian's surly orders. He had received nothing but angry looks from his masters. Now he listened to the soft voice of a woman, saw the tender warmth in her eyes.

Still, Old Wen got up betimes, put on his new clothes and

said goodbye to his new wife. He was off to town to find Mangzhong and join the army.

Now that he had a wife and son to care for, he felt responsible for protecting them. And his own happiness strengthened his determination to fight for his country's freedom.

57

His wife saw him to the gate. Their child on one arm, her other hand on the doorpost, she watched him step on to the road.

"Those clothes Chun'er made fit you well," she said. "I like the colour too."

"I don't suppose I'll be wearing them in the army. Once I'm in uniform I'll get someone to bring them home. It'd be a pity to lose them."

"No, don't lose your clothes, and don't go forgetting us either. Can you get photographs taken now in town? It would be grand to have a picture of you in uniform."

"No sense in wasting money," said Old Wen. "Go back in now, I must be off."

Out in the street he looked from left to right. It was still very early, but hired hands and peasants were up and about, as well as members of the defence corps getting ready for drill. To avoid attracting attention, Old Wen decided to slip away by a back street. But Old Chang by the well had already spotted him. He quickly hauled up his bucket, laid his pole to one side and strode over.

"Up so early? Had your breakfast? I meant to call you when I'd finished here. Our whole union's turning out to see you off."

"Don't do that." Old Wen grinned. "You've all got work to do."

"Not at this hour, we haven't. We didn't give Mangzhong a proper send off because we weren't organized then." Old Chang jumped on to a stone roller by the roadside and beckoned to some men with a shout. Several hired hands dropped their buckets and came at a run.

They were all sturdy fellows in their prime. Their jackets, unbuttoned although the air was fresh, showed their broad, sunburned chests. They bounded along like carters flourishing whips, dashed into the primary school and rolled out a big drum. The oldest among them followed behind the drum, whirling two sticks as large as rolling pins.

At the deafening noise he made, children came skipping out from their homes without stopping to put on their pants. Their mothers came at their heels. The men and women of the defence corps fell into line and marched briskly in step with the drum.

"Good Old Wen, off to the front!" they shouted. "Drive out the Japanese!"

What strength was it that stirred and inspired these villagers on the main street of Ziwuzhen, hardening their resolve to defend their home and country? Who was it that had led and taught them?

"Comrades and neighbours!" cried Old Chang from the stone roller. "Old Wen is off to join our Eighth Route Army. Like the rest of us, he's sweated long years for other people. He only got married yesterday, and today he's joining the army. He's a credit to all us working folk, an example to the rest of us. Why is he doing this? Let's ask Old Wen to tell us." With that he jumped down from the roller.

Old Wen tried to get out of speaking, but two hired hands

dragged him over to the roller. Standing up there, he said slowly:

"Why am I doing this? My mates will understand why. I was like a blind man for tens of years, but what's happened since last July has opened my eyes. The Communist Party and the Eighth Route Army have shown me the right way to take. If the Japanese or Zhang Yinwu came back, we'd have no future. The Eighth Route Army is defending our country and will drive away the Japanese. The only way for us working men to free ourselves and all those who have a hard life is by joining the Eighth Route Army."

"You go first, brother. We'll only be a step behind." Nearly twenty hired hands surrounded Old Wen and saw him out of Ziwuzhen.

The thunder of the big drum reverberated far and wide through the fresh morning air. It carried for a good ten *li* around, stirring the heart of the bride in her tiny courtyard.

The din of gongs and drums brought honour to that courtyard, to the listening mother and the babe in her arms. And its echoes would never die away until the victory was won.

At the ferry, Old Wen barred the way and forced his friends to go back. But he found another crowd waiting to welcome him on the dike at Five-dragon Temple.

It was eighteen *li* to town, and as he tramped that eighteen *li* Old Wen re-lived his whole life. By the time he reached town he was hungry. At the cross-roads he saw a small shop selling beancurd junket. He went in and sat down by a clean table near the street. The owner came over, wiping his hands on his apron.

"A bowl with hot sauce," said Old Wen. "And a catty of steamed bread."

He took out his pipe and lit up, watching the carts and soldiers on the road. In the past, if he went to a fair or out on an errand, it was carts and horses that caught his attention — the horses' condition and speed, the driver's skill, the way the awning was fixed, the state of the paint and axles. But today the troops held his attention. They'd changed since last winter. Their uniforms were a motley collection then, and they couldn't keep in step. Today they had standard uniforms, marched in good order and carried their rifles smartly. Their horses were properly saddled.

Who had trained and commanded these men? What had changed these peasants so quickly into a powerful rampart to guard North China? Old Wen would no longer be farming a few *mu* of land or tending a few mules and horses for his master. A higher task was now his. As a soldier in the people's army, he would defend this vast plain and watch over the fate of his homeland.

The food arrived and he ate slowly, keeping his eyes on the passers-by.

This road led to the North Gate and the highway to Baoding. Old faded signs hung from the doors of the inns on both sides. There was not much to be seen today, however, apart from two snack stalls further up the street and a few vendors with crates of vegetables. Old Wen watched an elderly man approach from the north. Unshaven, dusty, his heavily lined face bronzed by the sun. His black cotton suit was stained with sweat and the soles of his shoes were flapping loose — he had fastened them up with cord. He had obviously travelled far and was very weary. But he was the tough sort of fellow who stands out in a crowd. By the look of him, Old Wen reckoned that he'd be able to drive a five-horse cart.

Behind this man walked a middle-aged woman in dark blue. Her hair was as dusty as his, her face equally lined, and she had a tattered black bundle on her back.

At the cross-roads the man waited for her to catch up, then told her with a smile:

"We're nearly there now. It's only eighteen *li* from here. This is the busiest street in our county town. See that stone archway? Built in the Ming Dynasty."

"Let's rest a while then." She spoke with an outlandish accent.

"Whatever you say. We may as well eat something too. Come on, let's have a bowl of beancurd junket. It's seven or eight years since I last ate our local junket."

The old man made his wife sit down on the bench opposite Old Wen. She twisted slightly away and deposited her bundle at her feet.

Old Wen found the stranger's accent so familiar that he looked at him carefully. From the gleam in the old fellow's eyes when he smiled, he recognized his former workmate Wu Dayin, the father of Qiufen and Chun'er!

"You've come back then, Brother Dayin."

The old man stood up, staring, then seized Old Wen's hands.

As the shopkeeper brought the junket, Old Wen said:

"Bring another two catties of steamed bread. Charge it to me. Well, brother! Fancy having you back again with us — you've been missed."

He made Wu Dayin sit beside him. The old man said:

"Seven or eight years I've been gone, and not a day passed that I didn't think of you all. There I was, growing older every year with nothing to show for it, no money for the journey home. This year, after I heard the Eighth Route Army was here and the power had changed hands, I couldn't stay a day longer. Even if it meant begging my way, I had to come home. It's a hard journey, brother. If I hadn't got strong legs through working ever since I was a nipper, I'd

289

never have made it. How are Old Chang and Mangzhong?"

"Both well. Old Chang's chairman of our village Workers' Union. Mangzhong joined the Eighth Route Army last year. I can tell you we've had big changes here. And Qingshan's come back as a detachment commander, how d'you like that?"

"Hear that?" said Wu to the woman. "This detachment commander is our son-in-law."

The woman looked up from her bowl to beam at him.

"Who is this?" inquired Old Wen.

"Your new sister-in-law," said Old Wu. "At least I found a wife while I was away."

"The women here are coming on," Old Wen told her cheerfully. "Once you get home, sister, you must join the Women's Salvation Association. Chun'er is the chairman."

"Chun'er, that's my second girl," Old Wu reminded his wife.

58

In the county town Wu Dayin learned a good deal about his village, gaining a general idea of the new changes in his old home. Old Wen also told him of his marriage and decision to join the army. They didn't part until nearly noon when business picked up in the little shop.

Wu Dayin went on with his wife to Ziwuzhen, covering the eighteen *li* so fast that she had to ask him several times to slow down.

Early in the afternoon they reached Ziwuzhen. The old houses seemed unchanged, but the willows on the dike were taller and denser. Men and women, old and young, had gathered in the square by the cross-roads where a platform had been fixed up on four big stone rollers, with a strip of bright red cloth hanging over it. This didn't seem like a performance, for there were no musicians on the platform, no vendors crying their wares down below. The atmosphere was quiet and rather tense, as if some serious business were being transacted.

Wu Dayin was stopped at the east end of the village by two young militiamen, both carrying rifles, although he assured them laughingly that this was his home and he was able to call one of them by name. His travel-stained appearance and the strange clothes and accent of the woman with him made them cross-question him.

Someone was making a speech on the rostrum at the crossroads. Her shrill, girlish tones carried clearly to where Wu stood.

"Isn't that Chun'er speaking?" he cried. "I'm her dad."

At that one of the militiamen escorted them towards the meeting. Even so he was not fully satisfied and asked:

"Why didn't you get a pass, travelling all this way?"

"You think I flew back from the Northeast without a pass? I figured I wouldn't need one for my own home. How was I to know I'd meet a couple of youngsters who refuse to recognize me? By rights you ought to call me grandad."

"Ha!" The lad shifted his rifle to the other shoulder. "If my own grandad was away so many years, we'd have to question him when he got back. You wait here and don't disturb the meeting. When the woman chairman finishes, I'll tell her you're here."

As Old Wu and his wife waited, he stood on tiptoe to have a look at his daughter and hear what she was saying.

"Women comrades!" Chun'er was crying eagerly. "Today's meeting is to elect our village head and village administration. We must choose a head who'll go all out to resist

Japan, who'd rather die than turn traitor. He'll head our resistance work. In the old days we women couldn't join in elections. The village heads were chosen by a small clique. They had money and gave themselves airs, but they didn't do a thing for us common folk. We're able to vote today because we women have more rights now. We must take this seriously and vote for the one we think will do the best job resisting Japan."

Chun'er stepped back after this speech, and Old Chang came forward. The way he stood reminded Wu Dayin of the days when they'd had operas in the village and had to get a few men to keep order. For the country folk worked themselves into a ferment at a play. At the most exciting part — say that scene in *The Lover in the Chest* when the elder brother wants to open the chest but his younger sister won't — the audience would surge forward, pushing and jostling. Strong young fellows liked to clutch the edge of the stage, just as the rich men in town like to sit in the five front rows. Several would link arms to force their way through the crowd. And as soon as they had their hands on the stage they would heave back so hard that the whole audience staggered backwards and the stout poles supporting the awning threatened to crash down on the stalls outside. The stage started rocking so dangerously that the actors turned pale and the gonging and drumming stopped. Then one of the men responsible for order would step forward, a pipe in one hand, gesturing calmly with the other.

"Now then, friends," he would shout. "What's all this? Do you want to stop the show?"

His firm, reasonable manner soon restored order. Then, smiling, he'd step back behind the orchestra to go on smoking as he watched.

This task of controlling the disorderly crowd was not an

easy one. It could only be entrusted to men who were generally liked and respected and had plenty of self control. Today, though, Wu's old workmate had not stepped forward because of disorder below.

The villagers were clapping. Someone shouted a question and Old Chang answered it. Wu Dayin could contain himself no longer.

"Can't I go over there?" he asked.

"Not until the election's over," said the young militiaman. "I'm going to vote too."

"So am I," declared Wu. "Catch me passing up a chance like this! All those years I worked as a hired hand, I never helped to elect the village head."

"How would you know who to elect? You're only just back. I'll have to find out if you're allowed to or not."

With this the lad made his way to the platform, below which were some tables with two people seated at each, one to record the votes, the other to supervise. Workers, peasants, women and young people, all divided into different groups, took their ballot forms to a table and whispered the name of the man they wanted to elect. This was written down and put in the ballot box.

The young militiaman was so excited about casting his own vote that he forgot to come back. So Wu Dayin walked over to join the rest. Chun'er, the first to spot him, jumped down from the rostrum.

"Chun'er!" cried her father. "We'll talk when we get home, lass. Right now I want to vote."

The villagers agreed to this and gave him a form, which he took to one of the tables. The recorder there asked softly:

"Who are you voting for?"

"For Old Chang," was Wu's reply.

"His full name is Chang Dexing." The recorder smiled. "You've made a good choice."

Soon it was announced that Old Chang had been elected village head of Ziwuzhen. He stepped to the front of the platform to speak briefly about the resistance. Last winter in the fields he had thought Gao Qingshan was joking when he said a labourer could be village head. Yet now this had happened and he couldn't refuse the job but would shoulder the heavy task as best he could. Last of all he called on his old mate Wu Dayin for his impressions of this home-coming.

Wu Dayin went up to the rostrum. He told them he hadn't been long in the Northeast before Japan occupied it and the peasants became even worse off than before. Things were pretty grim up there, and by the time he left Japan had occupied so many other places that he'd had to come back by devious tracks and the journey had taken three months. But he'd seen many new things on that long journey. He'd discovered there were guerrillas everywhere — on both sides of the railways, in the plains, villages, hills and forests and beside every river and lake. Wherever the Eighth Route Army went, the peasants banded together against Japan and set up resistance bases large and small. Not all of these were linked up and sometimes the enemy drove a wedge into them, but in fact they formed one long continuous line, held together by the determination of the Eighth Route Army and the policy of mobilizing the whole people to join in the resistance. That long, long line stretched from Yan'an in Shaanxi, Chairman Mao's headquarters, to the guerrillas on the bank of the Yalu River. This was a line to attack the enemy, mobilize the people and set up political power for the resistance. This was the way they'd drive out the Japanese. After seeing how keen his neighbours here were to resist, he was glad to be able to tell them that there were huge parts of China just like Ziwuzhen. And he wanted to work for the resistance too.

As the villagers crowded round to listen to him, Gao Sihai and Qiufen arrived. Only One-eyed Tian and Old Jiang withdrew to a distance and smoked with lowered heads, not wanting to hear.

There was a family reunion that day in Chun'er's cottage. Big changes had taken place in Ziwuzhen and Five-dragon Temple during the last year. Gao Qingshan, Gao Xiang and Wu Dayin who had been forced to leave home had returned, while many like Mangzhong and Old Wen had left the village to fight. Those who had returned and those who had left, whether parted or together, were united by the same determination to defend their country and drive out the invaders.

Yet others, like Tian Yaowu and Gao Ba, had left, come back, then left again. But as they were doing nothing to defend their home and only making trouble for their own people, the village no longer needed or trusted them.

59

That afternoon Qiufen came over again with a basket of flour for her parents. Before leaving she took Chun'er aside and said:

"The time you've been waiting for has come. This evening."

"Where?" asked Chun'er, flushed and smiling.

"At our place, after supper. Don't be late."

"Why in your place? Is there no Party branch in our village?"

"There aren't many Party members yet, so our two villages

have a joint branch. What difference does it make, anyway? The Communist Party is one big family all over the world. It can't be divided by national boundaries, let alone by a single river."

"Will it be a big meeting?" Chun'er wanted to know. "Will I have to speak? Tell me, sis, what I ought to say."

"From today on we'll be revolutionary comrades. That means we'll be closer than sisters. Don't expect other people to tell you what to say. Just say what's in your heart."

Chun'er nodded, and Qiufen left.

The girl suddenly felt very solemn. For joining the Party was not just a cause for rejoicing, it meant shouldering heavy responsibilities too. From now on her life would belong to the revolution and she must take her share of the Party's responsibility to the people. She had given it her youth and future. The Party would train her and give her more strength to carry out the noblest, most glorious tasks.

Taking leave of her parents, she set off for Five-dragon Temple.

Dusk was falling but red clouds brightened the western sky as Chun'er walked through the fields. A bird with a green insect in its beak skimmed over the dense crops just in ear to where some fledglings were cheeping. The silky red tassels of the maize were as bright as the flowers a bride wears in her hair. A new look-out like a small shack on stilts had been built in a plot by the path, and there sat a young couple, swinging bare feet in the air. They were keeping an eye on their musk-melons which were now as large as rice bowls.

"Started picking them yet?" Chun'er smiled up at them.

"Not yet," replied the young woman. "The melons are ripe, we're just waiting for someone with good luck to spare."

"Aren't you lucky enough? Look at you — sitting pretty!"

The young man nudged his wife, who jumped down with a

smile, picked up a large yellow melon from beside the ditch and offered it to Chun'er.

"This year we're in luck. That mouth of yours was made for good fortune. You must take our first melon to give us a good start."

"What good fortune have I?" asked Chun'er.

"Anyone can see you're pleased about something today. If you eat this melon, we're bound to do well this year. We'll have no flood or drought, no pests of any kind."

"All right. Here's to the success of a handsome young couple." Chun'er split open the melon. "You take care of pests and I'll take good care that the Japanese don't overrun your melon patch."

"Didn't I say you were just the person we needed to bring us luck?" The young wife swung herself back on to the look-out.

Chun'er walked on happily, eating the melon, turning back for one last look at the husband and wife who were laughing as they crawled inside their shelter to sleep. It seemed to her that the ground beneath her feet, the sky overhead, the crops and local people, all expected great things of her.

By the time she had crossed the river and climbed the dike, the evening star was bright in the sky. Qiufen, waiting at her door, led Chun'er in.

Gao Sihai was watching gravely as Bian Ji fixed up a portrait of Chairman Mao. Presently the artist turned round to say with a smile:

"This took some doing, uncle. I asked everybody who came from Yan'an for a photograph of Chairman Mao, and finally Brother Qingshan borrowed one for me from a veteran of the Long March. I was so pleased, I bought the best paper and brushes and waited till my wife and the children were asleep and I could work in peace. Three whole nights it took me to do this. How do you like it?"

"You've done a good job." Old Gao nodded approvingly. "He's looking at us to encourage us. Through all those years of bitter struggle he's led the Party to victory. All that comes out in your picture."

"You mean that?" Bian Ji coloured up with pleasure. "You're my best critic, Uncle Gao. What d'you say, Qiufen? I'd like to have your opinion."

"It's grand," said Qiufen. "Looking at this portrait, I feel Chairman Mao is here directing us."

"And you, Chun'er? I drew this as well as I could for your admission to the Party today."

"I'm too happy for words." Chun'er's face was radiant. "I'm only a poor girl, but from now on Chairman Mao will be leading me."

"Let's start our meeting." Bian Ji drew himself up. "First I'll tell Chun'er who's who. Comrade Gao Sihai is secretary of the Five-dragon Temple and Ziwuzhen Party branch, I'm in charge of propaganda, and Comrade Qiufen's in charge of organization. Today, comrades, we're admitting Chun'er to the Party. We're admitting her because she's the daughter of a hired hand, Wu Dayin, who fearlessly opposed the landlords who oppressed us, because she's carried out her war work so bravely, because she loves the Party and is true to it."

"Chun'er, you're young," said Gao Sihai. "You must learn the history of our Party. Think of all the men and women who've worked hard and not been afraid to give their lives for the cause. Qiufen, show her the red flag we've kept."

Qiufen opened a battered red chest and took out the flag which her husband had carried twelve years before, during the peasants' revolt. Qingshan had planted it on the dike

298

when they fought the enemy there. One corner of it was stained purple with his blood. After Qingshan left, his father had told Qiufen to keep it safely. The flag, still in good condition, its colours unfaded, had inspired the villagers for all these years.

When Gao Sihai spread this red flag out on the table in front of Chun'er, all that it represented — that fierce struggle by the River Hutuo and the peasants' splendid ideals — made her heart beat even faster.

She raised her right hand and said softly yet resolutely:

"I mean to be a good, loyal Party member. I'll struggle hard and not be afraid to give my life."

After this ceremony, Old Gao explained the situation in Ziwuzhen, introduced the other Party members to Chun'er and assigned her to the group led by Old Chang.

Then her sister, seeing her down to the river, gave her some advice on the way to work from now on, the best way to unite and lead the villagers.

60

The cavalry company in Gao Qingshan's detachment had recently been brought up to regimental strength, and Mangzhong was one of its squad leaders. Old Wen was now assigned to this squad. He had not had high expectations and would have been satisfied with the job of a groom, but Mangzhong issued him with a new rifle and the best horse in the whole unit. For a new recruit in our army is treated like the youngest boy in a family — he gets preferential treatment. Not that Old Wen was young. He was the oldest man there.

During the twenty years and more in which Old Wen had worked as groom and carter, dozens of mules and horses had passed through his hands. Although bolting horses had kicked and knocked him down, he was known for his skill in breaking in the most unruly colt. He could tell a horse's age from its teeth, its temper from its eyes, its speed from its legs, and its strength from its shoulders. What's more, one crack of his whip could bring down a rearing animal without hurting one hair of its hide. All in all, he was an excellent horse-trainer who turned out strong, healthy and remarkably tractable animals.

As a cavalryman, Old Wen soon learned what was required of horses in the army and the difference between his present tasks and those of a hired hand. Feeding was just as important, but even more important was training the horse to be an extension of his master's body. To achieve this the rider had to show as much consideration for his mount as for his own legs. Old Wen treated his black horse as his best comrade-in-arms. And Blacky, a powerful four-year-old, soon came to understand his wishes and coordinate well with him during manoeuvres.

Old Wen and Blacky made a perfect team, each sensitive to the feelings and needs of the other. He taught Blacky to jump and charge when they stormed a position and to drop swiftly to the ground when they needed cover.

Soon a big campaign was to start. Meanwhile our forces in the Hebei plain were using this respite for intensive training. Before Gao Qingshan's detachment set off for Hejian, Old Wen asked half-a-day's leave to go back to Ziwuzhen and see his wife. The whole trip there and back took him less than four hours, and he only stayed a few minutes talking in the courtyard, for his main purpose had been to show his new uniform and Blacky to his old neighbours, workmates and wife.

The troops set off that evening, the cavalry heading the

way. At Manzhen they forded the Hutuo, at Wumaoying they crossed the River Sha, at Zhanggang they rested for fifteen minutes or so, and by midnight they reached Hejian.

The next day was July 7, the anniversary of the Lugouqiao Incident. Lugouqiao Bridge near Beijing still bore signs of the damage inflicted by the invaders, yet these had served to arouse a mighty nation and put fresh heart into it. Today Lugouqiao Bridge could see with content the heroism of China's sons and daughters.

The review of the troops of the Central Hebei Military Region took place on the old drill ground by the East Gate of Hejian. The dazzling radiance of the rising sun filled the clear sky above the plain. On the review stand a huge red flag flapped in the wind. As young, newly trained buglers blew the signal to fall in, a vulture took flight from the ruins of an old fort nearby. This scene filled the men with fresh hatred of the enemy and eagerness to do battle. It drew the eyes of the peasants ploughing in the fields around.

China's powerfully organized war of national liberation was being waged on a scale unknown before. Commander Lu Zhengcao, Detachment Commander Gao Qingshan and Political Commissar Gao Xiang took their places now on the stand to review the troops, the young Hebei peasants whom they had trained into a resistance force.

The review was followed by a political report from Gao Xiang. He explained the nature and course of the war, why it had to be protracted, and the way to fight a protracted war to a victorious conclusion. He refuted the theory of national subjugation, exposed the theory of capitulation, and criticized the theory of a quick victory. This report was more incisive and better substantiated than the one he had given the previous July. He pointed out the three stages of the protracted war, described its jigsaw pattern, stressed the importance of political mobilization, and carefully explained the principles of strategy and tactics in guerrilla warfare.

Gao Xiang's speech was lively and easy to understand. Soldiers who had fought for a year felt that the political commissar had summarized the experience of them all and clarified the fighting aims of the whole army and people. Each agreed completely with his summary, which redoubled their confidence and gave them fresh strength.

Because they could understand and were so stirred, they listened with close attention. Sitting on the ground, holding their rifles, they commented to each other on the political commissar's eloquence and analytical ability. The intellectuals among them, some of whom tended to be rather arrogant, were so impressed by Gao Xiang's brilliant, far-sighted analysis that they realized how low their own theoretical level was by comparison.

Gao Xiang's report was based on Mao Zedong's *Problems of Strategy in Guerrilla War Against Japan* published in May 1938, and *On Protracted War*, a speech delivered at Yan'an that same year.

These two speeches charted the way of the great War of Resistance. They were simple lessons on the decisive strategy for victory, the guarantee that national liberation would be won.

A few hundred copies of *On Protracted War* were first mimeographed in Hebei and then printed in large numbers. There were editions of every kind, on paper of every description. Cadres studied the work and relayed it to the soldiers, who in turn passed on its ideas to the civilians. As a result, our army advanced while the resistance bases were enlarged and went from strength to strength. This work filled the heart of every true Chinese with confidence in victory.

61

That July an Anti-Japanese Academy was set up in central Hebei. It consisted of a Mass Work College housed in the Number 10 Middle School in Jiuzhou, Shenxian County, and a Military College in the house of a Shenxian landlord who had fled to the interior for fear of the Japanese.

Mangzhong was to go to the Military College to study. Before leaving he sent a message to Chun'er informing her of his plans. He reached Shenxian with his letter of introduction only to find that few students had yet arrived and the buildings were still undergoing repairs. Classes would not be starting for several days. Having time on his hands, he went to Jiuzhou and asked if the Mass Work College was still enrolling students, and if so what the procedure was? He was told they hadn't yet got their full complement. In general, candidates must pass a test; but those recommended by their organization would be admitted even if their cultural level was rather low. On his way back Mangzhong sat down by the roadside, got out his fountain pen, tore a leaf from his notebook and wrote a letter to Chun'er advising her to come and take this test.

He folded the note and walked back to the county town. It was market day there, but because of the harvesting he met nobody from his home parts. Afraid the note would arrive too late if he gave it to the communications station, he waited at the cross-roads.

Towards noon he met a peach vendor who promised to deliver it to Ziwuzhen. To make sure of remembering, this man stuck the note under his peaches.

Chun'er was not too busy nowadays. She had hoed the fields three times, and this year there'd been plenty of rain. With the sorghum ripening there was a lull in the fighting.

The Party had stronger mass support in the village than ever before, and the work was going smoothly. Since her father's return Chun'er's life was much easier too, for her stepmother was very good to her, helping with the cooking and other household jobs. Sometimes Chun'er felt that she was being spoiled.

The morning had been fearfully hot and now most people were having a siesta. Chun'er was dozing when she heard a peach vendor crying his wares. She seldom bought anything good to eat but these peaches came from Shenxian, where Mangzhong was, and so she was tempted to try one. She ran out and found the vendor, just arrived, putting down his load in the shade. Both his crates were full of small peaches.

"How much a catty?" she asked.

"Five hundred." Squatting between his crates, the man was wiping his perspiring face.

"So much for such little ones?"

"These are Shenzhou peaches, I'd have you know — the sort sent as tribute to the Empress Dowager. Just taste one, sweet as honey."

"There's no need for that." Chun'er smiled. "I'll have half a catty."

As she started picking out the best, she saw Mangzhong's note sticking out of the pile of peaches. Chun'er recognized the handwriting at once.

Before the vendor could ask where this Chun'er lived, she'd opened the letter and was engrossed in it. She told the man she'd changed her mind about buying fruit, thanked him for bringing the note and offered him a drink and a rest in her home. When he declined, she ran back. The vendor was pleased by this coincidence, even if it meant selling half a catty less, for he could see that to this girl the contents of the note were sweeter than Shenzhou peaches.

Chun'er's first reaction to the prospect of studying was one of unadulterated delight. But the day before her departure she felt the misgivings of a child leaving home for the first time.

Having collected credentials from the village, district and county and said goodbye to her friends in Ziwuzhen, she dropped in to see her sister at Five-dragon Temple. She hardly closed her eyes that night, and before dawn her father urged his wife to get up and make dumplings for Chun'er's send-off.

Her sole baggage was a satchel with her precious writing brush and some papers, and a wrapper containing a change of clothes and a new pair of shoes.

It is sixty *li* from Ziwuzhen to Shenxian and the day was hot by the time she reached Shuangjing Village. She began to feel quite tired walking all alone, especially as from here on the road was sandy. Luckily it was flanked by fruit trees, in the shade of which she stopped several times to rest. Thanks to plentiful rain, the boughs were loaded with pears.

Chun'er reached Jiuzhou in the afternoon and found it smaller and quieter than she'd expected. The Number 10 Middle School stood in spacious grounds. An impressive pair of cypresses grew on either side of the big red gates above two marble lions. Chun'er had seldom seen such a cluster of substantial buildings, which threw even One-eyed Tian's mansion into the shade. In fact, the school reminded her of a large temple.

A sentry was marching up and down in front of the school gate. Chun'er flushed and her heart beat faster at the thought that she was coming here to study.

She was taken to the office of the dean of studies, a young man apparently fresh from the army, and handed him her letters of introduction.

The young dean questioned her in considerable detail about her work in the village and her life at home, before sending for one of the staff to give her a test. The teacher who did this was an elderly man and, much as he liked the girl's spirited appearance, he frowned dubiously over the result of the test.

"I've never been to school." Perspiration was pouring down Chun'er's face and dripping on to her paper. "I've just studied one book in our winter literacy class."

"Yet you're trying to get into college!" The old man chuckled. "Into university."

"She can make up her general education little by little," said the dean consolingly. "She's got some political understanding and practical experience."

"Well, you'll have to wait till the results are put up." Shaking his head, the teacher took Chun'er's paper, untouched except for some sticky finger-prints. The dean explained where she would find the results, then sent someone to take her off to have a meal.

Chun'er was too worried to eat. Would she be admitted? If not, how could she go back to the village again? Funny, the way sitting over a sheet of paper was more tiring than hoeing several *mu* in the hottest part of summer. Book learning really rather frightened her. Still, the fact that they'd kept her to a meal must mean there was hope. Encouraged by this thought, she got down the bowl of millet with which she'd been toying.

After the meal a slightly older woman in uniform offered to show her round.

"Leave your things in my room," said this woman, who had the same accent as people from Chun'er's district. "You'll be sleeping with me tonight."

She took Chun'er to the sports field, where a crowd of

students were clearing away the debris left here since the school evacuated to the south at the start of the war. Some boys and girls wore uniform, but these were a minority. Most of them came from secondary schools and colleges in Beijing and Baoding. There were barelegged girls in white frocks, others in white, shortsleeved blouses. These obviously came from well-to-do families, and some of them even wore make-up. Their hands were small and white, and they were careful to hold their skirts out of the dirt as they bent gingerly to pick things up. This job was much more in Chun'er's line than taking a test. Her energy and efficiency at once attracted the other girls' attention.

Later they formed a big circle and the girls joined hands with the boys as if this were the most natural thing in the world. But Chun'er found a place between two other girls. As they started circling round, Chun'er reflected that a poor peasant's daughter was lucky to have joined the ranks of these students. Once they began running, however, the students could see that Chun'er far surpassed them not only in her speed and grace but in the serious, whole-hearted way she threw herself into things.

62

When the results were posted up by the gate, Chun'er hurried there with the rest, her heart in her mouth, and started scanning the bottom of the list. To her surprise, her name was among the first. The term started immediately. Since they worked even on Sundays, Mangzhong could only come to see her one evening. He gave her a notebook he'd made himself and a quilt, which Chun'er accepted with a blush because they were not alone.

"Bring me any washing you want done," she said as she saw him out.

"I can do it myself," replied Mangzhong. "We're both studying, how can I waste your precious time?"

As this was a military academy, the discipline was strict. After seeing him off Chun'er went straight back to her class, and none of the girls asked who her visitor was. The young men, some of whom had felt attracted to her, realized from this glimpse of Mangzhong that she had a boy friend already.

They had a very full curriculum with political courses in the morning and military courses in the afternoon. Most of the instructors here were intellectuals who had joined the revolution early and served in the army. They took a keen interest in theory and were eager to do all they could for the resistance. They would hold forth for three hours at a stretch under the huge matting roof fixed up above a courtyard where five hundred students could gather.

Chun'er did well in the military courses, which held her interest completely. In the lectures on politics she could understand about the protracted war and united front, but not dialectical materialism or the role of art and literature in the resistance. Although the instructors did their best, these things were so far outside the range of her own experience that once the class ended all she could remember were the terms "contradiction" and "type".

Chun'er's reading vocabulary was limited and the characters she could write were even fewer. It was hard for her to take notes. To begin with she often sat silent in the discussion groups which met every afternoon under the willows on the sports ground. Her eyes strayed to the distant fields and she would think how much easier and more pleasant it was to sweat at farming than to join in these discussions. She'd gladly have talked about happenings in the villages, but at present their main task was memorizing rules. And in some ways she found the students hard to get on with. A number of them were good at talking and writing but didn't put their principles into practice. They lectured others but set a bad example themselves, or tried to shine not by helping others but by overshadowing them. Chun'er had patience enough not to quarrel over trifles, and she was helpful. If something they did made sense to her, she followed suit. For instance, the other students had high standards of hygiene and washed their hair every week or so by the well in the back yard. The result looked so attractive that, in addition to changing her clothes more often and wearing a skirt, she took to washing her hair more regularly. And everyone admired its glossy black. But some of the rest were only interested in personal cleanliness and would leave the wash-house dirty for other people. Chun'er never did this and she pointed out that it was wrong.

She never made fun of people. If she said something wrong during a discussion, many of the girls giggled surreptitiously. But Chun'er never laughed at them when they were scared by a passing plane or shrieked as if a scorpion had stung them when an insect crawled on their necks. She made allowances for such behaviour, knowing they had grown up in different surroundings from hers.

Some of the girls seemed to understand Chun'er and were good about helping her. After their drill they'd ask her to stroll to the fields. It was just before harvest, the sorghum stood red and tall. The students appreciated the sight without caring how large a harvest the peasants would reap. They would sing at sunset without troubling their heads about whether more rain was needed for the crops. They asked Chun'er:

"Which would you rather be doing, farming at home or studying here?"

"Studying here," was Chun'er's reply. "I'll be more use when I go back. I've too little education."

"What use is a good education?" asked one of the girls. "Production and fighting are the important things now. I'm sorry I've studied so long. I've written to my younger sister telling her to leave school and learn to weave. I envy people like you."

"You must be joking," said Chun'er.

"Not a bit of it. You come from the right sort of family."

"But book-learning is always useful," protested Chun'er. "I hate knowing so little. I mean to study hard, and I hope you'll all help me."

The others, impressed by her earnestness, said no more.

Sometimes Chun'er was puzzled by the strange questions they asked. As they strolled along one day, a girl pointed to a clump of trees and said:

"Which do you like better, Chun'er, willows or date-trees?"

Chun'er knew that each had its uses and replied:

"I like both."

The other girl found this an unsatisfactory answer. She said living in the country had been wasted on Chun'er. Then Chun'er reflected that dates bore fruit and the wood could be made into pegs and axle-trees, while willow wood was only fit to make ladles.

"I like date-trees," she said. "Sweet dates are good to eat."

Still far from satisfied, the other declared:

"Of all trees I dislike dates most. I think they're disgusting: the last to come into leaf, the first to lose their leaves, and always looking so angular, bare and dry. Willows are my favourite. Before spring's even here they start turning green, and they're a lovely sight with their soft tendrils.

They're harbingers of spring and give the plain most of its beauty. They're so hardy too they can live through flood and drought, in hills or on the plains, in hot climates as well as cold. You find them everywhere. And they shed their leaves later than any other tree...."

Chun'er nodded because there seemed to be something in this, but talk of this kind rather bored her.

63

College life was like being in the army. Every day before it was light they ran round the sports ground, there were set times for washing and eating, and one had to be constantly on the alert for the signal to fall in. Lights-out was at a fixed hour every night, leaving Chun'er no time to catch up with her studies. Sometimes she understood a lecture but couldn't remember the terminology and was afraid to speak up in the discussion. It always worried her when she forgot new terms. She worked hard to memorize them.

She lay awake at night thinking over her lessons, and if she suddenly remembered a new term she would get up and dress again. Taking her notebook from her satchel, she would tiptoe into the yard to write it down by moonlight.

One night when there was no moon, she went to the auditorium because there was an oil lamp on the desk there. Having lit the lamp, she carried it to a corner and laboriously wrote out the term.

At this hour her brain and memory functioned best. The whole place was empty except for her and row after row of benches lost in the darkness. A wood-pigeon nesting in the tall willows outside called out a couple of times, then went back to sleep.

The lamp showed how much weight Chun'er had lost in just one month at this college. By the time she had memorized all the terms in her book she was tired out and closed her eyes for a short rest before going back to sleep. But she couldn't help dozing off. As the oil was burnt up, the lamp flickered and went out.

Someone came in and stumbled over a bench by the door. Chun'er thought she was dreaming until she heard a man's voice:

"Come on in!"

"What's the hurry?" A girl laughed softly.

Chun'er was wide awake now, her heart pounding.

"This is a hell of a place, no time to have fun," swore the man. "Yet fresh batches of students keep pouring in, keen to mortify the flesh! Come over here."

"You scared me stiff, calling me in the middle of the night." Chun'er was dismayed to recognize the voice of a girl in her class.

"I told you why, didn't I?" said the man. "I love you."

"You're taking an unfair advantage."

"That's the essence of love, the last stage. Why did it take you so long to dress just now?"

"One of our class called Chun'er is not in her bed. I didn't want her to come back and see me. I suspect she's a Party member."

"Why should that worry you? Take my word for it, she's sneaked out to meet a lover. D'you think they're all holy virgins? To hell with them! They tricked us into coming here by claiming this was a university, but they're drilling us like common soldiers and making us mix with riffraff. I know you're from a good family and have been to a missionary college. We've the same background and education, you and I. That's a good foundation for love."

"You rotter!" The girl backed away. "Those old criteria have gone by the board. Nowadays girls love workers, peasants and old cadres."

"I'm not going to spend my whole life here. So why shouldn't I find a sweetheart in the old way?" He caught hold of her. "This is my idea of living."

Chun'er could have kicked herself for falling asleep and becoming involved in this sordid affair. When the man and girl got up presently to go, he gave her curt instructions.

"Tomorrow or the day after, a Kuomintang commissioner will be coming here. You must get the girl students to give him a big reception. Make them shout: 'Welcome to the delegate sent by the Central Government to lead our college.' Mind you do this. From now on you'll take orders from me."

The commissioner came neither the next day nor the day after. But a strange development threw the school into a ferment. An instructor named Hu had arrived not long ago from the Kuomintang army. According to him the die-hards there had attacked him because he was too radical, and so he had come over. He conducted no regular classes but gave supplementary lectures. He had brought a whole pile of Marxist books and seemed a serious theoretician, always using revolutionary terms. However, he vulgarized dialectical materialism by spicing it with fantastic examples of the lowest sort. Instead of using dialectics to expound the revolution or War of Resistance, he harped on his private life and even stooped to anecdotes about drinking, gambling and whoring.

One day he announced a lecture on free love. Many students felt this was out of place in the middle of their strenuous military training, for such a subject could only lessen young people's political enthusiasm, undermining their discipline and determination to fight. Still, a large crowd gathered in the auditorium. For Instructor Hu's specious arguments and impassioned delivery had convinced not a few that he was a distinguished professor.

As usual he opened with revolutionary phrases, then went on to quote from low-class novels and ballads, cracking jokes like a clown or sentimentalizing like the heroine in an old opera. Revolutionary theory, judging by him, was not the experience won in countless struggles at the cost of brave lives, not a guide for class struggle, the War of Resistance, social reform and cultural development, but a means for him to impress his listeners and win himself a name, a tool for rumour-mongering and trickery.

All students with any judgment, who had come here for the sake of the revolution, soon trooped out in disgust. Chuner was so behind with her classes that she seldom attended any of these outside lectures, but the topic "Free Love" had intrigued her. Squeezing into the back of the crowded hall, she immediately recognized the instructor's voice. This was the reactionary who had seduced a girl the other evening.

She reported this to the Party, then went back to her hostel shivering with malaria. Bouts of shivering alternated with high fever. She dragged herself out for a walk in an attempt to throw the illness off, but the attack only grew worse. In a few days she was the colour of wax, drained of all her energy.

Her class head and the doctor finally got her to the clinic, and after an injection she felt much better. In fact she now trusted the doctor so implicitly that she went back the next day of her own accord.

But now a new danger threatened. The traitor Zhang Yinwu, after robbing the peasants of Hengshui of their grain and recruiting a new force of brigands and riffraff, was marching in this direction.

64

In six months or so these two colleges trained nearly five thousand students for the resistance bases, which were desperately short of cadres with some knowledge of theory. The situation worsened on the Hebei plain soon after they plunged into practical work, but most of them stood up to the test and made a real contribution to the revolution. Because they were scattered far and wide, if their instructors had to travel through the border regions to Yanan they met former students all along the way. And being so well known they passed unchallenged, which made the troops nickname them "Live Travel Permits".

Chun'er learned a great deal during her three months' study. Most important, now that she had grasped the nature of the War of Resistance and the principles of protracted warfare, she was in a better position to lead the villagers. To start with there had been geography and chemistry classes, and although she was out of her depth here at least they gave her an inkling of the wide range of knowledge. She was also beginning to be able to size up people and arguments of every sort.

Once she was accustomed to her new surroundings and had found her feet, she stopped losing weight and her good looks came back. A new seriousness she had acquired made her just like a woman cadre of the Eighth Route Army.

At the end of the three months, Mangzhong graduated from the Military College and was told to rejoin his unit. Chun'er had done so well that she was kept on as a group leader for the next lot of students.

Before leaving, Mangzhong came to Jiuzhou to see her. This was a slack time for the college, and Chun'er asked leave to see him on his way. Her brigade leader asked:

"What relation is that young fellow to you?"

"A relative." Chun'er twinkled. "Why call him young? He'll be twenty at New Year."

"This is only the beginning of the tenth month, comrade. It's a long time yet till New Year."

First Chun'er took Mangzhong to a snack-bar near the college and used the money she had saved from her allowance to treat him to some fried cakes. Then they set off by a short cut to the highway leading north. They crossed some flats where the soil was too alkaline to grow anything but clumps of russet reeds. Sheep washed white in the ditches were sunning themselves on the sand in the clear, strong sunshine. Their path wound through meadows to a range of sand-dunes. Since the harvesting was done the track was almost deserted, but scores of huge grasshoppers, frightened by their approach, kept whirring out of the way. Chun'er couldn't think why they chose to lay their eggs here by the stony path instead of in the soft soil of the meadows.

"Give me your pack." She took hold of Mangzhong's neat kit. "Let me carry it for a while."

"Why should you?" Mangzhong protested. "It's not heavy."

"You can take it easy for a bit." Chun'er pulled the pack from him and slipped it over her shoulders. "Hmm, you must be thinner than me, your straps are so short."

She tugged at the straps which confined her breasts and made them stand out in relief.

"They're terribly tight."

"I can easily loosen them for you."

"There's no need." Laughing, she ran up a sand-dune.

These dunes were quite a height and stretched so far that you could not see their end. It must have taken centuries for the wind to pile up all this sand from deserts far away. Few trees grew here, but a tall wild pear with black bark and dense leaves, just reddening, shaded the path. The shadow it threw on the sand was as welcome today as a cool spring on a hilltop in mid summer.

"You mustn't come any further." Mangzhong halted. "Give me that pack."

"I'm tired." Chun'er dumped the pack in the shade and sat down beside it. "Let's rest a while before you go. I want to talk to you."

"Up here we're in full view of everyone around," said Mangzhong sitting down. "How can we talk?"

"Never mind who sees us." Chun'er hung her head. "Let's pretend we're on sentry duty."

But for several minutes she didn't utter a word, simply played with the plants in the sand. By her grew a small purple flower with vivid green leaves. Although autumn was nearly over, it had only just succeeded in putting out this flower no bigger than a copper coin. Its milky white roots must have thrust down at least a foot to find water and nourishment for it.

Chun'er scooped out a hollow in the damp soil below the sand, moulded a small mud ball and put it inside, then built a little tower beside it.

"Three months in university," commented Mangzhong, "and you still fool about like a child."

Laughing, Chun'er smashed the ball and tower and pounded out a small platform, on which she carefully planted three blades of grass.

"What's that?" demanded Mangzhong.

"Can't you see?" She looked up, both hands on her knees, and sternly ordered him, "Guess!"

"Looks like nothing on earth," he protested. "This is some

317

nonsense you've picked up from those girl students. I give it up."

"That's what's wrong with you — stupid!" she said disapprovingly. "Too lazy to use your mind."

"I know. That's my trouble." He grinned sheepishly.

"This is an altar table." Chun'er indicated the small platform and fingered the grass. "These are three sticks of incense — like we used to have at weddings in our village."

Smiling, she pulled Mangzhong to his feet and helped him on with the pack.

"You must go," she said, "or you won't make it. See how the tree's shadow has shifted."

From the top of the hill she watched him cross a pear orchard and reach the highway. An enemy reconnaissance plane was flying low overhead, circling round and round.

65

The next term, Bian Ji was admitted to the Mass Work College. At last he discarded his long gown for a new uniform. But he still shaved rarely and wore his puttees loose. With his height, shambling along as if still in a gown, he looked a very slovenly sort of soldier.

Bian Ji studied hard and threw himself eagerly into discussions, but what he liked best was debates with other students and extra-curricular activities. He often went for advice to Instructor Zhang, who took the course on art and literature. And in his eagerness to be of use, Bian Ji treated him with the old-fashioned deference shown to teachers in feudal times.

Zhang first asked him to draw head-pieces and illustrations for the wall newspaper, and then, seeing how well he

318

did this, got him to paint posters. Soon he was handling paints nearly all day long. When a spare-time drama troupe was organized, Bian Ji both acted in it and designed the sets. Whenever the orchestra was short of people he helped out with a gong. And since he showed special consideration for girls, who made up more than half the troupe, he became an unofficial stagemanager.

The college laid stress on keeping in close touch with life, so Bian Ji's drama troupe often gave performances in the villages. As he led the way there, carrying a red flag, he looked like a camel on a long trek hung about with impedimenta. On his back above the rolled-up curtain was his own pack; and on top of that, for safety's sake, was fastened a fiddle that nobody wanted to carry. As soon as they'd reached a village and put down their loads, he would have a look round and pitch in with a spade to help construct a stage, then climb on a stool to fasten up the curtains. Their plays were so short that in a single morning they could put on four or five, and Bian Ji figured in nearly all of them. The appreciative villagers boiled a great pan of water by the stage and brought over a basketful of coarse bowls for the actors. Bian Ji's energy was inexhaustible, he acted like a man inspired. When the curtain fell on the last item and the audience started dispersing, he would hurry to the front of the stage still in costume and make-up and shout:

"That's all for today, folks! Time to go home for a meal. Well, uncle, what did you think of our performance? If you liked it, try to behave like those model characters."

But by the time the old peasant nodded his approval, Bian Ji was already taking down the curtains.

Some students disliked his garrulous ways, thinking they weakened the impact of the play. However, he was so obviously motivated by enthusiasm not by any desire to make himself conspicuous, that no one objected. If one remarked jokingly that Bian Ji behaved just like a travelling showman, he would nod in full agreement, accepting this as a fair evaluation.

"We must learn from those showmen," he said. "They take enormous pains and know how to get close to the people. Have you ever watched a conjuror at a temple fair? When he starts sounding his gong only a few children gather round. But he doesn't waste a moment's time, he cracks jokes to set those kids laughing. He whisks out a white cloth and spreads it flat on the ground, then produces a frog from his pocket and makes it hop a couple of times before putting it back again. That's so as to draw a crowd. Between acts and at the end of the show, he makes the audience feel at home with him. They know this is sleight-of-hand, a way to earn money, but his skill is genuine and he's an honest fellow. In those days it wasn't as easy as it is now for an artist to fill his rice bowl."

Bian Ji's own memories of the past were bitter. But this only made him keener to do a good job of propaganda today.

One afternoon, cross-legged on a peasant's *kang,* he started writing a new skit for the next day's show. In a shack outside was a millstone which kept working, like the peasants, from dawn till dusk. A sturdy middle-aged woman had just finished grinding some maize and was starting on a measure of sorghum.

Up came a young woman with a sack half full of grain. Slight and graceful, she was strikingly pretty although very freckled.

"Let me have a turn, sister." Out of breath, she put down her sack.

"You must think you have big face," rejoined the elder

320

woman jokingly. "I've waited long enough myself. Why should I make way for you?"

"If you're just grinding middlings, I'll wait."

"I'm not. I'm grinding this fine to make pancakes for supper."

"Let me have a go first then." The young woman caught hold of the other's brush. "My baby's just this minute dropped off to sleep. I daren't leave him for long."

"What about me?" retorted the other woman. "My four imps are rolling in that muddy ditch south of the village. If you're in such a hurry, lend me a hand."

"Bah!" The younger woman dropped the brush and turned away. "Just my luck!"

"My luck's not up to yours." The middle-aged woman spread her sorghum evenly and started turning the mill. "You're pretty, you're young, you're smart. You use rouge and powder."

In embarrassment the young woman pointed to the window.

"Don't talk such rubbish. There's a cadre in there."

"What if there is? He's just like one of us."

Stamping her foot, the young woman picked up her sack.

"I wanted to hand in my grain in good time," she grumbled. "I didn't come here for a slanging match with you."

"What's that?" The mill ground to a stop.

"My public grain!"

"Why couldn't you say so before?" She swept her half-ground sorghum off the stone. "You've only yourself to blame if you don't make things clear. Here you are, get on with it."

The young woman poured her golden grain on to the mill-stone.

"Now you're half human." She giggled.

"I'm doing it for the men who've gone to fight Japan. In times like these whatever helps the war must come first."

One basket balanced on her head, another tucked under her left arm and the brush in her right hand, she started off. But she turned back after a few paces to call:

"Mind you grind it fine, sister! Your man and mine are both at the front. They're wearing cloth we've woven and eating the grain we've grown."

"Aren't you going to finish your sorghum?"

"It'll do as it is. To help our men, I'd gladly eat husks or wild herbs."

In silence the young woman spread her grain. Turning the mill was hard work for her. As dusk closed in, some sparrows alighted on the roof, cheeping and twittering as if to hurry her.

A girl came running along. She had grown out of her clothes and her trousers reached barely half way down her legs, but she looked strong and nimble. As soon as she lent a hand, the big millstone started turning much more quickly.

"Thank goodness you came," said the young woman cheerfully. "Why are you so late back this evening?"

"We had a test. Very difficult questions to answer. I came straight here after dumping my satchel at home."

"You must come and have supper with me."

It was so dark they decided to light the oil lamp hanging in the shed. The girl ran to Bian Ji's window to borrow a light.

"Are you two from one family?" he asked.

"No, we're not."

"Do you often help each other?"

"Yes." She chuckled. "She's an army dependent, it's only right I should help her. But why do you ask?"

"I may put you both in a play," was Bian Ji's reply.

66

Bian Ji wrote many short plays.

His topics were confined to young men's joining the army, women's aid for the front, the care for army dependents or delivery of public grain; yet each scene was true to life.

In playwriting, just as in painting, he had never been instructed by well-known masters but had virtually taught himself. As a boy, in the slack winter season, he got an uncle to teach him an old primer. For lack of paper and brush, he learned to write by scratching characters with a sickle on an old earthen rampart outside the village. He enlarged his vocabulary when he started painting, in his eagerness to learn treasuring every scrap of printed matter or paper with writing on it. All notices posted up in the village street, all lucky mottoes pasted on shop counters, received his careful attention. As an itinerant painter he took a keen interest in the poems or riddles scrawled with charcoal or chalk on ruined monastery walls, savouring them to the full and adding his comments. As for the old broken tablets lying by the roadside and the inscriptions hanging in temple halls, he looked up to these as great works.

The year of his marriage Bian Ji bought a few catties of old newspapers to paper his bridal chamber, for all village painters know how to paper a house. When bad weather kept him indoors he would lie or stand on the *kang* reading these sheets paragraph after paragraph, and long after the

323

words were too blackened by smoke to be read he could tell you what stories there were on the ceiling, what news items over the *kang*. He kept and pored over all pages torn from old books which the shops used as wrapping paper.

He loved to listen to stories. And he heard many fine ones during his wanderings, when in winter he put up for the night in small village inns with different travelling salesmen. Sometimes, however, they took advantage of him. One snowy day, the *kang* in the inn was so crowded that a packman, arriving late, had to squat on the floor. When he saw Bian Ji stretched out in comfort, he said:

"How about a story to cheer us up this cold evening?"

"Can you tell stories?" Bian Ji promptly sat up.

"I can tell the *Journey to the West*. Not that I often have time for story-telling."

"That's fine," said Bian Ji. "Go ahead, we'd all like to hear."

"Is it fair for all of you to lie on a warm *kang* while the story-teller squats on the cold floor?"

"He's got a point there," said Bian Ji. "Let's make room for him, friends."

But the others refused to move, preferring to forgo the story rather than sleep in discomfort.

"I tell you what," suggested Bian Ji. "Change places with me."

This done, the packman stowed his things away, undressed, burrowed under the quilt and closed his eyes.

"Go ahead," urged Bian Ji.

"Oh," said the packman. "What shall I tell?"

"*Journey to the West*." Bian Ji was shivering with cold on the floor.

"All right, here goes. The monk Tripitaka went to the

Eastern Heaven to look for a sacred canon. He rode on a white donkey that brayed. . . ." The packman was obviously no story-teller. He had simply posed as one to get a warm place on the *kang*. When the others protested he said sullenly:

"If you don't like my story, tell one yourselves."

But when someone did, the packman proved that he could neither tell stories nor appreciate them, for he fell sound asleep.

Even more than stories Bian Ji loved the theatre, which to him meant the troupes that toured the countryside. If there were good singers among them, he would travel more than twenty *li* in any weather to see an evening performance, not getting home until the day was light. He so admired an actress called Little Chuyun who toured that district that he made two cratefuls of toys as an excuse to follow her troupe wherever it went. After four days in one place, the actors piled on to a large cart and moved on, sometimes travelling more than a hundred *li*. Bian Ji followed them, carrying his trumpery wares: toy drums, red bridal sedan-chairs, yellow rollers and small wooden guns. He set up a stall by the stage, where he could hear Little Chuyun while selling his goods. For days he remained oblivious of hunger, thirst and the fatigues of the long way.

Bian Ji had a soft spot for travelling showmen and helped them whenever he could. At New Year, wandering minstrels and ballad-singers, story-tellers who sold needles or conjurors who peddled medicine, all got him to distribute chopsticks round the village. And when their performance was at an end, he would bring back the chopsticks stuck with New Year buns. In this way he earned their trust and gratitude.

325

67

In October, Wuhan fell. In November, the enemy launched a big offensive against the central Hebei plain. The Japanese were bringing pressure on Chiang Kai-shek to surrender, and as he retreated step by step they drew away their forces to attack the Eighth Route Army, well aware that there was the real threat to them. Bearing down from the Northeast, they occupied Poye and Lixian and patrolled the highway between their garrisons. Soon Shenxian fell.

The academy moved south. One day Bian Ji, Chun'er and Instructor Zhang received orders to make their way to the River Hutuo to welcome a force newly come to the Hebei plain — what force they were not told. They would have to cross the road held by the Japanese, and must plan ahead what local people they would rely on. On the way, Zhang proposed that they spend the first night in his home.

Instructor Zhang was very much in love with his wife and missed his family. When the army happened to march in the direction of his village he grew talkative and energetic, whereas marching in the opposite direction his legs soon ached and he had little to say. He tried to persuade Chun'er, telling her:

"She and I hit it off splendidly, you know. Only she's rather backward."

"Who is?" Chun'er was keeping a careful watch on the road.

"My wife. She's rather backward and doesn't want to leave home to work. The women cadres in our village haven't been able to persuade her and neither have I —she simply laughs at me. It struck me some time ago that you, with your rich experience of mass work, are just the person to help her."

This is an excellent opportunity. If we spend the night there, you can have a good talk with her."

When Chun'er simply smiled, Zhang turned to Bian Ji, who was carrying the instructor's pack in front. Although Bian Ji didn't know these parts he had as usual rushed ahead. Not liking to ask the way, he often went astray and had to retrace his steps, but at once he'd forge ahead of the rest again.

"Bian Ji!" called Instructor Zhang, bringing him to a halt. "I know you like books and paintings, but you haven't had a chance to see many good ones. I've a whole pile at home, enough to fill a suitcase and a crate. I barely had enough money to get through university, because my father's only a rich peasant; and while the average rich peasant can put his son through middle school he must scrimp and save to send him to college. So those books and paintings of mine weren't easily come by. You can have a good look at them — they'll give you some useful ideas. We've some coloured paper too at home of the sort you can't get nowadays, and we may as well take that with us."

Bian Ji's mouth watered at this prospect and he urged Chun'er to agree. But all she would say was:

"We'll see."

After the harvest the fields stretched bare as far as eye could see. The Japanese had burned so many villages that the peasants, instead of storing straw and fuel at home, had stacked it in the fields. The lanes were almost deserted, but hares were scurrying over the countryside. The setting aside of saltpetre for army use had stopped the usual early winter hunting, so emboldening the hares that they loped along the paths in full sight of people. But if you tried to grab one, it streaked off behind a pile of faggots.

Towards dusk they reached the highway — the first enemy highway they'd crossed on their native soil. The sky was cloudless, not a soul was in sight, and while still at some distance from the road they broke into a run. Bian Ji fell as he was crossing the trench beside it, while Chun'er stopped in the middle of the road to take a lingering look from east to west. This long road built by the Japanese was like a knife plunged into her mother's breast and made her own heart ache.

Instructor Zhang's village stood on sandy flats and was described in the local maps as a desert. Its few trees had been felled by the enemy and it would take years for the villagers to grow tall spreading trees here again. A vicious wind was whirling white sand towards the sky as if to blot out bushes, grave mounds and sand-dunes in its swirling advance. Suddenly black smoke eddied up, flames enveloped the village, and they heard shrieks and curses.

"Confound it!" exclaimed Zhang. "We must get under cover."

They dashed to some brick kilns southwest of the village. A batch of freshly baked bricks had just been turned out, and the workmen were lying on their stomachs watching the fire.

Instructor Zhang knew the old foreman, Zhang Laochong, who, stripped to the waist, a white beard streaming over his powerful brown chest, an embroidered sash round his middle, was standing under cover on the roof of one kiln. He motioned to the new-comers to lie down, and Chun'er felt the bricks hot beneath her.

"A squad of our men has been surrounded," the old man told them. "They could have left the village and gone into hiding, but they were so mad at the Japanese they stayed to fight. They're badly outnumbered, and now they can't get out."

The brickmakers' anxious eyes were fixed on the village. Their moulds and buckets lay scattered all around. It was not just the fate of their families that worried them, they were desperately concerned for the safety of that squad.

Although the Japanese had charged into the village, no sound could be heard except the crackling of flames, no one could be seen breaking out. There was something ominous about this silence. Tension gripped the whole countryside. Even the sun hung in suspense at the horizon, its red glow fading like iron taken out of the furnace. Everything in the vicinity of the kilns, down to the rows of moulds and stacks of firewood, seemed on edge with apprehension.

"One of our men's climbed up a roof!" shouted Old Zhang. "Damnit, he's been hit! He's lying there."

The others could not see this from where they were.

"He's done for. Two Japanese are up there." Old Zhang's voice trailed away. The next instant he yelled, "Good for him! He's up and going for them."

They heard the explosion of a hand-grenade. Black smoke billowed over that house.

Again the village was silent, petrified. But they knew that grim death was stalking its streets and houses.

"Someone's broken out!" cried Old Zhang.

This time all could see a soldier run south down a narrow lane. He was wounded in the legs and kept stumbling and falling. A Japanese was after him.

"This way!" yelled Old Zhang.

The soldier could hardly have heard but he did head in their direction, the Japanese clumping steadily after him. The soldier's blood was staining the white sand. He struggled to the side of the kiln, then fell dead at their feet.

The Japanese halted to eye the kiln warily.

"If we let him go back, they'll be after us," said Old Zhang. "That soldier has a pistol on him. Can any of you fellows shoot?"

He searched their faces, then sighed — none of the brick-makers could use a gun.

"I can!" Chun'er slid down the kiln, grabbed the soldier's gun and dropped behind a pile of rubble, unobserved by the Japanese. She took her time over aiming, and when she fired Old Zhang roared his approval.

They buried the dead soldier near the kiln.

68

At nightfall they entered the village. Instructor Zhang's home was a brick house built round a compound and they reached the black gate as his father was bolting it. His son's return startled yet pleased the old man, but the sight of two people behind made his face fall.

"What made you choose this day to come?" he exclaimed. "The Japanese have only just left. They turned the whole village upside down, burned a row of houses in the east and killed four or five people."

"We'd better go on," said Chun'er.

"Never mind." The old man was afraid his son would go with them. "Since you're here, we'll make shift to put you up. The enemy were here today, but that doesn't mean they'll be back again tomorrow. Come on in."

Outside the inner gate was a large grape trellis, and moonlight falling through the leafless vine gave the courtyard a ghostly look. Their hearts were heavy. Instructor Zhang's wife was waiting in the inner courtyard, a warm smile on her pretty face.

"Boil water for them to drink," said her father-in-law. "We've nothing good in the house to offer them."

Afraid to embarrass her husband and the guests, she whispered:

"Dad, can't you get some noodles from Old Ma?"

"All right." Zhang's father rummaged in a tattered sack lying by the stove. "The grocer likes books. See this one? It's not thick, but he'll give me a catty of noodles for it."

"Aren't those my books?" Zhang hurried over to the sack. "What are they doing here?"

"Don't talk to me about your books. They could have cost me my head." The old man's hands were trembling. "Your elder sister's house was burned by the Japanese just because she had a few books. They're dynamite."

Pulling out some more, he left with them under his arm.

"See this big pan of water?" Zhang's wife lifted the lid to show him. "We've been tearing up books and burning them since it grew dark. I know how you must feel — it hurts me too. Dad made quite a scene because I wanted to keep a few hard-backed ones with good paper to use as albums."

"Give me a few." Bian Ji was squatting down, busily rummaging. After filling his own pack, he asked Chun'er for hers. "We'll take these off with us to join the resistance."

"Give him my coloured paper and drawing paper too," said Instructor Zhang.

Presently his father came back with two catties of noodles. He took out some more books, weighed them in his hands and said:

"We'll get some scraps of pork for these."

It was a good meal, but both hosts and guests were too upset to enjoy it.

Then Zhang's wife plied the bellows while his father,

squatting beside her, tore up book after book and fed the stove with them.

"Have to burn them at night," he explained to his son. "It's dangerous in the daytime."

"Couldn't you bury them somewhere?"

"Burying isn't as safe as burning." The old man smiled bitterly. "You think I don't care? These books came out of my land. Load after load of grain it took to buy them."

The water in the pan was seething and bubbling. The young woman's heart ached as she worked the bellows. She loved her husband dearly and they had no child. Their most treasured possessions were his books and pictures, her patterns and embroidery. Her husband often put his newest book with her latest piece of needlework in the dressing-case that was part of her dowry. Now every page was being consumed by fire.

Her heart was so full as she approached the end that she stood up and went to her room, weeping over this vandalism. In the days to come she was to join the resistance and work at mimeographing. When that time came, she realized that culture suffered like everything else from the war; but the War of Resistance also created a fresher, more vigorous culture. For the new books they printed on coarse paper went to people who had never read books before, were taken to their hearts and contributed to the final victory.

"Fetch me his uniforms too," cried Zhang's father, who had taken over the bellows. "It's not safe to keep them either. The Li family got into trouble because of one pair of trousers. So bring me all his uniforms and we'll bundle them up and tie a big stone to them. While it's still dark I'll drop them in that well to the north."

"Yes, dad." Reluctantly she opened her cases.

332

"And those photographs he had taken outside...." The old man started coughing.

69

With heavy hearts they burned or threw into the well everything in the house that might arouse the enemy's suspicion. Then the old man told his daughter-in-law to fix their guests up for the night. Since they had only two *kang*, although Bian Ji suggested that husband and wife should have one, Mrs. Zhang would not hear of this and led Chun'er to her own room, leaving the three men to sleep in the western wing.

After the two young women had blown out the light, they talked for a long time in whispers. Zhang's wife made a good impression on Chun'er, who asked:

"Can you read and write?"

"I studied a primer with my brother when I was small," was the reply.

"Are you taking part in any work in the village?"

"I've joined the Women's Salvation Association. Sometimes I help round people up for meetings or work out figures for them, if you call that work."

"I do call it work. But why not find a job outside?"

"I'd miss home."

"Your husband's away, who's there to miss?"

"I'd miss my chest and red lacquered boxes, my dressing-case, mirror, flower vase and dining table. I'd miss this *kang* I sleep on." Having reeled off this list, she chuckled. "That's what home means for country folk."

She stopped short as firing burst out in the street.

It was a ragged fusillade, some bullets whizzing overhead,

others striking the ground or embedding themselves in houses. These were not regular soldiers but bandits.

Not far away someone yelled:

"Bullets don't have eyes. So if you're not called, better keep out of the way."

Another volley of shots.

"It's that renegade Gao Ba!" cried Chun'er.

Zhang's father, having roused his son and Bian Ji, dashed over to knock on the young women's window and urge them to climb over the roof and take cover south of the village.

Mrs. Zhang pulled Chun'er out with her.

"Come on!" she urged. "To the sand-dunes."

She gave Chun'er a leg up. But before Chun'er could pull her up too, a bandit jumped on to the roof of the next house and shouted:

"Don't move! Which is the girl student?"

As Chun'er jumped into the lane, a bullet whistled past her ear.

She tore along to the sand-dunes and ducked into brambles which cut her face and hands. There she waited for Mrs. Zhang, till a sudden scream told her that the young woman had been captured.

A pandemonium of shots, curses, shouts and sobbing had broken out behind her. Soon the bandits marched their prisoners out of the village.

Chun'er crouched in the pit left by an uprooted tree while the bandits passed almost on top of her on their way to the highest dune. There another shot was fired, and Chun'er heard Gao Ba cry:

"Sing out, you lot! Tell your folk to come and ransom you. Your men are soldiers in the Communist army. I'll finish you off, if your folk fail to produce cash here and now."

Among the cries for help, the faltering voice of Mrs. Zhang filled Chun'er with remorse. If Zhang's wife hadn't helped her to get away first, she wouldn't have been caught herself. The girl wondered if this method of kidnapping was something Gao Ba had learned from Zhang Yinwu.

Gao Ba fired more shots towards the village until a man approached with a lantern, shouting:

"Friends! I'm Zhang Laochong of the brick kiln. I've brought you money. Here it is. I'll put it under the big ailanthus tree."

"How much?" demanded Gao Ba.

"Four eights — 320. The Japanese looted the place today and pretty well cleaned us out."

"An old horse-dealer ought to know prices better," bawled Gao Ba. "You'd pay more than that for a mule."

"We're old gambling and drinking cronies. Give me a little face."

"What face have you got, you old bastard?" screamed a woman. "If you don't add twenty notes for each person we've captured here, we'll send for coffins."

Chun'er, recognizing Su'er's voice, nearly threw up in disgust. Gao Ba alone was bad enough without this she-bandit to egg him on.

"Our woman warrior!" Zhang Laochong laughed. "Why don't you put in a word for me with the regiment commander, instead of making things worse?"

"All right, leave it there," cried Su'er. "Go and tell the villagers Regiment Commander Gao isn't out for ransom this time, he's collecting funds for the army."

"Right." Zhang Laochong shook the sack so that the money clinked. "Come on and get it."

When Gao Ba, still cursing roundly, had taken the money

and fired a few more shots, he cantered off with his ruffians down the highway.

Lantern in hand, Old Zhang found the kidnapped villagers and untied them.

Back at home, Mrs. Zhang threw her arms around Chun'er and sobbed:

"Take me away with you. I can't stay here. I'm willing to leave everything behind."

Zhang Laochong, still holding his lantern, told Zhang's father:

"Don't take this too hard. Lives are more important than property. You can get money back again. But you're partly to blame for this, brother. When you took those books to exchange for pork, you let the cat out of the bag."

When he heard that Chun'er and the rest were leaving, he offered to see them on their way.

"I'm proud to have met you yesterday, comrade," he told Chun'er. "Let me introduce myself again. I'm Zhang Laochong, a well-known busybody in these parts. I stick my nose into everything, good or bad. I know Gao Ba, but I've no opinion of him. To hell with him! The Japanese butchers have just left and he comes to kidnap people — like a robber taking advantage of a fire. I'm no better than I should be. I started life as a carter, then took to horse-dealing and finally switched to the kilns. I've gambled and put the squeeze on people too. But I'm against Japan. You can tell Gao Ba's rotten to the core, picking on army dependents to get ransom money and sabotaging the resistance. I'm going to steer clear of the bastard. Don't get the idea that I belong to the same gang."

"What about your militia?" asked Chun'er as they left the village.

Zhang Laochong sighed. "Morale's slumped since that

336

highway was built and the Japanese started rampaging. We need a few victories. You can't blame folk in times like these. But we mustn't give up. A man must learn to swim against the tide. Sizing up the situation is like choosing friends — you have to take the long view. Not all is gold that glitters: it takes judgment to tell in advance which man will prove sound. I may seem to you to have frittered away my life, but I'm not one of those who drift with the wind. You saw the way Gao Ba carried on tonight. The lives of four people in his hands, and no one with the guts to stop him swearing at them or beating them up. Looked tough, didn't he? But I tell you the swine will come to a bad end. Of course the Japanese bastards are even worse. To my way of thinking, though, they're like the whirlwinds in these parts that spring up out of the blue. Just sit tight and you'll see them die down. The fiercer they blow, the sooner they subside. The Japanese have no more root on Chinese soil than the wind. They can get scum like Gao Ba to join them, but that isn't going to win them the war. The Eighth Route Army, now, gets hold of the salt of the earth, it has roots in these parts. Judging by people, the Eighth Route is sure to win. When the Japanese build a highway or burn a few houses and the Eighth Route disappears for a couple of days or has one or two defeats, some people say that it's no use resisting. I don't believe it. I've been around and seen all sorts of people. I've met Commander Lu Zhengcao. Not when he had several detachments and commanders under him, no, but last July when instead of retreating south he marched a small force back. We were used to seeing soldiers heading south, his was the first lot coming north. I'd been gambling in Dongchangshi Temple not far from Anguo that day. I was cooling off on the terrace in the afternoon when he and his men tramped up from the south. Shoes worn out, hollow-cheeked with hunger, they looked all in. Commander Lu strode along in front, his face burned black by the sun. Seeing me on the terrace, he called out, 'What village is this, friend?' I told him, 'Dongchangshi, eight *li* from the town.' He lined his men up just below me to speak to them. I've never forgotten what he said. If we want to resist Japan we mustn't be afraid of difficulties, he told them. Our strength may be small, but we have mass support. Just a few words, but each one went home. His men perked up, re-fastened their shoes and pushed on for Anguo. At the gate of the county *yamen* they fixed up two guns and collected a hundred rifles from the puppet merchants' guild. Soon their force was big enough to start skirmishing, and I saw with my own eyes the way they mopped up that brigand Gao Jianxun. That was when I made up my mind that Lu Zhengcao was one of the right sort."

The old man talked on and on, hardly pausing for breath, as he saw Chun'er and the others ten *li* on their way.

70

At dawn Chun'er and her friends reached the bank of the Hutuo. They were excited to hear that the troops they had come to welcome were the 120th Division led by General He Long, a well-nigh legendary division which they longed to meet.

Better still, the division headquarters was to be in Chun'er's own village Ziwuzhen. General He Long received them in the home of a poor peasant at the east end of the village. And at this first encounter Chun'er devoured him with her eyes, for to her he personified the splendid Red Army tradition and the heroic fighting men who had won such miraculous victories.

After thanking them, the general inquired after their health, asked if they liked their food at the academy and if they had sports in addition to military drill.

They also met the chief of staff Zhou Shidi, who, standing by a large military map on the wall, explained to them in some detail the war situation behind the enemy lines. For all their lack of military experience, they realized that the presence of this crack division heralded a fresh and fierce struggle in that area. Zhou Shidi told them that since the enemy was apparently aware of our main force's arrival, and the situation was changing from hour to hour, they had better not leave headquarters but form a mass work team and move away with the troops. That same evening, however, he calmly called a meeting to exchange experience and was particularly eager to learn from them something about the customs and people of central Hebei.

This meeting with veterans of the Red Army made this a red-letter day for Chun'er, who was sure that her village too must be glorying in the opportunity to entertain such fine revolutionary commanders.

Chun'er and Bian Ji went home to see their families. The soldiers billeted at Chun'er's home were surprised at first to find the visitor to their unit on such an intimate footing with their hosts. When they learned that this was Chun'er's home, they laughed.

"Fine!" they said. "In other words, you're not our guest. Hurry up and entertain us."

Some villagers asked Chun'er on the sly who the high commander was. Since this was a military secret, she simply told them with a smile that he was a brilliant general who had never been defeated. None of them knew who this general was, but they fully understood that this was a veteran Eighth Route Army contingent.

Then started a gruelling march. It was Chun'er's first experience of such marching. They set off each day at dusk and made camp the next morning. The girls, at the rear of one column, found it hard to keep up with the men. The troops swept along like a dragon rushing north, south, east and west, so that sometimes even Chun'er and the local people lost all sense of direction and could only follow blindly. Not until the next morning, ascertaining the name of the village, did they realize that they had covered well over a hundred *li*.

Day after day they marched. And Chun'er, footsore and weary, was afraid for the first few nights that she might drop behind. Later, she was able to take it in her stride. Falling in at dusk in fine trim, she found no difficulty in keeping rank. Only towards dawn did she begin to nod and dream as she trudged along.

The sun would be rising as they reached their destination and sat down in the village square, reluctant to move. But that was precisely when the girls' work began. The local people could not understand the dialect of many of the soldiers, whose customs often differed too. Chun'er helped the quarter-master to arrange billets, borrow what was needed, and procure grain and fodder. She had to explain matters to the country folk. Not till the men had found lodgings and the cooks had put on the rice, was there any rest for her.

The enemy was converging on this base from east and west, having mobilized a mighty force to pin down the 120th Division.

But the 120th Division had no intention of fighting a pitched battle. It simply slipped through the gaps in the enemy lines to attack his weak points, circling the base and fighting as it went. Moreover, in addition to campaigning, this division played an important political role and exercised a powerful attraction. Upon its arrival in the central Hebei plain, it comprised two regiments only; but in the course of this campaign it more than doubled in strength.

Chun'er covered the whole central Hebei plain with the troops. In the region of the Beijing-Hankou Railway, villages clustered close together and there were many waterwheels irrigating kitchen-gardens. The villages of Dingxian were surrounded by little runnels of clear water, and you could reach down to catch the fish in hiding below the rushes. The Tianjin-Pukou line ran through a more sparsely populated area, where the peasants lived in scattered cottages built of tamped earth. Clumps of bulrushes grew in the marshes outside their farms, and kites circled overhead.

Chun'er crossed rivers of very different kinds. Marching with the troops one night through a market-town bright with lights, she crossed the wooden bridge over the Ziya. Further east, they skirted the Grand Canal built for shipping tribute rice, both its banks covered with plump cabbages. More than once they forded the clear, shallow Shahe and went as far west as the railway almost at the foot of the mountains before circling northeast again to camp on the misty banks of the Daqing. Times past counting she picked her way gingerly over a swaying pontoon-bridge across the swift-flowing river, when her silhouette was reflected beside the moon and stars in the jadegreen water. On other occasions she stood waiting quietly on the shore for one of the ferryboats which were shuttling to and fro.

Across your broad, rich acres, dear motherland, flow the unruly Tanghe and untamed Hutuo. These rivers are your swiftly-coursing blood, your racing pulse, emblems of your fervent passion, the sons you have brought forth. Your daughters are the quiet-flowing Cihe and the translucent Liuli. They flow gently, almost noiselessly through soft meadows, lavishing all their care on the crops on either side, nurturing the region to ensure a good harvest. Who knows the whole tale of their loving kindness to men as they sway the dense reeds and bear small boats through the night? The sight of them brings home to us your beauty, your potential greatness and wealth.

Chun'er passed through "golden" Shulu and "silver" Lixian, two fine cotton-growing regions. She saw Shengfang, known as a smaller Suzhou and famed for its lotus, water-chestnuts, fish and rice. The peasants brought out their new autumn rice for the troops.

While on the march, she heard folk songs in every district and learned how rich our country is in music, with magic flutes able to convey the whole range of emotions. All she had heard before were cheerful wedding tunes or the sad songs of parting, but now the melodies were stirring and proud, inspired by the passionate resolve to defend our homeland.

At dawn Chun'er saw in the distance the old pagoda of Dingxian, the Great Buddha of Zhengding, the undulating twelve-arched bridge across the marshlands.

She saw the flickering lights of great cities, and heard the groans of those living there in despair.

Dear land of ours! Troops who won through the countless perils of the Long March, and showed their might by smashing so many "mopping-up" campaigns, are marching swiftly and tirelessly over your fertile soil.

Late at night Chun'er often caught glimpses of the com-

342

manders. Sometimes they alighted from their horses outside
a village and studied the map by the light of a dimmed lamp
before issuing fresh instructions. When they rode in the
middle of the column, Chun'er tried to guess how many soldiers there were before and behind them. Sometimes they
drew to one side to let the troops pass, calling words of encouragement to each in turn. When the army made camp
and the rank and file were asleep, the officers met to study
the enemy position and draw up their plan of action.

On and on they marched, changing course and covering
vast distances. Every night as they passed through village
after village, Chun'er heard the fitful barking of dogs, the
squawking of hens, or women working through the night to
cure leather, plait crates and baskets, or make copper sieves,
according to what the locality produced.

They found the militia assembled wherever they passed,
and the village cadres hard at work late in the night. Young
and old in the base area came to their doors to give the
troops a warm welcome, for they placed their trust in victory
in the people's own regular army.

She heard hammers clang on anvils, and in a secluded lane
saw sparks from a blazing furnace spatter the big black bellows. In the light of the flames, blacksmiths from southern
Hebei and Shandong, in tattered oilskin aprons, were making
the peasants shovels and picks to destroy the road before the
enemy's arrival, making rifles and mines for them too. Even
on nights of steady rain, the fires in those furnaces did not go
out, nor did the hammers fall silent.

Beloved country, whose children are legion, what sacrifices
you have made in the war! Holding your honour dear, you
will not brook the least insult but have arisen now, terrible in
your fury!

343

71

With the Japanese approaching, the presence here of Chinese troops of two completely different types made the people's struggle infinitely harder.

The enemy received support from wily scoundrels like Zhang Yinwu, who at the height of the Japanese offensive, came out with the slogan: "Change Red territory into occupied territory." And to win him over the Japanese cut their slogan: "Wipe out the Reds and destroy the Kuomintang" into "Wipe out the Reds." Zhang promptly responded with the declaration, "Resisting the Reds comes first." The Japanese held a rally in Beijing to celebrate winning over this "faithful" traitor.

In honour of Gao Ba's desertion from the Eighth Route Army, Zhang Yinwu wrote an article for the Kuomintang papers which was carried in full in the Japanese newspaper too. But Zhang treated Gao Ba just as he did the sanctimonious phrases which he used when it suited his book and then flung to the winds. He gave him neither supplies nor base, ordering him to fend for himself. So Gao Ba reverted to his old way of life.

As the Eighth Route Army fought running battles with the Japanese on the plain, Gao Ba raided the villages they evacuated. It was clear to him, however, that his days as a brigand were numbered, for the people's forces were growing steadily stronger. News reached him one day that Zhang Yinwu was in Five-dragon Temple helping the Japanese bridge the River Hutuo. With his small group of horsemen, Gao Ba forded the river and went to ask for supplies. But Zhang Yinwu refused to see him until he started firing towards the village.

Zhang Yinwu was staying in Gao Xiang's house, the most substantial building to the west of Five-dragon Temple.

Gao Xiang's father was at the market when the Kuomintang troops arrived and, without notifying the village cadres or asking permission from the owners, swarmed into the house. Gao Xiang's mother at once sent her daughter-in-law to lie low with a neighbour, undertaking to look after the soldiers herself.

Towards noon her grand-daughter came home for something to eat. She skipped along singing, a shuttlecock in one hand, and was delighted to see the house full of soldiers, for it was some time since the Eighth Route Army had left. She ran up to the sentry on duty.

"Uncle!" she cried. "What trophies have you brought me?"

"What trophies, you little bitch?" He glowered at her.

Taken aback by this answer she stared at him. Since he was in Chinese uniform, she tried again, asking:

"Have you seen my father?"

"How the hell should I know your father?"

The child was smarting over this when she heard her granny call. She decided to explain things to this soldier. For whenever the Eighth Route Army men heard who her father was, they'd pick her up and swing her in the air.

"My father's name is Gao Xiang," she said. "He's political commissar for his detachment."

"Uhh? So you're a damned little Eighth Router!" The soldier made such an ugly face that she nearly burst into tears.

She couldn't understand how China could have troops like these. She sat watching them from the doorstep, then went outside for a look. It dawned on her that this was a different army, at whose arrival the villagers closed their doors and streets were deserted, while even hens and dogs fled out of their way. The little girl hid herself inside the house.

When Gao Xiang's father heard these troops had come, he hurried home without finishing his purchases. He was a timid old fellow and, knowing that his son was this gang's enemy, cold as it was he broke into a sweat.

He reached home to find Zhang Yinwu conferring in the sitting room with Shi Yousan and Gao Ba. The courtyard was packed with horses and bodyguards, all in grey uniform. It was time for the midday meal and two pigeons alighted on the ash tree in the front yard. Oblivious of the change in this quiet courtyard, they were billing and cooing in the sunshine when one of the bodyguards quietly drew his pistol and brought one of them down. The other men crowded round, praising his marksmanship. But Old Gao's face clouded over at the sight of his pet pigeon dead on the ground. He was picking it up when the bodyguard scowled.

"Hands off! I bagged that bird."

The old man put it down and walked glumly inside. It was the male bird that had been shot. His mate soared swiftly up into the sky crying plaintively, then disappeared from sight.

Back in the west room, Old Gao sat on the *kang* with downcast eyes and told his wife:

"They say our boy's in charge of this district now. Stationed not far from here."

"You must write to him, then, at once." The old woman's face brightened. "Tell him to bring troops and drive away these brigands."

"Will he take orders from you? His job is to fight Japan. What you're asking for is civil war."

"If that's how you feel, go and make up to these devils,"

she retorted. "But be on your guard. The same field produces brambles as well as grain."

Zhang Yinwu was acting as host in the north wing, where Gao Ba was sitting in the lowest place. Plump Zhang Yinwu moved around restlessly, now pounding the papered wall with a pudgy hand, now hoisting himself on to the edge of the table to perch there precariously.

Shi Yousan was speaking.

"I've got hopes now of making contact with the Japanese. The head of the secret police in Baoding is an old friend of mine. A few days ago he wrote advising me to find connections in Beijing and Tianjin. I'm thinking of sending my brother Youxin to Beijing."

"An excellent plan," approved Zhang Yinwu. "We must pull all the strings we can. Let Youxin get in touch with all our fellow-provincials, old classmates or colleagues who have dealings with Japan. We'll give him funds for that."

"We should work for unity," was Shi Yousan's next proposal.

"Are you suggesting we don't?"

"Well. . . ." Shi Yousan's face darkened. "My brother Youxin has given me such outstanding help all these years that when we came to Hebei I made him a county head. He went to his post a few days ago only to find four men fighting for the same job."

"Had the Reds sent them?" asked Zhang Yinwu.

"No, our people had."

"Often the Civil Affairs Bureau appoints one man and the Provincial Government another," explained Zhang Yinwu. "I think in future we'd better all hand in our recommendations and let the Civil Affairs Bureau handle the appointments."

"One of these was apparently appointed by some special

commissioner," continued Shi Yousan. "If a commissioner can send one, I should have the authority to send two."

"One of them was appointed by me." Tian Yaowu rose from his seat.

"I hear your man is a scoundrel!" spluttered Shi.

"Now then, gentlemen," interposed Zhang Yinwu. "We must do everything in our power to extend our influence. We need more time and space in which to manoeuvre. I'm counting on you to do your best to carry out these decisions."

After the meeting Zhang Yinwu kept Tian Yaowu back to talk with Gao Ba.

"What do you want here?" demanded Zhang Yinwu.

"Reinforcements and supplies," was Gao Ba's answer.

"I can't produce soldiers for you or grow grain to feed you. You'll have to get both from the people."

"They won't give me any."

"Are you so helpless? There are plenty of ways and means. Just use your head."

"We can't ignore army discipline."

"Rubbish. Army discipline is for the Eighth Route Army, not for you."

"Can we put on Japanese armlets?"

"Not until I've fixed things up with them. Don't forget, I've given a great deal of thought to this collaboration policy, you need have no misgivings about it. But keep it a secret from the Eighth Route Army. Since you came over, Gao Ba, you haven't done much except make a bad impression. I've been lenient with you so far in the hope that you'll prove of some use later on."

"Please give me more instructions," said Gao Ba. "We're in a real tough spot now. Last time we ran into the Japanese, because no agreement had been worked out, they even stole my horse. I hope you'll issue me with a good horse, sir."

Ignoring this request, Zhang Yinwu marched out.

"Regiment Commander Gao." Tian Yaowu looked up. "Don't tackle the Japanese or you'll come to grief."

"I wouldn't think of it," protested Gao Ba. "But there's not always time to get out of their way."

"Don't get out of their way, try to join them. I shouldn't have to remind you that our aim in coming north wasn't to fight Japan. Other people can have the monopoly of those high-sounding slogans — we don't want them. Our job is to wipe out the Reds, and for that we've got to collaborate with Japan. You don't seem too clear about this basic line."

"I'm clear on it," replied Gao Ba. "Mr. Bai explained that the day he brought me here. But I can't join Japan without soldiers, horses and rifles. They mightn't take me with just this handful men."

"They'll take you," Tian assured him. "For the same reason we did. It's no military victory for them, but it's a political victory."

72

Gao Ba appealed to Tian Yaowu as well for men and supplies. But being only a commissioner in name, Tian was in no position to help. He advised Gao Ba to make use of his local connections and send Su'er back to Ziwuzhen, where she could be useful in a number of ways, including finding out news of the Eighth Route Army and keeping in touch with those who were against the Communists. Gao Ba had no alternative but to agree.

Dusk was closing in as Gao Ba left the room, his head

lowered in dejection. He cheered up a little, however, when he met a hired hand in the front courtyard furtively leading a black horse back to its stable.

"What have you got there?" asked Gao Ba.

"A colt." The man made haste to tether it in its box.

"Not bad." Gao Ba scrutinized its hind legs. "Why don't you tether it outside on a sweltering day like this?"

"Too skittish." The hired hand came out and shut the door. "The yard's full of troops. It would be no laughing matter if it kicked one of them."

"That's not the reason." Gao Ba grinned. "You're afraid they'd requisition it for the army, so you're hiding it away. If I were you, I'd put a lock on that door."

When the hired hand went that night to feed the colt, it had gone. He rushed to report this to his master, who fumed:

"What did I tell you? You'd no business letting those soldiers set eyes on it."

"It was parched, and I didn't water it until dusk. On the way back I met an officer who advised me to lock the door."

"That was Gao Ba. Don't try to make out they're real officers, that lot."

That evening Zhang Yinwu invited Shi Yousan to a good meal, including a dish of steamed pigeon which both host and guest ate with relish. They sat up late enjoying a good talk.

"It's not often one gets game in these parts," remarked Shi.

"This was a tribute from my bodyguard. They often go out and shoot hares or wild fowl for my table."

"Are there wild fowl here on the plain?" asked Shi in surprise.

"Certainly. As you know, I set an example to the troops by forbidding my guards to steal chickens or dogs. But they nd a way around that. By chasing hens out of their coops into the fields, they turn farmyard fowls into wild fowl. The situation's so out of hand, it's no use being too strict. One has to make allowances. And I'm lucky enough to have a cook who once worked for Yuan Shikai* and has a whole fund of anecdotes about President Yuan. I've learned a lot from him."

Just then, to their astonishment, their host came in.

"What is it?" asked Zhang Yinwu.

"I've lost a horse, general. Will you have a search made for it."

"Are you implying that my men have stolen your horse?" Zhang's face was stern.

"I'm making no accusations. Just asking you, as a favour, to help me find it."

"Cases of theft should be reported to the district or county head. Your county head is my neighbour, as it happens."

Old Gao stood there in silence, not daring to press the matter.

Zhang's face cleared a little as he turned to Shi Yousan.

"Our host used to be a draper," he said. "His son, Gao Xiang, is a celebrated political commissar. Gao Xiang once studied in my Four Virtues Middle School, but now he's joined the Eighth Route."

"That may be just a rumour." Old Gao made as if to go, but Zhang Yinwu stopped him.

"Your son is too famous, Mr. Gao, for you to hush up his whereabouts. But although he's with the Eighth Route, I still

---

* Yuan Shikai was the head of the Northern warlords. After the Qing Dynasty was overthrown by the Revolution of 1911, he usurped the presidency of the Republic by relying on counter-revolutionary armed force and on the support of the imperialists. The warlord government he organized represented the big landlord and big compradore classes.

look on him as my old pupil. I hope he'll see the error of hi. ways and come over to work for me. And the fact that Gao Xiang was my student puts the two of us on a special footing. I'm in the armed forces at present, but I come of a family of literati. My old home Boye has produced two eminent men, and I ran Four Virtues Middle School to preserve the traditional virtues. Now Generalissimo Chiang has sent me up north to resist the Communist Party and save substantial citizens from the painful situation they find themselves in. For months we have battled on against great odds. Has your son explained class struggle to you, Mr. Gao? The fact is, according to the Marxist teachings, you and I belong to the same class and should fight on the same side. If the Communists come to power, they'll share out your land, pull down your house and hold a big meeting to denounce you. Your son may be a political commissar, but I imagine during the last year and more you've had quite a bit to put up with in the village. You ought to understand why we're here, Mr. Gao, and co-operate with us. I must say I deplore your attitude to my army."

Zhang Yinwu kept his eyes on the old man as he spoke, and a crafty smile played round his lips. Some of his arguments did shake Old Gao; but a little sober thought soon restored him to his senses. For a long time, it is true, he had spent many sleepless nights worrying about his property, with painfully divided loyalties. One thing was clear, however. The Central Government had no intention of resisting Japan, and if China came to be enslaved that would be worse than losing his property. This latter possibility no longer preyed on his mind.

"Well, general," he replied. "I'll count it my bad luck that my horse has gone. But at noon today I saw your bodyguard shoot one of my pigeons. I hope you'll enforce better discipline among your men."

"You must be mistaken." Zhang Yinwu frowned. "I'll call my men together at once. If you can point out the man you say did this, I'll have him shot on the spot."

"What? Risk my neck over a pigeon?" retorted Old Gao. "No, I'm not asking for trouble. It's getting late, I'll leave you gentlemen to rest."

Returning to his room he sat in silence on the edge of the *kang* until his wife, snug in her quilt, urged him to turn in.

"This is the Central Army some people were longing for," muttered the old man. "It looks as if all that our son said was right."

He was slowly undressing when angry voices were raised in Zhang Yinwu's room. Old Gao went to the window. His wife, too, got up to listen. Apparently an urgent report had just come in.

"General, a small force of Japanese has gone to a village ten *li* or more to the east," announced an orderly. "They're conscripting men from every house to build roads."

"That's all right. Let them go ahead," said Zhang Yinwu.

"Some of the local gentry have come to ask for protection."

"Just ignore them."

"Our fellows want to fight. This enemy force is a small one."

"Who are you calling our enemy?" Zhang demanded. "Go and give the men this warning: Anyone who clashes with the Japanese will be shot."

"That's going to make us unpopular," his orderly protested softly.

"You fool! Unpopular? Are we popular now?"

"What if that unit heads this way?"

"If it does, we'll withdraw to the west. These are our strategic principles and we'll abide by them."

The orderly hurried out.

Before dawn Zhang Yinwu's headquarters evacuated Five-dragon Temple and moved west. As old Mrs. Gao heard the clatter of men and horses leaving the courtyard, she clasped her hands.

"Buddha be praised, they've gone!"

"That means the Japanese are coming," sighed her husband.

73

When conditions were ripe, one regiment of the 120th Division decoyed the enemy's main force into an impasse. Then the rest of the division surrounded the Japanese and launched an all-out attack. Never had the invaders met with such strong opposition. Not even the poison gas they resorted to could save them from destruction.

As a result of this battle, although the enemy still occupied some of our county towns, the position in the central Hebei plain was stabilized and the people gained in confidence. The local troops had learned enough in the course of this arduous campaign to adapt themselves to new circumstances, enlarge their forces and defend the resistance bases. Soon after this, the 120th Division received orders to take to the mountains.

Chun'er was drafted back to her district to work. Bian Ji was to work in the mountains west of the railway together with Instructor Zhang and had left two days earlier to pick up a few things from home before going to his new post. When Chun'er went to the regional office for fresh instructions she hoped to see Mangzhong again, but he was not there. She returned alone to her county.

This year the whole winter and the lunar New Year, so much enjoyed by young people, had been passed in fighting. Now spring was back again and, apart from the shabby padded army jacket over Chun'er's shoulders, few traces of winter could be found in the fields. Rich green wheat was shooting up, flocks of wild-geese searched for food and passed the night in the wheat fields, leaving prints like clustered bamboo leaves on the sand. A small peach tree was already in bloom, sheltered under a tall willow beside a big well. Waterwheels turned by donkeys and horses were creaking in all the fields around, while girls opening and closing irrigation ditches leaned on their spades in every conceivable posture, and yellow orioles trilled as they flitted in search of elm seeds. Bare-bottomed children turned somersaults on the sand dunes, and girls felt hot even in thin summer clothes. In the respites between battles, the people of the base went about their daily tasks as usual, and at dawn or dusk lovers still sought each other out by the stacks of grain or the ridges of the wheat fields.

That morning Chun'er walked to Wuren Bridge, a well-known market-town twenty-five *li* south of Anguo. While still some distance from the north gate, she could hear the noisy tumult of the market. The shouts of grain merchants weighing rice could be distinguished from the disputes over horses' speed and haggling over prices in the cattle market. Salesmen and customers alike seemed engaged in a ruthless struggle rather than met to do business. A tactless word from a buyer, who had already agreed to the price, might make a seller cling to his sack of grain and refuse to sell after all; or a cattle dealer might seize a calf by the horns and drag it away from the would-be purchaser.

After the enemy occupation of some county towns, the authorities in the bases encouraged merchants and tradesfolk to come to the market-towns. So the anti-Japanese markets grew larger and larger, and the fair at Wuren Bridge on the fourth and ninth days of the lunar calendar was so tightly packed that it was hard to squeeze your way through. Stalls of goods of every description stretched right down to the dikes.

The most popular Anguo eating houses and snack bars had become mobile too and moved here with the peasants on market days to do business. On the side of the south dike, a beancurd stall under a mat awning was doing a brisk trade. This shop had moved from the south gate of Anguo, where it had been opened by a famine refugee from Shandong, who, arriving with no more than two shabby crates, had succeeded in making money and settling down here. Now the old man was dead and his sons had joined the army; it was his wife who managed the business, while her daughters and daughters-in-law did the cooking and waiting. They were all good-looking girls. The eldest daughter, who served beancurd under the awning on market days, had neatly combed luxuriant black hair and wore a spotless white apron over her new blue cotton trousers and tunic. She bent over the stove as she cooked, stealing frequent glances from big, limpid black eyes at all the passers-by.

Chun'er stepped in here and sat down. She was hungry but could only afford a bowl of beancurd. The cook studied her eagerly as she filled a bowl and gave it to her small sister to carry over.

The neatly dressed little girl held the blue, flower-patterned bowl carefully in both hands, for it was filled to the brim and there were rich globules of fat and beancurd floating on the soup. She set it down with great care, only to spill some of the soup by bumping into the table.

"There you are, comrade! My sister specially added some pork stock for you," she confided softly, smiling.

"Why should I get such special treatment?" asked Chun'er, as she lowered her head to taste the soup.

"Why?" The little girl squatted beside her to explain. "We saw you coming along the dike. My sister said to me, 'There's a woman comrade from the Eighth Route Army that's just won another battle. Wouldn't it be nice if she stopped here for a snack?'"

"How pretty your sister is," remarked Chun'er. "Is she married?"

"Oh, yes. I've two little nephews. The Japanese burned our house by the south gate, so we had to move to this dike here."

She ran off then in answer to her sister's call, coming back with a dish of freshly made sesame cakes.

"Why don't you try one of these?" she asked.

Chun'er's only reply was a smile.

"I know you haven't much money." The child picked up a cake and slipped it into Chun'er's bowl, making another splash. "That's on the house — a present from my sister and me!"

As Chun'er left this likable family and hurried down the dike, her step was sprightlier and lighter than before.

Ahead of her rumbled an ox-cart, driven by a short, sturdy girl. She was wearing a baggy, faded red coat and trousers rolled up to her calves.

Some enormous round cabbages were rolling about in the cart. There were fine big turnips too, which kept threatening to pitch off the back. The girl turned and, catching sight of Chun'er, called:

"Here, comrade! Come and have a ride."

Chun'er wondered if the crisp sweetness of her voice came from eating fresh vegetables.

"I don't mind walking," she answered with a smile.

"I can't keep the cart from jolting on my own," said the girl. "It'll be much steadier if there are two of us."

Chun'er got up and sat beside her on the front shaft. The brown bullock pulling the cart was plump and glossy with short, curved horns. He flicked his tail indignantly at this increase in his load, but soon steadied down again.

The girl tucked her red-wood whip under her legs, picked up a knife and started carving a turnip. Presently she had made a charming flower basket.

Baskets like these are usually made as gifts for the lunar New Year. Girls sow wheat inside and hang them from the beams, so that the wheat sprouts just as the turnip flowers. For New Year they sometimes stick a candle inside, making a bright little lantern. But this year all that had been spoiled by the Japanese invaders.

"Which village are you from, little sister?" asked Chun'er.

"It's just over the river," said the girl, pointing ahead.

74

Perched on the cart, Chun'er reflected how good people were to her, not only today but ever since she'd joined the revolution. Surely it wasn't just because they liked her face?

Their cart soon reached the suspension bridge over the Shahe. Thanks to the fair, the approach was crowded with carts waiting to cross, and the old toll-keeper standing at the door of his hut was calling out greetings to carters whom he knew and collecting toll from those from far away. The ice in the river had melted and the current was swift. Both sides of the bridge were piled with sandbags and stone rollers had been propped up against the piers to hold the superstructure steady, but each time a heavy cart trundled on to the bridge it started swaying and creaking. Telephone wires for army use were attached to tall cedar poles at either end of the bridge, and through these the wind from the river set up a shrill whining.

Carters were disputing over the order of crossing when a soldier in full battle equipment appeared, his face streaked with mud and sweat, a small signal flag in one hand. He mounded up the dike and threw back his head like a tiger or panther mounting a peak at dawn to gaze down below. The contingent behind him was advancing in strict order along the dike. Their firm yet elastic tread made it seem as if the very hills were marching, as if the rushing waves had speeded up.

The man at the head strode up to the bridge and said something to the toll-keeper, who shouted to the carters:

"Move back there, fellows! Let these comrades cross first."

The cart Chun'er was on was behind a good many others which obstructed her view of the troops. And the girl driving the cart was in no great hurry, because her home lay just across the river. She sat there stripping the spoiled leaves off some cabbages and feeding them to her bullock.

On a sudden impulse, Chun'er stood up on the shaft to look at the troops. Clutching their rifles and ammunition tight, they were crossing the bridge at a run, directed by their commander from a pile of sandbags. The moment Chun'er saw who he was, she jumped off the cart.

"I'm crossing on foot, sister," she cried. "I can't wait."

Before the girl could reply, Chun'er was darting through the carts and horses to the bridge and calling:

"Mangzhong! Mangzhong!"

The commander turned.

"We've been drafted to the mountains," he told her in a low voice. "I never expected to see you before we left."

"I went to the district government for news of you," she panted. "They told me your troops had been reorganized."

"After the last campaign I was promoted to the rank of instructor," said Mangzhong. "We're organized now just like a regular army. There's a job waiting for us up there in the west. Are you on your way home? Tell them in the village that I've gone."

All his men as they passed stared curiously or winked to see him talking to Chun'er. The girl's cheeks burned, but Mangzhong paid no attention.

"Can't I go to the mountains too?" she asked eagerly.

"You'll have to ask your higher command. We may be coming back." With a last look into her eyes, Mangzhong turned and raced to the front of his troops again. Chun'er crossed at one side of the bridge, clambering over sandbags and millet stalks that threatened to trip her up. Once on the south bank of the river, the soldiers headed west. By now the sun was veiled by evening clouds.

Chun'er stood on the bank staring after the swift-moving column. The river swirled down from the west, buffeted the bridge and swept on. A large boat was battling its way up from downstream against the current and straining to negotiate the bridge. In her distress she put herself in its place and felt she too was grappling with a fierce current.

Mangzhong had not looked back. Only the soldier at the rear of the column, whom Chun'er belatedly recognized as Old Wen, kept turning to wave her back, but whether in fun or in earnest she could not tell.

The carts were crossing in turn now. Once over this tricky

stretch, men and horses brightened up and made briskly off with no thought to spare for Chun'er. Only the girl in the bullock cart swung her legs from the shaft and teased:

"So you couldn't wait, eh! It'll soon be dark yet you're still standing there. You can't fool me. Who was that talking to you just now?"

"A comrade I know." Tears stood in Chun'er's eyes.

"Come home with me." The girl tactfully pulled up. "You needn't go on tonight. I'll be glad of your company."

But Chun'er said she must hurry home and walked on alone towards the southeast. The sun just before setting was a glorious red, but when next she turned to look west it had disappeared completely behind the mountains. "If Mangzhong and his men make good time," she thought, "they'll reach the mountains tonight. They won't cross the Beijing-Hankou Railway without a skirmish." It seemed to her they were drawing apart all too fast.

Her steps began to drag, her heart yearned towards the west. The road was almost deserted, the fields and villages hidden in smoke and mist. The hazards of war made her reflect with a pang that she ought to lose no time in clarifying the relation between herself and Mangzhong.

On the road north of Ziwuzhen she met Bian Ji's wife, panting as she lugged along a branch and an armful of dry twigs for kindling.

"Where have you been?" Chun'er asked her.

"I'm learning the new ways." Mrs. Bian giggled breathlessly. "I've just seen my man off to the front. If he decides to go, who am I to stop him?"

"Has Brother Bian Ji left then?"

"He got an urgent summons, or I'd have made him hoe the fields before leaving. Anyway, he's not much of a farmer. The kiddies and I have to make shift for ourselves."

361

"Where did you see him to?"

"Liu Family Graveyard. Picked up this wood on my way back, because we're always short of firewood in spring. Well, well. Ten years and more we've been married, and his work kept taking him away from home, but when did I ever see him off before? This isn't the first time he's been up to the hills. Before it was to earn money painting temples, this time it's to work for the resistance; but he'll still only be painting and writing plays — I can't see that it's much improvement."

"Why did you see him so far then?" Chun'er laughed.

"Because of a visitor we had. My old man said his teacher was travelling to the west of the railway with him. Well, I wouldn't have put myself out for his teacher either, but he brought his wife along — such a pretty young thing."

"Our instructor and his wife!" exclaimed Chun'er.

"I've never set eyes on such a loving couple." Mrs. Bian smiled. "They must have come out from home and spent the previous night together. Couldn't finish all their billing and cooing at home, so she had to see him all this way. Sniffing and crying she was, till she had me crying too. I thought: All these years I've been married I've had the fields and the house on my hands, and no matter what the weather I took the children out to the fields so that he'd have more time to paint. I was the one to worry if there was no rice for the pot, no fuel for the stove. If we had anything good to eat, I gave it to him and the children. I tried to spare him all the heavy work. Now look at me, not yet thirty but ailing with asthma. How could I hold back my tears when that young wife cried? As if that wasn't bad enough, my old man said to his teacher: 'Look at her, how poorly she is. She's not known a single day's comfort in my house.' Why, sister, all these years we've been husband and wife that's the first kind

362

word he's said. It went to my heart and made me cry worse than ever!"

"Did you see him off crying all the way?"

"What if I did?" Mrs. Bian pouted. "I was seeing him off to study and resist Japan. You people keep telling us that once we've beaten Japan we'll be free and have a better life. I tell you, I'm just living for that day."

75

Some took the road of revolution with a light heart, others as if shouldering a heavy burden. For Bian Ji, and even more so for a poor peasant's son like Mangzhong, it meant exchanging a tattered padded jacket for a new uniform, the worry about his next meal for a generous issue of millet every day. He'd had no schooling, but here was a chance to study. He was really living better than ever before. Mangzhong had no wife and children to act as a drag. And if he thought of marriage he pinned his hopes on the victory of the revolution, when all things would be possible. Instructor Zhang's feelings were naturally more involved. At each step forward he felt something pulling him back. It took strong determination to overcome this.

His wife stayed close by his side each step of the way. She had never travelled so far and her feet often faltered. Her husband kept having to wait or help her along.

Mrs. Zhang had made up an outsize bundle for him: food for the road and clothes — thin, lined or padded — for every season. To show respect for his teacher, Bian Ji carried this pack in addition to his own which contained only the barest necessities. They counted on reaching the local government that evening to arrange to cross the railway. If necessary, they might run the blockade that night. Several times Bian Ji urged Mrs. Zhang to turn back, but she insisted on seeing them all the way, explaining that she had a relative in the local government.

They reached their destination at midnight. Because of the enemy's proximity, they were passed through several hands before a militiaman led them to the organization they wanted. But at last, in a shed by a threshing-floor, they found Li Peizhong.

Peizhong, not completely recovered from her wounds, had been transferred here to check up on the cadres crossing the enemy blockade and issue them with passes. They found her sorting out letters of introduction. Her face, in the light of an oil lamp, looked thinner and paler. Although she knew Bian Ji, for some reason her impression of this "local worthy" was not too favourable, and after taking their credentials from the Party committee of the academy she asked him a number of irrelevant questions. Tired and hungry after the journey, Bian Ji soon lost patience.

"I want to see the man in charge," he said.

"That's the Party secretary of the local government. Our section handles passes."

Bian Ji picked up his packs and left abruptly. He finally tracked down the Party secretary. It was Gao Xiang, and with him was Gao Qingshan.

"I knew we'd find friends here," said Bian Ji triumphantly.

Qingshan lost no time in getting them food and somewhere to rest. In addition to the ordinary pass he got Peizhong to write a letter in his name to the cultural officer on the other side, explaining Bian Ji's talents. Since they would not be crossing until the next evening, he urged the travellers to have a good rest.

The next morning Peizhong gave Bian Ji their passes together with his special letter of introduction. He put the passes carefully away before reading the other letter, which was a long one. Peizhong's style of writing irritated him: it was too flowery and fulsome for his taste. Much as he appreciated Gao Qingshan's concern, he thought this letter superfluous and tore it up.

That evening, when they assembled in a wood, the knowledge that Mangzhong's unit would be crossing with them made Bian Ji less nervous than he might otherwise have been. His eyes closed, he leaned against a willow tree conserving his energy as he listened to a report from their commander.

The Japanese had dug trenches on either side of the railway and at certain strategic points had built pillboxes and electric barricades. They enforced the *bao jia* system* in all the villages along the line and made severe reprisals wherever Eighth Army men crossed. We had several ways of running this blockade. The simplest, when our forces were strong enough, was to open fire and charge over. Another was to mine two sections of the line in order to hold up the enemy armoured trains and to cross between these mines. The puppet troops manning the pillboxes were not a serious menace. Complete secrecy, of course, was out of the question. There were too many villagers playing a double game, who might not cause serious damage but who tried to keep in with the Japanese by giving some information about our movements. Then armoured trains would thunder out to the mines, stop short of them, switch on searchlights, and keep that section under heavy fire. This had happened only a few days ago. But it would create a bad impression, if our mines blew up an ordinary passenger train.

---

* The administrative system by which the Japanese aggressors enforced their fascist rule at the primary level in the areas occupied by them.

So today they were trying out a new way of crossing.

It was early in the month by the lunar calendar, and a new crescent moon was rising behind the woods. Everybody swore at it and hoped it would soon be obscured by clouds; and, as those in command had foreseen, by the time they neared the railway the moon had considerately sunk behind the hills. Taking cover fifty yards or so from the track, Bian Ji watched Mangzhong and his men crawl forward.

The earth began to vibrate. An express roared up from the south. Soon red and green signals went on at the small station a little to their north. The express was still rolling by when Mangzhong's unit stood up. The second it had passed, they jumped on to the track. Someone smashed the poles of the barbed wire fence with a chopper, then they yelled to the others to cross.

As they rushed across, some who'd never seen a railway before stooped down to finger the tracks. Without warning the lights by the line and the station signals went out. The Japanese had spotted them. But the armoured train waiting in readiness found its way blocked by the express rolling into the station. The two drivers hooted and whistled furiously. By the time they had straightened things out our men were over.

Still the armoured train thundered out, only to be shot at by Mangzhong's men under cover.

Then a forced march began. Not only were they anxious to throw off pursuers, they had to run another blockade when they reached the foot of the hills. They sprinted over the wet sand and sharp stones beside the River Shahe. The ice in the water froze their veins when they waded through the shallows.

Bian Ji was carrying Instructor Zhang's pack, in addition to which he had to lend him a hand. And once safely in the hills they had no chance to rest, for it started to pour with rain — a gruelling test for those with no previous experience of climbing.

The thin shoes they wore on the plain were sopping wet. Soon they wore through and the jagged rocks cut their feet. Going downhill, the more nervous and tense a man was the easier it was to slip in the red mud. For Instructor Zhang this was a fearful ordeal. Bian Ji, looking back, would see his painting master toiling up painfully through the driving rain with no eyes for the beauty of the rugged peaks around him. Drenched to the skin, his face white, his teeth chattering, he seemed on the verge of collapse.

After they had crossed several ridges the rain let up. Down in the foothills the order came to halt. The men flung themselves down in exhaustion to sleep on the boulders or grass.

When they woke they ate some of their rations, changed their shoes and set off again. The sky had cleared. Forgotten now were the hardships, fatigue and fears of the previous night. Rested and fed, with new strength in their legs, they marched cheerfully on.

Only now did they gaze round with interest at the magnificent scenery of this base in the hills. The sun was shining on the mountain slopes, but the smoke of thatched cottages on the southern side could hardly be distinguished from wreaths of cloud. Women in light blue clothes stood at their doors. Men in coarse light blue padded trousers and sheepskin jackets were leisurely smoking the first pipe of the day. Children flung their arms round the necks of their big dogs to stop them from barking at these new arrivals.

367

76

With the rest of the troops, Mangzhong and Old Wen struck into the mountains, making for the northwest. The climb was a stiff one, as steep as a ladder to heaven. When the men looked back, their old camp in the plain seemed to have sunk to the bottom of a bowl.

In accordance with the regular practice, Mangzhong was marching at the rear of his company. Just in front of him, as it happened, was Old Wen, now second in command of the third squad. Old Wen always had plenty to say for himself and liked to crack jokes when the other men were tired. Although he constantly reminded himself that they had left One-eyed Tian's stable, Mangzhong was his superior officer, and army discipline must be upheld, he saw no reason to forget that they had been work-mates as close to each other as brothers, for that relationship had not changed to-day. So he never missed a chance for a good yarn with Mangzhong. He could see quite clearly how much his friend had changed, developing in a direction totally different from the one Old Wen would once have predicted. The lad seemed older and graver than his years, and Old Wen understood that this was due to the heavy responsibilities he had taken up while little more than a boy. It was rare now to see a mischievous smile on his face or catch him indulging in horse-play.

Old Wen remembered a day when they were reaping one of One-eyed Tian's fields. It was still very hot, that field was some distance from the house, and they had taken along an old pewter jug of water, mainly to whet their sickles but also to quench their thirst. Mangzhong put all his energy into reaping, keeping close at Old Wen's heels, not falling a pace behind. Old Wen reflected grumpily that if he were not second in the line the boy would have outstripped him. Old Chang, who was leading the way, turned back and called:

"Easy there, Mangzhong! What's the hurry, you young fool?"

"He wants to take over my rice-bowl." Old Wen gave a sarcastic laugh. "Use your head, kid. You can work yourself to death for One-eyed Tian, but he won't buy you so much as a willow coffin."

The next moment he felt he had spoken too harshly, so crestfallen and deflated did Mangzhong look. The lad obviously had very little idea of what being a hired hand meant or of the hard times ahead. He slouched off to the end of the field to whet his sickle.

He did not come back for some time, and Old Wen found him emptying their jug of water down a field-mouse's hole. He was lying on his stomach, one ear to the ground, as if to catch the sound of the field-mice scurrying to escape from this flood.

Old Chang's sickle needed sharpening too, and Old Wen was parched. But Mangzhong had emptied all their water away.

"You darned idiot!" swore Old Wen. "That hole's too deep for ten jugs of water to fill. How are we to get through our work, I'd like to know, with no water to whet the sickles?"

His eyes on the hole, Mangzhong paid no attention, clutching his sickle in readiness for the field-mice to dart out. But the water drained away and no field-mice appeared. Only a bloated mole-cricket crawled fearfully out. Mangzhong whacked it with his sickle and cried with a laugh:

"This mole-cricket is the living image of One-eyed Tian. Why should we wear ourselves out for a creature like that?"

At that Old Chang and Old Wen had to laugh. . . .

The troops toiled up and up. When those in front halted

to brush the sweat out of their eyes, it spattered the faces of men behind or fell on the rocky path. There was not a breath of wind in that ravine. The small patch of sky overhead was as blue as freshly dyed cloth.

"How high are we going?" demanded Old Wen. "We'll soon have reached the Southern Heavenly Gate."

Mangzhon made no reply, his eyes strained ahead. He was watching to see if any of his men looked fagged out, in need of a rest.

"Instructor!" tried Old Wen again, changing the subject. "Which is hotter in mid-summer, hoeing the sorghum or marching?"

"They're both equally hot," said Mangzhong. "But thers's a big difference."

"What big difference, instructor? A fellow sweats just the same."

"You sweat just the same. But we sweated before so that One-eyed Tian's family could have a soft life. Now we're sweating to liberate the whole Chinese nation."

"That's true," said Old Wen. "We must look at everything from the point of view of resisting Japanese imperialism. But tell me this, instructor: Do you count swine like One-eyed Tian in, when you talk about the liberation of the nation?"

"Anyone who resists Japan is counted in. One-eyed Tian is against resisting Japan, so of course he's out."

"Yes, leave him out. What's the use of our fighting Japan all this time if he cashes in on it. Right?"

"That's right. And because the war of resistance has liberated us, we must study hard and do our best to make progress."

Old Wen asked no more questions. There was no sign ahead that a halt was to be called, so they went on climbing.

But when Old Wen was not talking he had to amuse himself some other way. He started kicking stones over the cliff and listening to the clatter they made far below.

"Don't raise such a din," said Mangzhong. "What if there are people or goats down below?"

"On the north side of a mountain like this? I bet you there's nobody here but us," said Old Wen. "This is really what you call the back of beyond."

"You find people everywhere," protested Mangzhong. "When folk are hard pressed, they can't pick and choose where they'll live."

"Maybe. But I bet we're the only ones from outside to come this way. Only men tired of living would venture up here to be eaten by the wolves."

"How can you be so sure?" Mangzhong had no patience with such talk. "Men will go anywhere to make a living. If the Japanese can't stop them, neither can wolves."

"The Japanese can't stop *us*," retorted Old Wen gravely. "And neither can any mountain, no matter how high, any river, no matter how wide. All I'm saying is, this is a desolate place with no smoke from hut or cottage."

"There's smoke for you." Mangzhong pointed upwards with a grin.

They had halted now to rest. Some soldiers were sitting on the path gazing down towards the valley; some were leaning against the rocks looking at the peaks around; others were resting back to back, or sitting in small groups. They struck lights and lit their pipes. Tobacco was scarce but flints were plentiful here — any pebble on the road would serve. The men talked and laughed or sang. A cheerful medley of accents from all over China re-echoed through the lonely mountains.

The sun struck deep into the ranges of hills stretching out

in neat folds towards the west. Dense clouds of white heat vapour were billowing up from the fathomless valleys below. It was as if invisible fires were raging beneath, or magic geysers throwing up jets of steam.

"That's not smoke," said Old Wen to Mangzhong, pulling on his pipe. "Those are clouds. Didn't we often say, down in the fields, that the Western Hills produce clouds?"

They set off again, up and down through the endless mist which grew denser and denser as thunder started rolling.

"Without lifting a finger, we're going to get another shower and a chance to wash our clothes," exulted Old Wen.

Wind and rain held no fears for troops on the march in those days. In fact, like waterfowl they welcomed a downpour, glad to have their sweaty limbs doused by driving rain. Besides, the mountain paths here were so rocky that there was no danger of slipping.

They looked up, but impenetrable mist hid everything from sight. There was no way of telling how far it was to the top. Except for a few occasional big drops, the rain held off. Presently, as they rounded the right flank of the mountain, the stone path became wider and flatter and trees of a deep emerald green appeared on both sides. The scenery here was fantastically lovely. The slopes all around this dell hemmed in by peaks were thickly wooded with trees unknown to them, on whose broad, fleshy leaves wind and rain drummed softly. The massive bronze trunks were overgrown with moss, and the boulders on either side of the path were virtually swathed in moss too. Separated from both sides of the road by tinkling brooks, stood a number of cottages. And countless little waterfalls were cascading down from the hills above their roofs to flow into a pool further down. As the soldiers marched on, surrounded by streams and trees, they could hardly tell whether this water and greenery had its source above, all around, or in the pool below, deep as a well but covered with foam and floating water weeds.

"Well, see any sign of life?" Mangzhong teased Old Wen.

"Why, this is a fairy land!" exclaimed Old Wen.

77

For the people living here this was no fairy land, as Old Wen put it, for life high up in the mountains was very hard. The troops had not intended to have their midday meal until after the next pass, but now they were accosted by some old men from this remarkable village, who blocked the way and urged them to stop and rest. Women and children pressed excited, smiling faces against their thick window bars, but the water cascading down from their eaves prevented them from seeing the soldiers clearly, and this made them all the more eager for their menfolk to bring these visitors into their homes.

The order came to halt in the village for a meal.

The troops drew up in the "road" before being assigned to different homes. Old Wen and his squad went to a house overlooking the southern hill, whose builders had made the best use of the terrain. An overhanging boulder served as its roof, and the sheer cliff behind as its back wall. From the rafters hung large gourds filled with lentils and red pepper, switches of mountain bramble from which the bark had been peeled, and golden clusters of maize cobs. Two large orange pumpkins, one on each side of the door, were like the crimson lanterns hung up at New Year.

The cabin itself was a small place to house three generations, but the grandfather made the men welcome. Having told his wife and daughter-in-law to move his granddaughter, who was sleeping on the *kang*, to one corner, he cleared away the tobacco leaves that were being cured by the stove to make room for the men to sit down.

Since this was a small village and had no grain office, the soldiers produced some of their own ration of millet. There was no lack of fuel, for the pine and cedar wood stacked by every door burned well even if slightly damp. Although Old Wen was assistant squad leader, he had taken over the job of lighting a fire to cook during a march, having earlier on discovered that this was easy work during which he could smoke, while on cold or rainy days he was able to dry himself by the fire and get warm.

The old man told them that villagers had only recently heard about the resistance to Japan when a cadre from Quyang passed here on his way to Fanshi. This cadre, a former mason, was one of the very few visitors to have come there from outside. And this was their first sight of the Eighth Route Army.

"That mason gave us a good account of the Eighth Route Army," he said. "But we little thought you would come up all this way."

"There's nowhere we can't go, uncle," they assured him.

"It's seldom we leave the village," said the old man. "I'm sixty-seven this year, but I've never been out of the mountains."

A look round the room confirmed this. Everything the family ate, wore or used bore the imprint of the mountain. Their clothes were made of furs, skin, bark and straw. The only cotton jacket was worn by the daughter-in-law, sitting in bashful silence by the window. It was dyed a patchy black, and no doubt the dye came from acorns, cotton-grass, or the indigo plants that grew wild in the hills. The old man's pipe, his wife's hairpin, and the pegs their daughter-in-law used to plait ropes, were all carved from the bones of wild animals. Many of the utensils in there were made of stone, while handsome horns and skins hung next to plump pods on the wall. The necessities of their life were its ornaments too.

The cabin was very dark when first they entered. As the resinous pine faggots sputtered and sizzled in the stove, the room was filled with aromatic smoke. Just before the soldiers' millet was ready, the clouds and mist scattered and the sun shone in, flooding the room with light. An appetizing odour came from the millet bubbling in the pan.

The little girl, who had seemed asleep, sat up now and opened her eyes. Throwing off her black goatskin cover, she pointed one small hand at the pan and murmured:

"That smells good."

"She's better!" The mother smiled at the grandmother. "Beginning to be hungry."

"The child's been ill three days and not eaten a bite," her grandmother told the men. "Your coming's brought us good luck — now she's taken a turn for the better."

"We'd no idea the child was ill," said Old Wen, "or we wouldn't have made all this noise."

"Never mind," said the grandmother. "She's only a girl. No call for you to worry."

The child had just noticed the strangers. Drawing back the hand she had stretched out, she nestled up to her mother. Her mother smiled at her grandmother, who said:

"You mustn't be offended by an old woman. My granddaughter wants to eat some of your millet."

"Of course!" Old Wen whisked off the lid of the pan, took a rice bowl from the *kang*, filled it up and passed it over.

Her grandmother fed the little girl, who ate with evident relish, her merry eyes roaming over the soldiers' faces.

"It's not often we eat good grain like this," the mother told them shyly. She left the *kang* to fetch a big dish of pickles as a way of expressing her thanks.

"What's wrong with the little girl?" asked Old Wen between mouthfuls.

"A fever," her mother said.

"She ought to see a doctor. I'll go and get one." Old Wen put down his bowl and hurried to company headquarters. After hearing his report, Mangzhong told the medical officer:

"Go and have a look at the child. And don't just use aspirin or mercurochrome — give her something that works."

The medical officer went along with Old Wen and gave the child an injection from his small but precious stock of medicine.

When the villagers heard of this, all those with ailments came to ask for treatment. Some had suffered for years from ulcers, stomach trouble or eye disease which could not be cured overnight; but the medical officer did the best he could for them and told them what precautions to take. This made the people feel much closer to the army.

"We'll never forget how the Eighth Route Army cured our folk," they declared. "It's years since we last had a doctor up here."

The little girl's mother was distressed because she knew no way to show her gratitude. She insisted on washing the soldiers' pan and bowls, then swept the *kang* and urged them to sit down and rest. When Old Wen went out she stood watching at the door as if one of her own dear ones had just come home. This did not escape the attention of Old Wen, who decided to leave the mother and child some small memento. But the men of the Eighth Route Army had few personal possessions — what could he give? As he tidied up his kit before falling in, he drew from the bottom of his pack a portrait of Chairman Mao wrapped in several layers of paper which Bian Ji had painted for him before he joined up.

"Here's a portrait of Chairman Mao for you to hang on the wall," Old Wen told the mother. "We're his troops. He's the one who tells us to help poor folk in every way we can."

The whole family gathered round to look at the painting. The mother held it up with both hands and, laughing softly, exclaimed:

"So this is him? This is Chairman Mao!"

By the time the troops assembled, their propagandist had written an anti-Japanese slogan in big characters on the great boulder at the entrance to the village. And from this time on, from that village perched high up the mountain the word spread:

"Chairman Mao's troops passed this way!"

"Yes, to resist Japanese imperialism, they go wherever Chairman Mao tells them."

These troops of ours were not simply trail-blazers who marched thousands of *li* to swoop down on the enemy. It was their task as well to prepare the soil for revolution. At each step forward they took, at each new place they reached, they sowed the seeds of revolution in the hearts of the people there.

78

Campaigning here was hard in the extreme. The local people were too poor to provide the army with grain and cotton. Winter came early, but the extra clothes issued to the men were cut down from old uniforms and too short to cover the wrists and ankles of most of them. Their shoes and socks were made from old clothes as well, and day and night the women plaited hemp cords to make shoe soles for them, besides giving the fighters the thick soles they had put aside for their husbands.

These parts had always been sparsely populated, and after several of the enemy's "mopping-up" campaigns they became even lonelier and more desolate.

But the troops marched on, over wind-buffeted mountain tops, past the massive, crumbling Great Wall, along rocky river banks and stony tracks.

At dusk they would assemble among the boulders of a narrow bank, then climb to the summit of a hill and sweep down to storm an enemy stronghold. The stars in heaven glimmered faintly as they climbed up dizzy, twisting goat tracks, so high they could almost reach out and touch the sky. The going was rough and one false step would mean a fall thousands of feet to the valley below. More than once, on the march, they heard a clatter and slither as a heavily loaded mule slipped over the side and was lost.

Sometimes it was all the men could do to keep their footing in the teeth of a gale.

One night Mangzhong's company camped in a sheep-fold up on the hills. Now shepherds and sheep had gone. But the thick layer of dried sheep dung there made a warm, comfortable billet. Leaning against the fence, the soldiers cracked a few quiet jokes before lying down.

"People say our war of resistance is a peasants' war," remarked Old Wen to Mangzhong. "That's absolutely true. Apart from marching and fighting, we're still poor peasants."

"Yes, and it shows how close we are to the peasants. They're our own flesh and blood," replied Mangzhong. "We

378

depend on them for food and clothes, for billets and help on the march. Even deep in the hills here, we're sleeping in a sheep-fold some peasants sweated to make."

That night there were cold gusts of wind and a sudden squall of rain, but the soldiers did not even turn over in their sleep. They went on dreaming blissfully. Some laughed softly in their dreams.

Mangzhong and another man did sentry duty for the first part of the night on nearby peaks. A biting north wind tugged at the padded overcoat worn by all the company in turn. In the distance a pack of wolves howled. But Mangzhong's head was clear, his heart at peace. He stood with his shoulders thrown back.

He stood guard over those rugged hills as resolutely as he had once guarded his home in the Hebei plain. All his concern was for his comrades, now sound asleep. It was two years and more since he had joined the army, and each winter had been spent in gruelling fighting. In this time, he had made outstanding progress. He could give all his devotion now to this wild mountain region so far from his own native village.

That was why, above the howling of the wind, he seemed to hear every least sound from the neighbouring countryside: the scurry of a hare in flight, the bleating of a new-born lamb, the lullabies that mothers were crooning to their children, the endearments murmured by a young husband and wife as they woke from sleep. To him, so steadfast and true, the whole of life had become sheer poetry.

His watch over, Mangzhong went back to the sheep-fold and lay down beside Old Wen. Bitterly cold though it was, Old Wen was sleeping soundly, his contented snores rivalling the wind that blustered over the terraced fields and hillsides.

But his skimpy uniform could not cover him as he lay

sprawled out, and half his long limbs were exposed. Mang-zhong pulled his jacket over him before lying down at Old Wen's side to sleep.

79

For months now they had been cut off from news of home. Each time they camped in a new place, Mangzhong would take his squad leaders up the nearby hills to reconnoitre. Sometimes he went up with the men to collect firewood or pick herbs.

The guide for their reconnaissance today was a peasant who worked on the local monastery's farm. He was getting on in years, but these seasoned campaigners in their prime could hardly keep up with him when it came to climbing. He knew the whole district like the palm of his hand. He could describe every stick and stone on each mountain, and they found all his information accurate. He told Mangzhong with a smile:

"Instructor, why d'you suppose they sent me to you instead of a shepherd or a woodcutter? It's because shepherds only know the hills with good pasture, while woodcutters stick to the hills with trees. I'm a living map, I know every path out of here. I've been up and down these mountains since I was a boy. We're pretty high here, aren't we? But I could slide down to the bottom in next to no time."

The soldiers were eager to see him make good this claim. Mangzhong leaned out from the summit to have a look. No crops were planted on the mountainside, but the early morning sun was shining on a golden mass of wild chrysanthemums and clumps of fine trees and shrubs, some bearing purple bell-shaped flowers. Familiar insects were shrilling in the grass, and past them flashed birds they had never seen on the plain.

The old farm-hand tightened his belt and started his descent. Down he slid, now sitting, now standing, unimpeded by the trees and vines, but taking advantage of them to keep his balance.

Mangzhong and the squad leaders followed his example, to the detriment of their hands, feet and uniforms.

Although the foot-hills still lay in the shadow, they were a lovely and impressive sight. This central mountain was flanked by two others, covered with cedar saplings, which stretched in peaceful beauty to right and left like the two sides of a double door guarding this peak.

So many brooks wound down these hills, it was hard to know where they all had their source. Covered with a thick tangle of withered branches and dead leaves, the water tranquil as a girl sleeping in her lover's arms flowed with the faintest of murmurs.

They took off their shoes and socks to bathe their feet in the cool caressing water.

"You should feel at home, instructor," said the farm-hand. "This is the source of your River Hutuo. Anyone who's homesick can give this brook a message and it will carry it home to your wives and sweethearts."

"Doesn't look much like it to me." Old Wen was kicking the drift wood high up the bank. "The Hutuo's broad and big as it flows past our village."

"Of course, what's to stop it widening out down there? But I'll show you how it starts." The old farm-hand led them to the foot of the central peak where a spring welled through a crevice in the red rock and gurgled over the sand.

This was the main source of the Hutuo, which was swelled by other springs rising in the two nearby mountains.

The soldiers let themselves be convinced by the old farm-hand.

"After I heard you come from those parts," he told them, "I wanted to bring you here to have a look. We live so far apart, but all these years there's been this link between us."

"We're as close as folk drinking the same well's water." Old Wen chuckled.

"When I was young I walked along the bank of this stream out of the mountains, then took a boat down all the way to the sea," the farm-hand continued. "I remember your parts well, your people and their ways. How sturdily the sorghum was growing in well-spaced rows on both banks! Young fellows lugged great sheaves out from the fields, sweat pouring down the sorghum flowers sprinkled over them. Grey beards trudged with nets along the bank and cast them wherever they saw bubbles. Clods of soft earth from both banks kept plopping into the river. Fishermen holding nets stood stock-still in the eddies, looking for all the world like winnowing fans, not seeming to care if they caught anything. Our boat sailed on down the Hutuo past Raoyang and Xianxian to join the River Fuyang. Where it widens out and flows northeast, it's called the Ziya. But all the water in it comes from up here. Each time I looked at the river over there, I felt I was seeing somebody from home. In the lake district whopping mosquitoes came after us; so did sampans selling water-melons, musk-melons, sesame cakes and salted eggs. One evening the moon had risen and we were thinking of turning in when, at a bend in the river, we saw some girls bathing — stark naked! Hearing the boat, they ducked down and called out, as bold as you please: 'Look the other way!' "

"Yes, to be sure, it's a fine place, that grand, broad plain of ours." Old Wen looked up at the small patch of sky above and felt he was at the bottom of a well.

"I wouldn't care to live there," said the farm-hand. "Too many roads for my liking. Up here there's only one path leading anywhere — you needn't worry about losing yourself. Mind you, I'm only joking."

They waded along the brook down the sultry valley, where the decaying leaves underfoot were steaming. A huge black cloud loomed in the sky and bore down upon them like some enormous pestle.

"That's a bad look-out," said the farm-hand. "We must get on to higher ground before the storm breaks."

He sprinted out of the valley as if someone were chasing him and started up a mountain path, bounding quickly over the rocks. Old Wen, still barefoot, called after him:

"Who're you trying to fool? Even if it rains, you won't get the sort of flood that sweeps away houses."

"You don't know what you're up against, if you talk like that. Hurry up, or we'll not be able to ford the river!"

The peaks all around were muffled in dark clouds, and they could hear the swish of rain pouring down, yet not a drop fell where they were. They scrambled over a ridge and the farm-hand hurried them across the river. Here in the upper reaches of the Hutuo the water barely reached their knees, yet Old Wen stumbled several times while crossing, for the stream was sweeping down with such force that a rock the height of a man was tottering. Once across, they clambered quickly up to the peak. It was raining now and the farm-hand stopped to catch his breath.

"Look upstream," he told Old Wen, "and you'll see how the water rises in these hills."

Old Wen turned in the drenching rain and saw a torrent like a yellow mud wall rushing down the valley, rearing up higher and higher as it gathered momentum. At first they could hear nothing, but as the flood approached the foot of the massif, they felt the whole mountain shaking. The deluge bore with it branches and leaves that had lain for days in the gully. It had uprooted a great tree and sucked in wild animals, large and small, as well as cattle.

"We're well out of that!" Old Wen shuddered.

"This flood here is going to hit your folk down below," remarked the farm-hand.

"D'you think they've mended the dikes at home?" Old Wen anxiously asked Mangzhong.

But Mangzhong made no reply. He was gazing intently at the turbulent waters as they rushed headlong towards the east.

80

Our troops climbed up to a pass in the Great Wall. Its old keep, no higher than a small city gate, was strategically placed to command the steep slopes below.

The Great Wall built along the crest of the hills did not seem so very high either. Yet it was a powerful bulwark, winding along the undulating ranges on heights towering above the rest. And the forts set up on these sheer ridges were guarded in the old days by soldiers and bowmen.

Time had ravaged both the Great Wall and this keep. Their masonry, weathered by wind and rain, bore the scars of many battles. The feet of countless men and horses had hollowed out the stone causeway as they sweated up through the pass. On the stone wall by the entrance, blackened by the smoke of beacon fires, you could still make out verses and sketches scrawled by former garrison troops.

The wind roared up through the pass from the Yingxian plain. Between the towering peaks to north and south lay the broad, stony channel of the River Sanggan, which so often changes its course. The waves it threw up as it dashed against the rocks glimmered brown and murky under the setting sun. Long poles had just been laid across the river and villagers on both banks were busy fastening planks on these to make a bridge for our men.

Standing in the pass, looking back, Mangzhong could see nothing but serried peaks and valleys: houses, kitchen smoke and rivers were all lost to sight. Before the sun had gone down the full moon sailed up, scudding swiftly along the Great Wall. A flock of black goats, not yet folded for the night, skipped over boulders reddened by the setting sun. A shepherd, flask and wallet on his back, a crook in his hand, sat on one of the beacon towers gazing at the sunset sky. Did his mind run on the battles of long ago? Or was he glad because our troops' arrival meant safety for himself and his flocks?

After a short rest our men climbed up the wall, fingering its massive bricks. Some of them struck up *The March of the Volunteers,* and the next moment the whole company was singing. They felt a strength like that of the Great Wall surge through their veins with the force of the River Sanggan. The cold wind carried their singing down to the plain. The river that had witnessed so many wars in days of old joined in, beating time to the music. The strains eddied up to the setting sun and rising moon, racing along the whole length of the Great Wall. They filled countless valleys, melted the snow on the summit of Mount Wutai, and drowned all groaning and sighing. This was the triumphant marching song for which the land had been waiting.

The road down from outside the pass was precipitous, but the soldiers soon reached a valley and the rocky bank of the river. They crossed the swirling Sanggan and struck west through the hills. Far ahead was a sizable village and a great temple, its gilded roofs enclosed by a red earthen wall.

In that village they crossed a stone bridge with carved balustrades, and the clear stream that tinkled under it seemed to wash away the fatigues of their long march.

The large threshing-floor in front of the temple gate reminded Mangzhong and Old Wen of the old days when they worked as hired hands. Stacks of oat and maize stems stood here and there, while a dozen or more peasants were gathering up the grain which had been sunned. They were supervised by a middle-aged monk with a chaplet in his hands.

"These are the temple's tenant farmers," a man from Shanxi told Mangzhong. "All the big temples hereabouts are landowners."

The monk, raising clasped hands, greeted the soldiers in turn.

"You must be tired, comrades," he said with a smile. "Your regiment can put up in our humble temple and have a good rest."

Before the troops entered their billets, their officers reminded them to respect Buddhist customs and take good care of the temple property. This monk in charge of the temple also had the temporary job of purveyor for the army.

"We welcome all troops who resist Japan," he assured them. "Our temple can put up a whole regiment."

The monk showed each platoon in turn over the temple. The men refrained from entering the main hall but stood in the courtyard outside admiring the fine carving on the red-lacquered doors and the sparkling glazed tiles on the roof.

"Why use such big tiles?" asked Old Wen. "They must weigh five catties each."

"We get high gales here," was the monk's reply. "Lighter tiles would be blown away by the north wind."

To the troops, the monk seemed like any village cadre. For their supper he gave them oat noodles and fried parsley.

After supper, Old Wen wandered over to have a look at two horses tethered to the archway in the next courtyard, where some orderlies were standing.

"Whose are these?" Old Wen wanted to know.

"They're ridden by the local Party secretary and the commissioner."

"Lend me your torch to have a look at them."

The orderly obliged.

"Well cared for. The pasturage here must be good," said Old Wen. "I can see this white horse has speed, but he looks rather stupid."

He went back inside to turn in. They were sharing a huge *kang* with ten or more novices, who crowded round and wouldn't let the men sleep.

"How many of your age are there here?" asked Old Wen.

"Plenty," said one of the boys. "More than a hundred between fifteen and eighteen."

"Would you like to join the Eighth Route Army?"

"Yes!" they cried in unison. "We only came to the temple because our families were too poor to keep us. We'd like nothing better than to go with you."

That evening Old Wen remembered the Buddhist sacrifices of his young days, the prayers and the chanting of sutras. The litanies which sounded from the main hall kept him awake and reminded him suddenly of his wife in Ziwuzhen. Tomorrow, he decided, he'd ask Mangzhong to write her a letter about all the strange sights they'd seen up in the hills.

81

After Gao Ba deserted from the Eighth Route Army and went over to Zhang Yinwu, he and Su'er kept harrying the neighbourhood and the villagers regarded them as traitors; yet thick-skinned Old Jiang still swaggered about like the father-in-law of a regiment commander. In his eyes, serving in the Central Army was naturally a step up from being a brigand, and his son-in-law was not necessarily lower now in status than when in the Eighth Route Army. Let people gossip; he might come out top in the end. To his mind, Su'er had done right to follow her husband, reflecting as much credit on his household as if she had accompanied Gao Ba to some official post.

In the village Old Jiang still made up to One-eyed Tian. Now that Mangzhong and Old Wen had enlisted in turn and Old Chang as village head had duties outside, the scoundrelly landlord decided to cut down on farming. In times like these, he reasoned, each extra hired hand meant an extra enemy in his house, and why should he ask for trouble? But unless he got more help, who would work his land? Selling it went against the grain: he mustn't part with one inch of his property. Each time he studied the Tian family records, he preened himself on his own ability. It would never do to knuckle under to this riffraff. But he was finding life increasingly hard. Naturally, the reasonable levy imposed by the Eighth Route Army struck him as unreasonable in the extreme. When the Central troops launched their dastardly attack and the Japanese occupied the county town, Old Jiang, who was under his thumb, became village head; but even so the new authorities refused to let him off lightly. Anyone could see with half an eye that his was the wealthiest family in the village. The records showed that he owned 300 *mu*.

No matter how well he stood with the village head, he still had to pay his taxes.

One-eyed Tian decided he must cut his losses. He carefully devised a foolproof scheme that would neither reduce his real income nor disgrace his family. One evening he invited Old Jiang to a meal.

"It's a long time since I've drunk your wine." Old Jiang sounded quite apologetic. "What's put you in such a good humour today?"

"Good humour?" retorted One-eyed Tian. "I want to drown my sorrows."

Old Jiang pulled a long face out of sympathy, as he fell to greedily on the food and wine.

"Go easy," said One-eyed Tian gravely. "Let's make the wine and dishes last. I asked you here for a talk."

"What about?" Old Jiang promptly put his chopsticks down.

"I'd like to sell you some land." The landlord closed his one good eye.

This came as an utter surprise to Old Jiang after living for years as the Tians' hanger-on.

"You must be joking," he cried.

"Not a bit of it. I don't want to hire more hands. They'd only go off to meetings all the time and set me fuming by neglecting the fields."

"True enough." Old Jiang nodded agreement.

"That's why I thought of selling. My family has no poor land. We've always picked carefully and bought the best. I can only sell to a man after my own heart, I don't want to do a favour to any outsiders. You're the only man in the village that fits the bill."

"Even if that's how you feel, I've got no money."

"You can mortgage it. I'll lower the price."

"I haven't a cent."

"Then I won't ask you for money. You can pretend to have bought it, and farm it for nothing."

"What happens to the grain? Who pays the tax?"

After haggling until midnight, Old Jiang agreed as a favour to One-eyed Tian's terms. As he left he reflected bitterly that the landlord drove a hard bargain.

The two of them had agreed that One-eyed Tian should supply the draught animals, and the whole crop apart from the grain tax should be carried at night to his house. If this proved impracticable, Old Jiang should sell it on the market and hand over the proceeds. There was no profit in this for him, nothing but hard work. But for the sake of "friendship" he dared not refuse.

The plot was three *mu* of good land behind Old Jiang's house which had formerly belonged to his family. But in a year of flood, when he had nothing to eat and needed money for his elder daughter's marriage, he was forced to sell it cheap to One-eyed Tian. Now he would be posing as the owner of what had once been his own. Even Old Jiang found this difficult to stomach.

They went through the regular formalities. On a day appointed, Old Jiang invited his neighbours to a meal to celebrate his purchase of land. It was hard to find middlemen, but at last he succeeded. The wine and food were provided by Old Jiang, but One-eyed Tian footed the bill. After the meal they signed the deed of sale and counted out the money — more play-acting, this.

In a way Old Jiang was pleased. For now word would go round that One-eyed Tian was in a bad way, selling land north of the village to Old Jiang. Apart from the two free meals, this thought kept him happy for a couple of days.

When spring came, Old Jiang borrowed a mule from One-eyed Tian to plough his fields. The landlord stood watching him sceptically and asked:

"What are you going to grow here?"

"What do you suggest?" asked Old Jiang in a low voice. Unused to driving a mule, he was afraid she might bolt.

"Please yourself." One-eyed Tian started stumping home. "You've no more idea of ploughing than a dog. Good land is wasted on you."

A path to the village skirted this field and people kept passing by. One who knew Old Jiang was tickled to see him ploughing and stopped to ask:

"You working for the Tians now, Old Jiang?"

"Where d'you get that idea?" Old Jiang threw him a dirty look. "I can hardly get through my *own* work. Keep your eyes open for someone for me, will you? I want to hire a monthly labourer."

"You just bought this land?"

"Yes. Let me know if anyone in your village is thinking of selling. The size of the plot doesn't matter, but it would be handy if it were near our village."

"Have you bought that big mule too?" The other man grinned.

"I'm just trying her out. She does all right turning a mill but isn't too good with a plough. You might keep your eyes open for good draught animals too."

Old Jiang finally made shift to finish his ploughing. Having returned the mule to One-eyed Tian, he was too tired and hungry to go home and cook. Instead he trudged to the west end of the village where Widow He sold sesame cakes and fritters. The widow was sitting in her doorway counting the "goods" she had left. She saw Old Jiang out of the corner of one eye but decided to ignore him.

"Human nature's a funny thing," remarked Old Jiang loudly. "When a man has no land, he hankers after some; when he has a few *mu*, they're more trouble than they're worth."

"I hear you've bought land." The widow closed the box of cakes on her knees. "Is that true?"

"I had some money lying idle," said Old Jiang. "First I thought I'd deposit it here with you for sesame cakes, but someone advised me to invest in property. Now I've paid for my land I've just about enough left to keep me in sesame cakes for a year or two. One cake and one fritter, please!"

He opened the box on her lap, chose one of each sort, folded them together and started munching with relish.

"Let's have two more of the same," he said when he'd finished.

"I want cash down," said the widow.

"I shan't swindle you." Old Jiang stood up wiping his mouth. "I'll bring all my cash here tomorrow. It's safer in your hands. Have you done any match-making lately?"

"Why d'you ask that? Match-making's gone out of fashion."

Old Jiang sniggered.

"Well, these few *mu* of land are keeping me too busy to manage the house. Who wants to go home and cook after farming for hours? See if you can find me someone suitable."

"That won't be easy. If you've money, you can come and eat here every day."

"Maybe." Old Jiang started out. "But that won't do for long. So keep your eyes skinned. I'm too old for a girl, but a widow would do all right."

82

Old Jiang's behaviour gave rise to a good deal of gossip. Some villagers were of the opinion that Gao Ba had sent him money, and speculated as to the amount. There was so much talk that the village security officer paid him two visits.

At first Old Jiang had enjoyed keeping everyone guessing and had even supplied them with fresh material for gossip. He started to worry, however, when he heard that the security officer was coming. But it was too late by then to go into hiding.

Of all the village cadres this was the one he feared most. Although Old Chang was village head, he was an honest, tongue-tied, kindly fellow. Although Chun'er was on the district committee and didn't mince words, it was easy enough to set a girl like her blushing. He was not afraid of her either. But he found the security officer hard to handle. True, he was a peasant too, who had learned a trade outside but was no glib talker; yet his eyes were shrewd and appraising. Whenever they met, Old Jiang would put on a great show of respect while wishing with all his heart he were well away.

On his first visit, the security officer simply strolled round the compound in silence.

"Did you want something, security officer?" asked Old Jiang.

"I'm just having a look round." With that he left.

He came back the next day and sat on the *kang*, smoking one pipe after another. Old Jiang felt his eyes were boring through the wardrobe and wall behind it.

"Did you want me for something?" he asked.

"I hear you've bought some land."

"Just a few *mu*." Old Jiang had his answer ready. "I'm all for the resistance. I've learned a whole lot from the Eighth

Route Army. There's no place for slackers in times like these: we must all work for the resistance. I used to take life easy, as you know, just picking up a few crumbs at rich men's tables, but now I'm turning over a new leaf. That's why I bought these few *mu*."

"Where did the money come from?"

"I'd saved it up little by little. And I sold some of Su'er's clothes that day at the fair."

The security officer left without any comment. Old Jiang had reeled off his answers smoothly enough, yet still he felt uneasy. He could have kicked himself for making that agreement with One-eyed Tian. After brooding over the matter he decided he must get something out of the deal, not leave all the profit to the landlord and only arouse suspicion for his pains. He would sow those three *mu* with melons. That would bring him in spending money and enough water-melons to enjoy in the hot weather.

The trouble was he knew nothing at all about melons except which seeds were best to eat. He didn't even know whether to sow the seeds with the pointed end up or down. And his back ached at the mere thought of stooping all day to hoe between the vines. He must find someone else to do the work. After some reflection he hit on Chun'er's father, Wu Dayin. Since his return from the Northeast Old Wu'd had very little to do, but he was a first-rate farmer, honest and open-handed into the bargain. When Old Jiang sounded him out, he agreed at once.

Chun'er was against the scheme.

"Why pick a skunk like that to work for?" she asked. "Do you know how he came by that land? Or where One-eyed Tian comes in?"

"I'm not worrying about that," her father replied. "I need the money and I'll get paid by results. He can't wriggle out of it. We've not much land ourselves and your stepmother's another mouth to feed, but you're too busy outside to have much time to spin. We're feeling the pinch. Our bit of land doesn't take all my time. And I don't like idling."

"Well, talk it over first with Old Chang."

Old Chang's advice was:

"Go ahead. There's something fishy about that land. Just what, we'll find out by and by. But once the fruit ripens, Old Jiang will have to pay up. The power's in our hands now. We aren't afraid of him."

So Wu Dayin took on the job. And he was a dab at it. For musk-melons he chose only the seeds of superior varieties like Iron Skin, Toad Green and White Bowl. For watermelons he chose a variety with a dark skin, yellow flesh and red seeds which was sweet and drought resistant. He planted out his seedlings in neat rows.

Wu Dayin worked hard on that plot. And his melons came along at a splendid rate. Together they thrust through the soil and unfurled their seed-leaves towards the sun, like new-born infants searching for their mother's breast. Then suddenly, overnight, came the first foliage leaves. Soon fan-shaped leaves had covered the warm soil with thick green. Together again, overnight, they put forth tendrils identical in length, all growing in the identical direction. Wu Dayin spent hours tending these precious plants.

The Ziwuzhen villagers referred to the plot as Wu Dayin's melon plot, as if they had forgotten who its owner was. Old Jiang himself didn't have to lift a finger. In fact, Wu refused his few offers of help for fear he'd do some damage. That was a dry spring, but with ample watering the melongs grew well. In April the flowers faded and the fruit set in orderly rows like small school children neatly lined up in their playground.

They built a watchman's shack high on four poles. Because May is a busy month in the fields, Wu Dayin and Old Jiang took it in turns to spend the night there. These lookouts have been the scene of countless little dramas of village life. And now this one in the melon plot became the focus of Ziwuzhen's two opposing political forces.

During Wu Dayin's shift he was often joined by Old Chang and other village cadres, including Chun'er and her progressive friends. During Old Jiang's shift the look-out filled with his cronies, and sometimes One-eyed Tian was among their number.

One evening there was a full moon. After drinking a few cups, One-eyed Tian strolled over to the look-out in the mood for versifying.

"Let's make a few couplets," he proposed to Old Jiang.

"Couplets? Me? That's way over my head."

"Never mind. Have a try. I'll start with the first two lines.

When farm-hands go to meetings all day long,

The water vat stands empty in the yard.
Your turn now."

"Well, if I must, here goes:

The men go hoarse from bawling songs,

And women crick their backs, they dance so hard."

"The idea's all right, but the lines should be the same length. My turn now. . . ."

They were interrupted at this point by someone shouting from the end of the field:

"Who's on duty today?"

Old Jiang recognized the voice of one of the cadres.

"I am," he called back. "Come tomorrow."

Without answering, the other went away.

"Any word from your son-in-law?" asked One-eyed Tian softly.

"No, I've no idea where he's got to." Old Jiang sighed. "If he were in these parts, I wouldn't have so much to put up with."

"He's not far. Didn't you know? The Central Army's grown much stronger. Apart from Commander-in-Chief Zhang Yinwu, there's Commander Shi Yousan. You must know him, he used to be with your son-in-law. Then there are Pang Bingxun, Zhu Huaibing, Ding Shuben, Hou Ruyong and several others. They're combining all their troops now and will soon go into action. Then just watch! The Central Army will march north, the Japanese south, and the Eighth Route Army will be crushed between them."

"Is that true?" demanded Old Jiang.

"Yaowu sent me word." In high good humour One-eyed Tian went home to sleep.

83

In May, insects shrilled all over the melon plot where the fruit was ripening fast. The largest musk-melons were already turning soft and their heady fragrance at night made the mouths of passers-by water. Plump water-melons pearled with dew protruded from the leafy vines as they rested lazily on the dry ridges. And the vines were still thrusting up, flaunting sweet, nectar-filled flowers carefree and jaunty as girls tripping along the road with their heads in the air.

That evening Chun'er was up there watching the melons. Since her return from the army she'd been in charge of the district Women's Salvation Association, which entailed so much work that she seldom had time to sit down quietly and think. She'd taken on this task today because her father was busy.

She had just climbed on to the look-out and the cool breeze had just dried her perspiring face, when Old Wen's wife came along.

"Where's your baby?" asked Chun'er.

"Asleep in the courtyard at home." Mrs. Wen climbed up beside her. Both turned their heads towards the west where red clouds were still lingering at the horizon.

"Did you want me for anything, sister?" asked Chun'er.

"Not really. For some days I've been hoping to see you, but one or the other of us was always busy. It's pleasant, isn't it, sitting together like this? I feel you're my sister-in-law."

Chun'er took her hand.

"We're real sisters," continued Mrs. Wen. "Mangzhong and Old Wen are like brothers outside. I don't know if they're still together. I do hope so."

"I'm sure they are," said Chun'er.

"I wonder how far those hills are from here. They look close enough, just under those red clouds, but it must take days to walk there. If only we had wings like birds! We ought to write them a letter."

"I'll write one for you."

"Write one from both of us. We've the same things to say. Just put both our names at the end."

In companionable silence they gazed towards the west. The moon was racing through a drift of black clouds.

Mrs. Wen, who was easily satisfied, asked nothing better than to be with someone placed like herself who could share her feelings. She told Chun'er:

"Now I'm taking a keen interest in study and I'm learning a few characters every day. Tell me: what does that word 'defend' mean?"

" 'Defend' is pretty much the same as 'guard'. Only

stronger. The enemy's invaded our motherland and to defend her we must do all we can to drive the Japanese out. That's what defend means."

"I see. So Mangzhong and Old Wen have gone to defend the country. In a way, I suppose, we're defending this melon plot, aren't we?"

"That's right. The enemies of the melons are badgers, pigs and hedgehogs, and we're the fighters ready to drive them away."

"It's not a big plot, but your family's put a lot of hard work into it. And how pleasant it is, sitting here. Just sitting and not even talking."

Hugging her knees she looked up at the sky. The moon plunged behind a bank of black clouds and vanished from sight.

This plot was flanked by sorghum fields on two sides with a millet field to the north, from which the breeze was coming. As the temperature dropped, the insects quieted down. Mrs. Wen heard a rustling in the melon leaves next to one of the sorghum fields. This was followed by the sound of a vine being snapped.

"There's someone after your melons," she whispered to Chun'er.

"May be a badger," Chun'er whispered back. "Let's go and see."

"I'm scared to. It might bite."

Chun'er jumped lightly down and picked her way carefully through the vines, then softly parted the sorghum leaves and tiptoed to the spot. On the ground she saw something white, half in the melon plot and crawling backwards carrying a large melon. She planted one foot on the creature's back, and a startled cry rang out.

This was no badger or hedgehog. But after that one cry

399

there was no further sound. Disturbed by this, Chun'er shouted for Mrs. Wen, who after a while approached her nervously. Just then the moon came out again and Chun'er saw that it was a woman on the ground.

The woman kept her face down and didn't stir. Chun'er tugged at her, saying reassuringly:

"You can have a melon if you're thirsty. But it's wrong to steal, you know."

The woman turned towards her and laughed. Mrs. Wen and Chun'er fell back a step in dismay for it was Gao Ba's wife, Su'er.

Before Su'er could dash off, Chun'er caught hold of her.

"Stealing melons doesn't matter so much," she cried. "But you must tell me where you're from and what you're doing here."

"It's no business of yours where I'm from." Su'er slapped the dust off her clothes. "Who's been stealing your melons? You let go of me."

"I caught you red-handed. You'll have to come clean tonight."

"I've nothing to come clean about." Su'er took a comb from her pocket and slowly combed the long hair lying over her shoulders. A sickly odour of hair oil made Chun'er sneeze. Su'er, recovering her self-possession, went on: "This is my home. I can come back whenever I please."

"Your home?" Anger made Chun'er almost incoherent. "You kidnapped people in Shenxian."

"Did you catch me at it? You're always calling me names — it's nothing but slander. I'm not arguing with you, let's go to the district or county office and find Gao Qingshan or Gao Xiang. I know all the big-shots and we get on fine. Come on, I'm not afraid."

Chun'er kept close at her heels. In the street they met a

militia patrol and Chun'er handed her over to them. Su'er tried her blandishments on the young men, but they paid no attention. When they started to march her off, she got really worried.

"Sister Chun'er, you can't do this to me," she appealed over her shoulder. "Have a heart! Remember the two of us joined the resistance at the same time, one as head, one as deputy, both pulling together. And it's not as if I hadn't helped your family. That year Sister Qiufen wanted to find her husband, if not for me you'd never have discovered where Gao Qingshan was or had a family reunion. You should return a kindness a hundredfold. Virtue is its own reward. Get me out of this, Sister Chun'er!"

Chun'er made no reply. The militiamen took Su'er to a large room empty but for a big *kang,* covered by a mat with several holes burned in it.

"Want me to sleep here?" she asked coquettishly. "I'd be frightened all on my own. One of you must bring along a quilt and keep me company."

"Don't worry, we'll be on guard outside," they told her.

At the time of Su'er's arrest, Old Jiang was hobnobbing with One-eyed Tian and indulging in backward, reactionary talk. Nowadays when they had guests Mrs. Tian, who had seldom left the house before, would steal to the gate to keep watch on the street and pick up any information she could. She reported this development to Old Jiang. Being in a foul mood, he leapt to his feet with an oath.

One-eyed Tian restrained him, saying softly:

"This won't do, Old Jiang. We've got to humble ourselves. Go and see what's up and try to wheedle the cadres into letting Su'er out. I'm pretty sure she's come back on important business and she's bound to have brought us good news.

Tell her, secretly, she mustn't on any account give the show away again."

"I refuse to humble myself to them," roared Old Jiang. "Nabbing my daughter on her own doorstep — what the hell do they think they're doing?"

But by the time he reached the militia headquarters and saw the guard there, his courage failed him. His knees buckled and he nearly collapsed on the ground. After stammering out a few questions he went off to find Wu Dayin.

"Brother Dayin," he said, "your family and mine have hit it off well for generations. Now you and I are working a melon plot together. But just now Chun'er made the militiamen arrest my daughter. Do me a favour, brother, and get them to let Su'er go."

Wu Dayin, still half asleep, didn't know what had happened.

"What's the trouble about?" he asked.

"Su'er picked two melons from our plot."

"Is that all?" Wu Dayin dressed and got up. "She's welcome to ten melons, let alone two."

"But that's what they're like, arresting people for no reason at all."

"I'll go and see what I can do." Wu Dayin went out.

On their way Old Jiang called up Old Chang too, and together they went to the militia headquarters.

Chun'er told them of the kidnapping by Su'er and Gao Ba in Shenxian and proposed sending her to the district for careful cross-questioning. Su'er roundly denied this charge, maintaining that she'd divorced Gao Ba because he was no good. She'd arrived home hungry and thirsty and picked a melon at the edge of her own village. Chun'er was making a mountain out a molehill.

"Why send her to the district?" asked Old Jiang. "You

top cadres can surely settle any trouble in our village. Let me bail her out. You can send for her when you want her."

"Why not?" agreed Wu Dayin, reluctant to offend a neighbour. "That's fair enough, Chun'er."

But Chun'er protested:

"Dad, don't meddle in business you don't understand. Go back home to bed. What do you say, Uncle Chang?"

"I'm for sending her to the district," said Old Chang. "I'll go with the militiamen."

After Su'er had been detained a few days in the district, the river rose and the district cadres became extra busy. They notified Ziwuzhen that Su'er still maintained her innocence. They were sending her back to the village. She was a loose woman but could be released on bail.

84

That year flood devastated the Hebei plain. Overnight the River Hutuo rose in spate and rushed down from Daixian all the way to Pingshan in the central plain, swirling past Zhengding into Shenze. That same night it burst down in full force on Five-dragon Temple.

A torrential rain poured down all night on Gao Sihai's cottage on the dike. He sat on the *kang* by the window smoking his pipe and listening to the roar of the torrent. The fury of the rain and thunder of the water foretold a fearful flood.

Qiufen rose in the early hours.

"We'd better not wait till it's light." Old Gao got down from the *kang*. He put on a tattered straw hat and picked up a cracked gong from one corner of the room. Stepping out on to the dike he sounded the alarm.

This was the customary signal. The villagers waked from their sleep by the gonging jumped up, grabbed the straw hats, rags, shovels and crates which their womenfolk thrust at them and bursting out of their gates swarmed to the dike.

They gathered there, the women with glass lanterns which swung to and fro in the storm. They milled about on the river bank outside the dike and in the ditches inside it, carrying earth, looking for holes and filling up gaps.

The people of Ziwuzhen were bestirring themselves in the same way at the same time. Chun'er led the other women through the pouring rain to the dike.

Every household but that of "Mr. Jiang" sent volunteers. He alone lay snug in bed, heedless of this turmoil.

Halfway through the night Wu Dayin, on duty in the lookout, was roused with a shock by the gonging from Five-dragon Temple. He stared blankly at this plot he had sweated over for months. Disaster had struck just as the melons were ripening. He was sighing bitterly when Old Chang came to ask him to help organize a team to strengthen the dike. Wu trudged off with his shovel to the street. Passing Old Jiang's house on the way, he called him up.

"I'm off with the rest to man the dike," he shouted. "Go and keep an eye on the melons. If the water keeps on rising, you can pick the larger melons and salt them for pickles this winter."

Old Jiang refused to believe him and wouldn't stir.

"This is another rumour spread by the Eighth Route Army," he complained. "They're always up to this trick. Before the Japanese ever came, they called so hard for resistance that the Japanese really did come. Before there was a sign of enemy tanks, they were so set on demolishing the roads that then the Japanese trucks really charged in. They keep on looking for trouble. It's not time yet for the river

404

to rise, I tell you. But there they go calling everybody out. They won't be satisfied till a flood really comes. Listen to that gonging in Five-dragon Temple — that's going to bring bad luck."

When he knew he must either go to his field or the dike, he chose the former and squelched off sulkily. The rain was lighter now but the sky was pitch black. Old Jiang climbed on to the look-out and burrowed into the warm quilt left by Wu. Rain had driven all the mosquitoes under cover, and they bit him so mercilessly that he could not sleep. Shouting and the sound of digging could be heard from the dike. It did seem, after all, as if the flood was coming.

He jumped down and collected the largest melons he'd noticed earlier on. Bringing them back to the shelter he wiped them clean and ate them — this was how he carried out the task given him by Wu. He didn't care if the whole plot was flooded. It was One-eyed Tian's land and the loss would be his. Old Wu might be upset that his hard work had gone for nothing, but this didn't worry Old Jiang.

He bore Wu Dayin a grudge. It was typical of Old Jiang that he remembered every little detail of other people's faults. Before he even knew a man he would find out his shortcomings and then approach him, or even call on him, to gather fresh material of this sort to be stored up for future use. He remembered every single weakness, large and small. Whose forbears had begged for a living, who'd been a quarrelsome boy, who was hen-pecked, who couldn't keep accounts, whose reading was shaky, who mixed up people's names . . . he made a mental note of all these things. Instead of trying to make friends he prepared himself for possible disputes, and when a quarrel actually broke out he would reel off these shortcomings to make the other man lower his head in defeat. He could pride himself on several such encounters. Old

Jiang used other people's weaknesses to bolster his own self esteem. Looking down on others made him feel superior. So even if he met a stranger at the market or temple, he wouldn't let slip the chance to observe the fellow's faults. He called these dastardly tactics "getting a man by the short hairs" or "finding the skeleton in his cupboard".

Had this been all, one might have called Old Jiang realistic or at worst cantankerous. But this wasn't all. He fawned abjectly on those more powerful than himself. His servile cringing was laid on so thick that it even nauseated utter scoundrels and traitors like One-eyed Tian who were the objects of his flattery. And it was also his custom to run down those weaker than himself and level quite groundless accusations against them.

The existence of time-servers like Old Jiang might well lead even the kindliest person to believe the old saying that "human nature is evil". It is second nature for a fly to drop filth on a beautiful painting or for a rat to gnaw holes in a silken gown at night, but for the people concerned this may bring irrevocable loss and distress.

And Old Jiang had been unable to detect any faults in Wu Dayin. Although he asked several of the older villagers, all declared that Dayin had been a fine honest lad who had never done anybody an ill turn. Old Jiang was well aware that he hated him because he was Chun'er's father. But what could he do to discredit him in public? Any attempt to do this would merely recoil on himself.

He could only hope that some sudden disaster would strike Wu's family. And now it occurred to him that he might vent his spite by means of this melon plot. If One-eyed Tian were to insist that the rent on this land must be paid regardless of flood or drought, he could disclaim all obligations himself and leave the two of them to fight it out.

Pleased with this thought, Old Jiang clambered on to the look-out, pulled Wu Dayin's quilt up over his head and settled down to sweet dreams of revenge, oblivious of wind and rain, gonging and shouting, and the swarms of mosquitoes around him.

He dreamed that his shelter was rocking precariously, that he was floating in space. But he turned on his other side and was soon sleeping soundly. Then, without warning, an agonizing pain shot through his left cheek. Sitting up he saw a bedraggled black badger on his pillow. At his feet were several hares, also sopping wet and leaping about in panic, sticking their heads under cover only to withdraw again, shivering. As for his body, it was simply infested with little creatures and insects: the quilt swarmed with grasshoppers, dung-beetles, mole-crickets and centipedes, to say nothing of the field mice scurrying up and down with frightened squeals. At first Old Jiang imagined he must be dreaming, but it was no dream that his cheek was bitten and bleeding. He struck out savagely and the badger jumped away.

"Scram!"

The water outside was level with the floor of the look-out, which might be inundated any minute. Old Jiang peered round. He could see nothing but water. His look-out was a solitary storm-tossed island where birds and beasts had sought shelter from the fearful flood. He started shaking with terror.

The deluge, as far as eye could see, was swirling northeast. Here and there the tips of crops were being lashed about by the waves.

The melon plot had disappeared completely. The few melons he'd brought back but not yet eaten had been finished up by the hares. In his fury he hurled all the animals into the water.

The roaring flood surged onwards, razing everything in its path. Planks of rotten wood from gravemounds and beams of houses which had collapsed kept battering his look-out. Old Jiang crouched there waiting for it to fall, sure that his last hour had come.

When dawn broke, the sun shone on a scene of desolation.

85

Old Jiang stood up on the look-out and stared towards the village across the flood glimmering in the dazzling sunlight. He saw a gap as wide as a city gate in the northwest bend of the dike. Through this the river was swirling. The flood was steadily rising.

The villagers standing on each side of the breach in the dike seemed to have exhausted their last ounce of strength. Now all they could do was to stare helplessly at the ruin of their homes. But over the roar of the waters Old Jiang caught menacing cries. The crowd started milling about and some young men, naked to the waist, heaved up a black object and hurled it out into the torrent.

Like a wounded crow swallowed up in the clouds at dusk, the black object disappeared beneath the waves. Then it bobbed up, was caught in an eddy and carried back to the dike. The villagers rushed to that spot and the young men seized it again.

"Throw her further out! Drown the bitch!"

Old Jiang heard yells of fury and saw the village head, Old Chang, step forward to intervene.

"She's a traitor!"

"Nobody need feel sorry for her."

He could hear the shouts of the crowd, not what Old Chang

was saying. The struggling figure in black was thrown into the water once more.

Suddenly Old Jiang's legs gave way under him. He had recognized the figure in black as his daughter. He recalled that the previous evening, when the storm was at its height, Su'er had come into his room to ask:

"If the river rises and our dike gives way, how many villages will be flooded?"

"Why, plenty. Several counties."

"What's the likeliest place to cave in?"

"On the south bank, Five-dragon Temple. On the north bank, the southwest corner of our village. They keep a careful watch at Five-dragon Temple. And our dike's so thick, it's not likely to be breached. If it were, the old people say, there'd be the devil to pay."

Su'er lowered her head thoughtfully and then went out. Since she often left the house at night, her father thought nothing of it and went to sleep. Could she really have breached the dike?

Old Jiang stood up and shouted at the top of his voice to the people on the dike, but nobody answered. Then he tied Wu Dayin's tattered red quilt on to a stick and waved it in the air. At last the villagers saw him and signalled back. They seemed to have forgotten the creature in black, who was swept again to the dike and, having crawled up it, lay there without stirring.

Old Jiang signed to the villagers to come to his rescue, but they scattered as if going home to eat. Only then did he have a careful look at the village. Ziwuzhen was half submerged in swirling water. Many houses had collapsed, many more were tottering. The streets were full of flat grain-trays serving as little boats, in which sat women and children hugging the food and clothing they had salvaged. Falling on his knees, Old Jiang begged the river god to spare his house, but his few earthen rooms had already been swept away.

If this was really Su'er's work, he didn't care what the villagers did to her.

Two days and two nights Old Jiang was stranded there with nothing to eat. When the waters had subsided a little, Wu Dayin brought out a raft to take him and the bedding back. Although nearly dead with hunger, Old Jiang complained:

"The moment my back's turned, trouble starts. How could you be so careless and let the dike cave in?"

"*You* ask that?" cried Wu. "It was your daughter's doing."

"How could a woman breach such a solid dike? She's got a bad name so you blame everything on her."

"She may be only a woman." Wu Dayin sighed. "But she has Japanese and traitors behind her. She brought armed agents to blow up the dike. They got away, but she was caught."

"Is Su'er dead then?" Her father's eyes filled with tears.

"She'd have been drowned if not for Old Chang. He said she ought to stand trial. They've taken her to the district government."

What had happened that night was this. When the flood waters rose, Chun'er and some other young women had fought their way through the raging storm to guard the northwest corner of the dike. No one expected this solid section to give way, which was why Old Chang had entrusted it to the women.

Chun'er took the job seriously and didn't for a moment leave her post, snatching a bite of supper in the driving rain. She made careful tours of inspection, had the dam raised in places and gaps in the ramp filled in. The water was still

410

a foot or so from the top, and they had discovered no badgers' burrows or rat holes. The ground within the dike was full of pits because for years they'd taken earth from there. Chun'er warned the women:

"Be careful, everyone. It would be frightful if anything went wrong here."

It was a cold, eerie business guarding the dike at night. The water kept rising, the rain pouring down, the wind howling. The gale lashed the swollen river against the dike.

Suddenly Chun'er discovered Su'er in their midst. She was wearing black silk trousers and jacket and carrying a yellow oilskin umbrella.

"What are you doing here?" Chun'er demanded.

"Need you ask?" Su'er took a few steps forward, then halted. "You sound gongs and drums to call everyone to the dike. I've come to help. Aren't I welcome?"

"We've got enough people."

"It's everyone's duty to work for the resistance. You can't have too many hands. Those with money give money, those having strength give strength. That's the slogan from above. I've always been keen to work for the resistance. I may have slipped up half way, but I want to make amends now."

"We'll find some other work for you later," said Chun'er. "I've no time to waste chatting now."

"You call this chatting?" protested Su'er. "I want to turn over a new leaf and prove it in action. You've no right to stop me."

As Chun'er was concentrating on the flood she couldn't be troubled to argue with Su'er just then. She walked away, quietly detailing one of the militiawomen to keep an eye on Su'er, annoyed that this useless creature should take up the time of someone useful. But she guessed that Su'er was up to no good and might try to cause trouble at a time like this.

411

The storm increased in fury until it was too dark to see your hand before you. Their lanterns drenched by rain or blown out by the wind were hard to light again. Someone exclaimed:

"In a gale like this what we need is a storm-lantern."

"Has anyone in our village got one?" asked Chun'er.

"One-eyed Tian has. But who'll go and get it?"

Tian's big gate was not far from the dike, but no one wanted to go.

"If you won't, I will," offered Su'er. "As a public service, mind you. I'm not on good terms with him."

When the others agreed, Su'er hurried off. It seemed a long, long time before she came back.

"Did you get it?" shouted the women.

"Here it is," she answered slowly.

"Why haven't you lit it?" asked Chun'er.

"I was so flurried, I forgot. You can light it." Su'er climbed the dike and put the lantern down.

"Who's got a match?" asked the women crowding round.

"Stand round to keep the wind off while you light it. I'll be back in a second." Su'er ran down the dike into a field of sorghum.

The matches were damp, and in the pouring rain several women tried in vain to strike a light. Chun'er walked up impatiently, picked up the lantern and shook it.

"Is there any oil in this?"

"I wouldn't know," called Su'er from the sorghum field. "Where's one to find paraffin in wartime? But here's a light for you!"

From the bend in the dike came a series of tremendous explosions. As Chun'er rushed over, shots rang out below. The dike burst open and water came pouring in. By the time the men dashed up, the agents had escaped through the

sorghum fields and only Su'er was caught. They ⌐
best to save the dike, but it was too late. That was
the peasants clamoured for Su'er's blood.

The faint light of dawn showed the whole countrys
flooded — ruined houses, crops washed away. In a fur,
the young men dragged Su'er up the dike and hurled her into
the breach.

Finally Old Chang intervened.

Old Chang was so good himself that he always thought
the best of everyone else. He remembered every case he
had heard of people from ancient times to modern days who
had added to the glory of mankind or increased men's faith
in life. His mind was so full of such instances that he tried
to see good in bad people too, even in utter scoundrels. It
was hard for him to believe in wickedness. When the facts
proved him wrong he would be cast down, distressed to find
there were people like that in the world. And normally,
when Old Chang had dealings with scoundrels, he was the
one to lose out, the one to get hurt.

86

After crossing the Japanese lines, Bian Ji and Instructor
Zhang were assigned to a newspaper office.

Their office was in Three Generals Terrace near Kang
Family Gully in Fuping. The tiny village nestled against
the North Hill, with some houses at the foot, others half way
up. At the fold in the mountains here a stream gurgled so
loudly over its rocky bed that newcomers from the plain
were often woken by the sound and found it hard to get to
sleep again. Before the village was a reed-fringed pool and
by the street grew tall sweet cedrela trees.

...ji and Instructor Zhang lived in a solitary white cot-
...alf way up the hill. Instructor Zhang's task was
...ng, and at present he and his colleagues were compiling
...andbook for correspondents. Bian Ji, in charge of layout,
as designing a set of woodcut column heads and found this
so engrossing that he gave up writing plays and spent all his
time working with chisel and wood.

At the foot of the hill, by the entrance to the village, stood
a smithy run by a man from the Hebei plain who had married one of the local girls. They had settled down here and
had one daughter. Bian Ji found this household congenial,
and having done so much travelling in his time could enter
thoroughly into the feelings of other itinerant craftsmen. This
blacksmith used some first-rate steel he'd been hoarding for
years to make Bian Ji a set of knives identical with those used
by wood engravers in the North China Amalgamated University.

Bian Ji, who was also responsible for the mess, put in time
every day in the kitchen. Their diet was of the simplest:
nothing but millet and turnip soup twice a day. Apart from
helping to buy supplies, he sometimes went down to wash
millet on one of the stones in the middle of the stream. With
his good clippers brought from the plain he also gave his colleagues a haircut each month, and even intellectuals from big
cities admired his skill as a barber. In his spare time he
liked to sit on a stool in the yard, smoking his pipe and thinking, or get the cook to play the fiddle while he sang snatches
of opera.

Feeling specially close to people from his parts, he drew
portraits of the blacksmith's family and offered to make
woodcuts of them as well. Then the old, asthmatic blacksmith
started taking a keen interest in art. One day he lugged

414

home from ten *li* or more away a tree trunk about a foot across and gave this to Bian Ji, saying:

"We must borrow a saw from the carpenter. This ought to last you a lifetime."

"How did you get it?" asked Bian Ji, after bringing back a large saw worked by two men.

"Bought it as firewood." The blacksmith helped him operate the saw. "Listen to the sound of this timber — hard as copper."

They sawed whenever they were free. If the blacksmith was busy, his seventeen-year-old daughter took over. They sawed that trunk into blocks of different sizes, which Bian Ji took back to his billet and stacked against a wall. This pile of material for his new trade was the only ornament in that windowless room, originally a stable. He made his bed on what had been the manger, but he couldn't sit up straight in bed without banging his head against the oxen's yoke and plough hanging from the low ceiling. The narrow earthen *kang* he left to Instructor Zhang.

When he needed light, Bian Ji opened the door which overlooked the valley. Day and night he kept a work bench out there and would go on carving until his fingers trembled. On the mountain across the valley was a small pass leading to Pingyang. At this distance the blue sky above it was exceptionally light, and shouting drovers often brought teams of pack-animals down from the pass. The stars were unusually brilliant there at night, and the moon seemed to linger when she reached that point. Early in the morning soldiers went through their drill by the stream, their rifles and tin bowls clanking against the rocks, while great flocks of goats streamed up to cover the hills. And Bian Ji was a tiny part of all this exhilarating activity.

While making woodcuts of the blacksmith's family, he

found himself most dissatisfied with his portrait of the daughter. Her type of beauty appealed to him very strongly. She was the best model he'd ever had in all his years as painter and woodcarver. He studied his drawing carefully and changed it time and again, but still he could not bring out her charm to his own satisfaction. The eyebrows were like, so were the lips, but he couldn't reproduce the expression in the girl's eyes which animated her whole face. Would he be reduced to adding an inscription to explain this expression?

He observed the girl carefully and made many sketches, getting up early to watch her wash vegetables by the stream, or waiting at the fold of the hills at dusk to watch her carry down a load of firewood. Each day only increased his approval of the girl, but if she were out of sight he couldn't draw her.

Bian Ji pondered over the spell-binding power of art, the tortuousness of the pathway leading to it, the many obstacles in the way of one eager to storm its strongholds. He decided that, just as a fighter drills himself, an artist must carefully perfect his technique in order to achieve a seemingly effortless control of his brush.

In the afternoon he sometimes climbed alone to the highest peak to the east, where there was a tumble-down temple next to some ruins, relics of days gone by. There he would stand gazing east. Even on clear days the edge of the plain was nothing but a rosy haze. He missed his home so much that it seemed to him the best and dearest place in the world.

He knew the poverty of life in the hills. But although this poverty limited the outlook of the people here, he could appreciate their many fine qualities. At first he felt something oppressive about the mountains, but he soon adjusted himself to the surroundings: fold upon fold of hills, steep twisting goat tracks, countless brooks with stepping stones. The

416

craggy peaks often shut out the sun, and ⟨...⟩
be heard was the endless tinkle of water. ⟨...⟩
were black, black the prickly wild pepper tre⟨...⟩
paths, black the water and the slippery moss on th⟨...⟩

As he left home his wife had thrust into his hand th⟨...⟩
she'd saved by careful housekeeping. Each time he spe⟨...⟩
of it he thought of her, her poor health and the hards⟨...⟩
she'd put up with all these years for the sake of her usele⟨...⟩
husband. Kang Family Gully not far away was a rather larger
village with a shop selling beef and mutton. Some evenings he'd treat a couple of friends to supper there. They set
off cheerfully enough, as if bound for some rich banquet, not
feeling the cold as they waded through streams in the dark;
for once there they could eat hot chillis and relax on the warm
kang. On the way back, however, opinions differed. Some
of the youngsters bluntly criticized Bian Ji for not being able
to put up with hardships, saying this was bad for his work.
With a smile, Bian Ji would admit he was in the wrong.

87

Too little snow that winter caused a drought in the hills in
spring and held up the spring sowing. All cadres in the border
region were encouraged to help the peasants reconstruct,
plough and sow their terraced fields. Bian Ji was assigned to
the blacksmith's family. Many peasants were present when
the cadres were allotted tasks, and the shrewder among them
grabbed the strongest men. Bian Ji stood there sheepishly,
wanted by no one and conscious that he cut an unimpressive
figure, until the blacksmith's daughter arrived and asked for
him. At first he'd felt like a farm-hand hiring out his services, but it cheered him to be working for this family.

with the blacksmith's daughter.

...g him a mattock, she herself took a crate,
...ke, and asked her mother to bring them a meal

...e on," she said then. "I'll take you to our land."

...y climbed up a path barely wide enough for one,
...ked by withered grass and brambles. The path wound
...gher and steeper, till the village was far below them.

At last they reached a dell carpeted with light yellow sand,
where some date trees were growing. On the sunny slope
beside it were terraced plots. This was the blacksmith's land.

"Those date trees belong to us too," the girl confided.

The two of them set to work. Their job that morning was
to carry stones up to reinforce the parapets of the terraces
where these had been washed away.

The lowest of these plots was about the size of a *kang*, the
topmost even smaller than a kitchen range, but parapets to
retain the soil had to be built for each.

"How many plots like this do you have?" asked Bian Ji
as they worked.

"This is all. It comes to about three fifths of a *mu*. But
it doesn't belong to us, comrade. We have to give half our
produce each year in rent."

The girl took off her jacket and dropped it on the sand.
Wearing an old faded blouse, she climbed energetically up
and down putting the jagged stones carefully in place.

These few pockets of land were smaller than one corner of
Bian Ji's own fields, and how much could they harvest even
in the best years on this stony, sandy soil? No wonder the
people hereabouts relied all the year round on tree leaves pre-
served in a big vat in their yard. Realizing how much this
small allotment meant to the blacksmith's family, Bian Ji
redoubled his efforts.

418

"Comrade!" The girl surprised him by a frank, infectious laugh.

"What do you want?"

"Nothing. Let's knock off. You have clever hands but I can see you're no farmer. It's nearly time for lunch."

She straightened up and led the way to a spring on the shady slope. Its water was gurgling below a thin layer of ice. She broke the ice and cupped her hands to drink.

"If you can't drink cold water, just wash your hands." She made way for him.

By the time they got back to the sunny slope, the blacksmith's wife had arrived with a basket, a black pitcher of gruel, and the tools they'd be needing that afternoon. Bian Ji marvelled that she could carry so much on that steep, difficult path.

They sat down on the sand in the warm sunlight and the girl ladled out a bowl of gruel for Bian Ji, then removed the cloth covering the basket and produced some cornmeal cakes and a bowl of beancurd sprinkled with watercress.

"Eat up, comrade," said the blacksmith's wife. "It's not much of a meal, but I was up half the night grinding that beancurd."

Smiling, she inspected the work. Bian Ji had a keen appetite today and he found the cornmeal cakes delicious. He wondered if his morning's work was good enough to repay the blacksmith's wife for her trouble.

To show his appreciation, he harrowed the plots as hard as he could after lunch. It was hard work on the slope, and each patch was so small that after a few steps he had to jump outside the parapet to draw the harrow to the end.

It was dark by the time they finished. As they downed tools, the girl said with a smile:

"We've always worked for other people, comrade. Today

you've really sweated helping us. They say the Eighth Route Army first reduces rent and later on will give us all land. Is that true?"

"True as I'm standing here," Bian Ji assured her.

On the way back he asked a question that had been on his mind for some time.

"What do you think of that picture I did of you?"

"It's very good." She smiled.

He couldn't quite fathom the meaning of this smile.

"Good in what way?" he persisted.

"It's very like," she replied more seriously. "Still, I've one fault to find. There's something I don't care for about it."

"This is most important. Do tell me." Bian Ji was extremely modest about his work, always eager to improve. "Just tell me frankly what's wrong. I take the sitter's opinion very seriously."

"It's this." The girl smiled again. "It's not good-looking. I don't mean the eyes or eyebrows, but my hair — you've drawn it so untidy. You should have let me comb it first, and given me a chance to change into better clothes."

"I don't think that really matters." He tried to hide his disappointment. "Portraits are very difficult to do."

"I sometimes think it's funny," she went on, "all the time so many of you comrades spend writing and drawing. Strong young fellows too. What's the use? I think the higher-ups were quite right to send you to help in the fields. Growing grain is more important than anything else, don't you agree?"

"You're quite right." Bian Ji fell silent.

Back in their billet, although all his bones were aching, he lit his oil lamp and sat down to sketch his impressions of the day. Not until he could no longer keep his eyes open did he finally turn in.

420

The tiny villages scattered through the hills here were all filled with Eighth Route Army men. The soldiers and cadres depended on the hills and brought in much that was new to change the villagers' primitive way of living. The tough peasants who had eked out a wretched existence up here for so many years became organized. The men joined the army, worked with transport teams or tilled the fields. Women who had led very narrow lives flocked cheerfully to literacy classes and picked up a great deal of general knowledge too. The soldiers helped the villagers to repair their houses, clean the streets, open up waste land and plant trees. They turned the river flats into arable plots by digging up rich soil from several feet beneath the gravel and grew vegetables never seen here before. They helped to deepen the streams that had flooded their banks and made new ditches to irrigate the fields.

Fuping had always been a wretchedly poor district, known for its "barren mountains and turbulent streams". Yet now it became a base and source of strength for the whole Shanxi-Qahar-Hebei border region. It became a second, dearly loved home for many people from distant parts of the country. All its resources were utilized and expanded. New pits were sunk in the mines and more hands taken on, many students learned to be miners and transport workers. The paper mill in Gold Dragon Cave was enlarged to supply paper for newspapers and books.

At the warm springs they set up a quiet sanatorium. An architect designed an assembly hall which was built with local materials. An agronomist devised ways to wipe out the pests infesting the date trees here. . . .

All was new life, growth and struggle as the whole vast region developed its tremendous potential.

88

Every winter when the fighting started, the border region offices despatched most of their staff to the front. This admirable policy gave the cadres a chance to be steeled in battle, facilitated the movements of the offices with reduced personnel, and enabled the cadres to work better as they followed the armed forces. This year the newspaper office sent Instructor Zhang and Bian Ji to Yanbei to send in speedy firsthand reports on the front. The leadership valued Instructor Zhang's experience in writing and the revolutionary army always showed a high regard for intellectuals. But Zhang himself lacked tempering and politically was not too keen or progressive. Bian Ji was sent with him to learn a reporter's job and to help him along.

Instructor Zhang was delighted with this new assignment. Pleased because his former student and trusty friend was going with him, and because he'd grown thoroughly bored with the Fuping office and here was a chance to get out and have a change. The dangers and hardships of life at the front didn't even cross his mind.

The day they left he got up early to pack his rucksack, in addition to which he took a grey cotton satchel holding paper, pen, a bottle of home-made ink and a tattered volume of Tang poetry. He always carried a book about with him. When Bian Ji had collected their grain coupons, money for food and letters of introduction, the two of them set out.

They covered sixty *li* the first day, coming at dusk to an important communications post, a large house on the north bank of a stream. Its floor was strewn with straw, and a number of militiamen on active service were warming themselves round the stove. By the bridge were donkeys waiting to be loaded. Instructor Zhang and Bian Ji had a meal with the cadres at this post, after which they lay down on the straw to sleep. But the place was so busy and noisy all night, with a constant coming and going, that they got up and helped the cadres to register supplies and despatch men and donkeys. As soon as it was light they went on their way.

Inspector Zhang was very stirred by the wartime bustle of this communications post. The stacks of fuel, fodder and grain, the shouts of militiamen from all around, the clop-clop of donkeys trotting along the bank, symbolized to him the resistance outside the Pass. Before they turned in that night, sitting on a peasant's *kang*, he wrote an article called *The Communications Post*, and after getting it approved by Bian Ji sent it back to the newspaper office.

Instructor Zhang was rather tired the next morning after travelling so far the previous day and working late into the night. It was snowing too, which made the going harder. There was tension in the air as they travelled north. The roads were almost deserted, and they saw villagers running off into the hills. Apparently a Japanese force had come out, but no one could say how far away it was. They decided to put on a spurt and reach their destination that same night, as delay might prove dangerous. Bian Ji was the more anxious of the two, because the main responsibility was his. But on reaching a sizable village they were told that there was no sign of the enemy. And when they saw a small eating-house by the street, Instructor Zhang suggested going in for a snack.

They had been on rather short rations. The peasants supplied cadres on the road with buns made of coarse meal and a dish of chillis, but they had been too parched to eat much. They stepped into the shop and ordered two bowls of noodles.

The place was very warm, thanks to a brazier on the little *kang*. Instructor Zhang put down his rucksack and sat on the *kang*, taking off his wet shoes and propping them up against the brazier to dry.

The proprietress was an old woman who moved very slowly. When Bian Ji saw that it would take a long time for her to mix the dough and light the fire, he thought of cancelling their order, but she had already rolled up her sleeves and poured flour into the basin; and Zhang looked so hungry and tired that Bian Ji hadn't the heart to disappoint him.

"Let me mix the dough for you, granny," he suggested. "You can be lighting the fire."

When she agreed, he washed his hands and plunged them into the flour. Instructor Zhang leaned back against the wall, his eyes closed.

Smoke was just rising from the stove when an uproar broke out in the street and people started dashing past the door. Instructor Zhang woke with a start and looked out of the window. A big troop of men and horses was streaming down the mountain opposite.

"The Japanese are coming!" cried the old woman.

Instructor Zhang grabbed his rucksack and steaming shoes and rushed out with Bian Ji, whose hands were still covered with flour. They raced down a slope and waded through a stream at the bottom. At once their wet socks and padded trousers froze stiff. They had to break the ice before going on. But when they looked back all was quiet in the village and people were going home.

"A false alarm," said Instructor Zhang. "But a lesson to us not to be so greedy and careless. Let's go on."

They were now off the road, which lay across the stream, and they didn't want to go back to the village for a guide. So they pressed on, hoping to strike the highway again after climbing the next hill. It was a difficult climb. They had to heave their packs ahead of them, then Bian Ji would give Instructor Zhang a leg up, after which Instructor Zhang would pull him up. They were fagged out by the time they reached the top, but since there was still no sign of a road all they could do was to trudge along the ridge. It was growing late and the snow was still coming down.

Night fell. They hadn't met a soul or seen any village. They wondered what they would do if attacked by wolves. Neither man had a weapon with him.

"We joined the resistance with pen and ink," remarked Instructor Zhang. "Now it looks as if firing a gun would come in more handy."

This was stoutly said, but Bian Ji knew his teacher well enough to realize how low his morale had sunk.

"When I was young, wandering from place to place, I once lost my way in the mountains," he said reassuringly. "I was all on my own. But this time there are two of us. If we run into enemies or wolves we can bombard them with stones — there's no lack of such ammunition."

"Right you are." Instructor Zhang picked up two stones and carried them a short way. Finding them too heavy, he dropped them. But presently he picked up two more.

"We'll come across someone soon," said Bian Ji. "We should be glad it's snowing to light our way."

Then they saw a twinkling light far off in the hills, faint and fitful through the whirling snow. As they hurried eagerly yet fearfully in that direction it seemed like a lamp which a gust of wind might extinguish.

Hope gave them fresh energy, new warmth surged through them. Cold, hunger and alarm are often only temporary setbacks on the road to happiness.

At the foot of a cliff stood a solitary cottage crowded with refugees from nearby hamlets, with draught animals tethered outside. After some questions, the villagers invited them in.

Wind and snow were blowing through the broken door and windows of the cottage, yet women with babies in their arms were sleeping in the corners. Other children had snuggled up against their goats for warmth, while the hens brought by the old women were flapping their wings uneasily in the cold.

"The Japanese burned down our whole village," one old man told them. "They want to turn it into no-man's land. We'll have to spend the winter here. At least we'll be safe from the Japanese. You've travelled a long way, comrades. Sit down and rest a while. You can cover your feet with this old sheepskin of mine."

"Thank you, uncle," said Instructor Zhang. "We've brought quilts with us."

Seating themselves, they undid their packs and spread one of the quilts over some of the women and children sprawled on the floor. Instructor Zhang's eyes suddenly filled with tears. He was ashamed of his own weakness in the hills. The ones who suffered most in the War of Resistance were these women and children around him.

At daybreak the villagers kept them both to breakfast, which several families cooked on makeshift stoves. The cottage livened up, smoke curled up from its four corners. The children scampered about outside collecting fuel, while Instructor Zhang and Bian Ji fetched ice to melt in the pot and poured in some of their own ration of rice.

All gathered round to eat together. Some exchanged dry rations for gruel, some warmed up cakes on other people's stoves, some begged a bowl of congee for a child. They couldn't have been friendlier or kinder, helping those in difficulties. Trouble had united them. Those households who down in their village quarrelled over trifles were one big happy family up here.

After breakfast the country folk showed Instructor Zhang

and Bian Ji the way downhill, and on the road they met a unit bound for the front. As they were looking for somebody in charge to bring them up to date on news of the fighting, they saw Mangzhong and Old Wen and were thrilled to meet fellow villagers from the plain. Mangzhong took them to the regiment commander, who told them to follow this contingent to the front.

89

Together, the people of the Hebei plain and the soldiers of the resistance overcame the flood. They pumped out the water from the fields and sowed their wheat. The government supplied seed to the poorest peasants and the districts hardest hit, and the prospect of a good harvest raised everyone's morale. For the Hebei plain always yields a good crop of wheat after a flood. Since time was short and the earth too wet to plough, women and children worked in teams, sowing seeds in the clefts of the mud. Early in the morning, countless stooping figures moved up and down the great plain through the cold autumn dew.

The children carried nets to catch the plump locusts lurking in the ground now that the weather was chilly. They collected them in bags to take home and eat.

The mountain districts suffered the worst damage from the flood and the troops were fighting there. The peasants on the plain had suffered losses too, but they still had sufficient reserves to pay the grain tax and Chun'er helped the village cadres explain the need for this.

"Even if it means tightening our belts, we must help the folk up in the hills to tide over these hard times. We must see to it that our troops have enough to eat."

"Of course," said the villagers. "If each of us saves a fistful of grain a day, that'll feed a good many others. We'll ration ourselves until the wheat harvest."

Chun'er and the other cadres set an example.

But when they went to collect from One-eyed Tian, he refused to pay for the three *mu* "sold" to Old Jiang.

The cadres took this up with Old Jiang, who realized that the landlord had let him down.

"I was just going to see you about this," he said. "I bought those three *mu* from One-eyed Tian, I've the deeds to prove it. But I rented them to Wu Dayin, who's not paid me any rent. That means it's his business to fork out for the tax."

The cadres went to see Wu Dayin, who nearly choked with rage when he learned their errand.

"You've got it all wrong," he protested. "Old Jiang knows nothing about growing melons so I helped out, like a day labourer. Not a cent did he pay me for my work, yet now he expects me to pay the grain tax, does he? No matter whose land it is, you can't ask me to pay."

"Oh, yes we can," retorted Old Jiang. "I rent the land to you. That was clear from the start."

Soon the two of them were shouting, and Wu was too angry to eat any supper that evening. The cadres thought the matter over. No wheat had been sown on this plot, and in Old Jiang's hands it would never produce very much. Since Wu was short of land, they urged him to agree to renting it. The base had laws curtailing rents and rates of interest, so that even in a good year no landlord could recoup his losses: his tenants were too well protected. And as those three *mu* had not produced any melons, they would ask the authorities to exempt them from taxation.

Old Jiang was glad to agree to this proposal. That evening he told One-eyed Tian what had happened.

"You swindler!" swore the landlord. "So you're giving my land to Wu?"

"Who are you calling names?" For once in his life Old Jiang dared to answer back. "You've fallen into the trap you laid yourself. Don't try to trap me too."

"You must straighten this out."

"Who are you ordering about, you dirty traitor?" Old Jiang sprang to his feet. "Am I your slave? Your servant? Your *yamen* runner?"

"I've thrown away food and wine on a dog!" One-eyed Tian grabbed the pewter wine pot from the table and hurled it at Old Jiang's head. With blood running down his face, Old Jiang rushed off to complain to the district office.

First the cadres there put a poultice on his head. Then they made an investigation. They agreed to Ziwuzhen's proposal to help Wu Dayin get those three *mu* sown with wheat as quickly as possible.

Word of this threw One-eyed Tian into a frenzy. He dashed out with a chopper to the fields and bellowed:

"Let's see who dares touch my land!"

The district authorities had him arrested. Because of his many crimes, they decided he should have a public trial. The place chosen was the rubble-heaped ruins of Wudao Temple just outside Ziwuzhen. It was a clear windless day. All the peasants from that neighbourhood flocked to the meeting. Those who rented or had once rented One-eyed Tian's land, those who'd worked for him as hired hands or day labourers, squeezed their way to the front of the crowd. The air seemed quivering with the peasants' anger.

The village cadres enumerated One-eyed Tian's crimes: sabotage of the resistance; collusion with the traitor Zhang Yinwu; an assault on Old Wen, a worker; refusal to pay reasonable levies; and interpretation of the government's lenient

429

treatment as a sign of weakness. They urged the authorities to punish him with the utmost rigour of the law.

The peasants roared their approval.

"Down with the landlord!"

"Make the traitor eat dirt!"

The storm of the resistance brought in its wake determined opposition to feudal oppression. This was the start of the stupendous struggle, so long suppressed, which meant life or death to the peasants. Hearts ablaze, they poured out their just demands.

But other landlords trembled with fear as they saw One-eyed Tian, like a tattered flag over a dust-heap, brought low by this hurricane.

It was snowing hard in the twelfth month when a big convoy of carts loaded with grain set off for the mountains of the border region. This was far from being a smart or orderly convoy. There were few carts drawn by teams of mules or horses; most were yoked to a single ox, with maybe a small donkey as outrigger. Some had a rope tied to the cross-bar, and this was pulled by the carters anxious to spare their draught animals who had never travelled such a long distance before. But a bird's-eye view of the whole convoy, which stretched not only from the centre of the plain but from as far away as the Tianjin-Pukou and Beijing-Hankou railways, would have impressed you with the grit of these men pressing on so eagerly day and night, and the tremendous significance of this action.

The carts from Ziwuzhen and Five-dragon Temple formed one small team among many. Gao Sihai was its leader, Chun'er the instructor. Apart from political work, it was her job to keep in touch with all the carters and see to it that when the time came to rest men and beasts had food and a shelter from the storm. She was wearing a patched grey sheepskin jacket tied by a girdle and a new felt hat with earflaps. What was visible of her hair was silvered with hoarfrost.

Nothing could have been worse for the convoy than this snowstorm. The carters, who preferred to press on doggedly rather than stand still in the biting wind, were going all out to reach their destination — the railway ahead. They advanced like an army on the march: an obstruction in front caused a long delay behind. Each time this happened the carters yelled and shouted, tucking their whips under their arms as they thrust their hands into their sleeves, or lighting a fire below the cart to warm their fingers and melt the bottles of frozen axle-grease.

As they neared Dingxian, fields and woods reverberated to heavy bursts of gunfire and explosions from the Beijing-Hankou line. Draught animals reared or pricked up their ears in alarm. The carters had never heard such a furious bombardment, and the proximity of this fierce fighting made them forget the cold.

The thunder of this great offensive was the battle-cry of our army and the whole civilian population of North China as they plunged into the fight. That winter, as a result of fresh Japanese overtures, the Kuomintang was bent on capitulation. To help the enemy, Chiang Kai-shek launched a savage anti-Communist campaign.

Now we were fighting back to smash the enemy blockade, mop up his bases and destroy his communications. A powerful general offensive had started along all the railway lines.

Mangzhong's unit, accompanied by the two reporters, marched back to the Beijing-Hankou Railway. Militia and transport workers everywhere joined in the fighting or helped to destroy communications. They blew up or smashed the

431

tracks, and two men would carry off a rail while a third lugged away three sleepers. Overnight, the north sector of the Beijing-Hankou line vanished. Nothing remained but depressions or grooves in the ground.

"Get cracking! Up to the hills!" shouted the carters. The delivery of grain was going on steadily in two sunken roads by the railway. Countless porters with sacks of grain on their backs hurried over the ladders laid across the sunken roads, setting the ladders swaying.

In these strenuous days, although Mangzhong and Chun'er were within close distance of each other they never met. After a long separation, lovers are happy if they can exchange a few words or catch a glimpse of each other. But at this juncture neither even thought of such a thing. Both were too intent on their duties.

The artillery battle on the plain and the hills had not died down by the time the grain was safely delivered. It was raging more fiercely than ever.

90

One day Bian Ji climbed to the highest point in their position to gaze out over the plain. Standing there, he wrote these lines:

> I strain my eyes east through mist and smoke
> For a glimpse of my wife far away.
> Have the enemy atrocities made your blood boil?
> Has the gunfire of the resistance darkened your face?
>
> Is that cloud of dust
> Raised by enemy horses galloping past my home?
> I hear children crying,

See you breaking out of the village,
Dodging behind a mud wall
And taking deadly aim at the invaders.

The sun rising from your arms
Is racing towards me.
The struggle against Japanese imperialism
Has made dwellers on plains and hills one flesh and
    blood;
Our line is as long as the far-flowing Hutuo,
Strong as its turbulent waters.

Dear wife
Who appeared to me last night in a dream,
I must prize my soldier's honour
Just as I prize our love of all these years.

It was a plain simple poem. Yet men who've come
through that glorious war, when years later they read rough
unpolished lines like these, are drawn to the mimeographed
characters on coarse paper which carry them back to the days
of the resistance. In many respects such lines surpass more
substantial works based on hearsay or imagination, although
critics several generations to come may not be able to understand them.

I sometimes wonder how we can record history truthfully
in such a way that it will live in its entirety. At the time,
we wrote many poems on crumbling walls or cut them on
cliffs by the road. Are they still there after years of wind
and rain? The rivers bore off our songs, mountains echoed
them. Rivers and mountains will endure for ever; but just
as water flows away and mountains are transformed, songs
and echoes will change with the times as men's lives alter.
True accounts may be passed down by word of mouth, but
the differences in time and place, the inevitable additions and

omissions, make it hard for us to recall in full earlier scenes, events and emotions.

That is why I set such store by lines written at the time, on the spot. For however childish they may be, they are a true record of men's thoughts, feelings and aims.

Of course, we hope these humble compositions may fall into the hands of a genuine writer willing to make a careful study of the past, who will transform them in the crucible of his genius into one brick or stone of a masterpiece. We don't want them to be picked up by bogus craftsmen who try to produce a statue without quarrying and hard work. Their way is to add superfluous ornaments to the simple statues carved by others, giving them magnificent costumes to change them out of recognition, and then claiming these as their own work. Or, if they are more modest, as work they have "revised". When they revise a simple tune for a flute, they mobilize a whole orchestra, altering the melody completely and making it so involved that those who hear it are lost in the deafening medley of sound.

The simple originals are better than that.

Of course, the future of a work of art or a man can be pretty well predicted. The nature of the age determines the path men must take. And so long as you keep to the highway, you will every day meet other travellers who are bound in the same direction.

Our story seems to lack a conclusion. But the characters in it will keep appearing before us or walking by our side. I leave each reader to decide what became of them on the basis of his own knowledge, personal experience and ideals.

There's something I'd like to say here about Li Peizhong, however. She wasn't one of the main characters in our story; still, I don't think an author should discriminate between different characters as if he were the producer and they were actors in the old society. Some readers may wonder if Mangzhong and Chun'er have married, and a few may like to know what became of Peizhong. She never recovered completely from her wound. That winter during a fierce "mopping-up" campaign the local government was dispersed by the Japanese, and for a long time there was no news of Peizhong. Later it was rumoured that she had been captured and taken to Baoding; later still, that she had capitulated. The following spring a woman's corpse was discovered in a well some distance from a village near the railway. The body was unrecognizable by then, but in a hole scooped out a foot or more above the water was a package of documents. Secret documents, which proved that the dead woman was Peizhong. It was possible then to reconstruct what had happened. It was night when she and her colleagues fled in different directions, and Peizhong made for the railway, hoping to slip across and escape to the hills. Her colleagues recalled that a terrible dust storm was raging and the Japanese were scouring the countryside. Perhaps she was looking for a hiding place; perhaps she chose to kill herself rather than fall into enemy hands; or perhaps in her headlong flight she didn't see where she was going and fell into the well. The water wasn't deep but she didn't like to call for help, and she was cold, hungry and exhausted. Unable to climb out, she froze to death. But not before she'd found a safe place for the documents.

True, I sometimes made Peizhong appear a figure of fun. But her tall slim figure, long pale face and frank expressive eyes often rise before me. May she rest in peace!

In those stormy years and gruelling conditions, it was by no means easy for someone with all her faults and personal troubles — troubles which few others could understand — to leave her feudal family and stand up to fight her own father and father-in-law. Let us give her due credit and not expect perfection. Peizhong joined in the sacred War of Resistance Against Japan and laid down her life in the fight. She ranks among the finest sons and daughters of the Chinese people, one of the countless martyrs of the War of Resistance.

Her name is engraved on the memorial for martyrs of the resistance in her hometown.

About the Author

SUN LI was born in 1913 in the Hebei countryside. After finishing high school he went to Beijing but failed to find a steady job and had a hard time. During his wanderings from place to place he wrote some reviews and had a few poems published. Soon after the outbreak of the War of Resistance Against Japan he worked in an anti-Japanese base in the Shanxi-Qahar-Hebei area. In 1939 he was transferred to the Fuping mountain district, where he served as a correspondent and editor, taught literature and started writing stories. In 1943 he worked and studied in the Literature Department of the Lu Xun Academy of Art in Yan'an. There he wrote his famous short story *Lotus Creek.*

After the Japanese surrender he returned to the Hebei plain and took part in the land reform. Following the liberation of Tianjin in 1949, he became the editor of the literary supplement of the *Tianjin Daily.* He is now on the board of the Union of Chinese Writers, vice-chairman of the Tianjin Branch of the Writers' Union, and editor of the literary monthly *Xingang.*

Apart from his full-length novel *Stormy Years,* he has written a short novel *The Blacksmith and the Carpenter,* a collection of short stories entitled *A Village Song* and a selection of proses *Tales of Baiyangdian.* Some of his works have been translated and well received by readers abroad.

风 云 初 记

孙 犁 著

戴乃迭 译

*

外文出版社出版
（ 中国北京百万庄路24号 ）
外文印刷厂印刷
中国国际书店发行
（ 北京399信箱 ）
1982年（34开）第一版
编号：（ 英 ）10050—1066
000275
10—E—1647P